JOHN RUSSELL TAYLOR

THE PENGUIN DICTIONARY OF THE THEATRE

PENGUIN BOOKS

Penguin Books Ltd, Harmondsworth, Middlesex, England
Penguin Books, 625 Madison Avenue, New York, New York 10022, U.S.A.
Penguin Books Australia Ltd, Ringwood, Victoria, Australia
Penguin Books Canada Ltd, 2801 John Street, Markham, Ontario, Canada L3R 1B4
Penguin Books (N.Z.) Ltd, 182–190 Wairau Road, Auckland 10, New Zealand

—

First published 1966
Reprinted 1968
Revised edition 1970
Reprinted with minor revisions 1974, 1975, 1976, 1978, 1979

—

—

Made and printed in Great Britain
by Hazell Watson & Viney Ltd,
Aylesbury, Bucks
Set in Monotype Times

PENGUIN REFERENCE BOOKS

THE PENGUIN
DICTIONARY OF THE THEATRE

John Russell Taylor was born at Dover in 1935. After getting a First in English at Jesus College, Cambridge, he studied Art Nouveau book design at the Courtauld Institute for two years.

He has written regularly on theatre for *Plays and Players,* films for *Sight and Sound,* and television for the *Listener,* and was for ten years film critic of *The Times.* He is at present a professor in the School of Performing Arts, University of Southern California. His books include *Anger and After: A Guide to the New British Drama* (Pelican); *Anatomy of a Television Play*; *Cinema Eye, Cinema Ear: Some Key Film Makers of the Sixties, The Art Nouveau Book in Britain, The Rise and Fall of the Well-Made Play, The Art Dealers, The Hollywood Musical, David Storey, Directors and Directions, Hitch: The Life and Times of Alfred Hitchcock,* and *Cukor's Hollywood.*

NOTE

Most of the conventions used in this Dictionary are self-explanatory. Cross-references are indicated by SMALL CAPS. The titles of foreign plays are normally given in the form most familiar to English-speaking audiences. Entries for individual plays are therefore to be found under the established English title when there is one, with a cross-reference from the original: i.e. the entry would be found under *Ring Round the Moon*, with a cross-reference from *L'Invitation au château*. Where there is no established English title in currency – *Andromaque*, the *Oresteia*, *Ubu Roi* – the entry is given simply under the original; since there are at least three English titles for *Huis-clos*, this is also given under the original with cross-references for the various English titles. Date and place of first performance are given as for the official First Night, ignoring the odd weeks of pre-London or pre-New York tour for the same production; in cases where there was actually a different production beforehand, however, the date and place of that are given.

A

Abbey Theatre. The most famous of Dublin theatres and centre of the Irish Dramatic Movement founded in 1899 by W. B. YEATS and LADY GREGORY. The aim of the movement was to present Irish plays on Irish subjects, performed by Irish actors; the theatre was acquired with the aid of MISS A. E. F. HORNIMAN in 1904. The Abbey Theatre company functions as a specialized repertory group, partly amateur but mainly professional. In its time it has brought forward plays by almost all Irish dramatists of any note: Yeats and Lady Gregory (who continued actively involved in managing the theatre until 1939 and 1928 respectively), J. M. SYNGE, 'A.E.' (George William Russell), Edward Martyn, and later the young SEAN O'CASEY. From the beginning many of the plays drew on Irish traditions, though the accent came increasingly to be on modern subjects and poetic realism in the language, especially under the posthumous influence of Synge and the rule of LENNOX ROBINSON, regular producer at the theatre from 1910. On the production side, the Abbey has always stood for bareness and simplicity, partly to economize (it has been financially independent, but for a small subsidy, since 1910) and partly on principle: as a reaction to the elaboration in vogue when it was founded. Though in time the initiative in Irish drama passed elsewhere (from 1925 to the Gate Theatre – see MACLIAM-MÓIR – and later to other, newer groups), leaving the Abbey as a respected national theatre, it has continued to exert considerable influence on Irish drama in general, and especially to act as a nursery for most of the best Irish acting talent. In 1951 the theatre itself was badly damaged by fire, but the company continued to function elsewhere during rebuilding.

Abbott, George (b. 1887). American dramatist, director, and actor, best known for his work in musicals. Among those he has written, alone or in collaboration, are *On Your Toes* (1936), *The Boys from Syracuse* (1938), *Where's Charley?* (1949), *The Pajama Game* (1954), *Damn Yankees* (1955), *Fiorello* (1959). He has directed most of his own shows, and many others.

Abie's Irish Rose. Sentimental comedy by Anne Nichols, first produced at the Fulton, New York, in 1922, and famed principally as the classic case of the play no one believed in which yet went on to run for a record 2,327 performances.

Absurd, Theatre of the. Term applied to a group of dramatists in the 1950s who did not regard themselves as a school but who all seemed

7

to share certain attitudes towards the predicament of man in the universe: essentially those summarized by ALBERT CAMUS in his essay *The Myth of Sisyphus* (1942). This diagnoses humanity's plight as purposelessness in an existence out of harmony with its surroundings (absurd literally means out of harmony). Awareness of this lack of purpose in all we do – Sisyphus, for ever rolling a stone up a hill, for ever aware that it will never reach the top, is the perfect typefigure here – produces a state of metaphysical anguish which is the central theme of the writers in the Theatre of the Absurd, most notably SAMUEL BECKETT, EUGÈNE IONESCO, ARTHUR ADAMOV, JEAN GENET and HAROLD PINTER. What distinguishes these and other, lesser figures (ROBERT PINGET, N. F. SIMPSON, EDWARD ALBEE, FERNANDO ARRABAL, GÜNTER GRASS) from earlier dramatists who have mirrored a similar concern in their work is that the ideas are allowed to shape the form as well as the content: all semblance of logical construction, of the rational linking of idea with idea in an intellectually viable argument, is abandoned, and instead the irrationality of experience is transferred to the stage. The procedure has both its advantages and its limitations. Most dramatists of the absurd have found it difficult to sustain a whole evening in the theatre without compromising somewhat: Ionesco's full-length plays become more and more transparently allegorical, Beckett's get shorter and shorter, Adamov abandoned the absurd altogether in favour of Brechtian EPIC THEATRE, Pinter has moved towards a fusion of the absurd with high comedy. Indeed, by 1962 the movement seemed to have spent its force, though as a liberating influence on conventional theatre its effects continue to be felt.

Achard, Marcel (1900–1974). Prolific French writer of more or less poetic comedies; scored his first success with *Voulez-vous jouer avec moi?* (1924); most notable subsequent works *Jean de la lune* (1929), *Domino* (1931), and *Patate* (1956: translated as *Rollo*).

Acharnians, The. Comedy by ARISTOPHANES, first produced Athens, 425 B.C.

Ackland, Rodney (b. 1908). English dramatist, author of several good adaptations, e.g. *Crime and Punishment* (1945), *Diary of a Scoundrel* (1949), and *Before the Party* (after Maugham, 1949), as well as at least one capable psychological drama, *A Dead Secret* (1957).

Activism. A variety of EXPRESSIONISM which held that the drama should seek realistic solutions to social problems.

Actors' Studio, see STRASBERG, LEE.

Adamov, Arthur (1908–1970). Russian-born dramatist who lived in France and wrote in French. He began his career in Paris in the 1920s as a Surrealist poet, then withdrew from literature in the 1930s while undergoing a mental crisis described in his autobiographical volume *L'Aveu* (1938–43), in which he first expressed the deep sense of alienation which lies at the root of the Theatre of the ABSURD. In about 1945 he wrote his first play, *La Parodie*, and shortly afterwards *L'Invasion*, both of which are largely concerned with the impossibility of communication. They were finally staged in 1950. Among his other plays in the style of the Theatre of the Absurd are *La Grande et la petite manœuvre*, *Professor Taranne* (a literal transcription of a dream Adamov had), and *Le Ping-pong*, which sees life in terms of an endless, aimless contest at a pinball machine. By 1955, though, he was already abandoning the absurd in favour of Brechtian EPIC THEATRE which perhaps accorded better with his Marxist politics; his more important later plays are *Paolo Paoli* (1957), which examines the causes of the First World War in terms of the trade in butterflies and ostrich feathers, and *Printemps '71* (1962), a panoramic history of the Paris Commune.

A.D.C. Cambridge Amateur Dramatic Club, founded by F. C. Burnand in 1855. It acquired its own theatre in 1937, and has contributed a regular stream of recruits to the professional stage from its mainly undergraduate membership.

Adding Machine, The. Expressionist drama by ELMER RICE, first produced New York, 1923.

Admirable Crichton, The. Social comedy by J. M. BARRIE, first produced London, 1902.

Aeschylus (525–456 B.C.). Greek dramatist, author of over ninety plays, only seven of which survive complete, all of them tragedies, though he was noted as a writer of SATYR PLAYS. He was born at Eleusis, fought against the Persians at Marathon, and died in Sicily, at Gela. What may be his earliest surviving play, *The Suppliant Women*, is traditionally dated at *c*.490 B.C. Aeschylus can fairly be regarded as the father of European drama: it was he who took the lyrical alternation of single actor and CHORUS, which was the central ceremony at the Athenian tragic festival, and transformed it into drama proper by the addition of a second actor. (SOPHOCLES introduced a third, and in his later plays Aeschylus adopts this practice.) He also cut down the size of the chorus, and introduced the trilogy to the tragic festival competition, by the rules of which each competing dramatist had to submit three tragedies and a satyr-play. The only complete trilogy of his that we have is the *Oresteia* (458 B.C.), which consists of the *Agamemnon*, the *Choephori*, and the *Eumenides*. The three plays describe the offences of Agamemnon's family against the gods and the succession of vengeful acts whereby divine justice is finally achieved: Clytemnestra kills her husband, Agamemnon; their son, Orestes, kills his mother; and the Furies, after threatening Orestes and Athens, are finally appeased by Athena. Three other trilogies are represented by one play each: *The Suppliant Women* and *Prometheus Bound* (c.460 B.C.) are first plays and *Seven Against Thebes* (469), a third; *The Persians* (472), on the other hand, was a solitary play concerned with recent history and unconnected in subject-matter with the two other tragedies produced with it. Of the great Greek dramatists Aeschylus is the most severe and monumental in his effect, a major part in even his latest works being played by the great choric odes which hark back directly to the ritual role of drama. But his plays show sufficient penetration of human character to make them instantly comprehensible and moving today to audiences to whom the ritual background means nothing and for whom the poetry of the lyrical interludes is muffled in translation.

Affective memory. Technique, advocated by STANISLAVSKY and much elaborated in the METHOD, of re-creating emotions on stage by mental reference to experiences in the actor's own life.

Afore Night Come. Drama by David Rudkin, first performed by the Royal Shakespeare Company at the Arts, London, in 1962; one of the most successful British examples of the Theatre of CRUELTY.

After the Fall. Drama by ARTHUR MILLER, first performed by the Lincoln Center Repertory Company, New York, 1964.

Agamemnon, see ORESTEIA.

Agate, James (1877–1947). English dramatic critic (especially for the *Sunday Times* from 1923 until his death) and prolific autobiographer in the *Ego* series of volumes. Noted for his wit and for his persistent assertion that nothing, or almost nothing, which he saw after Bernhardt and Irving ever quite lived up to the standards they had set.

Ah, Wilderness! Small-town comedy by EUGENE O'NEILL, first performed New York, 1933.

Aiglon, L'. Romantic verse drama by EDMOND ROSTAND, first performed Paris, 1900.

Akimov, Nikolai (b. 1901). Russian designer and director, noted for his wild and experimental settings in the 1920s at the VAKHTANGOV THEATRE and especially for *Kabale und Liebe* in 1930. His most notorious work as a director was an eccentric reinterpretation of *Hamlet* at the Vakhtangov in 1932; later he worked, less controversially, at the Leningrad Theatre of Comedy, of which he became director in 1936.

Alarcón, Juan Ruiz de (c. 1580–1639). Spanish writer of moral comedies, sometimes in collaboration with TIRSO DE MOLINA. The best of his twenty-four plays exerted some influence on CORNEILLE and less directly on MOLIÈRE, his most famous play, *La verdad sospechosa*, being the type of several later French plays, including *Le Misanthrope*. He also wrote romantic dramas, the most popular of which was *El tejedor de Segovia*.

Albee, Edward (b. 1928). Eclectic American dramatist who has flirted briefly with the Theatre of the Absurd (*The Zoo Story*, 1958, and *The American Dream*, 1961) and with social criticism (*The Death of Bessie Smith*, 1959), and scored a major commercial success with his emotional melodrama *Who's Afraid of Virginia Woolf?* (1962), in which the predominant influences are TENNESSEE WILLIAMS and STRINDBERG. Later plays include *The Ballad of the Sad Café* (1963), based on the story by Carson McCullers, the puzzling allegory *Tiny Alice* (1964) and *A Delicate Balance* (1966), a return to tight-packed family drama more in the style of *Virginia Woolf*.

Alcestis. Tragedy by EURIPIDES, first performed Athens, 438 B.C.

Alchemist, The. Comedy by BEN JONSON, first performed at the Globe, London, 1610.

Aldridge, Ira (1804–67). Negro tragedian, billed as 'the African Roscius'. American-born, he acted mainly in England and on the Continent, one of his great roles being Othello (which on at least one occasion he played to the Iago of KEAN), though he was also a notable Macbeth and Lear.

Aldwych farces. A series of farces, mostly by BEN TRAVERS, which were played by a regular company headed by Tom Walls, Ralph Lynn, and Robertson Hare in succession at the Aldwych Theatre from 1925 (*Cuckoo in the Nest*) to 1933 (*A Bit of a Test*).

Aleichem, Sholom (1859–1916). Russian-born Jewish novelist (real name Rabinovich) who wrote mainly in Yiddish. He wrote no plays of his own (except a draft found after his death), but adaptations by others of his stories have been the staple of Yiddish theatre in Germany and in America, where he emigrated in 1905; among the most successful are *The Big Win* and *If I Were You*, comedies of Russian Jewish life, and *Tevie der Milchiger*, a drama about a farmer who cheerfully survives all reverses. (See FIDDLER ON THE ROOF.)

Alfieri, Vittorio Amadeo (1749–1803). Italian dramatist, remembered mainly for his severely classical verse tragedies, though he also wrote a number of undistinguished comedies. He was born in Turin, and brought up with French as his first language, but took up Italian in his twenties and was subsequently noted for his pure and musical use of the language. Most of his plays are based on classical and biblical subjects, the best-known being *Saul* (1784), *Mirra* (1786), and *Oreste*; the last achieved new fame as a result of a spectacular revival by Vittorio Gassman in 1962.

Alienation effect (often simply **A-effect**). One of the principal ideas in BRECHT'S 'theory' of drama, which requires the audience and actors to retain a degree of critical detachment from play and performance. From the playwright's point of view this involves the use of various techniques to keep the audience conscious of the fact that it is a theatrical performance they are witnessing, and to limit their emotional identification with characters and situations in the play. The actor also must contribute by the way he plays his part, implying an attitude to the character rather than attempting to lose himself in it and play it entirely from the inside.

Alleyn, Edward (1566–1626). Elizabethan actor and manager, considered BURBAGE'S chief rival, who appeared in a number of Marlowe's plays, including *Tamburlaine*, *Doctor Faustus*, and *The Jew of Malta*. After his retirement he founded and endowed Dulwich College.

All For Love. Verse tragedy by JOHN DRYDEN, first performed London, 1678.

All God's Chillun (or **All God's Chillun Got Wings**). Tragedy by EUGENE O'NEILL, first performed New York, 1924.

All My Sons. Social drama by ARTHUR MILLER, first performed New York, 1947.

All's Well That Ends Well. Tragi-comedy by WILLIAM SHAKESPEARE, written *c*.1603–04.

Altona (Les Séquestrés d'Altona). Drama by JEAN-PAUL SARTRE, first produced Paris, 1959.

Amazing Doctor Clitterhouse, The. Mystery thriller by Barré Lyndon, first produced New York, 1936; frequently revived and successfully filmed.

Amédée. Play by EUGÈNE IONESCO, first produced Paris, 1954.

American Dream, The. Play by EDWARD ALBEE, first produced New York, 1961.

Amphitheatre, see PLAYHOUSE.

Amphitryon '38. Comedy by JEAN GIRAUDOUX, first produced by LOUIS JOUVET, Paris, 1929.

Anastasia. Historical romance by Marcelle Maurette, first produced in London, adapted by GUY BOLTON, 1953; original version Paris, 1955.

Anatomist, The. Play by JAMES BRIDIE, first produced Edinburgh, 1930.

Anderson, Judith (b. 1898). Australian actress who has appeared chiefly in the United States. Important roles: Lavinia in *Mourning Becomes Electra* (1932), Gertrude to Gielgud's Hamlet (1936), Medea (1947), Hamlet *en travesti* (1970). D.B.E. 1960.

Anderson, Lindsay (b. 1923). British stage and film director. Most of his stage work has been done at the ROYAL COURT since 1957, often in plays which call for detailed realistic staging heightened by an unusual intensity of feeling. Among his most notable stage productions have been *The Long and the Short and the Tall* (1959), *Serjeant Musgrave's Dance* (1959), *Billy Liar* (1960), *The Fire Raisers* (1961) and David Storey's plays *In Celebration, The Contractor* (both 1969) and *Home* (1970). In 1969 associate artistic director of the ENGLISH STAGE COMPANY. His major films have been *This Sporting Life* (1963), based on a novel by David Storey, and *If . . .* (1969).

Anderson, Maxwell (1888–1959). American dramatist and advocate of modern verse drama. His first major success was the First World War comedy *What Price Glory?* (1924), written in collaboration with Laurence Stallings. A series of historical plays followed, among them *Elizabeth the Queen* (1930), *Mary of Scotland* (1933), and *Valley Forge* (1934), and then a group of poetic dramas on modern subjects, among which are numbered most of his best-known and most successful plays, *Winterset* (1935), *High Tor* (1936), *Knickerbocker Holiday* (1938), and *Key Largo* (1939). Though often written with some quiet distinction and with the skill of a practical man of the theatre, these plays probably lack the urgency of vision and excitement of language which might keep them in the repertoire. The most interesting of his later plays is *Lost in the Stars* (1950), a musical based on Alan Paton's novel *Cry, the Beloved Country* with music by KURT WEILL.

Anderson, Robert (b. 1917). American dramatist. Began dramatic career by winning a War Department prize for the best play written by a serviceman with *Come Marching Home* (1945). Best-known play *Tea and Sympathy* (1953), a smooth matinée study of a college boy unjustly suspected of homosexuality.

Andreyev, Leonid (1871–1919). Russian dramatist, friend of Gorky. The most famous of his plays are the symbolic *Life of Man* (1906) and *He Who Gets Slapped* (1914), although he also wrote a number of realistic pieces. His work was immensely popular in pre-Revolutionary Russia, reflecting in sensational style the prevailing pessimism and insecurity of the period: a quality that made it unsympathetic to Soviet authorities after the first experimental period of Soviet arts, but contributed to its European and American success (particularly for *He Who Gets Slapped*) in the 1920s. After a period of eclipse, Andreyev has recently been the subject of renewed interest for university and other experimental drama circles in Britain and America, his view of life, though differently expressed, being sympathetic to that of the Theatre of the ABSURD.

Androcles and the Lion. Comedy by GEORGE BERNARD SHAW, first produced Berlin, 1912; London, 1913.

Andromaque. Classical tragedy by JEAN RACINE, first produced Paris, 1667.

Anna Christie. Drama by EUGENE O'NEILL, first produced New York, 1921.

Anna Lucasta. Drama by Philip Yordan, first produced New York, 1944; one of the most successful and widely produced plays with an all-Negro cast.

Annie Get Your Gun. Musical by IRVING BERLIN, book by Herbert and Dorothy Fields, first produced New York, 1946.

Annunzio, Gabriele d' (1863–1938). Italian poet, dramatist, and novelist, the leading exponent of late Romantic drama. In 1898 he achieved major successes with two plays, *La Città morta* and *La Gioconda*, both of which enjoyed the powerful advocacy of Duse, and both rich in strong situations and violent action in their depiction of extravagant, tormented passions. These were to remain d'Annunzio's dramatic stock-in-trade through many plays, up to his last, *La Piave*, in 1918; the best of them are probably his retelling of the ill-fated love of Paolo and Francesca, *Francesca da Rimini* (1902), and *La Figlia di Jorio* (1904), a gloomy piece about a girl suspected of sorcery and her tragic love for a simple shepherd. The only one of d'Annunzio's plays which is still occasionally performed, in a truncated version, is his mystery play *Le Martyre de Saint Sébastien* (1911), largely because of its incidental music by Debussy.

Anouilh, Jean (b. 1910). Leading French dramatist of the Second World War and immediately post-war period. Born in Bordeaux, he studied law, worked briefly in an advertising agency and even more briefly as JOUVET'S secretary. According to Anouilh the turning point in his life as a writer was seeing GIRAUDOUX'S *Siegfried* in 1928, which showed him the possibility of an easy middle style of theatrical speech, at once colloquial and poetic. In 1932 the first of his plays to be produced, *L'Hermine*, successfully established him in the theatre with his own brand of melancholy romanticism. This was also evident, after a couple of failures, in *Le Voyageur sans bagage* (1937) and *La Sauvage* (1938, written 1934), plays which he subsequently published under the collective title *Pièces noires*. At about the same time, though, he was also writing a series of *Pièces roses*, in which the same obsessive themes (poverty in a world of riches, innocence in a world of experience, the role of memory in life) were treated less gloomily. Among these were *Le Bal des voleurs* (1938: written 1932), *Léocadia* (1939), and *Le Rendez-vous de Senlis* (1941, written 1937). During the 1930s Anouilh established two fruitful connexions: with the PITOËFFS and with the director André Barsacq, who remained his leading interpreter until *Médée* in 1953.

The war years saw the beginning of a new 'black' phase in Anouilh's work with three more reworkings of classic themes in modern terms, *Eurydice* (1942), *Antigone* (1944: written 1942), and *Roméo et Jeannette* (1946); from this he evolved two new categories: *Pièces brillantes*, which brought a hard glitter to the comic themes which earlier he had treated with romantic delicacy, and *Pièces grinçantes*, which offered a bitter mixture of savage humour and tragedy instead of the earlier misty fatalism of the first *Pièces noires*. Among the *Pièces brillantes* the best-known are *L'Invitation au château* (1947, adapted in English by Christopher Fry as *Ring Round the Moon*), *Colombe* (1951), and *La Répétition* (1950); among the *Pièces grinçantes*, *Ardèle, ou la Marguerite* (1948), *La Valse des toréadors* (1952), and *Pauvre Bitos* (1956). In 1953 Anouilh tried something new in *L'Alouette*, a fairly straightforward historical study of Joan of Arc, and followed this up with *Becket* (1959) and *La Foire d'empoigne* (1962: written 1959), which concerns Napoleon and Louis XVIII. In recent years, particularly since the advent of the Theatre of the ABSURD in the early 1950s, Anouilh's reputation has been somewhat in eclipse in intellectual circles, though some of his plays (*Pauvre Bitos* and *L'Hurluberlu* (1959) and *Cher Antoine* (1969) in particular) have been as brilliant as anything he has done, and his popularity, especially in Britain and the U.S.A., has continued to increase among the ordinary theatregoing public.

A.N.T.A. American National Theater and Academy. A body set up by Congressional charter in 1935 to encourage serious theatrical activities in the U.S.A. It was given no official grant, and did not really begin to function until 1945, when it was recognized as a sort of representative council of the American theatre to speak for American theatre internationally and to help develop experimental theatre, theatrical training and study schemes, and theatre outside New York. It aims to function as a privately financed trust on the lines of the Rockefeller and Carnegie Foundations.

Antigone. (1) Tragedy by SOPHOCLES, first performed Athens *c*.442 B.C. (2) *Pièce noire* by JEAN ANOUILH, based on the classical story; first performed Paris, 1944 (written 1942).

Anti-masque, see MASQUE.

Antoine, André (1859–1943). French director and theatrical manager. After spending several years as an enthusiastic amateur actor, in 1887 Antoine founded the Théâtre Libre, a company dedicated to introducing to the French public the works of Ibsen, Hauptmann, Strindberg, Verga, Becque, Brieux, and other leaders of the new naturalism and other movements following in its wake. Though the company itself failed in 1894, its influence in France and abroad was enormous; in particular Antoine's work and his ideas helped to mould COPEAU and through him the whole subsequent course of French theatre. After the failure of the Théâtre Libre Antoine worked for three years at the Odéon, then in 1897 he founded the Théâtre Antoine, run on similar lines to the Théâtre Libre and devoting itself particularly to the work of younger dramatists. From 1903 until his retirement in 1916 Antoine was director of the Odéon.

Antony and Cleopatra. Tragedy by WILLIAM SHAKESPEARE, written c.1606–7.

Anything Goes. Musical by COLE PORTER, book by P. G. WODEHOUSE, GUY BOLTON, Howard Lindsay, and Russel Crouse; first performed New York, 1934.

Apollinaire, Guillaume (1880–1918). French poet who dabbled briefly in the theatre with *Les Mamelles de Tirésias* (1917: mostly written 1903), a Surrealistic farce, and *Couleur du temps* (1918), an allegorical verse drama. *Les Mamelles de Tirésias* is best known today in the operatic setting by Francis Poulenc.

Appia, Adolph (1862–1928). Swiss stage designer and theorist. Along with GORDON CRAIG, one of the great proponents of symbolic, anti-realistic staging, Appia rarely worked in the professional theatre; in the whole of his career he designed less than a dozen productions. His major influence on the theatre of his day came from his books, particularly *Die Musik und die Inszenierung* (1899), in which he advocated a theatre of atmosphere rather than appearances, remarking that in *Siegfried* 'we need not try to represent a forest; what we must give the spectator is man in the atmosphere of a forest'. This he proposed to achieve by reducing the role of the actor to a mobile part of the stage picture, by staging drama rhythmically (his main interest was music and lyric theatre, and most of his theories evolved from the study of Wagner), and by more elaborate, non-realistic use of lights than had previously been attempted. Though Appia was not, as is often suggested, the first to use real shadows on the stage, created by lighting a three-dimensional set (IRVING and the Duke of SAXE-MEININGEN had both done so twenty years earlier), he was the first to work out a complete theory of stage lighting based on the possibilities of atmospheric effect in a constantly shifting, non-realistic play of light over simple, non-representational sets built up from solid masses of white or grey. Unlike Gordon Craig, who held rather similar ideas, he never tried to impose non-realistic staging on realistic drama, confining his ideas in practice to opera and to Shakespeare. His general theories of stage-craft have had little effect (though an echo of them may be found in recent Wagner productions at Bayreuth), but his ideas on lighting have had a profound influence on all modern stage practice.

Apple Cart, The. Comedy by GEORGE BERNARD SHAW, first performed Warsaw, 1929.

Apron stage, see STAGE.

Arbuzov, Alexey (b. 1908). Russian dramatist, author of one of the most popular plays in Soviet Russia, *The Irkutsk Story* (1960), a sort of Russian *Our Town*. The most interesting of his various other works are *The Twelfth Hour*, a macabre fantasy written in tribute to the memory of Meyerhold, and *The Promise* (1965), a romantic drama which had a great success when produced in the West.

Arcadians, The. Musical comedy by Lionel Monckton and Howard Talbot, book by Mark Ambient and A. M. Thompson, lyrics by Arthur Wimperis; first performed London, 1909. The overture and the song exhorting one to 'follow the merry merry pipes of Pan' remain part of the regular palm-court repertoire.

Archer, William (1856–1924). British critic, dramatist, and translator of Ibsen. He began his career as a journalist on the *Edinburgh Evening News*, moved to London in 1878 and was drama critic successively for the *London Figaro*, the *World*, the *Tribune*, and the *Nation*. He was a friend of Shaw, and in his critical writings stood for realism, good workmanship, and high seriousness in the drama (though oddly enough his own play *The Green Goddess*, 1923, was an absurd melodrama which enjoyed great success without any of these qualities). Ibsen was in many respects his model playwright, and his translations of Ibsen (collected 1906–8) did as much as his own writings to spread his ideas. He was also an enthusiastic supporter of the idea of a British National Theatre; among his critical works were *English Dramatists of Today* (1882), *Masks or Faces* (1888), and *The Old Drama and the New* (1923).

Ardèle, ou la Marguerite. *Pièce grinçante* by JEAN ANOUILH, first performed Paris, 1948, with *Épisode de la vie d'un auteur*.

Arden, John (b. 1930). English dramatist, born in Barnsley and trained as an architect. He first achieved notice with a prize-winning radio play, *The Life of Man*. He then had a play, *The Waters of Babylon*, produced without décor one Sunday at the Royal Court, and another, *Live Like Pigs*, publicly staged at the same theatre (1958). These plays show the bold, unpredictable mixture of verse and prose, the Brechtian use of song and ballad, and the unwillingness to draw general social conclusions from particular human situations which mark Arden's most famous play, *Serjeant Musgrave's Dance* (1959). This subtle and complex demonstration of the inextricability of pacifism and violence was a failure commercially but has subsequently continued to be produced all over the world and is generally regarded as one of the masterpieces of the British 'new drama'. None of Arden's subsequent plays – *The Happy Haven*, *The Workhouse Donkey*, *Armstrong's Last Goodnight* – has achieved wide critical or public acceptance, though the latter two have been produced at the Chichester Festival and *Armstrong's Last Goodnight* subsequently at the National Theatre (1965). In 1965 he was commissioned by the City of London to write a play commemorating the 750th anniversary of the signing of Magna Carta, *Left-handed Liberty*. Since then he has worked mostly with amateurs, improvisation groups and others outside the normal patterns of professional theatre, his most substantial later play being *The Hero Rises Up* (1969), about Nelson and the Nelson myth.

Arden of Feversham. Anonymous realistic prose tragedy based on a murder case of 1551. Once (incorrectly) attributed to Shakespeare. First performed *c*.1592.

Arena, see STAGE.

Aren't We all? Comedy by FREDERICK LONSDALE, first produced London, 1923.

Aristophanes (*c*.448–*c*.380 B.C.). Greek comic dramatist, chief figure of the Old Comedy (see GREEK THEATRE). Eleven of his forty-odd comedies survive complete, most of them fairly simple in plot, briefly sketching a comic–satirical situation and then elaborating it in a series of loosely connected scenes in various metres. The chorus still plays a prominent part in Aristophanes' early plays: *The Acharnians* (425 B.C.), *The Knights* (424), *The Clouds* (423), *The Wasps* (422), *Peace* 421), *The Birds* (414), *Lysistrata* (411), and *Thesmophoriazusae* (410). Its role frequently gave the play its title (it is the chorus that represents clouds, wasps, birds, etc.); it was regulated by a number of formal conventions, notably the parabasis, an address to the audience which permitted the dramatist to put over directly his own views of the subject at issue. In the later plays, *The Frogs* (405 B.C.), *The Parliament of Women* (392), *Ecclesiazusae* (391), and *Plutus* (388), the plots become more elaborate and the part of the chorus rather less prominent, more in the style of the Middle Comedy (GREEK THEATRE). Aristophanes' subjects are usually topical in their references, though the themes of some of them, notably the two concerned with women's powers and place in society, *Lysistrata* and *The Parliament of Women*, are sufficiently universal to have kept them in the repertory. *The Frogs* also has remained familiar, though for a rather different reason: it pictures satirically a contest in Hades between Aeschylus and Euripides with Sophocles standing by to take on Euripides if he wins, and therefore has considerable interest for the sidelights it throws on literary attitudes of the time. The very aspects of Aristophanes' work which made him more honoured in theory than in performance during the last few centuries, particularly his outspokenness in sexual matters (which has made 'Aristophanic' almost synonymous with 'Rabelaisian' in popular terminology), have particularly recommended him to modern audiences, and it seems likely that his plays have enjoyed more revivals in the last fifty years than in the previous 2,300.

Aristotle (384–22 B.C.). Greek scientist and philosopher, important in the history of drama for his *Poetics* (c.330 B.C.), in which he attempted to systematize the form and functions of tragedy and (more briefly) of epic, and possibly, in sections now lost, of the Old Comedy (GREEK THEATRE). The book was intended largely as a counterblast to the views of Plato and Socrates on the artist. Socrates emphasized the inspirational nature of the arts and suggested that the poet could not explain coherently what he did and how he did it; Plato criticized drama and poetry because their main aim was not propaganda for moral and social virtues. Aristotle answered the first criticism by attempting a coherent account of the poet's craft, and the second by explaining what drama did do and might properly be expected to do. His description of tragedy is based entirely on what he considered its highest point: the work of Sophocles, placed between the (for Aristotle) more primitive form of Aeschylus and the 'decadent' innovations of Euripides. A lot of what has subsequently been claimed as 'Aristotelian' in dramatic theory, especially by seventeenth- and eighteenth-century neo-classical critics, is not in fact present in Aristotle at all: the idea of the three unities, Time, Place, and Action, for example, is elaborated from Aristotle's view that the action of a play should be single, without diversification or sub-plot, and a passing remark that the action of Sophoclean tragedy is generally confined to about twenty-four hours.

Where Aristotle excels is as a practical critic of a particular type of tragedy and as a theorist of tragic effect. The effect of tragedy, he insists, should be *catharsis*, a purgation by pity and terror, or perhaps of the emotions of pity and terror, and essentially both. By our witnessing and imaginatively participating in a tragic action, certain emotions are purified or for the moment eliminated from our system, and in so far as these emotions are destructive this means that tragedy as an artistic experience (as opposed, that is, to the direct preaching and instruction envisaged by Plato) achieves a positive moral good. For it to do this the tragic hero and the action in which he is involved must have certain characteristics. The hero himself must be between the extremes of goodness and badness, because if he is completely good undeserved misfortune would be horrifying but not tragic, and if he is completely bad his misfortune would not induce pity and fear; moreover, he must come to grief on account of some error of his own. The action in which he is involved must be a single progression from fortune to misfortune, and ideally the fable should be complex, i.e. the catastrophe should involve a disclosure (*anagnorisis*) of some fact previously unknown, or an ironic reversal of events (*peripeteia*), or both, as in Oedipus's discovery that his wife Jocasta is his own mother and that the stranger he killed on the road was his own father. It should be noted that Aristotle's idea of an error leading to tragedy is not the same as that of the 'tragic flaw' often applied to Shakespearian tragedy; it is rather a false step often taken knowingly by the protagonist: he may well have the choice of two possible lines of action, each of which will lead to tragedy, and the morally right decision may do so all the more inexorably.

Arlecchino. Quick-witted servant character in COMMEDIA DELL'ARTE, found also in French comedy as Arlequin and in English pantomimes transformed into COLUMBINE's romantic young lover, as HARLEQUIN.

Arlen, Harold (b. 1905). American composer of Broadway shows and Hollywood musicals. His father was a famous synagogue cantor, and he began his career as pianist and singer. His first big success was the song *Get Happy*, contributed to *Great Day* (1929); among the shows for which he has written complete scores are *Hooray For What* (1937), *Bloomer Girl* (1944), *St Louis Woman* (1946), *House of Flowers* (1954), *Jamaica* (1957), and *Saratoga* (1959).

Arms and the Man. Comedy by GEORGE BERNARD SHAW, first performed London, 1894.

Arrabal, Fernando (b. 1932). Spanish-born dramatist of the ABSURD, who writes in French. Most of his plays are highly derivative, especially from Beckett; the most widely performed are *Pique-nique en cam-*

pagne (1952), about a picnic on a battlefield which ends in everyone's getting shot, and *Fando and Lis*, a sado-masochistic fantasy about love. *Le Cimetière des voitures* is his longest play, a two-act picture of life in a vast automobile scrapyard. He has also experimented in 'abstract theatre', a wordless action performed by the movement of abstract, three-dimensional shapes, in *Orchéstration théâtrale* (1959).

Arsenic and Old Lace. Comedy by Joseph Kesselring, first performed New York, 1941; classic case of a horror subject (two old ladies who turn out to be mass-murderers) played for laughs.

Artaud, Antonin (1896–1948). French director, playwright and theorist. Began as a poet under the influence of MAETERLINCK and as a film actor; in 1925 he became involved in the Surrealist movement as writer and organizer, and in 1927 founded with ROGER VITRAC the Théâtre Alfred Jarry, where he produced, among other things, Vitrac's Surrealist plays, Strindberg's *Dream Play*, and Claudel's *Partage de midi* (act three) as a farce. His own main work as a playwright was *Les Cenci*, based on versions of the story by SHELLEY and Stendhal and first performed in 1935, when he found backers for his Théâtre de la Cruauté (though the result was a disastrous critical and commercial failure); he also wrote the script for one of the most famous Surrealist films, *La Coquille et le clergyman* (1927). He was confined to a lunatic asylum in 1937 but released in 1946, two years before his death. Most of Artaud's influence in the theatre derives from his theoretical writings, particularly those gathered together in *Le Théâtre et son double* (1938), and from his personal influence on JEAN-LOUIS BARRAULT and ROGER BLIN, both of whom were associated with the production of *Les Cenci*. As a theorist Artaud stood for a theatre of myth and magic, casting aside narrative and psychological realism. The function of the theatre, for him, was to liberate forces in the audience's subconscious (here his Surrealistic background played its part) by giving direct expression to their dreams and obsessions, even, or perhaps especially, the least avowable. To do this the drama should relegate dialogue (which belongs to literature, not the stage) to a very subordinate role, and depend instead on gesture and movement – as do Balinese dancers, who made a deep impression on Artaud at the Paris Colonial Exhibition of 1931 – and on the play of lights and shapes. Drama's job was to express things which could not be put into words and the role of words in drama should be purely ritual and incantatory. Actors and audiences should be 'victims burnt at the stake, signalling through the flames'. Artaud thus forms a bridge between the SYMBOLIST drama and stagecraft of the 1900s and much theatrical practice of the 1960s, especially that of directors such as PETER BROOK, who have explicitly acknowledged him as their master.

Arts Council of Great Britain. Founded at the beginning of the Second World War as C.E.M.A. (the Council for the Encouragement of Music and the Arts), with grants from the Treasury (through the Ministry of Education) and the Pilgrim Trust, it was then designed to organize the arts in evacuation areas. From 1942 it was financed entirely by the Treasury, and at the end of the war was reorganized as the Arts Council, 'to develop a greater knowledge, understanding and practice of the Fine Arts, to increase their accessibility to the public and to improve their standard of execution'. In the field of drama this involves grants to a variety of theatres in the provinces and to some in London, particularly those like the Royal Court (the ENGLISH STAGE COMPANY) whose enterprises are regarded as non-commercial. The council also sponsors or participates in a number of schemes for training producers, stage managers, designers, etc., and encourages the staging of new drama and revivals of rarely-come-by older drama by direct guarantees against loss.

Ascent of F.6, The. Verse play by W. H. AUDEN and CHRISTOPHER ISHERWOOD, first produced London, 1936.

Ashcroft, Peggy (b. 1907). English actress; D.B.E. 1956. Trained at the Central School. Her first notable success in the theatre was in *Jew Süss* with Matheson Lang (1929); in 1930 she played Desdemona to Paul Robeson's Othello, and in 1932 Juliet in John Gielgud's O.U.D.S. production of *Romeo and Juliet*, a role she repeated in 1935 with Gielgud and Olivier alternating as Romeo and Mercutio and Edith Evans as the Nurse. In 1932–3 she played her first season at the Old Vic, in the middle of which she left to play the title role in Theodore Komisarjevsky's Schnitzler adaptation *Fräulein Else*, a personal *tour de force* which required her to be on stage throughout the play in a part twice as long as Hamlet's. In 1936 she played Nina in Komisarjevsky's production of *The Seagull*, and in 1937–8 played the Queen in *Richard II*, Lady Teazle in *The School for Scandal*, Irena in *The Three Sisters*, and Portia in *The Merchant of Venice* during Gielgud's season at the Queen's. Another notable Gielgud season in 1944–5 showed her as Ophelia, Titania, and the Duchess of Malfi. Among her more famous later roles are Catherine Sloper in *The Heiress* (1949), Beatrice in *Much Ado About Nothing* (1950, 1955), Hester Collyer in *The Deep Blue Sea* (1952), Cleopatra in *Antony and Cleopatra* (1953), Hedda Gabler (1954), Miss Madrigal in *The Chalk Garden* (1956), Rebecca West in *Rosmersholm* (1959), Queen Margaret in the Royal Shakespeare Company's sequence *The Wars of the Roses* (1963–4), the mother in Marguerite Duras's *Days in the Trees* (1966) and Beth in Pinter's *Landscape* (radio 1968, stage 1969).

Asmodée. Religious drama by FRANÇOIS MAURIAC, first performed at the Comédie-Française, 1939.

As You Like It. Comedy by WILLIAM SHAKESPEARE, written *c.*1599–1600.

Atelier, Théâtre de l'; École de l', see DULLIN, CHARLES.

Athalie. Tragedy by JEAN RACINE, first performed privately, Paris, 1691.

Atkinson, Brooks (b. 1894). For some years, up to his semi-retirement in 1960, doyen of American dramatic critics. In 1922 he was appointed literary editor of the *New York Times* and four years later became the paper's dramatic critic, a post he held, apart from five years as a war correspondent, until 1960.

Auden, W. H. (1907–73). English-born poet, later American citizen. During the 1930s wrote a group of verse plays in collaboration with the novelist CHRISTOPHER ISHERWOOD: *The Dog Beneath the Skin* (1935), *The Ascent of F.6* (1936), and *On the Frontier* (1938). These attempted modern social and political themes and mingled verse and prose, keeping verse in general to mark off passages of special significance and enforce special attention for them from the audience. Subsequently Auden's theatre work has been confined to opera librettos (notably Stravinsky's *The Rake's Progress* and Henze's *Elegy for Young Lovers*) and some contributions to *The Punch Revue* (1955).

Audiberti, Jacques (1899–1965). French poet, dramatist, novelist, and fantasist. His plays all mix comedy, satire, cruelty, and serious thought in varying and unpredictable measures. He had at least one major commercial success, *Le Mal court* (1947), a series of glittering, bitter variations on themes from eighteenth-century comedy, and in general his plays are most effective when removed in time from the present: *Quoat-Quoat* (1946), *Pucelle*, a strange reworking on the Joan of Arc story (1950), and *La Hobereaute* (1956). He also wrote some effective contemporary one-act pieces, notably *Les Femmes du Bœuf* (1948), first played at the Comédie-Française.

August for the People. Satirical comedy by NIGEL DENNIS, first performed Edinburgh Festival, 1961.

Aurengzebe. Heroic tragedy in rhymed couplets by JOHN DRYDEN, first performed London, 1675.

Aymé, Marcel (1902–1967). French novelist, humorist, and dramatist. For long a successful novelist before he attempted the theatre, Aymé achieved fair success with his first play, *Lucienne et le Boucher* (1946) and repeated it with *La Tête des autres* (1952), both comedies of a ferocity which in the case of the second provoked something of a literary scandal. In between came *Clérambard* (1950), a 'mystical farce' of considerable ambiguity which seemed to be saying something powerfully but left viewers mystified as to precisely what. Of his later plays perhaps the most effective is the fantastic tale *Les Oiseaux de la lune* (1955).

B

Bacchae, The. Tragedy by EURIPIDES, first performed in Athens after his death in 406 B.C.

Backdrop, see STAGE MACHINERY.

Back to Methuselah. Cycle of five plays by GEORGE BERNARD SHAW covering the history of humanity from the Garden of Eden to the remotest future. First performed in sequence by the Theatre Guild, New York, 1922; presented by SIR BARRY JACKSON at Birmingham, 1923.

Bad Seed, The. Melodrama by MAXWELL ANDERSON, based on a novel by William March; first produced New York, 1954.

Bagnold, Enid (b. 1896). English novelist, author of several plays, the most successful being the romantic drama *Lottie Dundass* (1943), and the glittering high comedies *The Chalk Garden* (1955), *The Chinese Prime Minister* (1963), and *A Matter of Gravity* (1976).

Bajazet. Tragedy by JEAN RACINE, first performed Paris, 1672.

Balcony, The (Le Balcon). Play by JEAN GENET, written 1956, first performed (in English) at the Arts, London, 1957; in French, Paris, 1960.

Balcony, see PLAYHOUSE.

Bald Prima Donna, The (La Cantatrice chauve, called **The Bald Soprano** in U.S.A.). One-act comedy by EUGÈNE IONESCO, first performed Paris, 1950.

Ballad opera. Popular form of drama with songs which evolved from the 'English opera' of the later seventeenth century, in which spoken dialogue took the place of Italian recitative. The ballad opera proper usually had a light romantic plot or, as in the most famous and familiar example, GAY'S *The Beggar's Opera* (1728), elements of satire; the music was sometimes specially composed, more often largely arranged from traditional and popular airs. Among the writers who worked in the form were Fielding, GARRICK, and SHERIDAN, whose ballad opera *The Duenna* (1775) is one of the best-known later examples of the genre.

Banana Ridge. Farce by BEN TRAVERS, first performed London, 1935.

Bankhead, Tallulah (1903–1968). American-born actress first seen in New York, 1918; London, 1923–33; thereafter in U.S.A. Though as noted for her off-stage eccentricities as her on-stage performances, she showed herself, on occasion, a powerful actress as well as a talented comedienne. Best roles: Julia in *Fallen Angels* (1925), Marguerite in *The Lady of the Camellias* (1930), Sadie Thompson in a revival of *Rain* (1935), Cleopatra in *Antony and Cleopatra* (1937), Regina in *The Little Foxes* (1939), Sabina in *The Skin of Our Teeth* (1942), the

Queen in *The Eagle Has Two Heads* (1947), Blanche in a revival of *A Streetcar Named Desire* (1956). Autobiography, *Tallulah* (1952).

Barker, Harley Granville (1877–1946). English director and playwright. Though a solid and serious dramatist in his own right (*The Voysey Inheritance*, 1905; *Waste*, 1907; *The Madras House*, 1910), it is mainly as a manager and director that Granville Barker exerted an important influence on the development of the British theatre. He was, in particular, closely associated with the works of SHAW, a personal friend: first at the Stage Society (where he played Marchbanks in the first production of *Candida*, 1900) and then during his period as manager (with John E. Vedrenne) and resident director at the Royal Court (1904–7). There he directed plays by Yeats, Maeterlinck, Hauptmann, Ibsen, Galsworthy, and Masefield, and two of Gilbert Murray's translations of Euripides, as well as sponsoring Shaw's own productions of *John Bull's Other Island, You Never Can Tell, Candida, Man and Superman, Major Barbara, Captain Brassbound's Conversion*, and *The Doctor's Dilemma*. After 1907, he continued until the 1914–18 war to bring the best of modern European drama to the London stage, as well as staging memorable versions of *Twelfth Night* and *The Winter's Tale* and helping the more interesting British dramatists. His productions were always attentive to the author's intentions and based as far as possible on understanding of the characters and teamwork among the actors. (In this respect he differed from his contemporary GORDON CRAIG whose theories tended to play down the dramatist's importance in favour of theatre as a director's art.) Immediately, therefore, Barker had a greater effect in the English theatre than Craig, confirming its tendency towards psychological realism. Barker's first wife, Lillah McCarthy, created many famous Shaw roles. In 1918 he married again, a rich *divorcée*, Helen Huntingdon, and virtually gave up practical participation in the theatre (mainly in obedience, it seems, to his wife's wishes), and from 1921 to his death his name appeared (and then only as co-director) on only two productions: *Waste* in 1936 and *King Lear* at the Old Vic in 1940. During this time he turned his energies instead to translation (with his wife he translated from the Spanish numerous plays by SIERRA MARTINEZ and the QUINTERO brothers) and to original writing; in the latter category his most important works were his series of *Prefaces to Shakespeare*, which for some years exerted a powerful influence, directly or indirectly, on English Shakespearian productions, advocating in the main an approach to Shakespeare through character and story-telling.

Barker–Vedrenne Company. Management which ran the Royal Court

Theatre, London, from 1904–7, and then for a few months the Savoy. See also BARKER, HARLEY GRANVILLE.

Barnum, Phineas T. (1810–91). American showman, associated mainly with the circus, and famous as the archetypal flamboyant show-business personality. His American Museum (built 1842) housed plays and spectacles of various sorts as well as cultural talking-points like Jenny Lind, curiosities of natural history, and all sorts of freaks and oddities. From 1871 until his death he was impresario of 'The Greatest Show on Earth', a vast circus which toured constantly, beginning its spring season each year at Madison Square Garden, New York.

Baroque theatre, see PLAYHOUSE, STAGE, STAGE MACHINERY.

Barrault, Jean-Louis (b. 1910). French actor and director. He began his studies as a painter, but attracted the attention of CHARLES DULLIN and was brought by him into the École de l'Atelier. Barrault soon achieved some reputation as a promising romantic juvenile, but already he was drawn to a deeper study of the actor's art and studied mime with Étienne Ducreux, as well as assisting ARTAUD in his short-lived Théâtre de la Cruauté. In 1935 he staged his first original production, *Autour d'une mère*, his own half-spoken, half-mimed adaptation of Faulkner's *As I Lay Dying*. His experiments in this direction continued with *Numance* (after Cervantes) and *La Faim* (after Knut Hamsun), but at the same time he set himself to master classical style and technique by playing in Molière. In 1940 he married the actress Madeleine Renaud and was engaged by Copeau for the Comédie-Française as actor and director, where he stayed until 1946, often raising eyebrows by his '*avant-garde*' interests; he extended the repertoire to take in such works as Claudel's *Le Soulier de satin* and Shakespeare's *Antony and Cleopatra*, both in memorable productions of his own. After his break with the Comédie-Française he and his wife set up their own company, the Compagnie Renaud-Barrault, and little by little, as much on tour in the provinces and abroad as in Paris itself, built up a spectacular repertoire of classics, modern plays, and even operettas (Offenbach's *La Vie parisienne* is one of the company's most reliable successes) and mime-plays. Among the most famous productions of the company are a series of Claudel plays, including *Le Soulier de satin*, *Partage de midi*, and *Christophe Colombe* (the latter one of Barrault's most remarkable essays in THÉÂTRE TOTAL), Barrault's own adaptation (in collaboration with André Gide) of Kafka's *The Trial*, and an experimental version of the *Oresteia* adapted by André Obey. From 1959 to 1968 Barrault was director of the former Salle Luxembourg of the Comédie Française, rechristened the Théâtre de France. He was dismissed from this post after the *événements* of May 1968, and shortly afterwards re-established himself in the independent theatre with his enormously successful *Rabelais* show, a singing–dancing extravaganza redefining *Gargantua and Pantagruel* in terms of total theatre. As an actor he is probably best known internationally for his appearance in the Marcel Carné–Jacques Prévert film *Les Enfants du paradis*, as the mime Baptiste.

Barretts of Wimpole Street, The. Romantic drama by Rudolph Besier about the love affair of Robert Browning and Elizabeth Barrett, first performed London, 1930. Musical version, *Robert and Elizabeth*, book and lyrics by Ronald Millar, music by Ron Grainer, first performed London, 1964.

Barrie, J. M. (Sir James Matthew Barrie; 1860–1937). Scottish dramatist and novelist, born in Kirriemuir, the son of a handloom-weaver. He first made a name as a novelist and essayist, drawing his material from the working-class life and backgrounds of his childhood. After some unsuccessful attempts at drama he had major successes with *The Professor's Love Story* (1894) and his dramatization of his own novel *The Little Minister* (1897). The most famous of his plays, though hardly the most characteristic, *Peter Pan*, appeared in 1904. It promptly made itself into an institution, and has remained one, finely regardless of those who subsequently saw in its story of a little boy who wouldn't grow up and a little girl with an overdeveloped maternal instinct all sorts of sinister Freudian overtones. The sometimes rather cloying whimsy of *Peter Pan* recurs in a number of Barrie's other plays, such as *A Kiss for Cinderella* (1916), *Dear Brutus* (1917), and *Mary Rose* (1920), all of them fantasies heavily tinged with sentimentality. More durable, perhaps, and certainly more appealing to later generations have been his social comedies, *The Admirable Crichton* (1902) and *What Every Woman Knows* (1908) or the lighthearted period romance of *Quality Street* (1902); one or two of his one-act plays, particularly the puzzle-piece, *Shall We Join the Ladies?* (1922), originally intended as the first act of an unwritten whodunit, also survive in the repertoire. After some years out of the theatre, Barrie returned in 1936 with a curious Biblical piece *The Boy David*, written for and acted by Elizabeth Bergner. Though a varied and prolific playwright, Barrie seems likely to be remembered by only a handful of pieces in which the impish humorist dominates the sentimentalist – and, of course, by *Peter Pan*, which whatever its faults seems to have entrenched itself permanently as part of the English Christmas, and therefore beyond criticism.

Barry, Philip (1896–1949). American playwright who wrote most sorts of play in his time, ranging from farce to heavy biblical drama. When produced, his most highly-thought-of play was the allegorical fantasy *Here Come the Clowns* (1938), but in retrospect the only plays of his which retain their appeal are his sophisticated light comedies, the best of which, *Holiday* (1928) and *The Philadelphia Story* (1939), are still as fresh as ever.

Barrymore, Lionel (1878–1954), **Ethel** (1879–1959), **John** (1882–1942). American family of actors, all children of Maurice Barrymore (1847–1905), an English actor who settled in New York in 1875, and Georgina Drew, an American actress of some note. The eldest, Lionel, achieved some reputation on the stage in his earlier years, but had increasing success in films after his debut in 1914 and soon gave up the stage entirely; to later generations of filmgoers he was chiefly familiar as crusty, lovable old Doctor Gillespie in a series of 'Doctor Kildare' films.

Ethel Barrymore, though she too had a long and distinguished career in films, never completely deserted the stage until relatively late in her career, and achieved a number of spectacular successes as a stage actress. One of her early appearances was with Irving in *The Bells*; later she appeared often both as a beauty (in plays like her first major success, *Captain Jinks of the Horse Marines*, 1901) and as an actress in roles like Nora in *A Doll's House*, Portia, Juliet, Marguerite Gautier, and Lady Teazle. She also created a number of roles in modern plays, notably *Whiteoaks* (1936) and *The Corn is Green* (1940). In 1928 a New York theatre was named after her.

John Barrymore, the youngest of the acting Barrymores, was noted for his romantic good looks (especially his famous profile) and, later, for his riotous living off-stage. His earliest successes were won as a matinée idol, but he also did well in more substantial parts like Falder in Galsworthy's *Justice* and Peter Ibbetson in the dramatic version of Du Maurier's novel. His Hamlet (1922, London 1925) was one of the most famous and highly regarded of his generation; his Richard III and Mercutio (which he also played in a film of *Romeo and Juliet*) were also well thought of. During the 1930s he appeared mainly in films (the most famous *A Bill of Divorcement* and *Grand Hotel* in 1932); one, *Rasputin and the Empress*, was the only time when all three Barrymores played together.

Bart, Lionel (b. 1930). British composer and lyric-writer. Began as composer of popular songs for Tommy Steele; wrote lyrics for *Lock Up Your Daughters!* (1959), lyrics and music for FRANK NORMAN's musical *Fings Ain't Wot They Used T'Be* (1959), and book, lyrics, and music for *Oliver!* (1960), based on *Oliver Twist*, and *Blitz* (book in collaboration with Joan Maitland, 1962). Later works include *Maggie May* (book by ALUN OWEN, 1964) and *Twang!!* (1965).

Bartholomew Fair. Comedy by BEN JONSON, first performed London, 1614.

Bat, The. Mystery play by Mary Roberts Rhinehart and Avery Hopwood, first produced New York, 1920, and frequently revived.

Baylis, Lilian (1874–1937). English theatre manager, founder of the Old Vic and Sadler's Wells. Trained originally as a musician, she assisted her aunt Emma Cons for a time in managing the Victoria Theatre, Waterloo Road, as a temperance music-hall, and took over the management herself in 1914. Her aim at the Old Vic, as it came to be called, was to provide opera and good drama for the masses (one of her first enterprises there was the production of all Shakespeare's plays between 1914 and 1923). Drama took up an increasing amount of the Old Vic's programme, and in 1931 she took over and rebuilt the Sadler's Wells Theatre as a permanent home of opera and ballet. She was appointed a Companion of Honour in 1929.

Beaton, Cecil (b. 1904). English designer, photographer, and writer. From 1935 has designed sets and costumes for a number of plays, musicals, and ballets, among them: *Lady Windermere's Fan* (San Francisco; 1946), *Aren't We All?* (London, 1953), *Quadrille* (New York, 1954), *The Chalk Garden* (New York, 1955), *Look After Lulu* (New York, 1959), *Saratoga* (New York, 1959). His most famous designs are the costumes for *My Fair Lady* (1956), and the costumes and sets for the film version (1964). Knighted 1972.

Beaumarchais, Pierre Augustin Caron de (1732–99). French dramatist, best remembered for having written the plays which formed the basis of Mozart's *The Marriage of Figaro* and Rossini's *The Barber of Seville*. According to his own memoirs he worked also as a secret agent, smuggler, financier, musician, and even watchmaker, the trade of his father for which he was trained as a youth. His first play, *Eugénie*, was produced at the Comédie-Française in 1767, but was not successful and was restaged in a rewritten version. His next, *Les Deux Amis* (1770), found more favour, but his first lasting success was *Le Barbier de Séville* (1775), a glittering comedy about an outspoken rogue of a barber which poked fun at the aristocracy and its ways. In its sequel, *Le Mariage de Figaro* (1784), his criticism of aristocratic society was even more outspoken, and the play was staged only after much opposition. His non-comic works, among them an opera *Tarare* (1757) and a tragedy *La Mère coupable*, are of little interest.

Beaumont, Francis (*c*.1584–1616). English dramatist, almost invariably remembered as half of Beaumont-and-Fletcher, from his regular collaboration with his contemporary JOHN FLETCHER. Though in seventeenth-century collections some fifty-three plays are attributed to the partnership, it is certain that Beaumont had nothing to do with most of them and likely that he collaborated on no more than ten. Two broad, extravert comedies, *The Woman-Hater* and *The Knight of the Burning Pestle*, are probably his own unaided work; in the trage-dies and tragi-comedies he wrote with Fletcher, among them *Philaster* (1610), *The Maid's Tragedy* (1611), *A King and No King* (1611), and *The Scornful Lady* (1613), he is generally supposed to be responsible for the more solid, serious, masculine sections, and to have excelled particularly in tragedy.

Beaux' Stratagem, The. Comedy by GEORGE FARQUHAR, first per-formed London, 1707.

Becket (Becket, ou l'honneur de Dieu). Historical drama by JEAN ANOUILH, first performed Paris, 1959. See also TENNYSON.

Beckett, Samuel (b. 1906). Irish dramatist and novelist, most of whose later works were written originally in French. Born in Dublin of Protestant Anglo-Irish parents (like Shaw, Wilde, and Yeats), Beckett had a distinguished academic career, and during two years as a *lecteur d'anglais* in Paris (1928–9) became closely associated with Joyce and his circle. In 1931 he gave up his job at Trinity College, Dublin, and wandered round Europe for several years, writing and doing various odd jobs until he settled permanently in Paris in 1937. His first novel, *Murphy*, was published in English in 1938. Practically everything else he wrote during the following twenty years was first written in French, because, according to Beckett, writing in an acquired language makes it easier to write without style. Towards the end of the war he wrote another novel, *Watt* (published 1958), followed by a trilogy *Molloy* (1951), *Malone meurt* (1951), and *L'Innommable* (1953). But it was his plays initially which established his international reputation: the first, *Eleutheria* (1946) remains un-published and unperformed, but *En attendant Godot* (*Waiting for Godot*), first performed in Paris in 1953, was rapidly performed all over the world and became unexpectedly a great popular success. It is an elusive tragic farce about two tramps for ever awaiting the arrival of the mysterious Godot, who will in some unexplained way make everything different but who never comes. Exemplifying as it does the existential absurdity of man's situation, the play became one of the cornerstones of the Theatre of the ABSURD. Beckett's second play, *Fin de partie* (*Endgame*) (1957) concerns the plight of a group of people: a blind master, his legless parents, who live in dustbins, and his ineffectually rebellious slave/son who is always trying to leave the tower in which they live cut off from a desolate lifeless world, but never does. *Endgame* was followed by a group of short plays in English (one for the stage, *Krapp's Last Tape*, and two for radio, *All that Fall* and *Embers*) and some short mime dramas, *Actes sans paroles*, and then by another full-length play, *Happy Days*, also written in English and first performed in New York in 1961. This seemed to represent the farthest refinement possible in Beckett's dramatic method, being virtually a monologue for a woman who is progressively buried alive till in the last act only her head is visible. But in *Play*, first performed in Ulm in 1963, even such remote concessions to theatrical convention disappear: here there are three characters, heads protruding from urns, and each speaks only when a shaft of light hits his or her face, the whole text being played through twice in twenty minutes. *Come and Go* (1965) also has three characters (female), a minimum of action, and indeed a minimum of everything else, running for only three minutes and containing only 121 words of dialogue. Beckett's exploration of the possibilities of one fringe of dramatic expression has been solitary and self-denying, and in his recent works he seems to be leaving more and more of the audience by the wayside until in *Play* and *Come and Go* he has reached some sort of *ne plus ultra*. *Waiting for Godot*, however, remains unarguably one of the most remarkable and influential plays of the twentieth century.

Becque, Henri François (1837–99). French dramatist in the naturalistic tradition of Zola, now remembered for two sharp pictures of amoral bourgeois life, *Les Corbeaux* (1882) and particularly *La Parisienne* (1885).

Beggar's Opera, The. Ballad opera by JOHN GAY, with music collected and arranged by Dr John Christoph Pepusch, first performed London, 1728, with a record run of sixty-three performances. The most famous subsequent production was Nigel Playfair's at the Lyric, Hammersmith, in 1920, in a new arrangement by Frederick Austin; in 1945 Benjamin Britten made a version, less romantic than Austin's. Brecht's THREEPENNY OPERA was suggested by Gay's work.

Behan, Brendan (1923–64). Irish writer and dramatist. After a stormy childhood and youth (chronicled in his autobiography *Borstal Boy*) which gave him experience of prison and the workings of the I.R.A., two recurrent subjects in his writing, he became a professional journalist and wrote his first play, *The Quare Fellow* (Dublin, 1954). Later it was accepted by Joan Littlewood for production at THEATRE WORKSHOP, and underwent the process of communal revision and elaboration usual there before production (1956). *The Quare Fellow* is a tragi-comic account of a hanging in an Irish prison; *The Hostage* (first written in Gaelic), which followed it in 1958, is a more strongly comic account of the goings-on at a decrepit brothel turned into a centre of I.R.A. activities, in which an English soldier is held as a hostage and finally, almost accidentally, shot. Behan's forte was lively invention rather than rigorous construction, and after *The Hostage* he proved unable to finish his long-announced third play, *Richard's Cork Leg* (edited from drafts and staged after his death, in 1973), though his highly publicized private life kept him before the public.

His brother **Dominic** (b. 1928) has also written plays, most notably *Posterity Be Damned* (1960), a shapeless satirical view of modern Ireland.

Behrman, S. N. (Samuel Nathaniel; 1893–1974). Prolific American author of light comedy who has occasionally tried his hand, with less success, at tragedy and heavy drama. A number of his most successful plays have been adaptations, notably *The Pirate* (1942), based on a play by Ludwig Fulda, *I Know My Love* (1949), based on Marcel Achard's *Auprès de ma blonde*, and *Amphitryon '38* (1938), after Giraudoux: all of them written for and played by the LUNTS. Of his original plays perhaps the best are *The Second Man* (1927), a comedy of manners with which he scored his earliest success, and *No Time for Comedy* (1939), about a playwright who, like Behrman himself, has the urge to write social tragedy but the talent only for light comedy.

Belasco, David (1859–1931). The great showman of the American theatre at the turn of the century. A playwright and actor-manager, he produced all kinds of plays from Shakespeare to *East Lynne* during his long career, though he is best remembered for his cosy accommodation of European naturalism to the sentimental ends of romantic melodrama. As a dramatist and adaptor he had a hand in dozens of works, at least two of which, *Madame Butterfly* (1900) and *The Girl of the Golden West* (1905), remain familiar through Puccini's operatic versions. The Belasco Theatre, New York, was built by and named after him.

Bel Geddes, Norman (1893–1958). American scenic designer and director. His work as a designer was much influenced by the ideas of GORDON CRAIG and ADOLPH APPIA, especially in the bold disposition of simple, often geometrical shapes about the stage, and the important role of lights playing over them in the creation of atmosphere. His characteristic abstract style of setting was exemplified by his sets for *Arabesque* (1925), *Lysistrata* (1930), *Hamlet* (1931), and Irwin Shaw's *Siege* (1937), as well as in a famous series of projects for an outdoor spectacle based on Dante's *Divine Comedy* in a specially constructed amphitheatre (1921). Bel Geddes also worked on occasion in more conventional styles, as in his extravagant cathedral-like setting for Reinhardt's New York production of *The Miracle* (1924) and in his elaborately naturalistic designs for his own production of Sidney Kingsley's drama of slum life *Dead End* (1934).

Bell, Marie (b. 1900). French actress and manager. Throughout her career she has managed to combine a successful career as a matinée star with a considerable reputation as a tragedienne. In the 1930s, for example, she was a popular film star; in the post-war years she has had major successes in such undemanding roles as the ageing *cocottes* in Félicien Marceau's *La Bonne Soupe* and Françoise Sagan's *Les Violins, parfois.* But at the same time she has been, on and off, a star of the Comédie-Française, and has played successfully such roles as Prouhèze in Claudel's *Le Soulier de satin* and Esther, Phèdre, Bérénice, and Agrippine (*Britannicus*) in Racine, as well as the Madame in Genet's *Le Balcon.*

Belle of New York, The. Musical comedy by Gustav Kerker, book by Charles McLellan, lyrics by Hugh Morton. First performed in New York, 1898, but most successful in its London production of the same year.

Bells, The. Melodrama by Leopold Lewis, based on Erckmann-Chatrian's *Le Juif polonais*; one of Henry Irving's greatest successes, first performed at the Lyceum, London, 1871.

Benefit. A performance of a play from which all the money taken goes to one or two members of the cast, or occasionally to a retired actor or to the family of a deceased actor.

Benevente, Jacinto (1866–1953). Spanish dramatist and translator of Shakespeare and Molière. Immensely prolific, Benevente figures in dramatic and literary history as the man chiefly responsible for popularizing Ibsen and Freud and other current trends of European thought and literature in Spain during the late nineteenth and early twentieth centuries, rather than as a dramatist of lasting interest in his own right. His vast output ranges from farce to intense symbolic drama, and is extremely eclectic in style; he has had little success outside Spain, though some of his one-act comedies collected in *Teatro fantastico* (1892) deserve to be better known. His chief success in translation has been *Los Intereses Creados* (*The Bonds of Interest*) (1907), an anti-materialist drama propounding the importance of artistic experience and love in the battle with the inane practicalities of the modern world. Benevente was awarded the Nobel Prize for Literature in 1922.

Benson, Frank (1858–1939). British actor-manager, specially noted for his championing of Shakespeare in the provinces. After studying at Oxford, where he was a leading light of the O.U.D.S. he became a professional actor in 1882, in Irving's company. In 1883 he formed his own company to play Shakespeare on tour and continued to do so for nearly fifty years, in the process producing all Shakespeare's plays except *Troilus and Cressida* and *Titus Andronicus*. In the intervals of touring, his company played a number of London seasons, the first in 1889–90; during one of them, to mark the Shakespeare Tercentenary in 1916, he was knighted for his services to the theatre. He was also noted as a great trainer of actors, many later distinguished in their profession passing through his company at the outset of their careers.

Benthall, Michael (1919–1974). British director. Member of O.U.D.S. at Oxford, actor 1938–9, co-director with Tyrone Guthrie of *Hamlet* for Old Vic, 1944. He subsequently specialized in Shakespeare and classical productions, as well as occasional operas. Director of the Old Vic in 1953–9. In general his productions placed prime emphasis on beauty of setting, and natural rather than formal delivery of verse.

Bentley, Eric (b. 1916). British-born American dramatic critic, director, and translator of BRECHT, whose principal spokesman and advocate in America he has been. As a critic of other drama he has been responsible for one of the best studies of Shaw (1948), and *The Playwright as Thinker* (1946, published in Britain as *The Modern Theatre*), a series of brilliantly perceptive and sometimes perverse essays on the major trends of twentieth-century drama. He has been drama critic of *Harper's* magazine (1940s) and of the *New Republic* (1952–62); since 1954 he has been Brander Matthews Professor of Dramatic Literature at Columbia University. In 1950 he assisted Brecht in his Munich production of *Mother Courage*; he has directed plays at the Abbey Theatre, Dublin, and elsewhere.

Bérard, Christian (1903–49). French stage designer, painter, and fashion artist. Worked extensively in ballet in the 1930s with the de Basil company and later with Roland Petit. In drama he collaborated with JOUVET and BARRAULT (particularly on stylish revivals of Molière and Marivaux) and with JEAN COCTEAU, for whom he designed *La Voix humaine* (1930), *La Machine infernale* (1934), *Les Monstres sacrés* (1940), *Renaud et Armide* (1943), and the costumes of *L'Aigle à deux têtes* (1946), as well as working on several of Cocteau's films. He was a master of romantic evocation as well as glittering period re-creation, and exerted a considerable influence on the whole field of fashion and design in wartime and immediately post-war France.

Bergman, Hjalmar (1883–1931). Swedish dramatist, generally regarded as STRINDBERG's successor. Starting about 1903, he wrote a number of folk comedies and lyrical, romantic, and historical dramas, each showing in varying degrees the influence of MAETERLINCK and IBSEN. His first mature work was the novel *Hans Nåds Testamente* in 1910, and from then on his work became more experimental, though the influence of Maeterlinck, coupled with that of Strindberg and even MUSSET, remains strong in his *Marionetspel* (1915–16), a group of three short plays, and *Sagan* (1919–20). An Expressionist phase followed with *Portea*, *Spelhuset*, and *Vävaren i Bagdad* (*The Weaver of Bagdad*), all of 1921. Bergman's most interesting play, and his most lastingly successful, was *Swedenhielms* (1923), a slightly Strind-bergian family drama about a Nobel Prizewinner. His later plays included successful dramatizations of his earlier novels, *The Markurells of Wadköping* (1929) and *Hans Nåds Testamente* (1931). He also worked in radio and the cinema, writing in addition to thirty stage plays over thirty film scripts and twelve radio plays.

Bergman, Ingmar (b. 1918). Swedish director and dramatist. While studying at Stockholm University he directed an amateur group and subsequently went as an assistant director to the Saga Theatre, where he staged Strindberg's *Ghost Sonata* with more scandal than success. In 1944 he turned to the cinema as a writer and later as a director, but continued to work in the theatre as well, and in 1947 directed Camus' *Caligula* and his own plays *Dagen slutar tidigt* and *Mig till skräck* at Göteborg Municipal Theatre. From 1947 to 1952 he was a freelance director, then he joined Malmö Municipal Theatre as resident direc-tor, and there directed a wide variety of plays, including Strindberg's *Dream Play*, Molière's *Don Juan* and *Le Misanthrope*, Goethe's *Urfaust*, Hjalmar Bergman's *Sagan*, Ibsen's *Peer Gynt*, and his own *The Barjärna Murder*. At this theatre his regular company included a number of players familiar from his films, among them Max von Sydow, Gunnar Björnstrand, and Naima Wifstrand. His own most successful play has been the one-act *Trämalning* (1955), subsequently the basis of his film *The Seventh Seal*. Among the notable films he has written and/or directed are *Frenzy* (1944), *Summer Interlude* (1950), *Smiles of a Summer Night* (1955), *The Seventh Seal* (1956), *Wild Strawberries* (1957), *The Virgin Spring* (1959), *Through a Glass Darkly* (1961), *Winter Light* (1962), *The Silence* (1963), *Persona* (1966), and *Hour of the Wolf* (1968). In 1965 he resigned his post at Malmö.

Berkeley Square. Play by John L. Balderston and J. C. Squire, based on

HENRY JAMES'S unfinished novel, *The Sense of the Past*; first performed London, 1926.

Berlin, Irving (b. 1888). American composer and author of musicals. Real name Israel Baline, born in Russia, emigrated to U.S.A. at the age of four. Began his musical career as a juvenile busker and then a singing waiter; in 1904 he became a staff lyric-writer to a music-publisher and in 1911 wrote words and music of his first lasting success, *Alexander's Ragtime Band*. His first complete score for a Broadway show was the revue *Watch your Step* (1914); during the 1920s he wrote songs for a series of *Music Box Revues*, which were presented at his own Music Box Theatre, and among his later successes on the stage were *Face the Music* (1932), *As Thousands Cheer* (1933), *This is the Army* (1942), *Annie Get Your Gun* (1946), *Call Me Madam* (1950), and *Mr President* (1963).

Berliner Ensemble. Theatrical company founded and directed by BERTOLT BRECHT in 1949 and directed since his death by his widow HELENE WEIGEL. It began as an off-shoot of the Deutsches Theater in East Berlin after Brecht had collaborated on a production of *Mother Courage* there; until 1954 it shared the Deutsches Theater's building and resources, and devoted itself entirely to works written or adapted by Brecht: *Herr Puntila and his Servant Matti* (1949), Lenz's *Der Hofmeister* (*The Tutor*) (1950), *The Mother* (1951), *Senora Carrar's Rifles* (1952), Erwin Strittmatter's *Katzgraben* (1953). In March 1954, the Berliner Ensemble moved to the Theater am Schiffbauerdamm as an independent State Theatre of East Germany. Its principal subsequent productions up to Brecht's death in 1956 were *The Caucasian Chalk Circle* (1954) and J. R. Becher's *Winterschlacht* (1955).

Bernanos, Georges (1888–1948). French religious novelist, author of one successful play, *Les Dialogues des Carmélites*, based on a novel by Gertrud von Le Fort. This was written in 1948 as the script for a film, but was first produced as a stage play in 1952, later turned into an opera by Poulenc, and finally filmed in 1960.

Bernard, Jean-Jacques (1888–1972). French dramatist, poet, and theorist of Theatre of SILENCE. Deriving his ideas somewhat from MAETERLINCK, Bernard stood in the 1920s for a reaction against verbose, rhetorical theatre: nearly all his plays deal with intimate subjects, mainly the problems of love, and place great emphasis on the spiritual drama which remains unspoken beyond the often slight and formal exchanges of what is actually said. The best-known of his many plays are *Le Feu qui reprend mal* (1921), *Martine* (1922), *L'Invitation au voyage* (1924), and *Le Printemps des autres* (1924); the most successful of his later works is the religious drama *Notre Dame d'en haut* (1952).

Bernhardt, Sarah (1845–1923). French actress, noted mainly for her appearances in tragedy and strong drama. Between 1862 and 1880 she appeared on and off at the Comédie-Française, though never settling happily there for long. Her first great success was won elsewhere, with Coppée's *Le Passant* (1869), but she established herself firmly as the leading actress of her day at the Comédie-Française in 1872 with her performances as Cordelia in *King Lear* and the Queen in *Ruy Blas*. Among her other famous roles were Phèdre, Marguerite Gautier in *La Dame aux camélias*, Hamlet (played *en travesti*), the King of Rome in Rostand's *L'Aiglon*, Doña Sol in *Hernani*, and the leading roles in Sardou's melodramas *Fédora, La Tosca*, and *Théodora*. She was noted particularly for her beautiful voice, which survived long after the slim figure and facial beauty which helped to establish her in youth were gone.

Bernstein, Leonard (b. 1918). American composer and conductor. Has composed symphonies and other substantial concert works and is permanent conductor of the New York Philharmonic Orchestra, but is most widely known for his scores to the Broadway musicals *On the Town* (1944), *Wonderful Town* (1953), *Candide* (1956), and *West Side Story* (1957).

Bespoke Overcoat, The. One-act play by WOLF MANKOWITZ, based on a short story by Gogol. First performed Arts Theatre, London, 1953.

Betterton, Thomas (*c*.1635–1710). Leading actor of the Restoration stage in England, skilled as both a tragedian and a comic. He was noted for his Shakespearian performances, his best roles being Hamlet and Sir Toby Belch. His sense of comedy was more robust than refined, but he had a great success in Congreve's *Love for Love* (1695), and created roles in plays by Dryden and other leading dramatists of the day. He was also a capable manager, and a passable adaptor of Elizabethan and Jacobean plays to Restoration taste.

Betti, Ugo (1892–1953). Italian dramatist and principal successor of Pirandello, by whom he was much influenced. He was a lawyer by profession, and legal considerations enter into many of his plays, particularly *Corruption in the Palace of Justice* (1949). His first play, *La Padrona*, won a prize in 1927, but his most important plays were nearly all written in the last five years of his life: *Crime on Goat Island* (1950), *The Joker* (1951), *The Queen and the Rebels* (1951), and *The Burnt Flowerbed* (1953). In all of these recur the same preoccupation with responsibility and identity, and the same flair for theatrical effect. Betti was discovered outside Italy only after his death, in Britain largely through the B.B.C.'s Third Programme; in 1955 three of his plays were running simultaneously in the West End.

Bibienas. A family of artists and architects who played an important part in the development of the Baroque theatre. **Ferdinando** (1657–1743) and his brother **Francesco** (1659–1739) were trained by Rivani, a stage engineer who worked on the construction of the court theatre at Versailles. Ferdinando had a hand in the equipment of Aleotti's Teatro Farnese at Parma, and later worked with his sons and Francesco on the design and staging of court entertainments in Vienna. Of Ferdinando's sons the most notable in stage history were **Giuseppe** (1696–1757) and **Antonio** (1700–74): Giuseppe built the court theatre at Bayreuth, and around 1723 pioneered the use of transparent scenery lit from behind; Antonio designed the Teatro Communale at Bologna (1763). Giuseppe's son **Carlo** (1728–87) was also an important stage designer. Among the most far-reaching innovations brought about by the Bibienas was the introduction of diagonal perspectives instead of the central perspective generally employed in the seventeenth century. Though their home and centre of activities was Bologna, they travelled all over Europe designing theatres, stage machinery, settings and pageants and spectacles of various sorts for powerful patrons, including, as well as kings and princes, city councils, educational establishments, and Jesuit colleges.

Bickerstaffe, Isaac (1735–1812). English dramatist, author of numerous ballad operas. His first, *Thomas and Sally, or The Sailor's Return* (1760) was followed by his most lasting success, *Love in a Village* (1762), based on Charles Johnson's *The Village Opera*, and by *The Maid of the Mill* (1765), based on Richardson's novel *Pamela*. He also collaborated on a number of occasions with DIBDIN and Foote, notably on *Lionel and Clarissa* (1768); in 1772 he was forced to flee to the Continent to avoid some trouble with the law, and lived there until his death.

Big Knife, The. Play by CLIFFORD ODETS, first produced New York, 1949.

Billetdoux, François (b. 1927). French dramatist. Began writing for radio, then wrote sketches for the theatre and finally a one-act play, *À la nuit la nuit* (1955), which achieved considerable critical success. His first full-length play, *Tchin-Tchin* (1959), is in effect a duologue for two characters, the partners of an adulterous couple, who gradually drift into alcoholism together. It was a commercial success in Paris and (considerably adapted) in London and New York. His subsequent play, *Va donc chez Törpe* (1961) confirmed his reputation for originality this side of *avant-garde*, without repeating the international career of the earlier play.

Bill of Divorcement, A. Play by Clemence Dane, first produced London, 1921. Created a great stir at the time for its boldness in urging that insanity should become a ground for divorce.

Billy Liar. Comedy drama by WILLIS HALL and Keith Waterhouse, based on the novel by Keith Waterhouse. First produced London, 1960.

Bio-mechanics. A system of training for the actor devised by MEYER-HOLD, intended to produce an almost acrobatic control of the body beyond the normal requirements of precise and authoritative movement about the stage, and reducing the actor to a sort of producer's puppet.

Birds, The. Comedy by ARISTOPHANES, first performed Athens, 414 B.C.

Birmingham Repertory Theatre, see JACKSON, SIR BARRY.

Birthday Party, The. Play by HAROLD PINTER, first performed London, 1958.

Bishop's Bonfire, The. Play by SEAN O'CASEY, first performed Dublin, 1955.

Bjørnson, Bjørnstjerne (1832–1910). Norwegian dramatist and novelist. A near-contemporary of IBSEN, he has always been overshadowed internationally by Ibsen, though in Norway he was found more easily accessible and was therefore more immediately popular. He was a prolific dramatist: in his earlier years he wrote a series of historical plays, among them *King Sverre* (1861), *Sigurd the Wild* (1862), and *Mary Stuart in Scotland* (1864); from 1865 to the mid 1880s he approached Ibsen more closely, with a group of contemporary social dramas: *The Newly-Weds* (1865), *The Bankrupt* (1875), *The New System* (1879), and *The Gauntlet* (1883). In his last period Bjørnson, like Ibsen, became increasingly preoccupied with spiritual questions, in his case usually with a specifically Christian tinge: the tendency is first marked in *Beyond Human Power* (1883), and continued, among others, in *Laboremus* (1901) and *When the Vineyards Bloom* (1905). In 1903 Bjørnson received the Nobel Prize for Literature.

Blacks, The (Les Nègres). Play by JEAN GENET, written 1957, first performed Paris, 1959.

Bless the Bride. Musical comedy by Vivian Ellis, book by A. P. HERBERT; first performed London, 1947. One of the long-running escapist successes of the immediately post-war period.

Blin, Roger (b. 1907). French director and actor. Was associated with ARTAUD in his short-lived Théâtre de la Cruauté, and worked as an actor with BARRAULT in a number of his early ventures into the *avant-garde* (*Numance*, *La Faim*). He is chiefly noted as director of various works of the Theatre of the ABSURD: Adamov's *La Parodie* (1952), Beckett's *En attendant Godot* (in which he played Pozzo), *Fin de partie* (1957), and *La Dernière Bande* (*Krapp's Last Tape*) (1959), and Genet's *Les Nègres* (1959).

Blithe Spirit. Comedy (described as 'an improbable farce') by NOËL COWARD, first produced London, 1941

Blood Wedding (**Bodas de sangre**). Peasant tragedy by FEDERICO GARCÍA LORCA, first performed Madrid, 1933. Also called *Marriage of Blood*.

Blue Bird, The (**L'Oiseau bleu**). Fairy play by MAURICE MAETER-LINCK, written 1905, first produced (in Russian) by Stanislavsky, Moscow, 1908; London 1909; New York 1910; Paris (in the original French) 1911.

Boland, Bridget (b. 1913). British dramatist. Most famous play *The Prisoner* (1954), a drama of conscience based remotely on the predicament of Cardinal Mindzenty.

Bolt, Robert (b. 1924). British dramatist. A teacher and sparetime writer for radio, he had a play, *The Critic and the Heart*, staged at Oxford in 1957, but his real success came with his first play to be produced in London, *Flowering Cherry* (1957), a slightly Chekhovian study of failure and self-deception. His historical piece *A Man for All Seasons* (1960) made discreet use of Brechtian devices to tell the story of Sir Thomas More; *The Tiger and the Horse* (also 1960) hovered awkwardly between realism and Expressionism in its study of a mental breakdown. After two years spent working on the film *Lawrence of Arabia* Bolt returned to the theatre in 1963 with *Gentle Jack*, a whimsical fantasy influenced by Barrie, which failed to find favour. Later plays include *Brother and Sister* (1969), a rewrite of *The Critic and the Heart* which never reached London, and *Vivat, Vivat Regina!* (1970), about Queen Elizabeth and Mary Queen of Scots.

Bolton, Guy (b. 1884). British dramatist and (particularly) author of 'books' for musical comedies, often in collaboration with P. G. WODEHOUSE. Most famous shows *Oh, Kay!* (1926), *Rio Rita* (1927), *Rosalie* (1928), *Girl Crazy* (1930), and *Anything Goes* (1934). Adapted Marcelle Maurette's play about the Romanov claimant, *Anastasia*, into English (1953).

Bond, Edward (b. 1935). British dramatist. His first play, *The Pope's Wedding*, was given a Sunday-night production-without-decor at the Royal Court. His first big critical success was *Saved* (1965), which caused a considerable stir because of its (marginal) scenes of gratuitous teenage violence. *Early Morning* (1968), a savage satirical fantasy in which Queen Victoria is shown having a lesbian liaison with Florence Nightingale and which concludes with a scene of cannibalism in heaven, was one of the last plays to fall foul of the Lord Chamberlain. *Narrow Road to the Deep North* (1968) took cruel happenings in medieval Japan as its subject, and seemed to mark a new confidence in Bond's command of his material. Later plays include *Lear* (1971), his variation on Shakespeare, and a strange comedy, *The Sea* (1973).

Booths. Family of Anglo-American actors. The earliest, **Junius Brutus Booth** (1796–1852) was already a prominent actor in England, more noted for the drive and forcefulness of his characterizations than for their finesse, when he emigrated to America in 1821. He played Iago to KEAN's Othello and Edgar to his Lear, and also made a name for himself as Shylock and Richard III. His elder son, **Junius Brutus Jr** (1821–83) was also an actor of some distinction, but the most famous members of the family are his other sons **Edwin** (1833–93) and **John Wilkes** (1831–65). The latter, also an actor, is chiefly famous as Lincoln's assassin, but Edwin seems to have been the genius of the family; specializing in Shakespearian and classical roles (Richard III, Hamlet, Romeo, Sir Giles Overreach in *A New Way to Pay Old Debts*), he had a fine presence and a beautiful voice perfectly controlled. He visited Europe on a number of occasions, and in 1881 alternated the roles of Othello and Iago with Irving at the Lyceum, London. He was a founder member of the New York Players' Club, and gave the club his house, which it still occupies.

Borchert, Wolfgang (1921–47). German short-story writer and dramatist. His play *Draussen vor der Tür* (1947; translated into English as *The Man Outside*) is one of the best-known German plays dealing with the Second World War.

Born Yesterday. Satirical comedy by GARSON KANIN, first performed New York, 1946.

Boucicault, Dion (1822–90). Irish dramatist and actor. Wrote or adapted (mainly from the French) some 150 plays, few of them entirely original. The most successful were *The Corsican Brothers* (1882) and *The Colleen Bawn* (1860, based on a novel, *The Collegians*). He spent much of his time in the United States, where his works were as popular as in London; even his slightest pieces have considerable gusto and a practical flair for theatrical effect which seldom deserted him.

Boulevard drama. Generic term for popular French drama from the 1850s on; for the most part realistic in general convention, embracing both fast-moving farce and solid domestic drama.

Box, see PLAYHOUSE.

Box and Cox. One-act farce by J. Maddison Morton, first performed London, 1847, and constantly revived ever since. Turned into a comic opera, book by F. C. BURNAND, music by ARTHUR SULLIVAN, under the title, *Cox and Box*, first performed 1867.

Boy Friend, The. Musical comedy by SANDY WILSON, first performed London, 1953.

Bracegirdle, Mrs (Anne) (*c.*1663–1748). Leading British actress of her day. Trained by BETTERTON, she had her greatest successes in the plays of CONGREVE, and created the role of Millamant in *The Way of the World*. She retired from the stage in 1707.

Brand. Verse tragedy by HENRIK IBSEN, published 1866, first complete performance Stockholm, 1885.

Brasseur, Pierre (1905–1972). French actor. For some years after his first great success in *Le Sexe faible* (1929) he specialized in handsome, turbulent, often cynical young heroes, with occasionally a more substantial role, especially in the cinema, where he gave remarkable performances in *Quai des brumes* and *Lumière d'été*. But it was the Carné–Prévert film *Les Enfants du paradis* (1944), in which he played the great romantic actor FRÉDÉRICK LEMAÎTRE, which marked the turning-point in his career. From then on he adopted a much more spectacular, flamboyant style, very much like a modern Lemaître, and when he found suitable roles proved one of the most powerful (if not exactly the most subtle) actors of his generation. Best roles: De Ciz in *Partage de midi* (1948), *Le Bossu* (1949), *Ornifle* (1955), *Kean* (specially written for him by Jean-Paul Sartre) (1958), *Le Diable et le Bon Dieu* (1958), Shaw in *Dear Liar* (1962).

Breadwinner, The. Comedy by W. SOMERSET MAUGHAM, first performed London, 1930.

Brecht, Bertolt (1898–1956). German dramatist, poet, director, and theoretician. Began his career as a dramatist with a series of experimental plays heavily influenced by EXPRESSIONIST techniques, of which *Baal* (written 1918: first performed 1923), *Jungle of the Cities* (written 1921: performed 1923), and *A Man's a Man* (1926) have been revived more or less successfully in recent years. The first play in which his Marxist preoccupations came to the fore is *The Threepenny Opera* (*Die Dreigroschenoper*, 1928), in which Gay's *The Beggar's Opera* is made the basis of a satirical attack on bourgeois society and its standards. This 'musical' with a score by KURT WEILL, who was to be one of Brecht's regular collaborators during the following years, rapidly achieved an international success and reputation, with productions in Moscow, Paris, and New York. For the next ten years or so most of Brecht's work was more or less didactic; increasingly he turned from the romantic, nostalgic, rather decadent imaginative world of his early plays to direct instruction, so that the works he wrote in this period have proved among his least lasting – the principal exceptions being his opera (with Weill) *The Rise and Fall of the City of Mahagonny* (1930), the opera-ballet spectacle (also with Weill) *The Seven Deadly Sins* (1933), and the play *St Joan of the Stockyards*, his first flirtation with the St Joan story, which continued to obsess him (written 1929–30, broadcast 1932, but not staged till 1959).

In 1933, with the advent of Hitler, Brecht left Germany, going first to Scandinavia, and then, when Scandinavia was overrun in 1941, to the U.S.A. for the duration of the war. Between 1937 and 1945 he wrote an almost unbroken succession of important plays, including several now recognized as masterpieces: *The Life of Galileo* (1937–9), *Mother Courage* (1938–9), *The Good Woman of Setzuan* (1938–41), *Herr Puntila and his Servant Matti* (1940), *The Resistible Rise of Arturo Ui* (1941), *The Visions of Simone Machard* (another St Joan story, 1940–3), *Schweik in the Second World War* (1942–3), *The Caucasian Chalk Circle* (1943–5). After this date his writing for the theatre was negligible, consisting mainly of adaptations and revisions; instead he devoted himself more to poetry and theoretical writing, and in the theatre to the direction of his own plays and, after his return to Germany in 1949, the running of his own company, the BERLINER ENSEMBLE. It was only at this relatively late stage that his stature as a dramatist and dramatic thinker came to be widely recognized. Up to 1949 a number of his major works remained unproduced and others (*Mother Courage*, 1941, *The Good Woman of Setzuan*, *Galileo*, 1942) were mostly seen only in a Zürich cut off from the rest of the cultural world by the war; indeed the only production of his work in these years to achieve any publicity and reputation at all was the Charles Laughton production of *Galileo*, translated by Laughton and Brecht, in Los Angeles in 1947. But with the appearance of *Mother Courage* in the repertory of the Berliner Ensemble, with Brecht's wife HELENE WEIGEL in the title role (1949) and the first professional production of *The Caucasian Chalk Circle* by the Ensemble (1954), Brecht came to be generally recognized as one of the most important figures in the contemporary theatre.

Brecht's importance made itself felt in two ways: through the production of his plays, and through the increasing influence of his theories about the theatre. His plays themselves can be roughly divided into four periods – romantic-nostalgic (1918–29), didactic

(1928–38), more generally humanist (1938–45), and again didactic (1945–56) – though in fact all the elements are present to a greater or lesser extent at all periods of his career. It seems safe to say that, apart from the group of collaborations on more or less equal terms with the composer Kurt Weill in the late 1920s and early 1930s (*The Threepenny Opera, Mahagonny, The Seven Deadly Sins*), all the works by which he will survive as a dramatist date from the third period. Here his social and political interests, while still a driving force in his work, are allowed to inform works far too complex in their human material and their attitudes towards character to be regarded as simple illustrations of a thesis. Characters like Mother Courage, the indomitable survivor of the Thirty Years' War, or Galileo, or Shen Teh, the good-hearted woman of Setzuan, and the ruthless *alter ego* she has to create in order to survive in a capitalist world, or Azdak, the rogue turned judge in *The Caucasian Chalk Circle*, are so fully imagined, so felt as intricate and contradictory human beings, that they escape all rigid formulations of their social and political significance.

As a theorist Brecht's most telling influence has been counterbalancing Stanislavsky as misunderstood by his American METHOD disciples. Instead of the complete absorption of the actor in his role Brecht demanded the retention of a critical distance: the actor should not attempt just to *be* the character, to present it entirely from the inside, but, while understanding its psychological workings, to present it in such a way as to imply an attitude towards it. Thus the audience, instead of identifying with characters in the drama, are encouraged to remain sufficiently outside what is happening on the stage to judge it critically and draw their own conclusions. (This is the much discussed ALIENATION, or 'A-effect'.) There has been much argument about the practicability of following Brecht's dicta on the subject to the letter, and it seems clear that as a practical man of the theatre he himself varied his directorial approach to suit the situation and the players he was dealing with. In fact his published ideas on the subject were intended only as rough guides and provocations rather than a cast-iron set of rules and regulations. Certainly his own best plays give scope for different types of production and do not depend for their effect on staging according to one particular theory, or even the models provided by Brecht's own productions with the Berliner Ensemble. See also EPIC THEATRE.

Bridie, James (real name Dr Osborne Henry Mavor; 1888–1951). Scottish dramatist and founder of the GLASGOW CITIZENS' THEATRE. Born in Glasgow, and early interested in the theatre, he studied medicine, continuing his practice throughout his writing career. He did not actually have a play produced until he was forty, and did not have a big success until *The Anatomist* (1930). Once started on a dramatist's career, he proved immensely prolific, turning out in the next twenty years at least thirty-four full-length plays (not including a number of rewrites so complete as to constitute new plays), as well as adaptations, one-act plays, and scripts for radio and film. The constant element in his plays is their immense vitality and gift for lively, speakable dialogue – usually applied with some carelessness of construction and an apparent impatience with the demands of simple story-telling in the theatre (many of his plays have one or two outstandingly good scenes rather too casually built into a theatrical whole, some start well but tail off). Probably the best and most lasting of his plays are those which draw extensively on his Scottish background and dramatize the conflicts between rigid Scottish puritanism and the world or the Devil (a figure in whom Bridie took a particular interest). In this series may be mentioned *The Anatomist*, which concerns the Edinburgh body-snatchers Burke and Hare and their relations with Dr Knox; *A Sleeping Clergyman* (1933), an elaborately constructed account of good and evil warring in one family through three generations; *Mr Bolfry* (1943), in which the Devil invades a Scottish manse; *Doctor Angelus* (1947), a Glasgow murder case; and *Mr Gillie* (1950), a quiet study of a village schoolmaster's life. Bridie's range extended also to broad comedy and farce (*What Say They?*, 1939; *It Depends What You Mean*, 1944), to biblical comedy and drama (*Tobias and the Angel*, 1930; *Jonah and the Whale*, 1930–32; *Susannah and the Elders*, 1937), to ballad opera, historical drama, and various unclassifiable plays. Outside the Scottish series, though, the most interesting is *Daphne Laureola* (1949) in which Edith Evans gave one of her best performances as Lady Pitts, a complex, capricious woman who is one of Bridie's best pieces of female characterization.

Brigadoon. Musical by FREDERICK LOEWE, book and lyrics by Alan Jay Lerner, first performed New York, 1947.

Brighouse, Harold (1883–1958). British dramatist of the MANCHESTER SCHOOL, associated with the Gaiety Theatre, Manchester, under the rule of MISS A. E. F. HORNIMAN. Wrote many realistic comedies of North Country life, the best known being *Hobson's Choice* (1916).

Britannicus. Tragedy by JEAN RACINE, first performed Paris, 1669.

British Drama League. Body for coordinating (in particular) amateur theatrical activity in Great Britain. Founded in 1919 by Geoffrey

Whitworth, it has over five thousand affiliated members involved in amateur theatre as well as membership among the smaller professional companies. Among the services it offers members are a library and an information service; it sponsors training courses for actors and directors, competitive drama festivals and play-writing competitions. The same sort of functions are performed in Scotland by an allied organization, the Scottish Community Drama Association.

Broadway. Street in New York on or near which are situated most of the important commercial New York theatres; hence Broadway as a generic term implies much the same as West End or Shaftesbury Avenue, suggesting commercial as distinct from experimental theatre. The latter is generally known as OFF-BROADWAY.

Broken Heart, The. Tragedy by JOHN FORD, first published 1633.

Brook, Peter (b. 1925). British director (and often also his own designer and composer). One of the most brilliant and inventive theatre men of his generation. His first London productions were *Doctor Faustus* in 1943 and Cocteau's *The Infernal Machine* in 1945. On leaving Oxford he directed an E.N.S.A. show and three productions at Birmingham Rep, and was already directing Shakespeare at Stratford when barely twenty. His early productions impressed mainly by their brilliant visual qualities and their extreme cleverness (sometimes demonstrated rather at the expense of the play): the culmination of this stage of his career was reached in 1949 with *Dark of the Moon*, an undistinguished play transfigured by Brook's staging, and Anouilh's *Ring Round the Moon*. In 1951, with his Stratford production of *Measure for Measure* (starring Gielgud), a more sober phase began, and since then he has been responsible for outstanding productions of such plays as *The Dark is Light Enough* (1954), *The Lark*, *Titus Andronicus* (1955), *The Tempest* (1957), *Irma La Douce*, *The Visit* (1958), as well as all the plays in the Brook–Scofield season at the Phoenix Theatre in 1956 (*Hamlet*, *The Power and the Glory*, *The Family Reunion*). Since 1956, when he directed *Cat on a Hot Tin Roof* in Paris, he has tended increasingly to divide his time between Britain and France, and has come more strongly under the influence of the ideas of ARTAUD; in 1962 he became a director of the Royal Shakespeare Company, and directed for them in particular a controversial *King Lear* with Paul Scofield and an enormously successful version of that director's play *par excellence*, the *Marat/Sade*. Among his later productions the most powerfully controversial was *US* (1966), a musico-dramatic polemic about the Vietnam war.

Brown, Ivor (1891–1974). British drama critic, particularly of the

Observer from 1928 to 1954. Author of numerous books on the drama and other topics, notably several on Shakespeare.

Brown, John Mason (b. 1900). American dramatic critic: of *New York Post* 1929–41, of *Saturday Review of Literature* 1944–55, and author of many books on the theatre, including *Two on the Aisle* (1939), a collection of his notices.

Browne, E. Martin (b. 1900). British director and actor, key figure in the modern revival of verse drama, especially religious verse drama. In 1935 he directed the first production of *Murder in the Cathedral* at Canterbury, and subsequently directed all T. S. Eliot's plays (*The Family Reunion*, 1939, *The Cocktail Party*, 1950, *The Confidential Clerk*, 1953, *The Elder Statesman*, 1958). In 1939 he founded the Pilgrim Players and ran the company, sponsored by the Arts Council, until 1948; in 1945 he staged a season of new verse drama at the Mercury Theatre, London, introducing Norman Nicholson's *The Old Man of the Mountains*, Anne Ridler's *The Shadow Factory*, Ronald Duncan's *This Way to the Tomb*, and Christopher Fry's *A Phoenix Too Frequent*. Director of the British Drama League, 1948–57.

Browne, Wynyard (1911–64). British dramatist and novelist. Began writing plays in 1947 with *Dark Summer*; major success *The Holly and the Ivy* (1950), a quiet sensitive piece about the relations between a clergyman and his grown-up children.

Browning, Robert (1812–89). British poet and author of several verse plays, mostly intended for reading rather than staging, though one of them, *Strafford* (1837) was written for and played by William Macready. Of his other plays the most frequently performed has been *Pippa Passes* (1841), although almost entirely by amateurs.

Browning Version, The. One-act play by TERENCE RATTIGAN, first performed with another, *Harlequinade*, in a programme called *Playbill*, London, 1948.

Büchner, Georg (1813–37). German poet and dramatist. His two principal plays *Dantons Tod* (1835) and *Woyzeck* (left unfinished at his death but in actable form) represent a reaction against the extravagant romanticism of SCHILLER and GOETHE, and anticipate at once the naturalist drama of the 1880s and, in their preoccupation with violence and morbid psychology, the EXPRESSIONIST theatre of the 1920s. They have been most widely performed since the 1914–18 war; *Dantons Tod*, a historical piece about the French Revolution, was revived in 1927 by Reinhardt and in 1938 by Orson Welles; *Woyzeck*, a gloomy picture of an illiterate soldiers' life and death, has achieved further fame as the basis of Alban Berg's opera *Wozzeck*. His only other surviving play, *Leonce und Lena*, a comedy written for a literary competition, is far less characteristic, though it contains passages suggestive of Büchner's better work.

Buckingham, George Villiers, Second Duke of (1628–87). Aristocratic dabbler in literature and the theatre; adapted FLETCHER'S comedy *The Chances* to Restoration taste in 1666 (this was the version revived by Laurence Olivier at Chichester in 1962) and in 1671 wrote a famous burlesque of the currently fashionable heroic tragedy in *The Rehearsal*. This has been revived itself on a number of occasions in the twentieth century, mainly by university groups, and also provided a model for SHERIDAN'S *The Critic* (1779).

Burbage, Richard (*c.*1567–1619). British actor. His father, James, was an actor and manager, and built the Blackfriars Theatre; his brother, Cuthbert, built the Globe on Bankside, where Burbage had his great successes. He began acting around 1584, and soon became recognized as the leading actor of his day, creating a number of important Shakespearian roles (Richard III, Hamlet, Othello, Lear) and also playing in works of Kyd, Ben Jonson, and Webster.

Burlesque. In eighteenth- and nineteenth-century usage a play parodying some current success or genre of the time, the most famous and lasting example being Sheridan's *The Critic* (1779). In America burlesque is a special type of show with a strong accent on sex and comedy, and designed for male audiences only. It began around 1865 (invented by one Michael Bennet Leavitt) and rapidly fell into a fairly regular form, consisting of a section of chorus numbers and comedy acts, a central section given over to conjurors, acrobats, sentimental songs, and other odds and ends, and a return to the chorus numbers and comedy acts with a finale of stomach dancers or 'leg-show'. The peak of burlesque's popularity was reached in the 1900s, and many of the most famous comics and singers of the period began in it, among them Sophie Tucker ('the last of the red-hot mommas'), Al Jolson, Fanny Brice, and W. C. Fields. After the First World War it came up against stiff competition from the cinema, and fought back by introducing striptease, which took over more and more of the shows and found its most famous practitioner in Gypsy Rose Lee. Burlesque throughout its career provoked the attacks of outraged moralists, and finally succumbed in the early 1940s, being banned from New York in 1942 and gradually fading away elsewhere to survive only in occasional club shows and cabarets devoted entirely to striptease.

Burnand, F. C. (Sir Francis Cowley; 1838–1917). British dramatist and editor of *Punch* (1880–1906). Wrote numerous ephemeral farces; is remembered in dramatic history mainly as founder of the A.D.C. at Cambridge and as adaptor of *Box and Cox* for Sullivan's operetta *Cox and Box*.

Burning Glass, The. Play by CHARLES MORGAN, first performed London, 1954.

Burnt Flowerbed, The (L'Aiuola bruciata). Play by UGO BETTI, first produced after his death, Rome, 1953; produced in London at the Arts, 1955.

Burrows, Abe (b. 1910). American dramatist and director; worked extensively in radio and television. Collaborated on musicals *Guys and Dolls* (1950), *Can-Can* (1953), *Silk Stockings* (1955), *First Impressions* (1959). Directed *Can-Can, First Impressions*, etc.

Burton, Richard (b. 1925). British actor. First success as Glan in *Druid's Rest* (1943); subsequently played in several Christopher Fry plays (*The Lady's Not for Burning*, 1949; *The Boy with a Cart*, 1950; *A Phoenix Too Frequent*, 1950), and Hamlet at the Old Vic (1953). His fine voice and striking presence seemed to mark him out as a possible successor to Laurence Olivier as an extrovert classical actor, an opinion supported by his Sir Toby Belch in *Twelfth Night* (1953) and his Othello and Iago (1956), but since then he has devoted himself almost entirely to the cinema, the principal exceptions being his appearance as Arthur in the Lerner and Loewe musical *Camelot* (New York, 1960) and his New York Hamlet (1964).

Business. An actor's smaller actions on the stage designed to illuminate character and/or occupy him believably when he is not the focus of attention.

Buskin. The thick-soled boot (*cothurnus*) worn by Greek actors in tragedy, and so, by extension, tragedy itself as written or acted.

Bus Stop. Play by WILLIAM INGE, first performed New York, 1955.

Buzzatti, Dino (b. 1907). Italian novelist and dramatist. His most important play, *Un Caso clinico* (1953), is related in technique to the Theatre of the ABSURD. It shows the decline and death of a middle-aged businessman by using the image of his gradual descent from a private ward on the top floor of a clinic to the bottom, where everybody dies. Buzzatti has subsequently written a powerful political satire for the stage, *Un Verme al ministerio*.

Byron, George Gordon, Lord (1788–1824). English poet and dramatist. Only one of his plays, *Marino Faliero* (1821) was performed during his lifetime, but he was on the committee of Drury Lane for a while and took an active and practical interest in drama. His plays, though in verse, are mostly less literary than those of his contemporaries (*Manfred*, a dramatic poem, is an exception, though it has been staged) and act better than they read. Of late there have been some spirited attempts (notably by G. Wilson Knight) to rehabilitate him as a dramatist.

C

Cabaret. An intimate entertainment, often in club surroundings, performed while the audience eat or drink. In a sense an offshoot of the traditional music hall, it takes place in a restaurant or a bar rather than a theatre, and is generally on a fairly small scale, with a minimum of props, although occasionally, as at a number of Las Vegas hotels and restaurants, or at the Talk of the Town (formerly the Hippodrome Theatre) in London, it can develop into a spectacular revue. The special advantages of the intimate form are that single performers – singers or comedians – can establish a very close relationship with their audiences and that the limitation of the audiences may permit a considerably more biting and outspoken sort of humour than is possible in entertainments intended for general consumption. Cabaret in pre-Hitler Germany was closely linked with the most advanced political and artistic groups, exerting considerable influence on the legitimate theatre of the time (notably on early Brecht). Most of the best American comedians of the 1950s (Mort Sahl, Shelley Berman, Lenny Bruce) have emerged from New York and San Francisco cabarets. Equally, the cabarets of the Establishment Club, London, have been the training ground for many of the people most closely associated with the popular boom in satire in the 1960s.

Caesar and Cleopatra. Historical comedy by GEORGE BERNARD SHAW, written 1898, first performed (by amateurs) Chicago, 1901; (professionally) Berlin, 1906.

Caesar's Wife. Drama by W. SOMERSET MAUGHAM, first performed London, 1919.

Calderón de la Barca, Pedro (1600–81). Spanish dramatist. He wrote his first play at the age of fourteen, studied mathematics at university, won a major poetry prize at the age of twenty, and after a period in the army entered holy orders. At the same time he wrote plays, and was eventually appointed Court Playwright and Master of the Revels to Philip IV. In this position one of his regular duties was to provide the texts of the *autos sacramentales*, religious dramas staged on Corpus Christi Day. Many of these survive, and are among his finest works; the most famous are *El gran teatro del mundo* (*c.*1645) and *La cena de Baltasar* (*c.*1634), but all of them contain exquisite poetry and witness his extraordinary ability to embody the dogmas of the Church in living drama. Though this and other forms of religious drama remained one of his major concerns throughout his life (for the last fifteen years of which he was Prior to the congregation of St Peter), he also wrote a great variety of secular entertainments for the court. These include a number of charming romantic comedies such as *El segreto a voces* (1626), *Casa con dos puertos mal es de guardar* (1629), which satirizes all the codes of honour and the extravagant jealousy which form the bases of Calderón's secular tragedy, and *La dama duende* (*c*.1629). Perhaps Calderón's most important works, however, are his dramas on religious themes (as apart from the *autos*) and one or two of his secular dramas. In the first class are *La devocion de la cruz* (*c*.1633), adapted into French by CAMUS, and *El magico prodizioso* (1637), a life of St Cyprian, partially translated in English by SHELLEY. In the second class, the most remarkable are *El alcalde de Zalamea* (*c*.1640), a drama of honour with a plebeian central figure, and the best-known of all Calderón's plays, *La vida es sueño* (*c*.1638), a strange play about a prisoner for whom the brief glimpse he is afforded of life outside the prison walls is nothing but a dream. In recent years there has been a considerable revival of interest in Calderón, represented by a number of productions in Britain and the U.S.

Call Me Madam. Musical by IRVING BERLIN, book by Russel Crouse and Howard Lindsay. First performed New York, 1950.

Camino Real. Dramatic fantasy by TENNESSEE WILLIAMS, first performed New York 1953.

Campbell, Mrs Patrick (1865–1940). English actress. First appeared in Liverpool in 1888; established herself as one of the leading players of her day with her performance as Paula in *The Second Mrs Tanqueray* (1893). Later she distinguished herself as a Shakespearian actress, playing Juliet and Ophelia opposite Forbes-Robertson, and also in Ibsen, particularly as the Rat Wife in *Little Eyolf* (1896), though Shaw thought her unsuitable for the role. Shaw was, however, fascinated by her personally, and had one of his platonic affairs with her, commemorated in a volume of letters which later formed the basis of Jerome Kilty's play *Dear Liar*. He wrote the part of Eliza Doolittle in *Pygmalion* for her and she played it in the first English production (1914). Later she was absent from the stage for long periods, and appeared in a number of films, but remained, and remains, something of a legend as an authentic *monstre sacré* of the English stage.

Campton, David (b. 1924). British playwright influenced by the Theatre of the ABSURD, the techniques of which he applies to directly political themes. His best works are two programmes of linked one-act plays, *The Lunatic View* (1957) and *Four Minute Warning* (1960).

Camus, Albert (1913–60). French novelist, philosopher, and dramatist. Born and educated in Algeria, he founded a company called Le Théâtre du Travail (later Le Théâtre de l'Équipe) in 1936, and there produced and sometimes acted in a wide variety of plays, including his own adaptations of Malraux's *Le Temps du mépris* and the *Prometheus Bound* of Aeschylus. During the war he lived in France, edited the underground magazine *Combat*, and wrote his first two plays *Le Malentendu* (1944) and *Caligula* (1945). *Le Malentendu* is a rather rigid demonstration of the 'absurdity' of existence (an idea already propounded in his novel *L'Étranger* and his essay *Le Mythe de Sisyphe*). *Caligula*, written earlier, but performed later, is more successful, though not much more dramatic; again the theme is man's struggles against the impossible and his unchangeable metaphysical solitude. *L'État de siège* (1948), evolved with Jean-Louis Barrault from Camus' novel *La Peste*, was an elaborately allegorical piece of *théâtre total*. *Les Justes* (1949) is another tragedy of conscience, this time with a background of the Russian revolution. Camus also made a number of adaptations, among them one of Faulkner's *As I Lay Dying* (1957), of Calderón's *La devocion de la cruz* (1953), and of Dostoyevsky's *The Devils* (as *Les Possédés*, 1958).

Can-Can. Musical by COLE PORTER, book by ABE BURROWS, first performed New York, 1953.

Candida. Play by GEORGE BERNARD SHAW, first produced South Shields, 1895; London, 1900.

Candide. Musical by LEONARD BERNSTEIN, book by LILLIAN HELLMAN, lyrics by Richard Wilbur, John La Touche, Dorothy Parker (based on the novel by Voltaire). First performed New York, 1956. New version, book by Hugh Wheeler, New York, 1975.

Cannan, Denis (b. 1919). British dramatist. His first play, *Max*, was performed at the Malvern Festival in 1949, but his main success came with *Captain Carvallo* (1950), a sophisticated and serious comedy, about military occupation. Subsequently he has written three elegant, perhaps too intelligent farces, *Misery Me* (1955), *You and Your Wife* (1955), and *Who's Your Father?* (1958), and has adapted Graham Greene's *The Power and the Glory* for the stage, in collaboration. He was also the writer principally involved in PETER BROOK's Vietnam show *US* (1966).

Čapek, Karel (1890–1938). Czech dramatist who often wrote in collaboration with his artist brother Josef. His best-known plays are perhaps the most lasting examples of Expressionist theatrical technique: *R.U.R.* (Rossum's Universal Robots) (1921) and *The Insect Play* (1921). The first is a piece of science fiction showing robots taking over the world, and the second an ironical picture of humanity under the guise of insects. Of his many other plays the most interesting is *The Makropoulos Affair* (1923), which poses the question whether the indefinite continuance of life is an unalloyed good.

Captain Brassbound's Conversion. Play by GEORGE BERNARD SHAW, first performed London, 1900.

Captain Carvallo. Comedy by DENIS CANNAN, first performed London, 1950.

Cards of Identity. Satirical comedy by NIGEL DENNIS, based on his own novel (1955), performed by the English Stage Company at the Royal Court, London, 1956.

Careless Rapture. Musical play by IVOR NOVELLO, lyrics by Christopher Hassall, first performed Drury Lane, 1936.

Caretaker, The. Play by HAROLD PINTER, first performed Arts Theatre, London, 1960.

Carousel. Musical by RICHARD RODGERS, book and lyrics by OSCAR HAMMERSTEIN II, based on FERENC MOLNAR's play *Liliom*. First performed New York, 1945.

Carroll, Paul Vincent (b. 1900). Irish dramatist, many of whose plays have been produced at the ABBEY THEATRE, Dublin, his second, *Things That Are Caesar's* (1932), winning a prize offered by the theatre for a new play. His greatest success outside Ireland was *Shadow and Substance* (1934), produced in New York in 1937. Later plays include *The Strings, My Lord, Are False* (1942), *The Wise Have Not Spoken* (1944), and *The Wayward Saint* (1955).

Casarès, Maria (b. 1922). French actress, specialist in intense, off-beat modern roles and in modern interpretation of classical tragedy. Her first major successes were in *Deirdre of the Sorrows* (1943) and the film *Les Dames du Bois de Boulogne* (1945); from them she went on to play Hilde in *The Master Builder* and leading roles in three Camus plays, *Le Malentendu*, *L'État de siège*, and *Les Justes*, as well as in a curious *avant-garde* work by Henri Pichette, *Les Épiphanies* (1947). In 1952 she joined the Comédie-Française, there playing a variety of roles, among them the Step-Daughter in *Six Characters in Search of an Author* and La Périchole in Merimée's *Le Carrosse du Saint-Sacrement*. The latter first revealed the comic side of her talents, subsequently brilliantly demonstrated in Marivaux's *Le Triomphe de l'amour* (1955), which she played with the Vilar company. More recently she has shone as Lady Macbeth, Phèdre, and Mrs Patrick Campbell in *Dear Liar*.

Caste. Comedy by T. W. ROBERTSON, landmark in English realism, first performed London, 1867.

Cat and the Canary, The. Comedy thriller by John Willard, first performed New York, 1922. Progenitor of many comedies involving murder and haunted houses; frequently revived and several times filmed.

Catharsis. Aristotelian concept of tragedy's function as a purgation by pity and terror (or perhaps a purgation of those emotions). See also ARISTOTLE.

Cat on a Hot Tin Roof. Drama by TENNESSEE WILLIAMS, first performed New York, 1955.

Catwalk. Narrow metal bridge over the stage, from which stage-hands can adjust scenery hung above the stage ('flown').

Caucasian Chalk Circle, The (Der kaukasische Kreidekreis). Play by BERTOLT BRECHT written 1943–5, first performed (in English) by students, Northfield, Minnesota, 1948; (in German) by the Berliner Ensemble, Berlin, 1954.

Cavalcade. Spectacular drama by NOËL COWARD, first performed Drury Lane, London, 1931.

Cenci, The. Verse tragedy by PERCY BYSSHE SHELLEY, written 1818, first performed (privately) London, 1886.

Censorship. Dramatic censorship in Britain, long the duty of the Lord Chamberlain, began in Tudor times as a function of the Master of the King's Revels, who organized dramatic entertainments for the court and incidentally saw to it that they contained nothing to offend royal susceptibilities. To these primarily political duties was added in the reign of James I a responsibility for the religious propriety of stage entertainments, and little by little the duties devolved on the Master of the Revels' superior, the Lord Chamberlain. Up to 1737, though, the position of the Lord Chamberlain remained undefined and without statutory recognition, and he did not interfere with the moral tendencies of the stage, but simply watched over its political and religious propriety. In 1737 the Lord Chamberlain's position in the theatre was defined by statute: he was made the dispenser of licences for dramatic performances and it was laid down that all new plays and additions to old plays had to receive his approval before they could be publicly performed. In 1843 the Theatres Act further codified the laws relating to theatrical performance: by this the Lord Chamberlain became the licensing authority for all theatres in London (apart from Drury Lane and Covent Garden) and in all places of royal residence, as well as continuing as the censor of all theatre scripts. Strictly speaking he had control over the productions of private theatrical societies and theatre clubs as well as over normal public theatre performances, but did not usually exercise this prerogative. He was not responsible for any of his decisions to anyone except the sovereign, and did not have to provide any explanations of his actions; there was no appeal against his decisions. During the 1950s and 1960s there had been ever-increasing agitation for reform, in response to which the Lord Chamberlain gradually liberalized his rulings, until finally in 1968 theatre censorship was abolished in Britain.

Centre 42. An organization of artists and writers founded by ARNOLD WESKER to stage arts festivals in parts of Great Britain usually neglected. Its first festival was held at Wellingborough in September 1962; further activities have been hampered by lack of funds. In 1967 it reappeared in a new form as the moving spirit in the arts centre set up in the Round House, Chalk Farm, London.

Centres dramatiques. A group of five state-supported provincial centres for the theatre set up in France between 1947 and 1952 to counteract the increasing centralization of theatrical activity on Paris. The centres are mostly based on university towns: the Strasbourg centre covers eastern France and Alsace-Lorraine; the Saint-Étienne centre covers the Rhone valley, Burgundy, and the Alps; the Toulouse centre south-west France from Bordeaux to the Rhone; the Rennes centre the north-west, Brittany, Normandy, and the Loire valley; and the fifth centre covers Provence and the Mediterranean coast. Each centre has at least one professional company touring for most of the year and playing in cinemas, village halls, or whatever offers, usually in a repertoire of the classics with a few modern plays.

César. Family drama by MARCEL PAGNOL, the third of a Marseilles trilogy begun with *Marius* and *Fanny*, first performed Paris, 1946. (Play based on the film of 1933.)

Chairs, The (Les Chaises). One-act play by EUGÈNE IONESCO, first performed Paris, 1952.

Chamberlain, Lord, see CENSORSHIP.

Chamberlain's Men. Elizabethan theatre company to which Shakespeare was attached for most of his career. Founded in 1594, it moved from James Burbage's theatre to the Globe in 1599, and later took over Blackfriars Theatre, where it played indoors in winter, while continuing to play outdoors at the Globe during the summer until this was burnt down in 1613. The company, known as the King's Men after 1603, opened the new Globe in 1614, but broke up after the death of Burbage in 1619. During its life the company first performed the majority of Shakespeare's plays, as well as a number of plays by Ben Jonson, Beaumont and Fletcher, and Webster.

Champion, Harry (1866–1942). British music-hall comedian, his most famous songs being *Any Old Iron, Boiled Beef and Carrots*, and *I'm 'Enery the Eighth I Am*.

Changeling, The. Tragedy by THOMAS MIDDLETON and WILLIAM ROWLEY, first performed London, 1622.

Chapman, George (*c*.1560–1634). English dramatist and poet, best remembered for his translation of Homer, the subject of a famous sonnet by Keats. In drama his most famous work was *Bussy d'Ambois* (*c*.1604), a Senecan melodrama full of blood and thunder showing a titanic, self-sufficient Renaissance man at odds with the world. In its sequel, *The Revenge of Bussy d'Ambois* (*c*.1610), on the other hand, Bussy's brother and avenger Clermont appears as the other sort of Senecan hero: the quiet, thinking stoic actuated entirely by a sense of duty. Perhaps more appealing to modern readers and worth stage revival are Chapman's comedies, especially *All Fools* (*c*.1604), which Swinburne called one of the best comedies in the English language and which is based on two plays by Terence. Chapman also collaborated on *Eastward Ho!* (1605) with Jonson and Marston, and shared their imprisonment when the play gave offence to James I.

Chapman, Henry (b. 1910). British dramatist, former building labourer, author of a group of realistic plays about building sites: *You Won't Always Be on Top* (1957), *On the Wall* (1960), *That's Us* (1961).

Charley's Aunt. Farce by BRANDON THOMAS, first performed London, 1892. Musical version, *Where's Charley?*, songs by Frank Loesser, book by GEORGE ABBOTT, first performed New York, 1948.

Charlot, André (1882–1956). British impresario, and C. B. Cochran's chief rival as deviser and presenter of elaborate musical shows in the inter-war years. *Charlot's Revue* (1924) marked Noël Coward's debut in revue, as writer and performer. The *Charlot's Revue* of 1925 included Gertrude Lawrence, Beatrice Lillie, and Jack Buchanan in its cast.

Chayefsky, Paddy (b. 1923). American dramatist. During the war wrote book and lyrics for army musical *No T.O. for Love*. First made a name in television with such plays as *Marty, Bachelor Party*, and *The Catered Affair*, all subsequently filmed. After the spectacular success of the film of *Marty* (1955) he turned increasingly to the stage and the cinema. His first stage play, *Middle of the Night* (1956), explored much the same sort of subject-matter as his television plays: it is a quiet, naturalistic examination of emotional problems in a modern urban setting. By contrast, his second stage play, *The Tenth Man* (1959), is a comedy drama based on the old Jewish legend of the dybbuk, a spirit which can take possession of a human body. A later play, *The Passion of Joseph D.* (1964) concerns a turning point in the life of Stalin.

Chekhov, Anton (1860–1904). Russian dramatist. Though of humble origins, he studied medicine at Moscow University and graduated in 1884. While still at university he wrote and published a number of short stories which attracted critical attention. Shortly after leaving he turned to drama, writing a group of one-act farces along the lines of French farces then popular in Russia, but adapted to the Russian scene and Russian character. Among the most popular of these are *The Bear* (1888), *The Proposal* (1889), and *The Wedding* (1890). But at the same time a tragic element in his talent, already evident in his stories, found expression in his plays: the very first, a one-act sketch called *On the High Road* (1884), is almost entirely tragic, and when in 1887 he tried his hand at a full-length play, *Ivanov*, it was a gloomy study of a bitter marriage based on a brief infatuation. This was produced, with no great success, and his second full-length play, *The Wood Demon* (1889), had no better luck, nor indeed did his third, *The Seagull*, when produced at the Imperial Theatre in 1896. (Another play from this period, *Platonov*, remained unpublished, and unperformed, until the 1920s.) In fact Chekhov had almost decided to give up drama for good when he was persuaded by NEMIROVICH-DANCHENKO to let the new Moscow Art Theatre, run by him and STANISLAVSKY, revive *The Seagull* in 1898.

This production first achieved the delicate balance of tragedy and comedy which is Chekhov's most individual contribution to drama. Though in many respects the situation of the characters is tragic, and the play ends with a suicide, from another point of view they are absurd, and the full tragic force of the play comes out only when its comic possibilities are given full scope: it is tragic *because* it is absurd. (A point until recently largely missed in British and American productions of Chekhov, which tended to play too much for a sort of elegaic poetry at the expense of the other equally important elements.) *The Seagull* also signals another revolutionary quality in Chekhov's work: it is essentially a play for a team of actors rather than for one or two star principals and supporting cast, and it therefore proved particularly fitting as a vehicle for the new approach to acting and production which characterized the Moscow Art Theatre at this time.

The success of the new production of *The Seagull* encouraged Chekhov to write more plays, the first of which, *Uncle Vanya* (1899), was a reworking of his earlier *The Wood Demon*, and in many ways the least satisfying of his mature works. It was followed in 1901 by *The Three Sisters* and in 1904 by *The Cherry Orchard*, which are

Chekhov's masterpieces. Both are atmospheric studies of groups of characters in the Russian provinces, and the plots, in so far as they have plots, are simply the interaction of the characters: the three sisters dreaming of Moscow but never going there, the drifting family brooding about whether the cherry orchard should or should not be sold. Hardly anywhere in either play does anyone take hold decisively of his or her own destiny: all are caught in the slack water between a hazy, nostalgically remembered past and an equally hazy but possibly heroic future (the latter, of course, being emphasized in current Soviet productions): waiting with greater or less apprehension for the world they have known to be swept away and replaced by a new. It is one of the fascinating unanswerable questions of literary history what Chekhov would have made of the Russian Revolution and its consequences; unfortunately he died in 1904, at the height of his powers and still at the beginning of general acceptance in Russia and abroad as one of the greatest precursors of modern drama.

Cherry Orchard, The (Vishnyovy sad). Tragi-comedy by ANTON CHEKHOV, first performed Moscow Art Theatre, 1904.

Chevalier, Albert (1861–1923). English music-hall entertainer, noted chiefly for his characterization of a cockney costermonger and his comic or sentimental songs, often written by himself. The best known are *My Old Dutch* and *Knocked 'Em in the Old Kent Road*.

Chichester Festival. Summer drama festival at the newly built Festival Theatre, Chichester, begun in 1962. Under the direction of Laurence Olivier until 1966, when John Clements took over. The festivals have included productions of plays by Chekhov, Beaumont and Fletcher, John Ford, John Arden, and Peter Shaffer, all on an open arena-type stage surrounded by spectators on three sides: the plan of the theatre being modelled on that of the Festival Theatre at Stratford, Ontario.

Chicken Soup With Barley. Jewish family drama by ARNOLD WESKER, first of the 'Wesker Trilogy'. First performed Coventry, 1958; first performed as part of the trilogy by the English Stage Company at the Royal Court, London, 1960.

Chikamatsu Monzaemon (1653–1725). The greatest Japanese dramatist, author of nearly 160 plays for the puppet (JORURI) or KABUKI theatre. Born into a family of hereditary *samurai*, he drifted in and out of court life and trade before settling down as a playwright, probably because of the success of his first known play, *The Soga Successors* (1683). This was a puppet play, and so were most of its immediate successors, the most notable of which, *Kagekiyo Victorious* (1686), revolutionized the genre with its bold departure from the stereotyped form and characterization normal at the time. Between

1695 and 1705 Chikamatsu devoted himself almost exclusively to Kabuki, working very closely with the actor Sakata Tojuro. Tojuro's approaching retirement and his own great success with his puppet-play *The Love Suicides at Sonezaki* (1703) persuaded him then to return to the puppet theatre, and from 1705 until his death he wrote nothing but Joruri. In this genre he specialized in two forms, domestic tragedy and historical drama. The historical dramas (the most famous of which is *The Battles of Coxinga*, 1715) are in general much longer and more elaborate than the domestic tragedies, in which his best work is to be found. Though some of Chikamatsu's puppet plays were later adapted to the Kabuki stage, he remains in general today a dramatist more read than performed, though the film *Chikamatsu Monogatari* was based on one of his love-suicide tragedies.

Children's Hour, The. Drama by LILLIAN HELLMAN, first performed New York, 1934.

Chiltern Hundreds, The. Light comedy by WILLIAM DOUGLAS HOME, first performed London, 1947.

Chinese Theatre. The origin of drama in China goes back at least to the sixth century A.D., and since that time there has been a continuous tradition of highly conventionalized dramatic performance up to the 1920s, when Western influences began to make themselves felt with a progressive vulgarization of traditional-style performances in the larger cities and a tentative introduction of stage realism. The characteristic form of traditional Chinese theatre is a drama in numerous short scenes, partly spoken, partly sung, and partly mimed. It is played with virtually no scenery, but with a great variety of symbolic props: a very formalized depiction of an archway on a cloth banner may represent a city, or an outline of a series of peaks painted on a light screen a range of mountains: a blue cloth agitated by stage-hands stands for water, four black flags fluttering for a strong wind, two yellow flags and wheels for a chariot and so on. Most of the burden of conveying time, place, and atmosphere therefore falls on the performers, who are trained from an early age in acrobatic control of their bodies and acquire in addition a wide range of conventional gestures.

The material of the plays is mainly drawn from traditional stories, legends and history, and is therefore familiar to the majority of the audience. Comedy and tragedy are freely mixed, though the endings are generally happy. The texts are usually mere outlines (composed in a special theatrical mixture of literary and colloquial Chinese) and are intended to be freely developed by the performers, rather as with Western COMMEDIA DELL'ARTE. The theatre itself has an almost square stage projecting into the audience, with a flat wall or curtain at the back, flanked by two openings: entrance on the left, exit on the right. The actors are divided basically into four classes: *sheng* (male characters), *tan* (female characters), *ching* (powerful or grotesque males), and *ch'on* (broad comics) – though each has numerous intricate sub-divisions. The female parts were until quite recently always played by men, but since the beginning of the twentieth century they have been played more and more often by women.

Chips With Everything. Service drama by ARNOLD WESKER, first performed by the English Stage Company at the Royal Court, London, 1962.

Chocolate Soldier, The (Der tapfere Soldat). Operetta by Oscar Straus, book by Rudolf Bernauer and Leopold Jacobson, based on GEORGE BERNARD SHAW's comedy *Arms and the Man*. First performed Vienna, 1908.

Choephori, see ORESTEIA.

Chorus. A group of actors in Greek drama. They were at first the main performers, tragedy consisting initially of a series of choric odes with interludes in which a single actor conversed with the chorus. Gradually, they came to occupy the role of commentators on the dramatic action, standing for the most part aside from it but representing townspeople and sometimes engaging as such in exchanges with the principal actors. In Elizabethan drama a 'chorus' sometimes occurs in the person of an individual actor, speaking a prologue and occasional explanatory linking passages (in *Henry V* and *Pericles*, for example). In the modern theatre there have been sporadic returns to the idea of a chorus (usually now a single actor) as commentator on the action, stepping in and out of it at will (in various plays by or influenced by Brecht: *The Caucasian Chalk Circle*, *A Man for All Seasons*, *The Entertainer*; the Women of Canterbury in *Murder in the Cathedral*; the narrator in Tennessee Williams's *The Glass Menagerie*). The term 'chorus' in the modern theatre more usually refers, though, to the singers and dancers in musicals and operettas, who play a more or less background role varying as the occasion demands.

Christie, Agatha (1891–1976). British crime novelist and dramatist. Several of her novels have been successfully dramatized, notably *Ten Little Niggers* (1943), but she did not write an original play until *The Hollow* in 1951. Her greatest success has been *The Mousetrap*, which opened in 1952 and is still (1977) running, holding the record for the longest continuous run in London of any play. Other plays include *Witness for the Prosecution* (1953), *The Spider's Web* (1954), and *The Unexpected Guest* (1958).

Chu-Chin-Chow. Musical extravaganza by Frederick Norton, book by Oscar Asche (based on *Ali Baba and the Forty Thieves*), first performed 1916, and for many years record-holder for the longest London run with 2,238 consecutive performances.

Church drama. In the Middle Ages the church in England played an important part in drama (see MEDIEVAL THEATRE), but at the Reformation it ceased for more than three hundred years to have any but the most occasional, casual connexion with drama (and indeed its more evangelical sections appeared more often as the theatre's most active opponents). At the beginning of the twentieth century, however, a revival of church interest in drama took place, beginning with a series of revivals of medieval religious plays (the first being William Poel's production of *Everyman* in 1901). In 1911 the Morality Play Society was founded to perform Mabel Dearmer's *The Soul of the World*, and was soon joined by other groups devoted to religious drama. In 1929 the Canterbury Festival of Music and Drama was instituted (and later produced T. S. Eliot's *Murder in the Cathedral*, Charles Williams's *Thomas Cranmer of Canterbury*, Dorothy L. Sayers's *The Zeal of Thy House*, and other plays), followed shortly afterwards by similar enterprises in other dioceses: Chichester, Bristol, Exeter. In the war years the Pilgrim Players under E. MARTIN BROWNE continued and extended the work, and religious drama is now generally recognized in the Church of England as an important and worthwhile activity.

Cibber, Colley (1671–1757). British dramatist, theatre manager, and actor. He initiated the vogue for sentimental comedy which succeeded the robuster humour of the Restoration with his *Love's Last Shift, or, The Fool in Fashion* (1696) and had other considerable successes with *The Careless Husband* (1705) and with *The Non-Juror* (1717), adapted from MOLIÈRE'S *Tartuffe*. He was for many years one of the three managers of DRURY LANE, and wrote a famous autobiography, *An Apology for the Life of Mr Colley Cibber, Comedian*, which is one of our best sources of information on Restoration acting. His second wife, Susanna Maria, was a notable actress in her day, appearing often with GARRICK.

Cid, Le. 'Heroic comedy' by PIERRE CORNEILLE, first performed Paris, 1636.

Circle, The. Comedy by W. SOMERSET MAUGHAM, first performed London, 1921.

Circus. Originally an arena in which Roman chariot races and gladiatorial combats took place. In modern terms, a species of entertainment involving trained animals, acrobats, and clowns, usually performed by touring companies in tents (the principal of which is known as the 'big top') or in specially prepared indoor halls, in which the audience sit all round the central 'ring' where the show takes place. In Britain the best-known circuses are Billy Smart's and Sanger's; in America circuses are always associated with the name of PHINEAS T. BARNUM. There have been occasional attempts to combine circus with the legitimate theatre, particularly in the spectacular melodramas of the nineteenth century; more recently Billy Rose included a circus in his musical extravaganza *Jumbo* (1935).

Clandestine Marriage, The. Comedy by DAVID GARRICK and GEORGE COLMAN the Elder, first performed Drury Lane, 1766.

Claque. Group of organized (and sometimes paid) applauders in a theatrical audience.

Claudel, Paul (1868–1955). French dramatist and poet. Devoutly religious after a sort of mystical revelation he underwent at the age of eighteen, he joined the French diplomatic service and achieved a considerable degree of wordly success, holding consular posts in various countries and becoming French ambassador to Japan (1921), the U.S.A. (1927), and Belgium (1933). During all this time he was a prolific author of plays, poems and prose, published at first anonymously, and all expressing his profound religious convictions. His first play, *Tête d'or*, was written as early as 1889 (though like all his work frequently revised) and is his only non-Christian play; it concerns a man who tries to rule his own destiny, and in the end fails. During the following years he wrote several plays, though none reached the stage until his modern miracle play *L'Annonce faite à Marie* in 1912. In 1906 he wrote one of his most important plays, *Partage de midi*, a tragic triangle drama based on an incident in his own life, but would not allow it to be published or performed until 1948, when it was staged by Jean-Louis Barrault. In fact, though he continued to write and usually to publish plays, none except *L'Annonce faite à Marie* had any great success in France until the production of *L'Ôtage* at the Comédie-Française in 1934. (He had been luckier abroad: *L'Ôtage* in particular scored a triumph in London in 1919 with Sybil Thorndike in the lead.) From then on he became increasingly well regarded by French critics and public, first through his successful collaborations with the composer Arthur Honegger on the opera-oratorios *Jeanne d'Arc au bûcher* (1935) and *La Danse des morts* (1938), and then through his collaborations with the PITOËFFS and particularly with BARRAULT, who staged *Le Soulier de satin*, his largest and most ambitious work (written 1919–24) in 1943, *Partage de midi* in 1948, and *Christophe Colombe* in 1953. Because of its complete commitment to the Roman Catholic faith and view of life Claudel's drama seems bound to provoke violent feelings of partisanship, for or against, but *Le Soulier de satin*, an enormous fresco of the Renaissance world across which stretches a great story of separated lovers and their way to salvation, and *Partage de midi*, a sketch of the same subject in modern, realistic terms, remain unique in dramatic literature and among the classics of twentieth-century French drama.

Clements, John (b. 1910). British actor and manager, noted mainly for his successful revivals of seventeenth- and eighteenth-century comedies, in which he has generally played with his wife Kay Hammond – *The Beaux' Stratagem* (1949), *The Rivals*, *The Way of the World* (1956) – and other classics, among them *Man and Superman* complete (1951), *The Wild Duck* (1955), *The Seagull*, and *The Doctor's Dilemma* (1956). In 1965 he took over the management of the annual Chichester Festival drama season. Knighted 1968.

Closet drama. Generic term for drama written to be read rather than acted. Most of the Romantic poets wrote at least one play of this sort, in effect if not always in intention: Shelley, *The Cenci* (1818), *Prometheus Unbound* (1819); Keats, *Otho the Great* (1820); Byron, *Manfred* (1817); Wordsworth, *The Borderers* (1796); Beddoes, *Death's Jest Book* (1825–49).

Clouds, The. Comedy by ARISTOPHANES, first performed Athens, 423 B.C.

Clown. Comic performer in theatre or circus. Some of the functions of the medieval and Renaissance court jester are carried over into the fools of the Elizabethan stage, such as the jesters in *Twelfth Night* and *King Lear*: these are professional humorists, as distinct from the comic butts of pastorals like *As You Like It*. Later these two traditions fused with alien strains from the COMMEDIA DELL'ARTE to make up the classic clown figure of pantomime, harlequinade, and circus: the cheery buffoon and tumbler with grotesque costume and make-up. Later still the opera *I Pagliacci* gave concrete form to a notion which had been vaguely present for some time: that the clown was in some way essentially pathetic as well as funny. Nowadays clowns proper are found only in circuses. See also GRIMALDI, GROCK.

Clurman, Harold (b. 1901). American director, manager, and critic. Began in the theatre at the experimental Greenwich Village Playhouse in 1924; worked as assistant stage-manager, actor and play-reader for THEATRE GUILD 1925–31. In 1931 founded GROUP THEATRE as an independent organization and became its managing director. In his book *The Fervent Years* he has told the story of this organization, its left-wing principles and its championship of the work of such dramatists as CLIFFORD ODETS, WILLIAM SAROYAN, Irwin Shaw, and SIDNEY KINGSLEY, many of whose plays were directed by Clurman himself or by such graduates of the Group as ELIA KAZAN. Since the break-up of the Group in 1941 Clurman has been one of the most successful of America's independent directors. He has written widely on the theatre, and has published *Lies Like Truth*, a volume of drama criticism.

Cochran, C. B. (Sir Charles Blake; 1873–1951). Leading British impresario of his day, specializing in musicals, revues, and comedy. He began as an actor, then became an agent and promoter, his first stage production being *John Gabriel Borkman* in New York (1897). In 1911 he presented Reinhardt's production of *The Miracle* at Olympia. In 1914 he began the vogue of intimate revue with a series of shows (*Odds and Ends, More, Pell Mell*) at the Ambassadors, and later, from 1918 to 1931, came into his own with a succession of more spectacular revues at the London Pavilion: *As You Were, This Year of Grace, Wake Up and Dream*, among others. He was for many years associated with Noël Coward's work, presenting *Bitter Sweet* and *Cavalcade*, and after the Second World War he concentrated mainly on musical comedies, his biggest success being *Bless the Bride*. In 1934 he was elected a governor of the Shakespeare Memorial Theatre, Stratford on Avon; he was knighted for services to the theatre in 1948.

Cocktail Party, The. Verse play by T. S. ELIOT, first performed Edinburgh Festival, 1949.

Cocteau, Jean (1889–1963). French dramatist, poet, novelist, filmmaker, and designer. Cocteau first made a name for himself as a poet, but in 1912 he struck up a friendship with Diaghilev, at that time visiting Paris for the first time with his Russian Ballet, and this led to his taking a greater interest in the theatre and producing a group of ballets and mimes (*Parade*, 1916; *Le Bœuf sur le toit*, 1920; *Les Mariés de la Tour Eiffel*, 1921) and then a series of reworkings of classic themes and materials (*Antigone*, 1922; *Roméo et Juliette*, 1924; *Orphée*, 1926). The most lasting success of his early stage works was *La Voix humaine*, a one-act monodrama first produced at the Comédie-Française in 1930; his first major play was *La Machine infernale*, a reworking of the Oedipus story which appeared in 1934. From then on he produced a bewildering variety of plays: transfigured boulevard melodramas like *Les Parents terribles* (1938) and *La Machine à écrire* (1941); romantic costume drama in the style of a modern Victor Hugo like *L'Aigle à deux têtes* (1946); the Arthurian tragi-comedy of *Les Chevaliers de la Table Ronde* (1937); the graceful love story in couplets of *Renaud et Armide* (1943). At the same time he made a succession of films, some adapted from his own plays, others, like *La Belle et la Bête* (1945) and *Orphée* (1950), original. All his works, despite their superficial differences, return to the same obsessive themes: love and death, the separation of lovers by one means or another, and all mirror his extraordinary personality. He is the supreme showman among French dramatists, and it has been suggested that his plays are really a succession of confidence tricks, all technique and no substance. There is something in this view, but it seems likely that at least a handful of his plays will survive the vicissitudes of fashion.

Cohan, George M. (1878–1942). American actor, dramatist, song-writer and manager, specialist in light comedy and musicals. His most famous shows were *Forty-Five Minutes from Broadway* (1906), *The Little Millionaire* (1911), and *Little Nelly Kelly* (1923); later he appeared as an actor in shows by others, notably O'Neill's *Ah, Wilderness!* (1933) and Rodgers and Hart's *I'd Rather be Right* (1937). Among his other claims to fame is having written *Over There*, the great 1914–18 American war song.

Collier, Jeremy (1650–1726). English non-juror and pamphleteer, re-membered as the author of a famous attack on the morals of the Restoration theatre, *A Short View of the Immorality and Profaneness of the English Stage* (1698).

Collins, Lottie (1866–1910). English music-hall performer, who owed her success entirely to one song, *Ta-Ra-Ra-Boom-De-Ay*, and the dance that went with it, which she first performed in 1891. Her daughter **José Collins** (1887–1958) was a star of musical comedy, her best-remembered role being in *The Maid of the Mountains* (1917).

Colman, George (the Elder; 1732–94). English dramatist and manager. His most famous plays, *The Jealous Wife* (1761) and *The Clandestine Marriage* (1766), both comedies, were written for, and in the latter case with, GARRICK. From 1767 to 1774 he was one of the lessees of COVENT GARDEN, during which time Goldsmith's plays, among others, were put on there. From 1776 to his death he was manager of the Haymarket, a position taken over by his son **George Colman the Younger** (1762–1836), a prolific dramatist whose best works were probably *The Iron Chest* (1796) and *John Bull, or, the Englishman's Fireside* (1803).

Colombe. *Pièce brillante* by JEAN ANOUILH, first performed Paris, 1951.

Columbine. The young girl in English harlequinades, daughter of

PANTALOON and in love with HARLEQUIN. In COMMEDIA DELL'
ARTE Columbine was a serving maid, as Arlecchino was a servant,
and they were not lovers.

Come Back, Little Sheba. Drama by WILLIAM INGE, first performed
New York, 1950.

Comédie-Française. French national theatre, founded in 1680, when
three existing companies, one of them Molière's, were combined. Its
original name was the Théâtre-Français, or Maison de Molière; the
name Comédie-Française apparently came into use to distinguish it
from a nearby company, the Comédie-Italienne. During the eighteenth century it moved twice to new quarters, and during the Revolution the company split into opposing factions, to be reconstituted in
the form it has today in 1803. It is still organized along cooperative
lines, according to the charter originally granted by Louis XIV and
revised by Napoleon. There are two grades of membership, the *pensionnaire* and the *sociétaire*; an actor is chosen on the merit of his
work, and if he succeeds in a special audition in a role of his choice he
becomes a *pensionnaire*, to be elevated to the level of *sociétaire* only
when a place falls vacant on the death, resignation or retirement of
another *sociétaire*. In theory a *sociétaire* is engaged to the company
for a long term, perhaps even for the whole of his acting life, but
most of the great French actors have had stormy, on-off relations
with the company, and in 1945 there was a major revolution in the
company which resulted in all the *sociétaires* at that time being left
free to stay or leave as they wished. A further reform of the company's
constitution took place in 1959.

Comedy of Errors, The. Farce by WILLIAM SHAKESPEARE, first recorded performance London, 1594.

Comic opera. Apart from its obvious meaning as an opera which happens to have a humorous plot, the term 'comic opera' often occurs,
like its French equivalent *opéra comique*, as applied to dramatic
shows with spoken dialogue and songs and dances (e.g., the works of
Offenbach or GILBERT and Sullivan). The plot of these need not be
essentially comic; it may be romantic and even, as with *The Yeoman
of the Guard*, have tragic elements. Towards the end of the nineteenth
century this *genre* came more generally to be known as operetta (see
MUSICAL COMEDY).

Command Performance. Performance of a theatrical show specially
commanded by the monarch and taking place in his or her presence.
Normally applied today to the annual royal variety show, the pro-
ceeds of which go to charity.

Commedia dell'arte. A form of popular Italian comedy which had its greatest vogue in the sixteenth and seventeenth centuries. It was performed by specially trained troupes of actors who improvised on prearranged synopses involving a group of familiar formalized characters (see ARLECCHINO, COLUMBINE, PANTALOON, PIERROT, PULCINELLA) and a series of stock situations (young wife deceiving old husband, servants and masters exchanging roles in the cause of intrigue, etc.). Though the *commedia dell'arte* proper died out in the mid eighteenth century, it exerted considerable influence on writers of the time, especially Molière and Marivaux in France, and left its mark on the English PANTOMIME, HARLEQUINADE, and PUNCH-AND-JUDY show. In France, too, it founded a tradition of mime performance which has had its exponents right up to JEAN-LOUIS BARRAULT and MARCEL MARCEAU in our own day.

Community Theatre. An amateur theatre movement in the U.S.A., started about 1910, and intended to create theatre away from the ordinary run of commercial theatre, with local talent and enterprise. Over the years, especially with the reduction of the professional theatre's touring circuits, community theatres have become increasingly general in their repertoire and increasingly professional in their personnel, even though they usually retain their non-profit-making status. Most community theatres nowadays have at least a professional director, and often a leavening of professional actors.

Compagnie des Quinze. A group of French actors which originated when JACQUES COPEAU took some of his troupe from the Vieux-Colombier to settle and work in Burgundy. Here they were first known as 'Les Copiaux', but in 1931 Copeau's nephew MICHEL SAINT-DENIS took over direction and they were reorganized as the 'Compagnie des Quinze'. The company had its resident playwright, ANDRÉ OBEY, and performed several of his works, most notably *Le Viol de Lucrèce* and *Noé*. These exploited to the full the company's varied aptitudes in speech and mime, and were designed to be played, according to Copeau's principles, with the minimum of naturalistic setting: the normal form of staging was a light, collapsible rostrum which could be assembled in various ways according to the requirements of the text with the occasional addition of one or two pieces of highly formalized scenery. The company appeared with great success in Paris and London before disbanding in 1934.

Complaisant Lover, The. Comedy by GRAHAM GREENE, first performed London, 1959.

Comus. Masque by JOHN MILTON, first performed Ludlow Castle, 1634.

Condell, Henry (d. 1627). English actor, editor with JOHN HEMINGE of the First Folio collection of Shakespeare's plays.

69

Confidential Clerk, The. Verse play by T. S. ELIOT, first performed Edinburgh Festival, 1953.

Congreve, William (1670–1729). English playwright, the greatest exponent of Restoration comedy. After studying at Trinity College, Dublin, where Swift was a fellow-student, he entered Middle Temple, but took up writing almost immediately, first with a novel, *Incognita*, then with a play, *The Old Bachelor*, which was staged with great success in 1693. He followed it in 1694 with another comedy, *The Double-Dealer*, and in 1695 with *Love For Love*, produced by and starring BETTERTON, which immediately established him as the leading dramatist of his day. Two years later he had an almost equal popular success with his verse tragedy *The Mourning Bride*, which remained for many years a favourite vehicle for the great tragediennes. Unfortunately his next and best play, *The Way of the World* (1700) was not well received (perhaps partly as a result of the controversy over the morals of the theatre initiated by JEREMY COLLIER in 1698) and Congreve retired to live the life of a gentleman – a claim which much irritated Voltaire when he visited him. His comedies, though criticized in their day and frequently since for their indelicacy, are still read and played, mainly for the exquisite elegance of their prose style and for Congreve's mastery of feminine psychology. Millamant in *The Way of the World*, especially, is one of the most captivating heroines in English drama.

Connection, The. Play by JACK GELBER, first performed New York, 1959.

Connelly, Marc (b. 1890). American dramatist and director. He wrote several comedies in collaboration with GEORGE S. KAUFMAN, *The Farmer Takes a Wife* (1934) in collaboration with Frank B. Elser, and, in 1930, *The Green Pastures*, a religious fantasy told in terms of Negro folklore and played by an all-Negro cast.

Cons, Emma (d. 1912), see OLD VIC.

Constant Nymph, The. Romantic drama by Margaret Kennedy and Basil Dean, first performed London, 1926. One of the great successes of the 1920s, providing the period with one of its most influential popular images of the artist and of romantic love.

Constant Wife, The. Comedy by W. SOMERSET MAUGHAM, first performed New York, 1926.

Conti, Italia (1874–1946). Founder of an important English school for child actors. She began her career as an actress, but after 1911, when she was employed to train the child performers in *Where the Rainbow Ends*, she devoted most of her time to her school, which produced a number of famous pupils, including Gertrude Lawrence.

Conversation Piece. Romantic comedy by NOËL COWARD, first performed London, 1934.

Co-Optimists, The. Long-running concert-party revue, London, 1921–7. Revived 1928 and 1935.

Copeau, Jacques (1878–1949). French manager and director. One of the second generation of the reaction against realism on the stage. Copeau read CRAIG and APPIA, but represents an opposite line of attack on the problem. For him, a literary critic before he came to the ~~theatre, the essential~~ the proper communication of the author's text with as little irrelevant elaboration as possible (in this he approaches closest the ideas and practice of GRANVILLE BARKER). If his earliest productions with his company (founded 1913) at the Vieux-Colombier theatre were a trifle mannered, he soon settled into his characteristic style, in which scenery was reduced to a minimum and the actors (who included Louis Jouvet and Charles Dullin) played with a lightness and ease nurtured by Copeau's meticulous training in both clear delivery and precise, economical stage movement. The company specialized particularly in Molière and Shakespeare; from 1917 to 1919 they played in New York as part of France's national war propaganda campaign and then from 1919 to 1924 they again made the Vieux-Colombier their base, with visits to London, New York, and elsewhere. In 1924 they retired to Burgundy to 'renew contact with the soil', studying their art and performing entertainments of various sorts for the peasants. In 1931 Copeau handed over direction of the group to his nephew and assistant MICHEL SAINT-DENIS, who reformed them as the COMPAGNIE DES QUINZE. Copeau returned to Paris, and in 1936 was appointed a director at the Comédie-Française, from which he retired in 1941.

Coquelin, Constant-Benoît (1841–1909). French actor, noted chiefly as the creator of Cyrano de Bergerac in Rostand's play, and as the author of two important books on acting, *L'Art et le comédien* (1880) and *Les Comédiens par un comédien* (1882). He is sometimes called 'Coquelin aîné' to distinguish him from his brother Ernest ('Coquelin cadet') and his son Jean, both also actors.

Coriolanus. Classical drama by WILLIAM SHAKESPEARE, written c.1607–8.

Corneille, Pierre (1606–84). French dramatist. Though considered in many ways the founder of French classical drama and especially tragedy, Corneille began as an author of farcical comedy with *Mélite* (1629), inspired by the arrival of a touring company in his home town, Rouen. This, when played in Paris in 1630, had some success, and encouraged him to write several other comedies, as well as his first tragedy, *Médée* (1635). For a while he was employed by Richelieu as an official dramatist, but a quarrel sent him back to Rouen, where he wrote his most famous play *Le Cid*, first produced at New Year, 1637. This was an 'heroic comedy' concerning the stormy love of Chimène and Rodrigue, interrupted by an insult offered by Rodrigue to Chimène's father, but at the last achieving a happy conclusion. The play become a centre of controversy because, while nominally observing the unities (see ARISTOTLE), at that time a major issue in critical discussion, it was really a romantic drama roughly forced into a classical mould. However, the play was enormously successful with the public, and established Corneille as the major dramatist of his day, a position he held with little real competition (despite some ups and downs in popularity) until the arrival of RACINE in the mid 1660s. His plays of this period include a series of tragedies on classical themes – *Horace* (1640), *Cinna* (1641), *Polyeucte* (1642), *La Mort de Pompée* (1643) – and at least one excellent comedy, *Le Menteur* (1643). The failure of *Pertharite* in 1652 sent Corneille back to Rouen for seven years, and after that his fortunes were in decline, though he had a number of successes still to come, particularly the spectacle play *La Toison d'or* (1660), the tragedy *Tite et Bérénice* (1670), which appeared in direct competition with Racine's treatment of the same subject, *Bérénice*, and *Psyché* (1671) written in collaboration with Molière and Quinault. Though one of the most important and influential figures in the establishment of classical tragedy in France, he seems not to have found the form particularly congenial himself, and no doubt his failure to turn its limitations into advantages was responsible for his replacement in popularity and critical esteem by Racine. However, his major tragedies are still played, and his reputation as a classical tragedian remains second only to Racine's.

His brother, **Thomas** (1625–1704), was also a dramatist, but his works, although fairly popular at the time, particularly his tragedy *Timocrate* (1656), do not survive in the repertoire today.

Cornell, Katharine (1898–1974). American actress. Made her debut New York, 1916; played a variety of roles, among them Candida (1924) and Leslie Crosbie in *The Letter* (1927), but came into her own after 1931, when she went into management on her own account. Her most famous roles, all of which she played in several revivals, were Candida, Juliet, and Elizabeth in *The Barretts of Wimpole Street* (1931). She also played St Joan (1936), Jennifer Dubedat in *The Doctor's Dilemma* (1941), Cleopatra in *Antony and Cleopatra* (1947), the Countess Rosmarin Ostenburg in *The Dark is Light Enough* (1955), and Mrs Patrick Campbell in *Dear Liar* (1960).

Corn is Green, The. Comedy by EMLYN WILLIAMS, first performed London, 1938.

Costume. Special costumes have been used in drama to tell audiences certain things about the characters they are seeing since the earliest times. In ancient Greece tragedy and comedy each had its own particular costumes, unlike those normally worn by theatregoers at the time: apart from the MASKS, the actors wore the robes of the priests of Dionysus while playing AESCHYLUS, and archaic Ionian costume for the tragedies of SOPHOCLES and EURIPIDES. Gradually each role in tragedy came to have its own particular costume, which could be recognized at a glance, and in addition the actors (though not the chorus, since they were required to be mobile) took to wearing the *cothurnus* (buskin), a long boot with a very thick sole, like a small stilt. In comedy there were different dress conventions for the Old and New Comedies (see GREEK THEATRE). In the Old Comedy a heavily grotesque costume was worn, with a lot of padding and, for the male characters, a large phallus in red leather; birds and animals were distinguished by characteristic costume accessories (heads and tails, wings, etc.). The New Comedy being more naturalistic, actors wore the ordinary street clothes of the day, though the various regular types were distinguished by the colour of their clothes. Roman costume convention in drama was much the same, though with ordinary Roman dress naturally taking the place of Greek in the comedies of TERENCE and PLAUTUS.

With the reappearance of drama in medieval times in the mystery and miracle plays, costume became increasingly prominent as an important part of the dramatic experience, especially towards the end of the Middle Ages, when the guilds responsible for different parts of the Biblical cycle would vie with each other in the splendour and fantasy of their mounting of the supernatural elements and their detailed realism in the rest. Morality plays also were often very grandly mounted, with rich and elaborate costumes to characterize the various allegorical characters. In the secular, Renaissance theatre conventions were much the same: historical accuracy counted for little, and the norm for costume was contemporary dress with occasional fantastic variations in the way of accessories. The Jacobean masque and the baroque theatre, however, generally evolved their own forms of costume, mingling contemporary elements with classical and exotic ones according to the taste of the designer, the aim always being the utmost luxury and extravagance. The COMMEDIA DELL'ARTE, too, had its own forms of costume, each of its regular characters having a formalized and immediately recognizable way of dressing. These special genres had little influence on the costume of the normal run of dramatic performance, however, which remained much closer to contemporary fashion. A tendency to increased fantastication in the early eighteenth century was corrected by 'realists' such as GARRICK, who brought back stage costume to a close approximation to everyday eighteenth-century dress and made some attempt at geographical exactness in the costumes of exotic characters.

Towards the end of the eighteenth century a call for historical accuracy in stage costumes was more persistently heard, and during the first quarter of the nineteenth an increasing number of period accessories were used, generally added rather incongruously to costumes reflecting the everyday modes of the period. It was not until the work of the DUKE OF SAXE-MEININGEN in the 1870s that archaeological accuracy became the norm in historical plays, but this period, represented in England by the productions of IRVING and TREE, did not last long before the arrival of Symbolism and Expressionism in the theatre, each with its own sorts of stylization. In the modern period there has in fact been no question of a consistent approach to costume design (except, of course, in realistic contemporary drama, which has never presented any problems): in Shakespeare, for instance, symbolic sets, costumes and scenery may vie with productions dressed in Elizabethan style, vague attempts at accuracy to the period in which the play is set rather than that in which it was written (this especially with the classical plays), or modern and variously 'fancy' dresses (a Victorian *Hamlet*, a 1920s *Troilus and Cressida*). Never before has so much been left to the individual fantasy of the designer, with such varying and unpredictable results.

Countess Cathleen, The. Verse play by W. B. YEATS, written 1889, revised and first performed Dublin, 1899.

Count of Clerembard, The (Clérambard). Tragi-comedy by MARCEL AYMÉ, first performed Paris, 1950.

Country Girl, The. Drama by CLIFFORD ODETS. See WINTER JOURNEY. See also next entry.

Country Wife, The. Comedy by WILLIAM WYCHERLEY, first performed London, 1674. From 1766 to 1924 usually played in David Garrick's adaptation *The Country Girl*.

Courteline, Georges (1861–1929). French dramatist (real name Georges Moineaux), specialist in sophisticated farce. His first great success was *Les Gaietés de l'escadron* (1886), which was followed by a number of others on military themes. Many of his later plays were first produced at the Théâtre Libre (see ANDRÉ ANTOINE), his masterpiece being probably *Boubouroche* (1893), a cunning variation on the classic theme of the deceived husband. Among his other plays, all full of keen and malicious observation, are *Le Gendarme est sans pitié* (1899), *Le Commissaire est bon enfant* (1900), and *La Paix chez soi* (1903).

Covent Garden. The first theatre on the site opened in 1732, under the management of John Rich, but did not achieve glory until it was taken over in 1767 by a management including GEORGE COLMAN the Elder, and saw the first production of *She Stoops to Conquer* in 1773. In 1808 the theatre was burnt down, and rebuilt on much grander lines as the home of four companies: opera, ballet, and players of tragedy and comedy. Among the actors to perform there during this period were Kemble, Mrs Siddons, Kean, Macready, and Madame Vestris. Since the 1850s the theatre has been devoted almost entirely to opera and ballet; it was burnt down again in 1856, and the present building, the Royal Opera House, Covent Garden, dates from 1858.

Coward, Noël (1899–1973). English dramatist, actor, and composer. Began his career as a child actor in 1911. When he appeared as a dramatist with comedies like *The Young Idea* (1921) and *Fallen Angels* (1925) and dramas like *The Vortex* (1924) he was hailed at once as the spokesman of the younger generation of the early 1920s, and his plays were often roundly condemned as immoral. With *Hay Fever* in 1925, he showed his real talents with an elegant high comedy in the tradition of CONGREVE and WILDE, and continued through the years to produce his best work in this vein, with *Private Lives* (1930), *Blithe Spirit* (1941), and *Present Laughter* (1942). During the same period he ventured also into a wide variety of genres with revue (*On with the Dance*, 1925, *This Year of Grace*, 1928), romantic musical (*Bitter Sweet*, 1929, *Operette*, 1938), patriotic drama (*Cavalcade*, 1931), the one-act play (*Tonight at 8.30*, three bills of three, 1935), farce (*Nude with Violin*, 1956), adaptation (*Look After Lulu*, based on Feydeau's *Occupe-toi d'Amélie*, 1959), and sentimental comedy-drama (*Waiting in the Wings*, 1960). In 1966 he returned to act in the West End in a group of three new plays, *Suite in Three Keys*, one of which, *A Song at Twilight*, was among his best. In all these genres he has shown at least enormous professionalism as a writer and (in revue and musical) composer, but it seems likely that he will be remembered almost entirely as the most polished author of high comedy since the death of Wilde, an opinion borne out by the successful revival of several of his earlier comedies in the 1960s. Knighted 1970.

Cox and Box, see BOX AND COX.

Craig, Edward Gordon (1872–1966). English director, designer, and theorist. Son of ELLEN TERRY and the architect and designer Edward

William Godwin, he was brought up in the theatre and first appeared as an actor at the age of sixteen. After a career of modest distinction as an actor he took up direction in 1900 with a revival of Purcell's opera *Dido and Aeneas*, which he restaged the next year with *The Masque of Love* from Purcell's *Diocletian*. Nearly all his career as a practical director in the theatre was crowded into the following two years, when he staged *Acis and Galatea*, *Bethlehem*, and parts of *Sword and Song* (1902), and *The Vikings at Helgeland* and *Much Ado About Nothing* (1903), his mother appearing in both the latter. Subsequently he was associated with only four productions, *Venice Preserved* at Berlin in 1904, *Rosmersholm* with Duse in 1906, *Hamlet* at the Moscow Art Theatre in 1911, and Ibsen's *The Pretenders* at Copenhagen in 1926. In each of these last productions, he worked with a more practical man of the theatre (Stanislavsky for *Hamlet*), who was charged with translating his vague and grandiose visions into workable realities. During this time and later he rejected all other offers, often on fantastic grounds (one, to take over a Paris theatre, he would agree to only if the theatre could be closed for ten years while he prepared his opening production), and became increasingly involved in the elaboration of his theories on the theatre. There seems, in fact, little doubt that the practicalities of the theatre never interested him very much, and that he had little aptitude for them: his real role was as a theatrical prophet and seer, a thrower-out of pregnant notions which could be brought to birth by other men. His most important and influential book is *On the Art of the Theatre* (1911), which puts forward in a readable and provocative form ideas akin to those of ADOLPH APPIA about the subjection of all elements in a theatrical production to the director's will and the importance of lighting and colour in the creation of theatrical atmosphere, as against the realistic, representational settings then general. In particular, Craig advocated a view of the theatre as an extension of dance and mime, in which words should be allotted a less important role than the visual effect, and the actor be virtually reduced to an easily movable, manoeuvrable part of the scenery, a sort of elaborate marionette. Craig's ideas have had particular influence on certain elements in the French theatre, especially on those devoted to the notion of THÉÂTRE TOTAL, and on JEAN-LOUIS BARRAULT, who acknowledges him as one of the principal shapers of his own view of the theatre. More generally, Craig's experiments with non-representational décor and atmospheric, non-realistic lighting have passed into the general vocabulary of the modern theatre.

Crazy Gang, The. Group of English comedians, consisting of Flanagan and Allen (up to Allen's retirement in 1946), Nervo and Knox, Naughton and Gold, and 'Monsewer' Eddie Gray, first assembled in 1932 for 'crazy weeks' staged by George Black at the London Palladium. These shows developed into such elaborate revues as *Life Begins at Oxford Circus* (1935), *O-Kay for Sound* (1936), *London Rhapsody* (1937), and *These Foolish Things* (1938). In 1947 they began again, at the Victoria Palace, with *Together Again*, and continued with *Knights of Madness* (1950), *Ring Out the Bells* (1952), *Jokers Wild* (1954), *These Foolish Kings* (1956), *Clown Jewels* (1959), and *Young in Heart* (1960).

Creighton, Anthony (b. 1923). Scottish actor and dramatist. Wrote two plays in collaboration with John Osborne, *Personal Enemy* (1953) and *Epitaph for George Dillon* (1956), and later *Tomorrow With Pictures* (1960), in collaboration with Bernard Miller.

Crime passionnel (Les Mains sales). Drama by JEAN-PAUL SARTRE, first performed Paris, 1947.

Critic, The. Satirical comedy by RICHARD BRINSLEY SHERIDAN, first performed Drury Lane, London, 1779.

Criticism, Dramatic. Dramatic criticism in the sense of descriptive writing about dramatic performances has existed as long as dramatic performances themselves. (The earliest known example is the Egyptian actor I-kher-nefert's comments on his production of the Passion Play of Osiris, which date from before 3000 B.C.) Theoretical consideration of drama as such, what it is and what it should be, began as far as we know with the *Poetics* of ARISTOTLE in the fourth century B.C., and continued, at least incidentally, in such later classical treatises on the arts as Horace's *Ars Poetica* (first century B.C.). The elaboration of general theories on drama revived with the professional theatre during the Renaissance, producing, among works that are still read, Dryden's *Essay of Dramatic Poesy* (1668) and a spate of works by neo-classical theorizers in France in the seventeenth century. The end of the seventeenth century, though, saw a move away from this sort of theoretical study to more practical criticism of particular dramatists and their works, as well as of dramatic performances. In Britain Colley Cibber's *Apology* (1740) gives vivid pictures of the actors of the day, and rather later Charles Lamb, William Hazlitt, and Thomas De Quincey all wrote usefully about the actors of the Romantic heyday. In France theoretical criticism held its place rather later, with Diderot's *Essai sur la poésie dramatique* (1767) and Beaumarchais's *Essai sur le genre dramatique sérieux* (1767), and even later Victor Hugo's preface to *Cromwell* (1827), the clarion call of Romantic drama. The nineteenth century was predominantly the century of practical criticism: in it, in particular, the practice of regular newspaper criticism of the drama became general, and some of the best work of such important critics as GEORGE HENRY LEWES, WILLIAM ARCHER, and GEORGE BERNARD SHAW began in this form. The end of the nineteenth century and beginning of the twentieth saw a revival of general theoretical writing on the theatre, though now often by directors and designers rather than dramatists and *littérateurs*: from this era date the influential writings of ADOLPH APPIA, GORDON CRAIG, STANISLAVSKY, GRANVILLE BARKER, COPEAU, and ARTAUD. At the same time popular writing on the theatre became more and more widely disseminated by newspapers, magazines, and books, the volume of which continues to increase every decade.

Crommelynck, Fernand (1885–1970). Belgian dramatist writing in French. His early plays, such as *Nous n'irons plus au bois* (1906) and *Le Sculpteur de masques* (1908) showed no great originality (the influence of MAETERLINCK was much in evidence), though the latter had some success. The real revelation of his talents did not come until 1920, when *Le Cocu magnifique* was staged in Paris. This savage tragicomedy concerns a husband whose misery at the doubts engendered by the possibility of his wife's unfaithfulness drives him to force her into infidelity, so that he can be sure, and at the same time test his own fidelity. The bitterness of the play, and its unpredictable mingling of tragedy and farce, recur in Crommelynck's other plays, among them *Les Amants puérils* (1921), *Tripes d'or* (1925), *Une Femme qui a le cœur trop petit* (1934), and *Chaud et froid* (1934), though never quite so successfully.

Crucible, The. Historical drama by ARTHUR MILLER, first performed New York, 1953.

Cruelty, Theatre of. Theory advanced in his book *Le Théâtre et son double* (1938) by ANTONIN ARTAUD.

Cuckoo in the Nest, A. ALDWYCH FARCE by BEN TRAVERS, first performed London, 1925.

Cure for Love, The. Comedy by Walter Greenwood, first performed London, 1945; a long-running play about the return of the soldier to civilian life.

Curtain. Introduced with the proscenium arch (see PLAYHOUSE) in the seventeenth century: at first used only at the beginning, when raised after the prologue, and at the end. In the mid eighteenth century it came to be dropped between acts, though it was soon replaced for this purpose by a flat painted cloth called the Act-drop. In the 1880s Irving revived the use of the curtain between acts, and also began the practice of dropping it during scene changes. In recent years scene changes in full view of the audience have become common again, and the curtain is less frequently seen even on proscenium stages. Of course on the newly popular arena and in-the-round stages it does not exist at all.

Curtain-raiser. One-act play used in a theatrical bill to precede the main full-length drama, often a comedy before a tragedy. Seldom used now except in French classical revivals, and even there not regularly.

Curtmantle. Historical verse-drama by CHRISTOPHER FRY, first performed (in Dutch), Tilburg, Holland, 1961; first produced in English by the Royal Shakespeare Company, London, 1962.

Cyclorama. A curved, plain backing to the acting area of the stage, either solidly built or movable, upon which varying light patterns can be thrown as part of a stage setting.

Cymbeline. Tragi-comedy by WILLIAM SHAKESPEARE, first performed Globe, London, 1611.

Cyrano de Bergerac. Romantic verse drama by EDMOND ROSTAND, first performed Paris, 1898.

D

Dada. Artistic movement of the early 1920s. Precursor of SURREALISM, with which it had much in common – a taste for shock, outrage, and unlikely disruptions and juxtapositions – though lacking Surrealism's occasional earnestness about its psychological and philosophical pretensions. Dada was founded in Zurich in 1916, and included among its manifestations drama and cabaret. After the war its centre moved to Paris, and it gradually merged into Surrealism – André Breton, a leading Surrealist, supported Dada and wrote some dramatic sketches for Dada evenings – while the early Dadaists who went back to Germany became involved in theatrical EXPRESSIONISM. The first play presented by Dadaists was the painter Oskar Kokoschka's *Sphinx und Strohmann*, in 1917; later the most notable works produced by the movement were *Le Cœur à gas* by its founder Tristan Tzara (1921) and two plays by the poet Ribemont-Dessaignes, *L'Empereur de Chine* (1916) and *Le Bourreau de Pérou* (published 1928).

Daddy Long-Legs. Comedy by Jean Webster, from her novel of 1912; first performed New York, 1914. Classic story of the successful mating of December and May.

Dame aux camélias, La. Romantic drama by ALEXANDRE DUMAS *fils*, based on his novel (1847); first performed Paris, 1852.

Damn Yankees. Musical with book by GEORGE ABBOTT and Douglas Wallop, based on Wallop's novel *The Year the Yankees Lost the Pennant*; music and lyrics by Richard Alder and Jerry Ross. First performed New York, 1955.

Dancing Years, The. Romantic musical play by IVOR NOVELLO, first performed Drury Lane, London, 1939.

Dandy Dick. Farce by ARTHUR WING PINERO, first performed London, 1887.

Dangerous Corner. 'Time play' by J. B. PRIESTLEY, first performed London, 1932.

Daphne Laureola. Drama by JAMES BRIDIE, first performed London, 1949.

Dark at the Top of the Stairs, The. Drama by WILLIAM INGE, first performed New York, 1957.

Dark is Light Enough, The. Verse play by CHRISTOPHER FRY, first performed London, 1954.

Dark of the Moon. Fantastic drama by Howard Richardson and William Bernay, first performed New York, 1945. Given one of Peter Brook's most brilliant productions in London, 1949.

Darlington, W. A. (b. 1890). Dramatic critic of the *Daily Telegraph* from 1920 to 1969; also dramatist and novelist, notably as author of *Alf's Button* (as a novel 1919, as a play 1924) and various sequels.

Davenant, William (1606–68). English dramatist and theatre manager, according to legend Shakespeare's god-son and illegitimate child. He first came to prominence as a deviser of court masques for Charles I and was made Poet Laureate in 1638, but his main claim to fame is as the 'father of English opera'. His play-with-music *The Siege of Rhodes* (1656), thought up as a ruse to evade the Puritan ban on dramatic performance during the Commonwealth, is generally regarded as the originator of the genre. When the Restoration came he shared with Thomas Killigrew a monopoly of London theatre. He set up a company (which included the young BETTERTON) at the Duke's House, Lincoln's Inn Fields, but died before the company could be installed in their new home in Dorset Garden. Most of his own later dramatic works were adaptations of Shakespeare to the taste of the time.

Day by the Sea, A. Drama by N. C. HUNTER, first performed London, 1953.

Day in the Death of Joe Egg, A. Drama by PETER NICHOLS, first performed London, 1967.

Dear Brutus. Fantastic comedy by J. M. BARRIE, first performed London 1917.

Dear Liar. 'Comedy of letters' by Jerome Kilty, based on the correspondence of GEORGE BERNARD SHAW and MRS PATRICK CAMPBELL, first performed New York, 1960.

Dear Miss Phoebe, see QUALITY STREET.

Dear Octopus. Comedy by DODIE SMITH, first performed London, 1938.

Death of a Salesman. Drama by ARTHUR MILLER, first performed New York, 1949.

Deathwatch (Haute surveillance). One-act prison drama by JEAN GENET, first performed Paris, 1949.

Deburau, Jean Gaspard (1796–1846). French pantomimist and originator of the familiar melancholy Pierrot figure in the white floppy costume. He was born in Bohemia, and in 1811 joined the troupe of actors and jugglers in Paris at the Funambules, where he remained for the rest of his life, soon becoming the theatre's principal attraction. He is most familiar today from the Carné–Prévert film, *Les Enfants du paradis*, in which he figures as Baptiste, the role played by Jean-Louis Barrault.

Décor, see SCENERY.

Deep Blue Sea, The. Drama by TERENCE RATTIGAN, first performed London, 1952.

de Filippo, Eduardo (b. 1900). Italian actor, dramatist, and director, born in Naples of a theatrical family, his father being the actor Eduardo Scarpetta, and his brother and sister, Peppino and Titina, both distinguished actors. He and his brother and sister founded a company in the late 1920s and achieved national success in 1931. De Filippo continued to direct and write for this company exclusively until 1946, with occasional incursions into the cinema. His own most famous and popular plays are *Napoli milionaria*, *Filomena Marturano*, and *Questi fantasmi*.

Deirdre of the Sorrows. Poetic tragedy by J. M. SYNGE, first performed Abbey Theatre, Dublin, 1910.

Dekker, Thomas (*c*.1572–*c*.1632). English dramatist who wrote mainly in collaboration with other Elizabethan and Jacobean writers. His best play, and the only one revived nowadays, is *The Shoemaker's Holiday* (1599), a rough, robust and fairly realistic piece of urban comedy. Otherwise his plays are not now very interesting: the best known are two comedies he wrote in collaboration with MIDDLE-TON, *The Honest Whore* (1604) and *The Roaring Girl* (1610), and *The Virgin Martyr* (1610–20), a tragedy he wrote with MASSINGER. He also wrote a number of lively satirical pamphlets, the best of which is *The Gull's Hornbook* (1609).

Delaney, Shelagh (b. 1939). English dramatist, born in Salford. Her first play, *A Taste of Honey*, was written at the age of seventeen, and accepted at once by THEATRE WORKSHOP. Somewhat revised in production by JOAN LITTLEWOOD and the cast, it was first staged in 1958 at Stratford, East London, and later successfully transferred to the West End. Her second play, *The Lion in Love* (1960), boldly chose as its heroine a mature woman who drinks and whose husband cannot quite resolve to leave her, instead of the seventeen-year-old girl at the centre of *A Taste of Honey*. *The Lion in Love* was less successful than *A Taste of Honey*, and subsequently Shelagh Delaney has devoted herself mainly to narrative prose and film scripts.

Dennis, Nigel (b. 1912). British novelist, dramatist, and critic. The first novelist tempted to try his hand at drama by the English Stage Company, first with an adaptation of his novel *Cards of Identity*, played in their first repertory season (1956), and then with two original plays, both satirical comedies, *The Making of Moo* (1957), about religion, and *August for the People* (1961), about power and publicity.

Deputy, The. American title of THE REPRESENTATIVE.

Desert Song, The. Musical play by SIGMUND ROMBERG, book and lyrics by OSCAR HAMMERSTEIN II, Otto Harbach, Frank Mandell; first produced New York, 1926.

Design for Living. Play by NOËL COWARD, first performed London, 1939.

Desire Caught by the Tail (Le Désir attrapé par la queue). DADAIST play by Pablo Picasso, written 1941, first read publicly Paris, 1944.

Desire Under the Elms. Drama by EUGENE O'NEILL, first performed New York, 1924.

Deus ex machina. Literally a god from a machine, come to sort out the action of a play at the end. The 'machine' is the crane used in Greek theatre to give actors the appearance of flying, but the term was later applied to the elaborate chariots in which deities would descend in the Baroque theatre. The phrase is usually used now figuratively, of a character who arrives from outside the main action of a play at its end and sets matters to rights.

Devils, The. Historical drama by JOHN WHITING, based on Aldous Huxley's book *The Devils of Loudun*, first produced by the Royal Shakespeare Company, London, 1961.

Devine, George (1910–66). British actor, director, and theatre manager. Began his career acting in 1932; from 1936 to 1939 he was director and manager of the London Theatre Studio; his first directing job in the West End was Daphne du Maurier's *Rebecca* in 1940. After the war his first important post was as director of the Young Vic, a second company of young actors run for five years by the Old Vic. His principal importance in the modern British theatre, though, comes from his part in the founding of the ENGLISH STAGE COMPANY and in his direction of it at the Royal Court Theatre from 1956 to 1965.

Dexter, John (b. 1925). English director. First came to prominence working with the English Stage Company, especially in his productions of the plays of ARNOLD WESKER: the *Trilogy* (1958–60), *The Kitchen* (1961), and *Chips With Everything* (1963). Specialist in meticulously organized physical action on the stage, the most spectacular instance being his British and American productions of *The Royal Hunt of the Sun* (1964–5) and *Equus* (1973).

Dial 'M' for Murder. Thriller by Frederick Knott, originally written for television; first stage production London, 1952. Considerable international success; filmed by Hitchcock.

Diamond Lil. Comedy melodrama by Mae West, first performed New York, 1928, and frequently revived as a starring vehicle for the author, whose risqué, voluptuous image of comic temptation it helped to perpetuate.

Dibdin, Charles (1745–1814). English dramatist, actor, and song-writer, most of whose best known works have a naval background, like his song 'Tom Bowling'. His most popular theatrical work was the ballad opera *The Waterman* (1774). His younger son Thomas wrote songs and theatrical extravaganzas in much the same style.

Diderot, Denis (1713–84). French philosopher, novelist, dramatist, and theoretician on the drama. Diderot's plays are unimportant – stolid *pièces à thèse* cast in the currently fashionable mould of sentimental bourgeois drama – but the writings on the theatre to which they gave rise are still of interest. The most famous of them is his *Paradoxe sur le comédien*, but he also wrote an *Essai sur la poésie dramatique* and various essays on the actors of his day. The subject which most interested him in his theoretical writings was the relation between the actor and his role, and the general argument of them all was in favour of a closer and more intelligent understanding between the dramatist and his interpreters, and a nearer approach to ensemble playing in dramatic production.

Dinner at Eight. Play by GEORGE S. KAUFMAN and Edna Ferber, first produced New York, 1932.

Dinner with the Family (Le Rendez-vous de Senlis). *Pièce rose* by JEAN ANOUILH, written 1937, first performed Paris, 1941.

Director. The title, general in the U.S.A. and becoming so in Britain (but see also PRODUCER), of the man responsible for the actual staging of a theatrical production. The function of director as such is a fairly recent development in theatrical history. Of course someone has always had to be in general charge of productions, rehearsing actors in their roles and ordering movement on the stage, but until the mid nineteenth century the convention was that the stage manager should be mainly responsible for hiring actors and making the physical arrangements for sets and costumes, while the leading player put the finishing touches to the production at one or two rehearsals, mainly to see that nothing interfered with his reading of his own part. In the 1820s directors (or producers as they were then called) began to be credited with the staging of pantomimes and spectacles, and by the 1870s it was fairly general practice to credit a 'director' on the programme, though he would always be someone otherwise connected with the play – author, leading man, stage manager. The first man employed exclusively as a director in Britain seems to have been Lewis Wingfield, who directed Lily Langtry's production of *As You Like It* in 1890. The term 'producer', incidentally did not come into general currency until the 1900s (GORDON CRAIG, for instance, still writes in *The Art of the Theatre*, 1905, of the 'stage manager') and began to be ousted by 'director' shortly after the Second World War.

The first full-time directors in the modern sense of the term were a Continental phenomenon: one of the earliest was the DUKE OF SAXE-MEININGEN, whose work was directly influential on the aspirations and careers of such important figures in the twentieth-century theatre as STANISLAVSKY, REINHARDT, and ANTOINE, as well as on the elaborately realistic productions of IRVING and TREE in Britain. Already in the 1890s and 1900s theorists such as APPIA and GORDON CRAIG were elevating the director's role to that of prime creator in the theatre, and his prestige has been further enhanced by such developments as THÉÂTRE TOTAL.

Dock Brief, The. One-act comedy by JOHN MORTIMER, originally written for radio; first stage production London, 1958.

Doctor Faustus. Tragedy based on the Faust legend by CHRISTOPHER MARLOWE, first performed London, c.1588.

Doctor Knock (Knock, ou le triomphe de la médecine). Satirical comedy by Jules Romains, first performed Paris, 1923. English adaptation by HARLEY GRANVILLE BARKER, first performed London, 1926. Classic satire on the doctor–patient relationship; one of LOUIS JOUVET's most famous vehicles.

Doctor's Dilemma, The. Drama by GEORGE BERNARD SHAW, first performed Royal Court, London, 1906.

Doll's House, A (Et Dukkehjem). Tragedy by HENRIK IBSEN, first performed Christiania (Oslo), 1879.

Don Carlos. Tragedy by SCHILLER, first performed Hamburg, 1787.

Don Juan. Character of the wilful, self-indulgent lover, derived from Spanish legend and first fully explored in literature in TIRSO DE MOLINA's *El Burlador de Sevilla y Convidado de Piedra* (1630), a two-part play with all the main ingredients of the story, including the hero's ironic invitation of a statue to dinner and the latter's acceptance and punishment of him. The theme has subsequently been used innumerable times in literature and in drama, notably Molière's *Le Festin de Pierre*, Goldoni's *El dissoluto*, Dumas *père*'s *Don Juan de Manara*, Rostand's *La Dernière Nuit de Don Juan*, Shaw's *Man and Superman* (Act III, *Don Juan in Hell*), Tennessee Williams's *Camino Real*, Ronald Duncan's *Don Juan* and *The Death of Satan*, Frisch's *Don Juan, or the Love of Geometry*, and Ingmar Bergman's film *The Devil's Eye*: not to mention Mozart's opera *Don Giovanni*.

Don Juan in Hell, see MAN AND SUPERMAN.

Double-Dealer, The. Comedy by WILLIAM CONGREVE, first produced London, 1694.

Douglas. Verse tragedy by John Home, first produced Edinburgh, 1756. Long famous as the most consistently successful of eighteenth-century neo-Shakespearian dramas.

Downstage. Towards the front of the stage, near the audience.

D'Oyly Carte, Richard (1844–1901). British impresario and theatre manager, notable chiefly for his long collaboration with Gilbert and Sullivan. He presented nearly all their comic operas, latterly at his own new theatre, the Savoy, which was the first in London to be lit with electricity.

Dramaturg. German term which resists determined attempts at acclimatization, despite its usefulness. A *dramaturg* is a sort of reader-cum-literary editor to a permanent theatrical company; his prime responsibility is the selection of plays for production, working with authors (when necessary) on the revision and adaptation of their texts, and writing programme notes, etc, for the company. The NATIONAL THEATRE appointed KENNETH TYNAN to just such a position, giving him the title 'Literary Manager'.

Draper, Ruth (1884–1956). American monologuist who always performed alone in a variety of character sketches of her own devising. (Henry James once wrote a monologue for her but it is recorded that she never used it.) She performed with a minimum of props and no changes of make-up, and toured widely, playing in London and New York once every two or three years. The complete text of her repertoire has been published in *The Art of Ruth Draper* (1960).

Dream Play, The (Ett Drömspel). Symbolic drama by AUGUST STRINDBERG, first performed Stockholm, 1907.

Dress Circle, see PLAYHOUSE.

Drinkwater, John (1882–1937). English poet, dramatist, actor, and director. An important figure in the twentieth-century revival of verse drama but, unlike most of those involved in it, also a practical man of the theatre, since he was a founder-member of SIR BARRY JACKSON's Pilgrim Players and later for some time actor, producer, and general manager of that company's successor, the Birmingham Repertory Theatre. As a writer his major successes were in the field of historical drama, particularly with *Abraham Lincoln* (1919). His comedy *Bird in Hand* (1927) was also popular in both London and Birmingham.

Drury Lane. The Theatre Royal, Drury Lane, was built by Thomas Killigrew under royal charter and opened in 1663. It was burnt down in 1672 but rebuilt and reopened by 1674. In the new theatre DRYDEN was resident playwright, but it soon ran into difficulties over the management. Wrangles continued, with occasional periods of distinction, until 1746, when GARRICK became joint manager of the theatre, where he remained for thirty years of glory. On his retirement SHERIDAN took over management, his first production being *The School for Scandal*. In 1791-4 the theatre was again rebuilt, and Sheridan remained in control (usually more or less bankrupt) until it was burnt down in 1809. When the theatre was rebuilt in 1812 it began another chequered period in its history, in which the high points (KEAN's seasons in 1814-20, MACREADY's in 1841-3) were interspersed with pantomimes, spectacles, promenade concerts, and all sorts of miscellaneous entertainments. From 1880 onwards the theatre was under the control of Augustus Harris, who specialized (like his assistant Arthur Collins, who succeeded him in 1896) in large-scale productions of opera, the classics, and especially the elaborately staged Drury Lane melodramas, which made the fullest possible use of the theatre's technical resources to show horse-races, train-wrecks, waterfalls, and all manner of spectacular highlights in popular drama. After Collins's retirement in 1923 the theatre became the regular home of large-scale musicals, among its biggest successes being *Rose Marie*, *Cavalcade*, a succession of IVOR NOVELLO shows including *Glamorous Night*, *Careless Rapture*, *Crest of the Wave*, and *The Dancing Years*, also *Oklahoma*, *Carousel*, *South Pacific*, *The King and I*, and *My Fair Lady*.

Dryden, John (1631-1700). English poet and dramatist. As well as being the leading poet of his day, both on his own account as author of a series of great verse satires and as translator of Virgil, Dryden was a prolific dramatist, alone or in collaboration. He essayed almost all the popular genres of the time: comedy, tragi-comedy, 'opera' (i.e. plays with spectacular musical interludes), blank-verse tragedy, Shakespearian adaptation and – the form of which in English he was originator and leading exponent – 'heroic tragedy' in rhyming couplets. Of his comedies *Marriage à la Mode* (1672) is still occasionally revived, and others, such as *Sir Martin Mar-All* (1667) and *Amphitryon* (1690), have a certain rough vigour. His tragi-comedies are of little interest, and his heroic tragedies, full of rhetoric and large-scale conflicts between love and honour, are now museum pieces, though *The Conquest of Granada* (*Almanzor and Almahide*, 1669-70), an enormous two-part play, and *Aurengzebe* (1675) still hold much to entertain the reader. By general consent the best of his plays is the blank-verse tragedy *All for Love* (1678), a retelling of the story of Antony and Cleopatra; it has, however, despite its merits, been overshadowed since the beginning of the nineteenth century by Shakespeare's *Antony and Cleopatra*.

Duchess of Malfi, The. Tragedy by JOHN WEBSTER, first performed London, *c.*1619.

Duel of Angels (Pour Lucrèce). Drama by JEAN GIRAUDOUX, first performed (edited and directed by LOUIS JOUVET) Paris, 1953; English version by CHRISTOPHER FRY first performed London, 1958.

Duenna, The. Ballad opera by RICHARD BRINSLEY SHERIDAN, music by Thomas Linley, first performed Covent Garden, London, 1775. New version with music by JULIAN SLADE first performed London, 1953.

Dukes, Ashley (1885–1959). English dramatist and theatre manager, founder and owner of the Mercury Theatre, Notting Hill Gate, at which many important new foreign and British plays were first produced. After the Second World War it was for a while the principal home of new verse drama in London, as well as providing a permanent base for the ballet company run by Dukes's wife, Marie Rambert. As a dramatist he was responsible for the translation and adaptation of many foreign plays; the best of his own plays is *The Man with a Load of Mischief* (1924).

Dullin, Charles (1885–1949). French director, actor, and theatrical manager. Much of his early experience was gained with COPEAU – he was a founder-member of the Vieux-Colombier company – and when in 1918 he founded his own troupe his approach was very similar to that of Copeau. After touring for some time the company finally settled in Paris at the Théâtre de l'Atelier, and rapidly made a reputation for itself as one of the most enterprising and imaginatively organized groups in France. Though he presented some new plays, Dullin's most famous productions were revivals of classics by Shakespeare, Ben Jonson, and Aristophanes; among contemporary foreign dramatists he particularly favoured Pirandello. Like Copeau, he sought in his productions to combine music, disciplined movement, dance, and stylized décor into an exciting experience of theatrical poetry. He was also an outstanding teacher of acting, and many of the subsequent generation of French actors either passed through the school attached to his theatrical company or underwent his influence in one way or another. In 1936 he became a director at the Comédie-Française.

Dumas, Alexandre (père) (1803–70). French novelist and dramatist, for many years the most successful author of romantic melodrama on the Paris stage. Altogether he wrote, alone or in collaboration, nearly a hundred plays, most of them costume dramas and many adapted from his own novels. His first great success was *Henri III et sa cour* (1829) which as much as any other play established the theatrical ascendency of Romanticism. Thereafter most of his plays were cast in the same mould, the most popular of them all being *La Tour de Nesle* (1832) and *Kean* (1836) (the latter rewritten in 1952 by JEAN-PAUL SARTRE). Almost equally popular were his adaptations, often in collaboration with Auguste Maquet, of his most popular novels, among them *Les Trois Mousquetaires*, originally called *La Jeunesse des mousquetaires* (1849), *Le Comte de Monte-Cristo* (1848), and *La Reine Margot* (1847). The novels, incidentally, have continued to provide material for the dramatist, the most successful and famous recent dramatization being Roger Planchon's of *Les Trois Mousquetaires* (1959). On at least one occasion Dumas took time off from historical drama to write a modern-dress middle-class drama, *Antony* (1831), which had no great success at the time but pointed the way towards the sort of drama favoured by the next generation of dramatists.

One of the most successful of these was Dumas's natural son **Alexandre Dumas fils** (1824–95). His first great success was the romantic drama he adapted from his own semi-autobiographical novel *La Dame aux camélias* (1852), and this tearful story of a repentant prostitute has continued to provide flamboyant actresses with a meaty role right up to the present. His later plays are quite different, being mostly moral tracts in dramatic form on the sanctity of marriage and the home – a theme understandable enough considering his own stormy childhood, but hardly one designed to make lasting drama. Among these works are *Le Demi-monde* (1855), which gave the phrase general currency, *Le Fils naturel* (1858), *Le Père prodigue* (1859) and *Françillon* (1887).

Du Maurier, Gerald (1873–1934). English actor-manager, son of the novelist and cartoonist George du Maurier and father of the novelist and dramatist Daphne du Maurier, author of *Rebecca*. Primarily a naturalistic actor, neither romantic nor classical, he shone particularly in light drama and comedy, often playing gentlemen crooks (Raffles, Arsène Lupin) or gentlemen detectives (Bulldog Drummond). Among his more important creations were Mr Darling and Captain Hook in *Peter Pan*.

Dumb Waiter, The. One-act drama by HAROLD PINTER, first performed in German, Frankfurt Municipal Theatre, 1959; first English production London, 1960.

Duncan, Isadora (1878–1927). American dancer and choreographer who revived a form of pseudo-Greek dancing in flowing robes and bare feet and exerted considerable indirect influence on the development of modern ballet.

Duncan, Ronald (b. 1914). Prolific English author of verse dramas, the most famous of which are his religious 'masque' *This Way to the Tomb* (1945) and the double bill *Don Juan* and *The Death of Satan*, which figured in the first repertory season of the ENGLISH STAGE COMPANY (1956). He has also translated a number of French plays, notably Cocteau's *L'Aigle à deux têtes*.

Duras, Marguerite (b. 1914). French novelist and dramatist. After making a considerable reputation with a series of increasingly rarefied novels which associated her vaguely with the French *nouveau roman* group, she made a dramatic version of one of the novels, *Le Square* (1955), and wrote the original screenplay for Alain Resnais's film *Hiroshima mon amour*. There followed a number of stage plays, the best known of which are *Des Journées entières dans les arbres* (*Days in the Trees*), based on an earlier story, and *Les Viaducs de la Seine et Oise* (*The Viaduct*), based on a real-life murder in which two old people apparently killed a relative for no reason and distributed her body in sections on trains going all over France. This subject seems to fascinate her, as she has since written another play on the same theme, *L'Amante anglaise*, in a much more experimental style.

Dürrenmatt, Friedrich (b. 1921). Swiss dramatist and novelist, writing in German. Son of a Protestant pastor, Dürrenmatt was originally intended for the Church and studied theology, but he soon became involved in writing – first fiction and then drama. His first play, *Es steht geschrieben* (*All As It Is Written*, 1947) was a rather chaotic revivalist drama, but soon after he had some success with an 'unhistorical comedy', *Romulus der Grosse*, a satirical picture of life in the Roman decadence. The religious theme occurs again directly in *Ein Engel kommt nach Babylon*, a parable play, but with *Die Ehe des Herrn Mississippi* he hit on his characteristic mature style: a comedy full of menace and black humour, reflecting the fears and tensions of the modern world in the shape of an ironic, essentially nihilistic thriller. This style recurs in Dürrenmatt's two most famous plays, *Der Besuch der alten Dame* (*The Visit*, 1955) in which an old woman returns to a town to take revenge on one of the inhabitants, buys over all the other villagers, exacts her revenge and leaves, and *Die Physiker* (*The Physicists*, 1962), in which the world's three greatest physicists take refuge in a lunatic asylum to keep their discoveries from the world. The 'message' of Dürrenmatt's plays is always ambiguous, the ironies cancelling each other out so neatly that finally no coherent meaning emerges, but he is one of the most skilful technicians in the modern theatre.

Duse, Eleonora (1859–1924). Italian actress, Bernhardt's chief rival in the international theatre as the great tragedienne of her day. Bernhardt was more spectacular, Duse more subtle and analytical in her approach. Her first big success was in *Les Fourchambault* in 1878, and she rapidly established herself as a leading figure on the Italian stage. She was long associated with the plays of D'ANNUNZIO, in which she had some of her greatest successes: *La Gioconda, La Città morta* (both 1898), *Francesca da Rimini* (1902). One of her most famous productions was *Rosmersholm* (Florence, 1906) directed by EDWARD GORDON CRAIG; she also appeared in many of the same romantic roles as BERNHARDT, among them Sardou's Fédora, Tosca, and Théodora, and Marguerite Gautier in Dumas *fils's La Dame aux camélias.* She retired in 1913, but made a brief return to the stage in 1923, just before her death.

Dutch Courtesan, The. Satirical comedy by JOHN MARSTON, first performed London, *c.*1605.

Dynasts, The. Historical verse drama by THOMAS HARDY, written 1904–8, first performed in a stage adaptation by HARLEY GRANVILLE BARKER, London, 1914.

E

Eagle Has Two Heads, The (L'Aigle à deux têtes). Romantic costume drama by JEAN COCTEAU, first performed Paris, 1946; English version by RONALD DUNCAN, first produced London, 1946.

East Lynne. Melodrama by John Oxenford, based on Mrs Henry Wood's novel, first performed London, 1866. (This is the most famous and frequently played dramatization; there was an earlier one, *The Marriage Bells* by W. Archer, first produced 1864, and there were several later ones.) The archetype of the Victorian melodrama.

Eden End. Drama by J. B. PRIESTLEY, first produced London, 1934.

Edinburgh Festival of Music and Drama. Annual international festival, instituted in 1947. Along with concerts, opera, and ballet there is always a group of official festival drama productions, usually including performances by visiting foreign companies, a production by a local Scottish company, and at least one important new play. Among the plays first seen at Edinburgh have been T. S. Eliot's *The Cocktail Party*, *The Confidential Clerk*, and *The Elder Statesman*, Charles Morgan's *The River Line*, Thornton Wilder's *The Matchmaker* and *A Life in the Sun*, and Ray Lawler's *The Unshaven Cheek*. Another regular feature has been the series of open-stage productions in the Assembly Hall, instituted with Tyrone Guthrie's production of *The Three Estates* (1947, revived three times). In later years a sort of unofficial festival called the 'Fringe' has grown up alongside the official festival; it consists of more or less experimental productions by amateur and small professional companies.

Edwardes, George (1852–1915). English theatrical manager, associated for most of his career with the Gaiety Theatre, which he took over in 1885; in 1893 he built Daly's for Augustine Daly, and later took it over himself. At these two theatres, and sometimes elsewhere, he presented innumerable musical comedies and revues, among them many of the most famous of the period – *The Geisha*, *The Merry Widow*, *The Quaker Girl*; indeed he virtually established the popularity of the genre.

Edward, My Son. Drama by ROBERT MORLEY and Noel Langley, first performed London, 1947. Its principal oddity was that the title character was never seen.

Edward II. Historical drama by CHRISTOPHER MARLOWE, first performed London, 1593.

Elder Statesman, The. Verse play by T. S. ELIOT, first produced Edinburgh Festival, 1958.

Electra. (1) Tragedy by SOPHOCLES, first produced Athens, 409 B.C. (2) Tragedy by EURIPIDES, first produced Athens, *c.*413 B.C.

Eliot, T. S. (Thomas Stearns; 1888–1965). English poet and dramatist, born in America. His first work in dramatic form was *Sweeney Agonistes* (1927–8), fragments of an Aristophanic comedy. In 1934 he wrote the script for a religious pageant, *The Rock*, for which, he said, he merely put words to the detailed outline provided by E. MARTIN BROWNE. In 1935 came his first real play, *Murder in the Cathedral*, which was commissioned for the Canterbury Festival and first performed in the Chapter House of the Cathedral. This was the first of many very successful productions of the poet's drama by E. Martin Browne, and the first example of the revival in religious drama really to outlive the original occasion of its performance and to break out of the church setting for which it was conceived. Despite this, the play itself is not particularly theatrical in form and does not play so well in a theatre. It tells the story of Thomas Becket's martyrdom with elaborate use of a chorus of Women of Canterbury, includes a long sermon by Becket, and then at the end puts up a series of arguments about the murder addressed directly to the audience by the four knights who killed Becket (doubling the roles with those of four tempters in the first half). Once interested in the drama, though, Eliot decided to evolve for himself a type of poetic drama which would work in the modern theatre, and in 1939 he wrote *The Family Reunion*, which tries to apply dramatic techniques vaguely suggested by classical drama (and specifically by the ORESTEIA) to a subject drawn from recognizable everyday life. Eliot himself subsequently said that he was dissatisfied with the play's methods and solutions, feeling that the supernatural machinery – the Eumenides who torment the hero Harry for some mysterious transgression – was too obtrusive and that the use of the characters sometimes as individuals and sometimes as a sort of Greek Chorus was excessively self-conscious. But to other judges the highly wrought poetic style of *The Family Reunion* is more interesting and effective than the plain, unnoticeable verse of Eliot's three post-war plays: *The Cocktail Party* (1949), *The Confidential Clerk* (1953), and *The Elder Statesman* (1958), all commissioned by and first performed at the Edinburgh Festival. In these Eliot assumed a variety of popular styles – respectively drawing-room comedy, farce *à la* LONSDALE and realistic drama *à la* RATTIGAN – to disguise the religious designs he had on his audience and (incidentally) the classical origins of the plots: the *Alcestis* of EURIPIDES, the *Ion* of Euripides and the *Oedipus at Colonus* of SOPHOCLES. In the process he produced plays which are hardly ever appreciable by the unwarned ear as *verse* plays, and stand or fall primarily by their interest as examples of their chosen genres with something added. Probably the most successful in these terms is *The Cocktail Party*, though even here the characters remain shadowy and the writing lacks tension. Even so, T. S. Eliot, both by the distinction of his name and the very real interest and enterprise of his plays, probably did more than any other writer to establish verse drama as a living part of the modern English-language theatre.

Elizabethan theatre. The precise form taken by the Elizabethan PLAY-HOUSE – highly important, naturally, for a full understanding of the techniques and intentions of Shakespeare and his contemporaries – has been the subject of much debate during the last fifty years or so, ever since William Poel's first attempts (1895) to reconstruct a stage setting for Elizabethan drama approximating as closely as possible to that of Shakespeare's own day. Despite one or two spectacular divergences (among them Leslie Hotson's theory that in some Elizabethan theatres at least the stage was in the centre of the audience), the general lines of Elizabethan theatre design are fairly widely agreed.

There were two types of theatre building: the public (represented most famously by the Globe) and the private (such as the Blackfriars and Whitefriars). The public type was roughly circular, enclosing a public yard open to the sky and surrounded by galleries. To one side was the stage, which projected into the audience and seems to have had a curtained alcove behind, which could be used for intimate scenes (though the very existence of the recess is open to doubt), and a balcony above, which may possibly have been used as another acting area when required (e.g., the Balcony scene in *Romeo and Juliet*). Somewhere behind the stage was the 'tiring house', or actors' dressing room, and below the stage was a store-room, with a trap through which ghosts and devils could appear. Scenery was kept to a minimum – conventionalized representations of a wood by a single tree, a throne-room by a throne and so on – though costumes were frequently elaborate. Audiences sat in the galleries, or stood in the yard on three sides of the actors, where they paid less and were called 'groundlings'. Performances took place in daylight, usually at 2 p.m.

The private theatres were rather different: they were indoor halls, rectangular and with permanent seats for all the audience (which was smaller than in the public theatre). The exact form of staging adopted is more mysterious than in the public theatres; it seems likely, though, that scenery played a more important part and that the action of the play, scene by scene, was more localized: one scholar has suggested that the stage of the Blackfriars was divided into three 'mansions', left, centre, and right, with any scenes required by the play which could not be fitted into this arrangement played unlocalized between the mansions.

A third sort of theatrical presentation existed at the same time as these two normal public or semi-public forms: the court MASQUE, which reached its height in Jacobean times. This, unlike the other two, was very elaborately presented and depended largely on visual spectacle, with rich sets and costumes, large casts and spectacular additions like chariots with real horses. This sort of presentation had an important influence on the professional theatre of the Restoration period and the more literal, representational form of theatre it exemplifies supplanted the more economical, less literal production style of the normal Elizabethan theatre almost universally until the twentieth century.

Emperor Jones, The. Drama by EUGENE O'NEILL, first performed 1920.

Empire-Builders, The (Les Bâtisseurs d'empire). Drama by BORIS VIAN, first performed Paris, 1959.

Endgame (Fin de partie). Drama by SAMUEL BECKETT, first performed (in French) Royal Court, London, 1957; (in English) Royal Court, London, 1958.

Enemy of the People, An (En Folkefiende). Drama by HENRIK IBSEN, first performed Christiania (Oslo), 1883.

Enfant prodigue, L'. Mime play with music, book by Michel Carré, music by André Wormser; first performed Paris, 1890, and thereafter on a world tour by the same company, who made it something of an international institution.

English Stage Company. A theatrical management set up in 1956 by GEORGE DEVINE in collaboration with the poet-dramatist RONALD DUNCAN, Lord Harewood, and others. It took the ROYAL COURT THEATRE, London, as its permanent home and instituted a repertory season with the avowed intention of providing a platform for established writers who wanted to try their hand at drama and for new writers, as well as for the best of current drama from abroad. The first repertory season illustrated this policy with two plays by established novelists: Angus Wilson's *The Mulberry Bush* and Nigel Dennis's *Cards of Identity* (adapted from his own novel), one notable foreign play: Arthur Miller's *The Crucible*, a double bill by Ronald Duncan: *Don Juan* and *The Death of Satan*, and one play by a new writer: John Osborne's *Look Back in Anger*, the eventual success of which really set off the revival in British drama. Subsequently the repertory form was dropped, but otherwise the company remained true to its initial policy, and up to the closure of the theatre for renovation in

1964 had presented (often for the first time) works by virtually every important new British dramatist (among them nearly all John Osborne's plays and plays by John Arden, Ann Jellicoe, N. F. Simpson, Harold Pinter, Shelagh Delaney, Arnold Wesker, and Henry Livings) and by many major foreign dramatists, such as Beckett, Ionesco, Sartre, Genet, Tennessee Williams, Brecht, Edward Albee, and Max Frisch. These have been interspersed with a handful of notable revivals, among them *The Country Wife*, *Lysistrata*, *Major Barbara*, *Rosmersholm*, and *Platonov*. In addition, the company has brought forward several of the most notable directors in the modern English theatre – TONY RICHARDSON, JOHN DEXTER, WILLIAM GASKILL – and given chances to many young actors and designers. After the first season it has run as a permanent company only in the sense that it has a permanent administrative staff, a number of contract directors, and a theatre of its own: the productions have been cast, like normal West End commercial productions, from the London pool of actors, with little or no continuity from one to the next. The first season under the direction of William Gaskill, after the retirement of George Devine (1965) attempted a return to the stricter repertory principles, both in the arrangement of programmes and in the retention of a permanent nucleus of actors from production to production, but the experiment was short-lived.

As a sideline the company has also run a club, the English Stage Society, for whom private productions without décor were given on Sunday nights. These served as a workshop for the company, allowing them to try out new talent inexpensively; in particular a number of plays first seen this way – *The Kitchen*, *Progress to the Park*, *A Resounding Tinkle* – have subsequently been given full-dress productions, there or elsewhere. Since 1969 a somewhat similar function has been served by small-scale productions in a new intimate theatre upstairs at the ROYAL COURT.

E.N.S.A. Entertainments National Service Association. A body set up just before the war to come into operation at the outbreak, providing entertainments of all sorts – dramatic, cinematic, and musical – for the troops at home and abroad.

Entertainer, The. Drama by JOHN OSBORNE, first performed by the English Stage Company at the Royal Court, London, 1957.

Entertaining Mr Sloane. Comedy by JOE ORTON, first performed London, 1964.

Entr'acte. A diversion, generally musical, between the acts of a play.

Epicoene, or The Silent Woman. Comedy by BEN JONSON, first performed London, 1609.

Epic theatre. Type of theatre advocated by BERTOLT BRECHT, ERWIN PISCATOR, and other German theatre men of the 1920s. According to Brecht 'the essential point of the epic theatre is that it appeals less to the spectator's feelings than to his reason'. The term is derived from Aristotelian usage, for a narrative not governed by the unity of time, and in the theatre epic drama usually means a series of incidents simply, clearly presented without restrictions of conventional theatrical construction. These elements stay constant throughout the various, fluctuating interpretations of the term Brecht employed in different phases of his career, which sometimes also stressed the political significance of the genre and its complete exclusion of empathy.

Epilogue. Speech, usually in verse, delivered from the stage by a member of the cast, sometimes in character or sometimes as a direct representative of the author, at the end of a dramatic performance. Its heyday (along with that of the **Prologue**, its counterpart at the beginning of a performance) was in the Restoration period. Its popularity gradually waned towards the end of the eighteenth century, and it is now used only very rarely, on gala occasions. 'Epilogue' may also mean a final scene summarizing or commenting on the main action, as in *Saint Joan*, but the usage is exceptional.

Epitaph for George Dillon. Drama by JOHN OSBORNE and ANTHONY CREIGHTON, first performed Cambridge A.D.C., 1956.

Equity (British Actors' Equity Association). The actors' trade union in Britain, which regulates conditions of employment, negotiates rates of pay, etc. Set up 1929.

Equus. Drama by Peter Shaffer, first performed National Theatre, London, 1973.

Ervine, St John (b. 1883). Anglo-Irish dramatist and for a time manager of the ABBEY THEATRE, Dublin. Author of many plays, several of the earliest of which, *Mixed Marriage* (1911), *The Critics* (1913), *John Ferguson* (1915), *The Island of the Saints* (1920), were first produced at the Abbey. *Jane Clegg*, an emotional drama first produced at the Gaiety, Manchester, with Sybil Thorndike, in 1913, has been revived on occasion, but for the most part his later plays, except perhaps for *Robert's Wife* (1937), have proved ephemeral. He has also written several books on the theatre and been a dramatic critic, notably on the *Observer* 1919–23, 1925–39.

Etherege, Sir George (1634–91). English dramatist and pioneer of Restoration comedy of manners. His first play, *The Comical Revenge, or Love in a Tub* (1664), mixed drama and comedy, the main plot being written in serious verse and the sub-plot in robust comic prose. This latter style (in which he was probably influenced by MOLIÈRE, with whose work he had become familiar while living in France during the Commonwealth) he later developed in *She Would If She Could* (1668) and his masterpiece *The Man of Mode* (1676), which contains his most famous character, Sir Fopling Flutter, a satirical picture of the Restoration dandy. Etherege was surpassed by his successor CONGREVE, but his works, especially *The Man of Mode*, continue to be revived from time to time.

Eumenides, see ORESTEIA.

Euripides (484–406 B.C.). Greek dramatist, third in time of the three great tragic poets of the Greek theatre. He is said to have written ninety-two plays, of which we have seventeen tragedies and one SATYR PLAY complete. In contrast to AESCHYLUS and SOPHOCLES, Euripides represents a critical, sceptical mind at work on the myths and legends which form the subject-matter of his plays, more interested in individual psychology, and further from the ritual origins of drama. In this he looked forward and, after his death, his reputation continued to rise while that of Aeschylus and Sophocles, considered more archaic, fell sharply. He generally takes as his subjects individual dramas of personal emotions rather than cosmic dramas of principle; sometimes, too, his argumentative nature led him to deal quite directly in his plays with questions of war and politics. He has been called the first of the realists. His plays are always in danger of breaking out of the fairly rigid mould of Greek tragedy both in emotional climate, which pushes them now towards sensationalism, now to sentimentality, and in form, where Euripides was constantly forced to introduce not altogether satisfactory innovations, such as the PROLOGUE to explain directly to audiences what had gone before, and the DEUS EX MACHINA to sort things out summarily at the end. He also varied the formula of classical tragedy by introducing romantic, even comic elements, as in his earliest extant tragedy, *Alcestis* (438 B.C.). Most of his later plays have women as their central characters, usually involved in extreme situations – mixed marriage and infanticide in *Medea* (431), incestuous passion in *Hippolytus* (428), matricide in *Electra* (413). In his later plays, particularly *Helen* (412) and *Iphigenia in Tauris* (414), he evolves a new style, and almost a new genre: the romantic adventure story with a happy ending. In his very last plays, *The Bacchae* and *Iphigenia in Aulis* (both posthumously produced) he found a new maturity of vision; *The Bacchae* especially, a wild, ecstatic picture of a situation in which the emotional and irrational may triumph over reason, has come to be regarded in this century as one of the most relevant of all Greek plays to our own situation. Far more than Aeschylus and Sophocles, Euripides was influential in later drama, both in the Greek 'New Comedy' (see GREEK DRAMA) and in the sensational tragedies of the Roman SENECA.

Eurydice, see POINT OF DEPARTURE.

Evans, Edith (1888–1976). English actress (D.B.E. 1946). Though she occasionally played with some success in tragedy, by temperament she seemed best suited to comedy, and it was her gallery of classic comedy roles which was mainly responsible for assuring her position as one of the leading actresses of her day. She first appeared on the London stage in an amateur production of *Troilus and Cressida* by William Poel, in which she played Cressida (1912). Her first great critical success did not come until her Cleopatra in Dryden's *All for Love* (1922), rapidly consolidated by her series of roles in the first British production of Shaw's *Back to Methuselah* (Birmingham, 1923) and by her Millamant in *The Way of the World* at the Lyric, Hammersmith (1924). In 1925–6 she played her first season at the Old Vic, as Portia, Cleopatra, Rosalind, Katharina, Mistress Page, Beatrice, Queen Margaret in *Richard III*, and the Nurse in *Romeo and Juliet* (among other roles). Important later roles in classic comedies included Mrs Sullen in *The Beaux' Strategem* (1927), Lady Fidget in *The Country Wife* (Old Vic, 1936), Lady Bracknell in *The Importance of Being Earnest* (1939), Mrs Malaprop in *The Rivals* (1945), and Lady Wishfort in *The Way of the World* (1948). Other classic roles included Irena Arcadina in *The Seagull* (1936) and Madame Ranevsky in *The Cherry Orchard* (1948), and the Countess of Rousillon in *All's Well That Ends Well* and Volumnia in *Coriolanus* (both Stratford, 1959); important modern plays she played in were *The Apple Cart* and *Heartbreak House* (1929), *The Millionairess* (1940), *Daphne Laureola* (1949), *Waters of the Moon* (1951), *The Dark is Light Enough* (1954), *The Chalk Garden* (1956), *Gentle Jack* (1963), a revival of *Hay Fever* at the National Theatre (1964), and Enid Bagnold's *The Chinese Prime Minister* (1965). In later years she acted principally in films.

Everyman. Morality play, perhaps translated from the Dutch, written *c*.1500; first modern revival by WILLIAM POEL, London, 1901; spectacular new version by HUGO VON HOFMANNSTHAL, *Jedermann*, first produced by Reinhardt, 1920.

Every Man in His Humour. Comedy by BEN JONSON, first produced London, 1598.

Evreinov, Nikolai (1879–1953). Russian dramatist and theorist, proponent of theatricalism and a determined opponent of theatrical NATURALISM, which he pilloried amusingly in *The Theatre of Life*.

His most famous play, *The Theatre of the Soul* (1912) exemplified his theories of what the theatre should be: sub-titled 'a monodrama', it illustrates in generally comic terms the diversity of personalities which any one person may assume in the eyes of various observers by having these different aspects played by different actors. A number of his other plays were directly concerned with the theatre: among them *Revizor* (1912), which offered burlesqued views of what STANIS-LAVSKY, REINHARDT, and GORDON CRAIG might do with GOGOL's classic comedy; and *The Fourth Wall* (1915), in which an ultra-naturalistic assistant director creates havoc in a projected production of *Faust*.

Expressionism. Theatrical movement which dominated German theatre for a while in the 1920s. A reaction against theatrical REALISM, it sought to mirror inner psychological realities rather than physical appearances. The direct origin of Expressionism may probably be found in the later work of STRINDBERG: *The Dream Play* overtly tries to translate into drama the logic and movement of the dream; *The Ghost Sonata* mingles realism and fantasy quite unpredictably, so that we never know for sure which characters 'really exist' and which do not. In Germany WEDEKIND's drama developed along similar lines, and after the First World War the German theatre received a powerful infusion from DADAISTS returning from Switzerland. The result of these various influences was a sort of theatre in which extreme and often morbid psychological states were obsessively explored via a bold use of symbolic settings **and costumes** (Expressionism was in many ways primarily a designer's theatre), and abrupt, extravagant playing in which gradations of tone and mood tended to be suppressed in favour of sharp, uncompromising transitions from extreme to extreme. Later in the 1920s the 'subjectivist' phase of Expressionism, which was dominated by the symbolic embodiment of states of mind and soul on the stage, gave way to a more formalist, social phase, which applied the same sort of techniques to the study of society at large, with man himself represented as a counter in the larger pattern. Most of the best-known Expressionist plays are of this latter type: those of TOLLER in Germany, and of ČAPEK and ELMER RICE among others, elsewhere.

Expresso Bongo. Musical, book by WOLF MANKOWITZ and Julian More, lyrics by Julian More, David Heneker, and Monty Norman, music by David Heneker and Monty Norman; first performed London, 1958.

Exton, Clive (b. 1930). English dramatist who has worked up to now almost entirely in television. His first play, *No Fixed Abode* (1959), was written for the stage but first performed on television, and it was followed by two other plays in the same meticulously naturalistic style, *The Silk Purse* and *Where I Live*, then by two more highly-wrought symbolic dramas, *Hold My Hand, Soldier*, and *I'll Have You to Remember*, and several black satires, among them *The Big Eat*, *The Trial of Doctor Fancy*, and *The Close Prisoner*. His first produced stage play was *Have You Any Washing, Mother Dear?* (1969), a satirical fantasy about the workings of a Parliamentary committee.

F

Fabbri, Diego (b. 1911). Italian dramatist. Brought up in a devoutly Roman Catholic family, he studied law, but soon became a professional writer and teacher of philosophy. After a brief flirtation with amateur theatre decided to devote himself to the drama full-time. In all his drama religion is prominent, and indeed his main object as a dramatist seems to be to give expression to his religious beliefs. His first play, *The Flowers of Sorrow*, was written when he was seventeen; his first important play, *The Knot* (1935) suffered from the disapproval of the Fascist government, and was rewritten in 1942 as *The Swamp*. By 1950 he was regarded as the leading poet of the modern Italian theatre. His two most widely played works are *Inquisition* (1950), a study contrasting two priests who find themselves counselling the husband and wife respectively in an unsatisfactory marriage, and *Family Trial* (1955), a sharp attack on egoism and hypocrisy in family life.

Faithful Shepherdess, The. Pastoral drama by JOHN FLETCHER, first performed London, 1608–9.

Fallen Angels. Comedy by NOËL COWARD, first performed London, 1925.

Family Reunion, The. Verse drama by T. S. ELIOT, first performed London, 1939.

Fanny. (1) Family drama by MARCEL PAGNOL, first performed Paris, 1931. (2) Musical by Harold Rome, book by S. N. BEHRMAN and JOSHUA LOGAN, based on PAGNOL'S *Marius*, *Fanny* and *César*; first performed New York, 1954.

Fanny's First Play. Comedy by GEORGE BERNARD SHAW, first performed London, 1911.

Farce. Species of humorous drama, usually distinguished from comedy by its tendency to extract amusement from the ingenious manipulation of a series of intricate situations in which stereotyped human figures are involved, rather than from the reactions of more complex, credible characters to one another and to their situation. The incidents are often amatory involvements, in and out of wedlock – hence the term 'bedroom farce'. Farce as we know it today is virtually a nineteenth-century invention perfected by LABICHE and FEYDEAU in France and by PINERO in England. The dividing line between farce and comedy has never been clear, though, and many 'comedies' of earlier epochs might equally well be considered farces in the modern sense – e.g. Shakespeare's *The Comedy of Errors*. In general the term 'farce' in earlier periods is taken to signify a particularly broad sort of comedy, involving a lot of physical knockabout: this is found in Greek satyr plays and in both Old and New Comedy, while the plays of PLAUTUS and TERENCE are primarily farcical in their machinery. There are farcical incidents in medieval religious drama, and the rise of the professional theatre produced a spate of brief farces, often played as preludes or after-pieces to tragedy – a function they continued to perform up to the middle of the nineteenth century. British theatre in the twentieth century has seen two notable series of farces associated with a particular theatre: in the 1920s and early 1930s at the ALDWYCH, and in the 1950s and 1960s at the WHITEHALL.

Farmer's Wife, The. Comedy by EDEN PHILLPOTTS, first performed Birmingham, 1916.

Farquhar, George (1678–1707). Anglo-Irish comic dramatist, writing largely in the tradition of Restoration comedy, though coming later to the stage than ETHEREGE and CONGREVE and moderating the outspokenness of their comedy of manners somewhat in response to changing tastes and standards in the first decade of the eighteenth century. His earlier plays are not now remembered, but the two works of his maturity, *The Recruiting Officer* (1706) and *The Beaux' Stratagem* (1707), have been revived as often as any plays of their period and still remain fresh in their backgrounds and lively and vivid in their characterization, as well as being more acceptable in later, more prudish eyes than the majority of Restoration comedies.

Father, The. Drama by AUGUST STRINDBERG, first produced Copenhagen, 1887.

Faust. Two-part drama by JOHANN WOLFGANG VON GOETHE. Part I begun 1774, published 1808, first performed in an adaptation by Klingemann, Brunswick, 1829; Part II published 1832; portions used in various stage adaptations, notably Witkowski's, designed to be played on two consecutive nights (1910). The *Urfaust* which has been performed by INGMAR BERGMAN'S Malmö Theatre and elsewhere is an earlier, simpler draft of Part I, posthumously published.

Faust legend. Concerns a character who sells his soul in exchange for knowledge and is then involved more or less disastrously in trying to retrieve matters at the last. The origin of the legend is medieval: the historical Faust was a fifteenth-century conjurer, and the first coherent literary version of the story was published in 1587. The first dramatic treatment of the story was MARLOWE'S *Tragical History of Doctor Faustus*, written around 1588. This passed into popular folklore as a puppet play, and in the eighteenth century the subject attracted the attention of GOTTHOLD LESSING, who sketched a drama on it. The most famous dramatic version (see above) is GOETHE'S two-part drama; others have been written by Lenau, Heine (as a dance-drama), Valéry (*Mon Faust*), and STEPHEN PHILLIPS and J. Comyns Carr.

Feed line. A line of dialogue the whole purpose of which is to invite a funny reply; normally delivered by the straight man to the comic in a double act ('I don't know; why did the chicken cross the road?'), but the device is not unknown in drama.

Feuillère, Edwige (b. 1907). French actress. Studied at the Conservatoire and then began her career with a brief period at the Comédie-Française (1931–3). She was soon drawn to the cinema, and for a while seemed to be settled happily as a lightweight performer in romantic melodrama on stage and screen, but in 1937 she first played two of the roles which made her name, in BECQUE'S *La Parisienne* and in *La Dame aux camélias*. Since then she has made few stage appearances which were not distinguished, picking her roles carefully and returning often to *La Dame aux camélias*, a play she has made peculiarly her own. Her major attempt at the classics, *Phèdre* (1957), was not a great success, her reading being found too romantic and undisciplined. Plays she has created roles in include Giraudoux's *Sodome et Gomorrhe* (1943), Cocteau's *L'Aigle à deux têtes* (1946), Claudel's *Partage de midi* (1948), and the French version of Arthur Kopit's *Oh Dad, Poor Dad, Mamma's Hung You in the Closet and I'm Feelin' So Sad* (1963). In 1967 she had a great success in a revival of Giraudoux's *La Folle de Chaillot*.

Feydeau, Georges (1862–1921). French comic dramatist, perhaps the most brilliantly adroit of all devisers of bedroom farce. His father was a novelist of some slight note, and his own first piece, *Tailleur pour dames*, was produced when he was twenty-four. His output was vast, stretching right through from the *belle époque*, to which most of his best work belongs, up to the 1920s. His last play, *Cent millions qui tombent*, was produced posthumously in 1923. For the twenty years after his death Feydeau was regarded for the most part merely as an efficient, undemanding light entertainer, but subsequently his best plays have been recognized as masterpieces of theatrical contrivance and elegantly economical style, and have been taken into the repertory of the Comédie-Française, the Renaud–Barrault company, and other dignified groups. His masterpieces, perhaps, are *Occupe-toi d'Amélie* (1908), later unhappily adapted by Noël Coward as *Look After Lulu*, and *Le Dindon* (1898), brilliantly played by the Comédie-Française. Other farces of his in the same exacting tradition survive in the repertoire, among them *Un Fil à la patte* (1894), *La Dame de chez Maxim's* (1899), *La Puce à l'oreille* (1907), and *On purge bébé* (1910).

Fin de partie, see ENDGAME.

Finney, Albert (b. 1936). English actor. Began his career at Birmingham Repertory Theatre, made his first West End appearance in 1958, had his first big success in the title role of *Billy Liar* by WILLIS HALL and Keith Waterhouse (1960). Major subsequent stage parts have been the title role in JOHN OSBORNE'S *Luther* (1961), Armstrong in JOHN ARDEN'S *Armstrong's Last Goodnight* (1965), and Bri in *A Day in the Death of Joe Egg* (New York, 1968); has also appeared in films, most notably *Saturday Night and Sunday Morning* (1960), *Tom Jones* (1963) and *Charley Bubbles* (1968), which he directed himself. Member of the National Theatre Company 1965–6.

Fire-Raisers, The (Biedermann und die Brandstifter). *Comédie noire* by MAX FRISCH, first performed Zürich, 1958 (based on a radio play of 1953).

Five Finger Exercise. Drama by PETER SHAFFER, first performed London, 1958.

Flare Path. Drama by TERENCE RATTIGAN, first performed London, 1942.

Flats. Units of stage scenery, generally stretched canvas or hardboard, used in various combinations to make up three-dimensional sets.

Flecker, James Elroy (1884–1915). English poet and dramatist, author of two poetic plays, *Hassan* and *Don Juan*, the first of which had a considerable vogue when first produced after his death (1922) with great scenic elaboration and incidental music by Delius. These latter contributed much to its success; for later generations its luxuriant pseudo-Oriental decadence has proved something of an acquired taste.

Fletcher, John (1579–1625). English dramatist and, alone or in collaboration, one of the most prolific of the Jacobean period. His name is generally coupled with that of FRANCIS BEAUMONT and the blanket term 'Beaumont-and-Fletcher' used to cover more than fifty plays, of which only six or seven seem in fact to be collaborations between the two men. These include, however, the most important and influential, among them *Philaster* (1610), *A King and No King* (1611), and *A Maid's Tragedy* (1611), which established the popularity of a distinctive genre, the romantic tragi-comedy (and incidentally seem to have influenced SHAKESPEARE in his later plays). Fletcher also collaborated with Shakespeare on *Henry VIII* and *The Two Noble Kinsmen*, and frequently with MASSINGER, but apart from the Beaumont plays his most notable works seem to have been written unaided. Among them are the delicate and sophisticated pastoral *The Faithful Shepherdess*, the melodramatic tragedies *Bonduca* and *Valentinian*, and the broad comedies *The Wild Goose Chase* and *The Chances* (the latter revived as recently as 1962 at the Chichester Festival).

Flies, see PLAYHOUSE.

Flies, The (Les Mouches). Drama by JEAN-PAUL SARTRE, based on the story of the ORESTEIA, first performed Paris, 1942.

Float, see STAGE LIGHTING.

Flower Drum Song. Musical by RICHARD RODGERS, book by OSCAR HAMMERSTEIN II and Joseph Field, lyrics by Oscar Hammerstein II; first performed New York, 1958.

Flowering Cherry. Drama by ROBERT BOLT, first performed London, 1957.

Folies-Bergère. Parisian music hall, built in 1869, specializing in spectacular revues with a lot of beautiful, lightly clad girls. MISTINGUETT, Maurice Chevalier, and many other greats of French entertainment have appeared there.

Fontanne, Lynn, see LUNTS.

Fool. Licensed jester, especially at court in late medieval times. The characters of the fools in Shakespeare's plays (*Twelfth Night, King Lear*) are based on the court jester, and take over his function of satirical, deflating comment on the splendours and follies of the great. The costume of the fool, known as motley, is traditionally particoloured, with bells attached to cap and shoes, though this is perhaps not what was intended in Elizabethan times, some modern scholars arguing that 'motley' at that period meant a sort of dark green.

Foote, Horton (b. 1916). American dramatist, author of several television plays, one of which, *The Trip to Bountiful*, has successfully transferred to the stage (1953). The same sort of easy small-town naturalism also characterizes *The Travelling Lady* (1954).

Footlights, see STAGE LIGHTING.

Footlights Club. A Cambridge University dramatic society, founded in 1883, which presents an annual revue written and performed by undergraduates. Formerly an all-male society, it admitted women to the revue in 1957, and to membership in 1965.

Forbes-Robertson, Sir Johnston (1853–1937). English actor-manager, noted for his flawless elocution. He played both classical and modern roles, but is best remembered for his Shakespearian performances. In 1880 he played Romeo to Modjeska's Juliet, and in 1895 to Mrs Patrick Campbell's under his own management. He was considered the great Hamlet of his day; his major success in a modern role was as The Stranger in Jerome K. Jerome's *The Passing of the Third Floor Back* (1908). He retired in 1913. A number of other members of the family were actors, the best known being Sir Johnston's daughter, Jean, the most famous of all PETER PANS.

Ford, John (1586–c.1639). English dramatist. Almost nothing is known of him apart from his plays, of which, collaborations apart, the most important are a restrained and dignified historical drama, *Perkin Warbeck*, and two tragedies of violent and often unnatural passions, *The Broken Heart* and *'Tis Pity She's a Whore*, all written between 1625 and 1634. Ford excels especially as a student of morbid states of mind; in particular his masterpiece, *'Tis Pity She's a Whore*, is a full and sympathetic account of an incestuous passion between brother and sister. It has frequently been revived, notably in a spectacular production in Paris by Luchino Visconti (1961); *The Broken Heart* was revived at the first Chichester Festival in 1962.

Forestage, see STAGE.

Formalism. Any pronounced form of conventionalization or stylization in a production, notably that practised by MEYERHOLD in Russia shortly after the Revolution. The term has a particularly derogatory ring in the Soviet theatre today, where it is used to castigate anything in a production which seems to obscure the social significance of the text.

Forsyth, James (b. 1913). Scottish dramatist who first made his mark at the Glasgow Unity Theatre and was subsequently taken up by the Old Vic, where *The Other Heart*, an historical play about François Villon, was staged in 1952. He has written plays in a wide variety of styles: others in costume, like *Heloise*, symbolic fantasy (*Trog*, first staged at the Belgrade, Coventry, in 1959), and realistic social drama (*The Pier*, 1958).

Fort, Paul (1872–1960). French director and theatre manager, leading theatrical symbolist and founder of the Théâtre d'Art (1890), which began the reaction against ANTOINE, by abandoning realistic perspective backdrops in favour of formalized, symbolic designs. Fort wanted to make the theatre an abstract art, and regarded the humanity of actors as an obstruction; after only two years he gave up the theatre and was succeeded at the Théâtre d'Art by LUGNÉ-POË.

Four Saints in Three Acts. Musical play by GERTRUDE STEIN, music by Virgil Thomson, first performed Hartford, Connecticut, 1934.

Fourth wall. Concept of the naturalistic theatre, according to which the proscenium arch represents the fourth wall of the room in which the action of the play takes place, removed for the benefit of the audience but without any of the performers taking cognizance of the fact.

Fraser, Claude Lovat (1890–1921). English stage designer and book-illustrator, specialist in his own brand of prettified, whimsical eighteenth-century fantasy. His most famous designs were for Nigel Playfair's revival of *The Beggar's Opera* at the Lyric, Hammersmith, in 1920.

French Without Tears. Light comedy by TERENCE RATTIGAN, first produced London, 1936.

Fresnay, Pierre (1897–1974). French actor. He began his professional career rather spectacularly by being, at the age of eighteen, the first actor engaged by the Comédie-Française after the start of the First World War. Here he rapidly established himself as a powerful and intelligent actor, played Britannicus in 1915, and was named a *sociétaire* in 1923, but chose instead to resign (in 1926) and pursue his career independently, on stage and in films. His first great popular success was the title role in MARCEL PAGNOL'S *Marius* (1930), a role he repeated in the cinema (1931) and played again in the two sequels *Fanny* (1932) and *César* (1936). Meanwhile on stage, he played for a while with the COMPAGNIE DES QUINZE in *Noé* and *Don Juan*; in 1934 he appeared in London in Noël Coward's *Conversation Piece* with his wife, Yvonne Printemps, and had one of his greatest successes with her in Paris in the operatta *Trois valses* (1937). A notable later play starring him and produced under his management was Anouilh's *Léocadia* (1940). He continued to appear regularly on the screen, his best roles being in Renoir's *La Grande Illusion* (1937), Clouzot's *Le Corbeau* (1943), Anouilh's *Le Voyageur sans bagage* (1943), and *Monsieur Vincent* (1947).

Friml, Rudolph (1881–1974). Czech-American composer of operetta and musical comedy, mostly in an expansive romantic style. His biggest successes were *The Firefly* (1912), *Rose Marie* (with Herbert Stothart, 1924), and *The Vagabond King* (1925).

Frisch, Max (b. 1911). Swiss dramatist and novelist. Apart from *Als der Krieg zu Ende war* (*When the War was Over*), which is largely realistic and even rather romantic in style, Frisch has devoted himself almost exclusively to symbolic drama in which the question of identity figures prominently. His very first play, *Santa Cruz* (1944), is a fantasy about freedom and marriage; *Die chinesische Mauer* (*The Chinese Wall*, 1946, 1955) is a cosmic fantasy about man's inability to learn by experience, set in an imaginary China; *Biedermann und die Brandstifter* (*The Fire-Raisers*, 1953, 1958) concerns the small beginnings of large disasters; and *Graf Öderland* (1951, 1956, 1961), *Don Juan*, and *Andorra* (1962) all concern people variously trapped in their public images, as peace-loving philanthropist, omnicompetent lover, and

Jew respectively. All Frisch's plays are technically adventurous, and he is noted for his endless revision of them (hence the double and triple dates); they have great diversity and drive, but lack (apart from *The Fire-Raisers*) the immediate appeal which has made the plays of his compatriot Dürrenmatt so widely successful.

Frogs, The. Comedy by ARISTOPHANES, first performed Athens, 405 B.C.

Frost at Midnight (Plus de miracles pour Noël). Drama by ANDRÉ OBEY, first performed (in English) Oxford, 1957.

Fry, Christopher (b. 1907). English dramatist and poet. Began his career alternating periods of acting with periods of teaching; wrote a short religious play in verse, *The Boy with a Cart*, in 1938, though it did not attract much attention until revived in 1950. In 1940 he was appointed director of the Oxford Playhouse, and took up the post again in 1944 after war service. His first success with the public was *A Phoenix Too Frequent*, a witty one-act comedy in verse produced in E. MARTIN BROWNE's season of verse plays at the Mercury Theatre in 1946; it was followed in 1948 by *The Lady's Not for Burning*, a romantic comedy in medieval setting which began life at the Arts Theatre Club and was subsequently a surprise success in the West End with John Gielgud in the leading role. Having established something of a vogue for his brand of bubbling, easy eloquence, Fry followed in rapid succession with a play for the Canterbury Festival, *Thor, with Angels* (1948); *The Firstborn*, a biblical drama for the Edinburgh Festival (1948); a tragi-comedy *Venus Observed* (1950), written for Laurence Olivier; another religious play, *A Sleep of Prisoners* (1951), written for performance in a church; and a 'winter piece', *The Dark is Light Enough*, written for Edith Evans (1954); as well as some translations of Anouilh, notably *Ring Round the Moon* (*L'Invitation au château*), 1950, and Giraudoux. After this the vogue for his sort of extravagant, romantic, verbally prodigal drama began to pass, and it was not until 1961 that another play by him was seen, the historical drama *Curtmantle*, followed in 1970 by the 'summer play' *A Yard of Sun*. Recently he has devoted himself increasingly to film script-writing.

Funny Face. Musical by GEORGE GERSHWIN, book by Fred Thompson and Paul Gerard Smith, lyrics by Ira Gershwin; first performed New York, 1927.

G

Galileo (Leben des Galilei). Historical drama by BERTOLT BRECHT, written 1937–9, first performed Zürich 1943; second (American) version written 1945–7, first performed (in English translation by Brecht and CHARLES LAUGHTON) Los Angeles, 1947.

Gallery. Upper balcony of a theatre (see PLAYHOUSE) and by extension those who sit there, in the cheapest, unreserved seats (known also as 'the Gods') and who are traditionally noted for their direct and uncompromisingly expressed reactions to plays and performers.

Galsworthy, John (1867–1933). English novelist and dramatist, best remembered today for his novel-sequence *The Forsyte Saga*. He was encouraged to try his hand at drama by the success of Shaw's plays and the Barker–Vedrenne management at the Royal Court, where his first play, *The Silver Box*, was produced in 1906. This was a sober, well-observed social drama, and Galsworthy continued to develop the style in *Strife* (1909), a scrupulously fair study of industrial unrest, and *Justice* (1910), an equally balanced study of the process of law. After a group of relative failures he returned to form in *The Skin Game* (1920) and *Loyalties* (1922), and continued to write plays on and off for some years, none of them specially interesting except perhaps *Escape* (1926), in which he experimented with a free, almost cinematic construction. Galsworthy was essentially an old-fashioned dramatist, writing 'well-made' realistic dramas on social topics of the time, but at his best had sufficient force and intelligence to produce something durable.

Gammer Gurton's Needle. Farce by 'Mr S., Master of Art' (possibly William Stevenson, *c*.1521–75), published in 1575, first performed Cambridge *c*. 1553–4. One of the earliest secular prose farces in English.

Garden District. Double bill by TENNESSEE WILLIAMS, consisting of *Suddenly Last Summer* and *Something Unspoken*, first performed New York, 1958.

Garrick, David (1717–79). English actor, theatre manager, and dramatist; the dominant figure on the London stage of his day. Child of a prosperous Huguenot family, he studied under Doctor Johnson and accompanied him to London; there he entered the wine trade, but soon deserted it for the stage. After a few chequered years he scored a great success as Richard III in 1741, and from then on he continued to lead his profession until he retired in 1776. His great innovation as an actor was to reintroduce an easy, natural style, even in his great

110

tragic roles (Hamlet, Macbeth, Lear), in place of the elaborate, histrionic style then in favour. He was also successful in comedy, his best roles being Benedick in *Much Ado About Nothing*, Bayes in *The Rehearsal*, and Abel Drugger in *The Alchemist*. As an author he wrote a number of forgotten plays on his own adaptations of Shakespeare, and a new version of Wycherley's *The Country Wife*, retitled *The Country Girl*. The work for which he is best remembered now, *The Clandestine Marriage* (1766), is a spirited comedy on which he collaborated with GEORGE COLMAN the elder. He also managed DRURY LANE from 1747 to his retirement, during which time he made it the leading playhouse in Europe, virtually every actor of any importance playing there. As well as acting himself, Garrick introduced a number of important new features, particularly by concealing stage lighting from the audience, encouraging the experiments of Philippe Jacques de Loutherbourg with naturalistic painted backdrops (see SCENERY), and banishing spectators from the stage itself: thus ending a practice begun in Elizabethan times.

Gascoigne, George (*c.*1542–78). English dramatist, satirist, and pamphleteer. Highly prolific in writing of all sorts, particularly diverting autobiography and fiction, his main claim to note as a dramatist is his comedy *Supposes* (1566), a free translation of Ariosto's *I Suppositi* (1509; itself based on plays by Plautus and Terence). *Supposes* is remembered as the first English comedy entirely in prose, a fashion-setter for Italian backgrounds in comedy, and the source of the Bianca–Lucentio plot in *The Taming of the Shrew*.

Gaskill, William (b. 1930). English director. First made his mark with the ENGLISH STAGE COMPANY, which he joined in 1957; in 1959 he became associate director; in 1963 he became a resident director at the National Theatre. At the Royal Court he directed John Osborne and Anthony Creighton's *Epitaph for George Dillon* and three plays by N. F. Simpson, *A Resounding Tinkle*, *The Hole*, and *One Way Pendulum*. Subsequently his most important productions have been Brecht's *The Caucasian Chalk Circle* for the Royal Shakespeare Company and Farquhar's *The Recruiting Officer* for the National Theatre. In 1965 he became director of the ENGLISH STAGE COMPANY in succession to GEORGE DEVINE.

Gaslight. Melodrama by PATRICK HAMILTON, first produced Richmond, 1938.

Gatti, Armand (b. 1924). French dramatist. Vaguely *avant-garde*, he made his name with a group of odd, poetic, symbolic pieces, including *Le Poisson noir*, *L'Enfant-rat* and *La Vie imaginaire de l'ébloueur August G.* The last played with great success at the Cité de Villeurbanne in 1962. In 1965–6 his *Chant publique devant deux chaises électriques* was outstanding at the T.N.P. He has also written and directed films, most notably the prize-winning prison-camp drama *L'Enclos*.

Gay, John (1685–1732). English poet and dramatist, best remembered as author of *The Beggar's Opera* (1728), which began the whole vogue of the BALLAD OPERA in England. Much of its popularity at the time was due to its elements of political satire, and its sequel, *Polly*, remained unproduced until 1777 because of its political aspects. Gay also wrote the libretto of Handel's *Acis and Galatea*, and a number of comedies in collaboration: one of them, *Three Hours After Marriage*, with Alexander Pope and Dr John Arbuthnot.

Gay Divorce. Musical by COLE PORTER, book by Dwight Taylor, first performed New York, 1932.

Gay Lord Quex, The. Comedy by ARTHUR WING PINERO, first produced London, 1899.

Gelber, Jack (b. 1931). American dramatist, author of two curious plays – *The Connection* (1958) and *The Apple* (1961) – which combine techniques suggestive of the Theatre of the ABSURD with an elaborately detailed naturalism designed to encourage audiences' imaginative participation in the performance. Of the two *The Connection*, which pictures a group of drug addicts waiting for a 'fix', is much the more successful.

Genet, Jean (b. 1910). French novelist, dramatist, and poet. Noted as much for his bizarre private life as for his literary works, Genet was illegitimate and spent years in and out of prison, stealing and living in a homosexual underworld, before he began in the early 1940s, while still in prison to write poems and fiction. In 1947 he wrote his first play, *Haute surveillance* (*Deathwatch*), a long one-act drama set in a prison cell concerning the tensions, erotic and otherwise, among three dazzlingly beautiful men, with the unseen presence of their idol, a Negro murderer called Snowball, brooding over them. In *Les Bonnes* (*The Maids*), written later but produced first (by JOUVET), Genet told another tale of violence and unnatural passion. This involved two maids, sisters, whose hatred of their mistress makes them first try to kill her in fact and then do so in play-acting, with one of them dying in the mistress's place. This ritual act is the key to all Genet's drama, which is one of ritual, dream and fantasy, in which realities are replaced by 'absurd' reflections which are perhaps just as real as the realities they mirror. Thus in his next play, *Le Balcon* (*The Balcony*), the characters who satisfy their fetishes by playing the roles of general, judge, and bishop in a brothel house of illusions actually take on their roles in reality when a revolution comes, and the leading revolutionary finally finds himself taking on the role of the chief of police. *Le Balcon* was produced in London in 1957, but not in Paris till 1960. Since *Le Balcon* Genet has written two plays, *Les Nègres (The Blacks)*, a '*clownerie*' written in 1957 and first acted by an all-coloured cast in 1959, which is a ritual enactment of Negro grievances against the whites; and *Les Paravents (The Screens)* (1961), a similar but less effective dramatization of Algerian grievances against the French. He is said now to be engaged in writing a cycle of seven plays, of which *Les Paravents* may or may not be one. Genet has been classified both as a dramatist of the ABSURD and as a follower of ARTAUD in his ritualistic Theatre of Cruelty. But essentially he is an original, making his own solitary and unpredictable way through modern French drama.

Gentleman Dancing Master, The. Comedy by WILLIAM WYCHERLEY, first performed London, 1671–2.

George, Mademoiselle (1787–1867). French actress and great beauty of the Napoleonic era, Napoleon's mistress for a short time. She excelled in the more spectacular tragic roles, such as Lady Macbeth, Agrippine, and Jocasta; later she made a new career for herself in the flamboyant historical dramas of Dumas and de Vigny, her greatest success being in Dumas's *La Tour de Nesle* (1832).

George and Margaret. Comedy by GERALD SAVORY, first performed London, 1937.

Georges Dandin, ou le mari confondu. Comedy by MOLIÈRE, first performed Versailles, 1668.

Gershwin, George (1898–1937). American composer of musicals. He was born in New York, published his first song at the age of eighteen and had his first big hit, *Swanee*, when he was twenty. He contributed many songs to the annual *George White's Scandals* from 1920 to 1924, and in 1924 had his first success with a musical entirely his own, *Lady, Be Good* (the lyrics of which, like most of his later work, were by his brother, Ira), and his first concert work in a jazz-influenced style, *Rhapsody in Blue*. From then on there was an almost unbroken succession of Broadway hits from the two Gershwins: *Tip-Toes* (1925), *Oh, Kay* (1926), *Funny Face* (1927), *Strike up the Band* (1930), *Girl Crazy* (1930), *Of Thee I Sing* (1931), and in 1935 the Negro opera *Porgy and Bess*. Gershwin was one of the first composers to persuade serious musicians to pay attention to popular music, partly by his concert works and partly by the enterprise of his works in the popular theatre, notably *Of Thee I Sing*, a political satire with book by GEORGE S. KAUFMAN and Morrie Ryskind, which was the first musical to be awarded the Pulitzer Prize. More recently the strictly musical importance of his popular songs has been reaffirmed by a number of intellectual critics, and his place as the genius of the American musical stage seems secure.

Getting Married. Play by GEORGE BERNARD SHAW, first performed London, 1908.

Ghelderode, Michel de (1898–1962). Belgian dramatist of Flemish origin but writing in French. The spirit of his plays owes much to that of Breughel and the medieval grotesquerie of his school, which still finds direct theatrical expression in the traditional dramas of Belgian puppet-theatres today. Ghelderode has been much influenced by these, and has written a number of plays for puppets as well as for live actors. His subjects are often religious, though in his plays, as in medieval drama, the comic and grotesque and the reverent are boldly mixed and mingled. Of his nearly fifty plays a number remain unpublished or unperformed, and several have been performed only in Flemish translation. His first play, *Les Víeillards*, was written in 1919; his best-known plays are those in which he has rewritten perennial subjects of drama in his own style – *La Mort du Docteur Faust* (1926), *Don-Juan* (1928) – and *Pantagleize* (1929), *La Ballade du Grand Macabre* (1934), and *Sire Halewyn* (1934), farcical tragedies full of poetry and violence. The vogue for his drama, long little known, began in Paris, in 1949, when his *Fastes d'enfer* (written 1929) caused a scandal; it has subsequently continued to grow, particularly in the U.S.A.

Ghéon, Henri (1875–1944). French dramatist (real name Henri Vangeon) of primarily religious interests. His first play, *Le Pain*, was written in 1900 but was not produced in Paris until 1911; his first real success was *L'Eau de vie* (1914) produced by Copeau at the Vieux-Colombier. Many of his later plays are based on saints' lives, among them his masterpiece *Le Pauvre sous l'escalier* (1921) about St Alexis, *L'Histoire de jeune Bernard de Menthon* (*The Marvellous History of St Bernard*, 1925), *Le Comédien et la grâce, ou le comédien pris à son jeu* (1941), about St Genest, and *Jeanne écoute* (posthumously produced, 1954), about Joan of Arc.

Ghosts (Gengangere). Drama by HENRIK IBSEN, published 1881, first performed Helsingborg, 1883.

Ghost Sonata, The (Spöksonaten, also known as **The Spook Sonata).** Drama by AUGUST STRINDBERG, first performed Stockholm, 1907.

Gibson, William (b. 1914). American dramatist, author of the two-character emotional drama *Two for the Seesaw* (1958) and of *The Miracle-Worker*, based on the education of Helen Keller and written originally for television. He has also written *The Seesaw Log*, a ruthless account of a playwright's tribulations in getting his play on to the American commercial stage.

Gielgud, John (b. 1904). English actor and director, knighted 1953. Studied at R.A.D.A. and made his first stage appearances in small parts at the Old Vic in 1921. He was soon recognized as a classical actor of exceptional promise; he played Romeo for the first time in 1924, and in 1925 took over from Noël Coward the lead role in *The Vortex*. In 1929 he joined the Old Vic again, playing among other roles Hamlet, Macbeth, Romeo, Richard II, and Mark Antony in *Julius Caesar*. Next he appeared for the first time in one of his most famous roles, John Worthing in *The Importance of Being Earnest* at the Lyric, Hammersmith, and then returned to the Old Vic to play Hotspur, Prospero, Benedick, and Lear. The year 1932 brought one of his best performances, as Joseph Schindler in Ronald Mackenzie's drama *Musical Chairs*, and one of his most popular, Richard in Gordon Daviot's *Richard of Bordeaux*, which established him in the popular West End theatre. In the following years he appeared several times as Hamlet, being widely regarded as the finest Hamlet of his day, as Romeo and Mercutio (in 1935 he alternated roles with Laurence Olivier), and as John Worthing, as well as managing a season at the Queen's in which he played Richard II, Shylock, Joseph Surface in *The School for Scandal* and Vershinin in *The Three Sisters*. In 1943 he directed and appeared in a memorable revival of *Love for Love*; in 1949 he played the lead in his own production of Christopher Fry's *The Lady's Not for Burning*, and in 1950 at Stratford played Benedick and Lear, two of his most famous roles which he has frequently played since, and Angelo in *Measure for Measure* and Cassius in *Julius Caesar*, both for the first time. Other notable appearances include Mirabell in *The Way of the World*, which he also directed, and Jaffeir in *Venice Preserved* (both 1953), James Callifer in Graham Greene's *The Potting Shed* (1958), Wolsey in *Henry VIII* (1958), Gayev in *The Cherry Orchard* (1961), Othello (1963), Ivanov (1965), Seneca's Oedipus (1967) and Harry in David Storey's *Home* (1970), his first role in an example of the new British drama. His most remarkable qualities as an actor are his musical and flexible speaking voice and his acute intelligence in the analysis and re-creation of character; though he excels in tragedy, he is by no means lacking comic skill, as his success in Congreve, Sheridan and Wilde suggests.

Gilbert, W. S. (Sir William Schwenk; 1836–1911). English dramatist and humorist. Though he wrote many comic and fantastic dramas himself, often successfully, his fame today rests on his collaboration with Sir Arthur Sullivan (1842–1900) in the 'Savoy operas', a succession of light operas with spoken dialogue which began in 1875 with *Trial by Jury* and ended with *The Grand Duke* (1896). Most of them – *H.M.S. Pinafore* (1878), *The Pirates of Penzance* (1880), *Patience* (1881), *Iolanthe* (1882), *The Mikado* (1885), *Ruddigore* (1887), *The Yeoman of the Guard* (1888), and *The Gondoliers* (1889) – are still in the repertoire of the D'OYLY CARTE Opera Company and are constantly revived by amateur groups all over the country. Gilbert's gift for resourceful rhyming and excruciating puns, though now very evidently of its period, is still appreciated by modern audiences.

Giraudoux, Jean (1882–1944). French dramatist. From his very first play, *Siegfried,* a symbolic drama of Franco-German rapprochement produced in 1928, he collaborated closely with the actor-director LOUIS JOUVET on nearly all his theatrical work. Noted above all for his elegant prose style and critical intelligence, he was capable of graceful light comedy (*Amphitryon '38,* 1929), fairy-tale fantasy (*Ondine,* 1939), drama of contemporary reference based on history or legend (*Judith,* 1931; *La Guerre de Troie n'aura pas lieu,* 1935; *Sodome et Gomorrhe,* 1943), graceful poetic drama (*Intermezzo,* 1933; *La Folle de Chaillot,* produced 1945), and intricate moral drama (*Pour Lucrèce,* produced 1953). In all his work the hand of a superb theatrical technician is evident – even leaving out of account the great deal he owed to Jouvet – but it has been suggested that the shallowness of his plays, and their intellectual coolness, will finally prove them ephemeral.

Glamorous Night. Musical play by IVOR NOVELLO, first performed Drury Lane, London, 1935.

Glasgow Citizens' Theatre. Repertory theatre founded by JAMES BRIDIE in 1942, with the backing of C.E.M.A. (later the Arts Council) to give Glasgow a permanent theatre company and to encourage the work of modern Scottish dramatists.

Glass Menagerie, The. Drama by TENNESSEE WILLIAMS, first performed New York, 1945.

Glenville, Peter (b. 1913). English director, son of the Irish comedian Shaun Glenville, and the English principal boy Dorothy Ward. Began his career as an actor; started directing for the Old Vic in 1944 and went over completely to direction in 1947. Has worked mainly in a realistic style, directing several of Terence Rattigan's plays, Tennessee Williams's *Summer and Smoke,* and Graham Greene's *The Living Room,* as well as his own adaptation of Feydeau's *Hotel Paradiso* (1956). Of late has also directed a number of films.

Globe Theatre. Elizabethan theatre on the south bank of the Thames, built 1599, burnt down 1613, rebuilt 1614, demolished 1644. First home of many of Shakespeare's plays (see also ELIZABETHAN THEATRE).

Goethe, Johann Wolfgang von (1749–1832). German poet, dramatist, novelist, and man of letters. Among his vast output were several influential plays, starting with *Götz von Berlichingen* in 1773, a wild, romantic, action-packed portrait of a robber baron, influenced by Shakespeare and the first play to introduce full-blooded Romanticism and STURM UND DRANG on to the German stage. His next important play was the idealistic (and highly idealized) historical drama *Egmont*, best remembered now for Beethoven's overture. A visit to Italy in 1786 produced two dramatic poems, *Iphigenie auf Tauris* (loosely based on Euripides) and *Torquato Tasso*. These were not really intended to be staged and from this time on Goethe took less and less interest in the practical possibilities of the theatre. However FAUST, the major work of his maturity, was cast in dramatic mould, and has been successfully staged in various adaptations, though the immense length of the whole two-part text virtually precludes staging. The first part, published in 1808, is the more practicable; it retells in Goethe's own fashion most of the Faust story as traditionally handed on. The second, published only after his death in 1832, is an elaborate philosophical fantasy of cosmic proportions which has had far more influence on literature than on drama. In the main adaptors have preferred to keep as far as possible to the first part, even on occasion going back to the simpler, posthumously published *Urfaust*, an early draft of the work.

Gogol, Nikolai (1809–52). Russian novelist and dramatist, famed in the theatre almost entirely for one work, his satirical comedy *Revizor* (*The Government Inspector*) of 1836. This scathing picture of municipal corruption, set off by the arrival in a village of a clerk pretending to be the inspector-general, got past the censors because the Tsar enjoyed it. Gogol's other plays were not so lucky: his first, *The Decoration of Vladimir of the Third Category* (1832) was destroyed and partly used in two others, *The Servants' Hall* and *The Law Suit*, neither of which found favour. His other farce, *The Marriage* (1837–42), did not find favour either, though its vividly grotesque characterization has enabled it to be revived successfully in the twentieth century, and it seems to have influenced the early plays of CHEKHOV.

Golden Boy. Drama by CLIFFORD ODETS, first produced by Group Theatre, New York, 1937; musical version, book by Odets and WILLIAM GIBSON, music by Charles Strouse and Lee Adams, first performed New York, 1964.

Goldoni, Carlo (1707–93). Venetian dramatist and stage reformer. He wrote nearly three hundred plays in French or Italian, and sometimes in both (he lived in Paris from 1761 until his death). All his works were comedies, usually firmly founded in realistic observation and directed mainly at a popular middle-class audience, hence perhaps his rather critical attitude towards his aristocratic characters. The main theatrical reform he encouraged by his work was the substitution of written drama for the decadent tradition of actors' improvisation represented by the COMMEDIA DELL'ARTE, his chief opponent being Gozzi, who wanted to reform the *commedia dell'arte* itself, instead of replacing it. The most famous of his plays today are *La Locandiera* (1753), which provided Duse with one of her favourite roles, and *I Rusteghi* (1760) a Venetian dialect piece turned into an opera by Wolf-Ferrari in 1906. Other plays of his include *Il Moliere* (1751), *Un Curioso accidente* (1757), and *Le Baruffe Chiozzotte* (1762).

Goldsmith, Oliver (1730–74). Irish dramatist, novelist, and man of letters, friend of Doctor Johnson and author of two comedies, *The Good-Natured Man* (1768) and *She Stoops to Conquer* (1773), both of which survive in the modern repertoire. Both are robust and individual, lacking the painful gentility of most of their contemporaries and the coarseness of Restoration drama, though in certain respects they suggest the works of FARQUHAR. The role of Tony Lumpkin in *She Stoops to Conquer* has long been a favourite part of comic actors and Goldsmith's amiability and lightness of touch ease us over some highly improbable plotting to a happy conclusion.

Goll, Yvan (1891–1950). Franco-German dramatist and poet, writing in both languages. Early involved with DADA and Surrealism, Goll was one of the first to use film techniques in the theatre (*Die Chaplinade, Der Unsterbliche*, both 1920). His most ambitious work, a satirical drama called *Methusalem, oder der ewige Bürger* (*Methusaleh, or the Everlasting Bourgeois*, 1924) contains filmed sequences, as well as flat exchanges of nonsensical clichés which anticipate Ionesco.

Gondoliers, The. 'Savoy opera' by Arthur Sullivan (music) and W. S. GILBERT (book and lyrics), first performed Savoy, London, 1889.

Good-Natured Man, The, Comedy by OLIVER GOLDSMITH, first performed Covent Garden, London, 1768.

Good Woman of Setzuan, The (Der gute Mensch von Sezuan). Drama by BERTOLT BRECHT, written 1938–41, first performed Zürich, 1942.

Gorky, Maxim (real name Alexei Maximovich Pyeshkov; 1868–1936). Russian novelist and dramatist. Of working-class origins, he began writing short stories and prose-poems of revolutionary tendency in early manhood, and was a well-known writer by the time CHEKHOV induced him to try his hand at drama in 1901. His first play, *Scenes in the House of Bessemenov*, later called *Smug Citizens*, was produced by the MOSCOW ART THEATRE in 1902, much censored and with no great success. With his next play, though, *The Lower Depths* (1902), the company scored a triumph; Gorky's ruthlessly detailed and realistic depiction of the down-and-out inhabitants of a doss-house was matched by STANISLAVSKY's elaborately naturalistic production, and the work has remained in the world repertoire ever since. Meanwhile a gap opened between Gorky and the Art Theatre, who rejected his next play, *The Vacationists* (1904). Gorky continued to write plays, several of them, like *The Enemies* (1907) and *The Last Ones* (1909) banned from the Russian stage until after the Revolution. At the Revolution Gorky gave up drama, to return to it only in the 1930s with a projected sequence on the fall of the tsarist regime, only the first two of which, *Yegor Bulychev and the Others* and *Dostigayev and the Others* (both produced at the Vakhtangov Theatre in 1932), were completed. These, particularly the first, were the best plays he had written since *The Lower Depths*, but it is that alone which keeps his reputation as a dramatist alive outside Russia.

Government Inspector, The (*Revizor*, also known as **The Inspector-General**). Satirical comedy by NIKOLAI GOGOL, first performed St Petersburg, 1836.

Grand guignol. Term derived from Théâtre du Grand Guignol, Paris, used to describe a genre of brief plays each built round a sensational situation – rape, murder, hauntings – exploited entirely in terms of the pleasurable horror it can excite in an audience. 'Guignol' originally was a puppet in a sort of French Punch-and-Judy show. The genre of the play to which he lent his name flourished particularly in Montmartre in the 1890s and 1900s; London saw a famous season of *grand guignol* plays starring Sybil Thorndike in 1920–2.

Grass, Günter (b. 1927). German novelist and dramatist. Began as a painter, then took to the theatre and since 1957 has more or less given up the theatre in favour of the novel. All his plays belong to the Theatre of the ABSURD tradition, given a distinctively grotesque twist. His first, *Onkel, Onkel* (*Uncle, Uncle*), is a story of an absurd obsession – with murder – by a man who cannot even scare little children; his second, *Zweiunddreissig Zähne* (*Thirty-two Teeth*), is about a teacher obsessed with dental hygiene. His most ambitious play, *Die bösen Köche* (*The Wicked Cooks*), is a strange religious allegory about a group of cooks looking for the secret of a mysterious soup which seems to represent the eucharist, and is described by its inventor as 'an experience, not a recipe'.

Greek theatre. Drama in Greece, and specifically in Athens, is the earliest of which we have an extensive record and remains. It was acted in open-air theatres built into hillsides, consisting of a central acting area overlooked by a semi-circle of tiered seats and backed by a permanent architectural setting. The dramatic performances had their beginning in religious ritual and remained part of a religious festival. The two principal dramatic forms, tragedy and comedy, evolved separately with little or no interaction, comedy rather later than tragedy.

The earliest complete surviving play is probably AESCHYLUS'S tragedy *The Suppliant Women*, if its dating at *c*.490 B.C. is correct, and it shows tragic form already somewhat evolved from the most primitive form we know of: the play for one actor only and a CHORUS. *The Suppliant Women* already has two actors, and the importance of the chorus must therefore already be slightly diminished, though its lyrical episodes still play a vital part in the whole. Aeschylus's drama is still concerned with general moral judgements, the relations of mankind to the gods and the universe; that of SOPHOCLES takes as its subject more the problems of the individual and of relations between individuals: hence the importance of the chorus is even further diminished, and a third actor is introduced. (Roles might, incidentally, always be doubled: it is a question of how many actors appear on the stage simultaneously.) In his later works Aeschylus adopted the third actor, and made use of rather more intricate situations, but his plays remained throughout essentially depictions of catastrophes. Sophocles, on the other hand, made room for much more exploration of individual character; his chorus is used largely to make lyrical comment on the action, and is directly involved in it very little. This innovation was taken up by EURIPIDES, the third great tragic poet of Ancient Greece, and carried to its logic conclusion by a later, Agathon, who, we are told, reduced the chorus to a mere provider of lyrical interludes quite unconnected with the plot. Euripides was not so much a technical innovator as an explorer of new subject-matter, particularly in the realms of abnormal and morbid psychology; his plays are more 'romantic' in their construction than those of Sophocles, being often a succession of startling or sensational events (sometimes widely differing in mood) with more characters and less discipline in the ordering of plot. Towards the end of his career Sophocles seems to have introduced a fourth actor (in *Oedipus at Colonus*) and he is also credited with the introduction of painted scenery, though elaborate props and machines had been used by Aeschylus (see also COSTUME).

Comedy followed a different line and evolved later (the first comedy competition was nearly fifty years later than the first tragedy contest), though the general tendency of its development was much the same. The so-called 'Old Comedy' of ARISTOPHANES was still in many ways close to its ritual origin, with the chorus playing a prominent role in the action and the accent being on topical satire directed at individuals rather than elaborate plotting. Aristophanes' last two plays, however, the *Ecclesiazusae* (392 B.C.) and the *Plutus* (388 B.C.), already have a more developed plot and are more generalized in their satire – a state of affairs which seems to have been characteristic of the 'Middle Comedy', which survives only in fragments. 'New Comedy', which developed out of this (MENANDER being its principal dramatist), was pure comedy of manners, the chorus taking part only as an occasional irrelevant musical relief. The New Comedy was the basis of the Roman comedy of PLAUTUS and TERENCE.

Green, Julien (b. 1900). French dramatist and novelist of American origin, writing in French. His first play, *Sud* (*South*), was not written until 1953; it is a psychological drama concerning a young man's recognition of his own homosexuality, set, rather uncomfortably, against a political background of the outbreak of the American Civil War. The following year *L'Ennemi* (*The Enemy*) was staged; another psychological drama, this time about a battle between physical desire and the force of divine Grace, it provoked exaggerated partisanship on both sides. There is little sign in either play that Green's gifts are genuinely dramatic.

Green Bay Tree, The. Drama by Mordaunt Shairp, first performed London, 1933; famous in its time for its 'daring' treatment of decadence and the moral corruption of a young man by an older.

Greene, Graham (b. 1904). English novelist and dramatist of the Roman Catholic persuasion and usually concerned in his writing, more or less directly, with religious questions. His first play was an adaptation, in collaboration with Basil Dean, of his own novel *The Heart of the Matter* (1950); in 1953 he wrote his first original play, *The Living Room*, about suicide, and in 1957 another, *The Potting Shed*, about the recovery of faith. His third, *The Complaisant Lover* (1959), was a comedy with serious undertones about adultery, and it was followed by *Carving a Statue* (1964), a tragical farce about a sculptor with an obsession but no talent. He has also written a number of film-scripts (notably *The Third Man*, 1948), and his novel *The Power and the Glory* has been adapted to the stage by Pierre Bost and Denis Cannan.

Greene, Robert (*c.* 1560–92). English dramatist, poet, and pamphleteer whose most famous work was his deathbed tract *A Groatsworth of Wit Bought with a Million of Repentance*. His *James IV* (of Scotland, that is) is a highly unhistorical historical drama; his *Friar Bacon and Friar Bungay* a weird concoction of comedy, tragedy, fantasy and sentiment supposedly based on the history of the alchemist Roger Bacon. He may also have written the bright rustic comedy, *George a Greene*.

Green Goddess, The. Melodrama by WILLIAM ARCHER, first performed Philadelphia, 1923.

Green room. Actors' common-room backstage, now obsolete except at Drury Lane.

Gregory, Lady (Augusta; 1859?–1932). Irish dramatist and dominant figure in the Irish dramatic revival. An author and friend of W. B. YEATS, she was associated with Yeats and Edward Martyn in the planning and setting up of the Irish Literary Theatre (1898–9). This became the Irish National Theatre Society in 1902 and in 1904 moved into the ABBEY THEATRE, of which Lady Gregory was the patent-holder, and with which she remained closely connected, through all its trials and triumphs, until she retired in 1928. Largely as a result of her practical theatre work she tried her hand at play-writing, first with two plays written in collaboration with Yeats in 1902, *The Pot of Broth* and *Cathleen ni Houlihan*, then on her own. She attempted a wide variety of forms and styles, but her best plays remain her one-acters, notably *The Gaol Gate* (1906) and *The Rising of the Moon* (1907); and her peasant comedies *Spreading the News* (1904), *Hyacinth Halvey* (1906), and *The Workhouse Ward* (1908). She was also a successful translator of Molière into Irish terms (*The Kiltartan Molière*).

Grenfell, Joyce (b. 1910). English actress and writer. Specialist in humorous and lightly ironic monologues concerning the vagaries of a certain type of upper-middle-class English woman, which she writes and performs herself; originally as a contributor to revues (*Sigh No More*, 1947; *Tuppence Coloured*, 1947; *Penny Plain*, 1951), later in one-woman shows, starting with *Joyce Grenfell Requests the Pleasure* (1954). Published autobiography with same title, 1977.

Griboyedov, Alexander (1795–1829). Russian dramatist. Began as a translator and adapter of Molière; his own major work, the satirical verse comedy *Wit Works Woe*, written in 1823, is heavily influenced by *Le Misanthrope*, showing, in the author's own words, Moscow society in terms of 'twenty-five fools to one reasonable man'. The play was read at literary gatherings in 1824, but its production was not allowed, even in a heavily cut form, until 1831, when it was allowed to be played only in the two capitals; the complete text was not staged until 1869, so explosive was it thought to be. The author himself, who was also a diplomatist, died mysteriously in Teheran at the age of thirty-four.

Grid, see STAGE MACHINERY.

Grillparzer, Franz (1791–1872). Austrian dramatist of the most extravagantly Romantic STURM UND DRANG school. His first play, *Die Ahnfrau* (*The Ancestress*, 1817) is an elaborate piece of Gothick nonsense about a vengeful ghost bringing ruin on a family; *Sappho* (1819) deals emotionally with an imaginary episode in the love-life of the Greek poetess; *Die Jüdin von Toledo* (*The Jewess of Toledo*), his best play, was written in 1837, when his Romantic fervour had abated somewhat, but it was not acted till 1888.

Grimaldi, Joseph (1778–1837). The most famous of clowns, born in London of an Italian father and an English mother and trained in pantomime from earliest youth by his father, a ballet-master at Drury Lane. He is said to have appeared on the stage first as a dancer at the age of two. His great success came at Covent Garden in 1806, and he reigned there continuously until his retirement in 1823. He was a singer, dancer, actor and acrobat as well as comedian and mime, and originated the type of clown known after him as 'Joey'.

Grock (real name Adrien Wettach; 1880–1959). Swiss clown. Toured Europe in partnership with a clown called Brick, and then, with another called Antonet, he attempted to invade the music hall, where finally his greatest successes were achieved. The point of his act was a battle with a succession of musical instruments, none of which for one reason or another he succeeded in playing (though in fact he could play them all well). He first appeared in London in 1911, under the aegis of C. B. Cochran, and performed there regularly after this.

Grossmith, George (1847–1912). English actor and entertainer; regular performer in the Savoy operas from 1881 to 1889, author with his brother **Weedon** (1852–1919) of *The Diary of a Nobody*, and father of **George Grossmith Junior** (1877–1944), star of musical comedy and revue.

Groundling. Member of the audience in an ELIZABETHAN THEATRE who stood in the central promenade area nearest the stage and, paying least, was regarded as part of the most rowdy and least intelligent element.

Group Theatre. American theatre company founded in New York in 1931 as an offshoot of THEATRE GUILD and dissolved in 1940. See also HAROLD CLURMAN; CLIFFORD ODETS.

Gründgens, Gustav (1899–1963). German actor and director. Studied at drama school in his native town of Düsseldorf, and early came to the fore as a forceful romantic actor, his Hamlet being particularly admired. He appeared in a number of notable films, among them Fritz Lang's *M* (1931) and Max Ophüls's *Liebelei* (1933), but his career was mainly on the stage, where his gifts as an organizer and director were explored to the full as director of the Preussisches Staatstheater, Berlin (1937–45), the Deutsches Theater, Berlin (1946–7)), the Stadtische Bühnen, Düsseldorf (1947–51), the Schauspielhaus, Düsseldorf (1951–5), and the Deutsches Spielhaus, Hamburg (1955–63). Among his most famous achievements as actor and director were his productions of *Faust* (in which he played Mephisto), *Hamlet*, *Richard II*, *Wallenstein*, and the *Oresteia*.

Guardsman, The (A Testór). Comedy by FERENC MOLNAR, first performed Budapest, 1910.

Guerre de Troie n'aura pas lieu, La, see TIGER AT THE GATES.

Guinea Pig, The. Drama by Warren Chetham-Strode, first performed London, 1946; concerned the fate of a working-class boy introduced as a 'guinea pig' into a public school.

Guinness, Alec (b. 1914; knighted 1959). English actor, first appeared on stage in 1934, first made his mark at the Old Vic in 1936–7 playing Osric in *Hamlet* and Sir Andrew Aguecheek in *Twelfth Night*. By 1938 he was playing Hamlet there himself (complete and in modern dress). After his war service his first role was Mitya in his own adaptation of *The Brothers Karamazov* (1946); a further season at the Old Vic (1946–8) saw him as the Fool in *King Lear*, Abel Drugger in *The Alchemist*, Richard II, and Hlestakov in *The Government Inspector*, among other roles. Later parts included Sir Henry Harcourt-Reilly in *The Cocktail Party* (1949), Richard III (Stratford, Ontario, 1953), the Cardinal in *The Prisoner* (1954), Boniface in *Hotel Paradiso* (1956), T. E. Lawrence in *Ross* (1960), the King in Ionesco's *Exit the King* at the Royal Court (1963), Dylan Thomas in *Dylan* (New York, 1964), Macbeth at the Royal Court (1966) and his original role in a revival of *The Cocktail Party* (1968). Later theatre roles have included appearances in John Mortimer's *A Voyage Round My Father* (1971) and Alan Bennett's *Habeas Corpus* (1973). Recently he has devoted himself with rare exceptions to the cinema, where his gifts as a brilliant mimic and character-actor have been exploited more fully than on the stage; he is essentially a character-actor rather than a true star, and has generally been at his best playing roles most evidently remote from his own personality.

Guitry, Sacha (1885–1957). French actor and dramatist, son of the actor Lucien Guitry. Author, and often director and star, of innumcrable plays and films, mostly lightweight if not entirely comic. In particular he specialized in intriguing and often faintly saucy glimpses behind the scenes in the lives of the great – *Jean de la Fontaine* (1916), *Deburau* (1918), *Mozart* (1928), *Frans Hals* (1931), and his spectacular films, *Si Versailles m'était conté* (1953) and *Si Paris nous était conté* (1955). His best works were his simplest comedies, *Le Grand Duc* (1921) and his films *Le Roman d'un tricheur* (1936) and *Ils étaient neuf célibataires* (1939).

Guthrie, Tyrone (1900–1971). British director. His first job was as a director with the Scottish National Players 1926–7, then with the Cambridge Festival Theatre 1929–30; his first London production Bridie's *The Anatomist* (1931). He was a director at the Old Vic 1933–4, 1936–7; administrator of the Old Vic and Sadler's Wells 1939–45; back at the Old Vic 1951–2. Founder of the Shakespeare Festival, Stratford, Ontario, and regular director there from 1953 (though he resigned as artistic director in 1955), he has continued to direct drama and opera in London, New York, and elsewhere in the meantime. From 1962 to 1965 he was director of the new theatre at Minneapolis, built, like that at Stratford, Ontario, to his own specifications. Guthrie's stock-in-trade as a director was always inventiveness, sometimes in the service of the play, at others in the play's despite, generally a bit of both. Much of his best work was done with Shakespeare and Elizabethan drama in general: there have been a number of modern-dress productions – *Hamlet* with Alec Guinness (Old Vic, 1938), *All's Well That Ends Well* (Stratford, Ontario, 1953), *The Taming of the Shrew* (Stratford, Ontario, 1954), *Troilus and Cressida* (Old Vic, 1956), *The Alchemist* (Old Vic, 1963) – and many more conventionally costumed, among them *Tamburlaine* (Old Vic, 1951), *Timon of Athens* (Old Vic, 1952), and his notoriously eccentric *Henry VIII* (Old Vic, 1953). One of his most successful productions was Sir David Lindsay's medieval Scottish play *The Three Estates*, directed on an apron stage at the Edinburgh Festival in 1948. He was knighted in 1961.

Guys and Dolls. Musical by Frank Loesser, book by ABE BURROWS and Jo Swerling after stories and characters of Damon Runyon; first performed New York, 1950.

Gwynn, Nell (1650–87). English actress of no particular talent but great charm and vivacity, who began by selling oranges at Drury Lane and became Charles II's mistress, retiring from the stage in 1669.

H

Habimah. Jewish theatre company, founded in Moscow in 1917 to perform plays in Hebrew. The enterprise was started under the aegis of STANISLAVSKY, the training of actors was confided to VAKHTANGOV, and after the company's first performances of a group of one-act plays in 1918 they became an affiliated studio to the MOSCOW ART THEATRE. Before his death in 1922 Vakhtangov staged one of their most famous productions, *The Dybbuk*, which remained for many years a staple of their repertoire. The company toured America in 1926 and visited Palestine for the first time in 1928. In 1931 they settled in Palestine, becoming, as originally intended, a Jewish national theatre on the setting-up of Israel, with a permanent base at Tel Aviv.

Haigh, Kenneth (b. 1932). English actor. His most famous role is Jimmy Porter in *Look Back in Anger*, which he created at the Royal Court in 1956 and later played in New York. Later roles include the title role in Camus's *Caligula* (New York and London) and Franz in Sartre's *Altona* (London).

Hair. Musical, book and lyrics by Gerome Ragni and James Rado, music by Galt McDermot, first performed New York 1967. A virtually plotless attempt to capture in music and movement the characteristic tone of life among the American younger generation, helped to international success by a mild injection of nudity.

Halévy, Ludovic, see MEILHAC, HENRI.

Hall, Peter (b. 1930). English director and theatrical manager. Began directing while at Cambridge, and on leaving started directing professionally at once, first in repertory, then in 1954 at the Arts Theatre, of which he was appointed assistant director (director 1955–6). At the Arts he directed, among others, *The Lesson, South, Mourning Becomes Electra, The Burnt Flowerbed, Waiting for Godot,* and *The Waltz of the Toreadors*, the last two of which transferred successfully to the West End. In 1957 he formed his own production company, International Playwrights' Theatre, and directed for it *Camino Real*; meanwhile he continued to direct Shakespeare at Stratford (*Cymbeline*, 1957; *Coriolanus*, 1959; *Twelfth Night*, 1960; *Romeo and Juliet*, 1962), opera at Sadler's Wells, and dramas of all sorts elsewhere (*Cat on a Hot Tin Roof, Traveller Without Luggage, The Wrong Side of the Park*). In 1960 he was appointed director of the Shakespeare Memorial Theatre, which subsequently became the ROYAL SHAKESPEARE COMPANY, took over the Aldwych as its London home, and branched into experimental seasons at the Arts and Lamda Theatres. With all these enterprises to control, he had less time for direction and in 1968 he stepped down from sole directorship of the R.S.C., though remaining one of the four governing directors, in order to direct more himself. As a director he has shown a considerable range and eclecticism of style, though perhaps happier with the intenser sort of contemporary drama, and his productions have been more notable for all-round efficiency than for personal eccentricities or erratic brilliance. Became director of the National Theatre 1976; knighted 1977.

Hall, Willis (b. 1929). English dramatist, prolific author of television and film scripts, often in collaboration with the novelist Keith Waterhouse, as well as of stage plays. The most notable of his solo works is *The Long and the Short and the Tall* (1958) a military drama of vaguely liberal sentiments in the tradition of *Look Back in Anger*; of his various collaborations with Waterhouse the most successful has been their adaptation of Waterhouse's novel *Billy Liar*.

Hamilton, Patrick (1904–62). English novelist and dramatist, author of three highly successful essays in the theatrical macabre, *Rope* (1929), *Gaslight* (1938), and *The Governess* (1945), all of them extremely well-made thrillers with a dash of *grand guignol*, and a curious, grim psychological drama, *The Duke in Darkness* (1942).

Hamlet. Tragedy by WILLIAM SHAKESPEARE, written *c.* 1600–1.

Hamlet of Stepney Green, The. Jewish comedy by BERNARD KOPS, first performed Oxford, 1958.

Hammerstein, Oscar, II (1895–1961). American dramatist and lyric-writer, son of Oscar Hammerstein I, a theatrical manager and impresario. Though trained for the law, he became involved in the theatre at university. His first Broadway show as book- and lyric-writer was *Always You* (1920) and his first major hit was *Wildflower* (1923), in which he collaborated with Otto Harbach on the book and lyrics while Herbert Stothart and VINCENT YOUMANS wrote the music. In his next hit, *Rose Marie* (1924) he again collaborated with Otto Harbach, the music this time being by Herbert Stothart and RUDOLF FRIML. Hammerstein also collaborated with Harbach in writing such later shows as Jerome Kern's *Sunny* (1925) and Romberg's *The Desert Song* (1926). Under Hammerstein's influence *Wildflower* and *Rose Marie* attempted a closer integration of song and dance into the dramatic structure than was usual at the time, but he became increasingly associated with the old-fashioned, operetta type of musical until *Show Boat* (1927), which he wrote on his own, with music by JEROME KERN; this made a real move in the direction of musical comedy as a sort of American folk opera, such as had always been Hammerstein's ambition. During the next few years Hammerstein had considerably fewer successes (the most notable was *Music in the Air*, with Kern, 1932), and did not really come back to the limelight again until his first collaboration with RICHARD RODGERS on *Oklahoma!* (1943), in which again he had the chance to develop his ideas of American folk opera and the complete integration of music and drama. *Oklahoma!* was the first of an almost unbroken string of successes in collaboration with Rodgers, among them *Carousel* (1945), *South Pacific* (1949), *The King and I* (1951), *Flower Drum Song* (1958), and *The Sound of Music* (1959).

Hannele (Hanneles Himmelfahrt). Drama by GERHART HAUPTMANN, first performed Berlin, 1893.

Hansberry, Lorraine (1930–65). American dramatist, author of the successful Negro family drama *A Raisin in the Sun* (1958) and a play about a Jewish intellectual in New York, *The Sign in Sidney Brustein's Window* (1964).

Happiest Days of Your Life, The. Farce by John Dighton, first performed London, 1947.

Happy Days. Drama by SAMUEL BECKETT, first performed New York, 1961; Paris (as *Oh, Les Beaux Jours!*), 1963.

Hardy, Thomas (1840–1928). English novelist and poet, author of two original plays, *The Tragedy of the Queen of Cornwall* (1923), based on the legend of Tristan and Iseult, and *The Dynasts* (1904–8), a vast historical fresco in nineteen acts of the Napoleonic Wars, written in verse and not initially intended for the stage, though an adaptation by Harley Granville Barker was successfully performed in 1914.

Harlequin. Character of the young lover in English harlequinades, suitor of the beautiful COLUMBINE, and generally distinguished by his costume patterned in bold diamonds of colour. His name is derived from that of the *commedia dell'arte* character ARLECCHINO.

Harlequinade. Hybrid English form based on elements from the COMMEDIA DELL'ARTE, involving young lovers (HARLEQUIN and COLUMBINE) escaping from persecution with the aid of magic and all the stage machinery that could be managed. It was a mixture of music and mime, with a lot of character transformations and disguises. The form began in the early eighteenth century: a century later the clown character, PANTALOON, became the principal figure, and the section devoted to his antics became longer and longer until the romantic intrigue was relegated to a mere formal epilogue. This had disappeared entirely, even in pantomimes, by the early twentieth century.

Harlequinade, see BROWNING VERSION.

Hart, Lorenz (1895–1943). American lyric-writer, life-long collaborator of the composer RICHARD RODGERS. He has good claims to be the wittiest and most dexterous of all lyric-writers in the inter-war heyday of the American musical, being able to range easily from deep feeling expressed with great directness and simplicity to the most complex word-plays and intricate conceits. His best work is to be found in such shows as *On Your Toes* (1936), *I'd Rather Be Right* (1937), *Babes in Arms* (1937), *The Boys from Syracuse* (1938), and *Pal Joey* (1940).

Hart, Moss (1904–61). American dramatist and director, author of an excellent theatrical autobiography, *Act One*. Most of his best-remembered plays were written in collaboration with GEORGE S. KAUFMAN, among them *You Can't Take It With You* (1936), *I'd Rather Be Right* (1937), and *The Man Who Came to Dinner* (1939), all of them comedies with strong satirical overtones.

Hasenclever, Walter (1890–1940). German dramatist closely associated with the EXPRESSIONIST movement. His first big success was *Der Sohn* (*The Son*, 1914), fairly conventional in form but embodying powerfully one of the key Expressionist themes, enmity between the generations. His *Antigone* (1917) was a reworking of the classical story as an anti-war parable; after one or two more extreme experiments in Expressionist style he turned to conventional comedy with *Ein bessere Herr* (*A Man of Distinction*, 1926).

Hassan. Spectacular Oriental drama in verse and prose by JAMES ELROY FLECKER, first performed, with incidental music by Frederick Delius, London, 1922.

Hastings, Michael (b. 1938). English dramatist and novelist. His first play, *Don't Destroy Me*, about a wild Jewish family in Brixton, created a stir when produced at a London theatre club when he was only seventeen. A later play, *Yes, and After*, about the reactions of a fourteen-year-old girl to rape, was staged by the English Stage Society in a production-without-décor (1956). Another large-scale work, *The World's Baby*, was given a similar Sunday-night performance in 1963, though with Vanessa Redgrave in the lead. His documentary *Lee Harvey Oswald* (1966) marked a new departure in his style.

Hatful of Rain, A. Drama about drug addiction by Michael V. Gazzo, first performed New York, 1955.

Hauptmann, Gerhart (1862–1946). German dramatist often bracketed in his lifetime with IBSEN and STRINDBERG, though his reputation has declined considerably since. He began as a naturalist, and had great success with his first play *Vor Sonnenaufgang* (*Before Sunrise*, 1889), a drama of degradation in a village of Hauptmann's native

Silesia. A series of similar naturalistic dramas followed, and then in 1892 he wrote a spectacular historical drama, *Die Weber* (*The Weavers*), about the revolt of Silesian weavers in 1844. This, one of the earliest plays in which the crowd was the hero, and highly influential on German drama of the 1920s, was followed by an ironic comedy, *Der Biberpelz* (*The Beaver Coat*, 1893) and then by a fantasy, *Hanneles Himmelfahrt* (*Hannele*, 1893), which represents the dreams of the dying Hannele in a fashion a little similar to that of Strindberg's later plays. *Die versunkene Glocke* (*The Sunken Bell*, 1896) was another essay in symbolic drama, and from then on Hauptmann continued to alternate, or sometimes to mix, the various styles he had already mastered, the best of his many other plays being probably *Der rote Hahn* (*The Red Cock*, 1901), another ironic comedy; *Rose Bernd* (1903), an essay in grim naturalism; and *Die Ratten* (*The Rats*, 1911), a scarcely more cheerful 'Berlin tragicomedy'.

Hayes, Helen (b. 1900). American actress; has appeared on the stage since the age of five, when she played Prince Charles in *The Royal Family*. Her most famous youthful roles were Pollyanna (1917–18) and Margaret in *Dear Brutus* (1918). Her first fully adult success was in *To the Ladies* (1922), and in 1925 she played Cleopatra in Shaw's *Caesar and Cleopatra*. A more important role was Mary of Scotland in Maxwell Anderson's drama (1933), after which came her greatest success, Queen Victoria in Laurence Housman's *Victoria Regina* (1935–8). Among her later roles have been Portia (1938), Maggie Wylie in *What Every Woman Knows* (1938), Amanda Wingfield in *The Glass Menagerie* (1948), Mrs Antrobus in *The Skin of Our Teeth* (1955), the Duchess in *Time Remembered* (1957), and Nora Melody in *A Touch of the Poet* (1958). She is widely regarded as the American theatre's leading actress, and had a New York theatre named after her in 1958.

Hay Fever. Light comedy by NOËL COWARD, first performed London, 1925.

Hazlitt, William (1778–1830). English essayist and dramatic critic, who wrote about the current theatrical scene mainly between 1813 and 1818, a period of great acting but with little of note as far as new drama was concerned. He wrote vividly about actors, and as a literary critic was able always to measure theatrical actualities against his ideal theatre, as described particularly in *The Characters of Shakespeare's Plays* (1817). The best of his dramatic criticism was collected in *A View of the English Stage* (1818).

Heartbreak House. A 'fantasia in the Russian manner, on English themes', by GEORGE BERNARD SHAW, first performed New York, 1920.

Hebbel, Friedrich (1813–63). German dramatist. Specialized in bitterly pessimistic studies of suffering womanhood victimized by the oppressive forces of contemporary life, starting with his first mature work, *Maria Magdalena*, in 1844. He also wrote a number of historical dramas (though with the characters treated in a very 'modern' fashion), among them *Genoveva* (1843), *Herodes und Mariamne* (1850), and *Gyges und sein Ring* (*Gyges and his Ring*, 1855), as well as a florid and extravagant trilogy *Die Nibelungen* (1862), based on the same materials as Wagner's *Ring*. Hebbel was also a dramatic theorist, his main tenet being the necessity of replacing individual by social tragedy. His wife, Christine Enghausen, was his chief interpreter on the stage.

Hecht, Ben (1894-1964). American dramatist, novelist, and film-writer. Most of his best-known works were written in collaboration with Charles MacArthur, notably *Front Page* (1928), a tough comedy-drama of newspaper life, and *Twentieth Century* (1932), a satirical comedy about New York society.

Hedda Gabler. Drama by HENRIK IBSEN, first performed Munich, 1891.

Heiress, The. Drama by Ruth and Augustus Goetz, based on the novel *Washington Square*, by HENRY JAMES. First performed New York, 1947.

Hellman, Lillian (b. 1905). American dramatist, author of a succession of dramas, usually thoroughly well-made and neatly plotted, on intricate family relations and over-heated and unnatural passions. Her first play was *The Children's Hour* (1934), about the effects of a rumour of lesbianism on two young schoolteachers and the community in which they live. Other plays include *The Little Foxes* (1939) and its sequel *Another Part of the Forest* (1946), which chronicle the chequered fortunes of a Southern family, a musical version of *Candide* (1956), and *Toys in the Attic* (1960), another family drama. Autobiographies: *An Unfinished Woman* and *Pentimento*.

Hello, Dolly!, see THE MATCHMAKER.

Heminge, John (1556–1630). English actor, reputedly the first player of Falstaff, and editor with HENRY CONDELL of the First Folio of Shakespeare's plays (1623).

Henry IV. Historical drama by WILLIAM SHAKESPEARE, in two parts. Written c.1597–8.

Henry IV (Enrico Quarto). Drama by LUIGI PIRANDELLO, first performed Rome, 1922.

Henry V. Historical drama by WILLIAM SHAKESPEARE, written *c.*1598–9.

Henry VI. Historical drama by WILLIAM SHAKESPEARE, in three parts, written 1589–91. Usually performed in modern times in two-part versions (e.g. at the Old Vic in 1923, Stratford 1963).

Henry VIII. Historical drama by WILLIAM SHAKESPEARE and JOHN FLETCHER, first performed London, 1613.

Henslowe, Philip (d. 1616). English theatre manager, owner of the Rose, Fortune, and Hope playhouses in Elizabethan London, and keeper of a diary which throws much light on Elizabethan theatre organization.

Herbert, A. P. (Sir Alan; b. 1890). English dramatist, novelist, and politician. Prolific author of light comedies and operettas, among them *Tantivy Towers* (1931), *Derby Day* (1932), *Bless the Bride* (1947), and *The Water Gypsies* (1955).

Herbert, Victor (1859–1924). English-born American composer of operettas and musical comedies. Best-known works *Babes in Toyland* (1903) and *Naughty Marietta* (1910).

Hernani. Verse tragedy by VICTOR HUGO, first performed Paris, 1830.

Heroic tragedy. A species of large-scale tragedy on grand themes of love and honour, written in heroic couplets, which enjoyed a brief vogue (largely under French influence, particularly that of CORNEILLE) in England during the latter half of the seventeenth century. Its chief exponent was DRYDEN, who wrote the only plays of the type still of literary interest (none of them has remained in the repertory), including *The Conquest of Granada* (1669–70) and *Aurengzebe* (1675). The short career of heroic tragedy was shortened still further by BUCKINGHAM's satire of the genre in *The Rehearsal* (1672).

Herr Puntila and His Servant Matti (Herr Puntila and sein Knecht Matti). Comedy by BERTOLT BRECHT, written 1940, first performed Zürich, 1948.

He Who Gets Slapped (To, kto poluchaet poshchoching). Symbolic drama by LEONID ANDREYEV, first performed Moscow, 1915.

Heywood, John (*c.*1497–1580). English dramatist whose works form a bridge between medieval drama and Elizabethan comedy. His best-known work is *The Playe Called the Foure P.P.* (*c.*1520), a lying contest among a palmer, a pardoner, an apothecary, and a pedlar.

Heywood, Thomas (*c.*1570–1641). English dramatist, possibly related to John Heywood. He himself claimed to have worked on nearly 220 plays. His best works were domestic dramas, tragedies and comedies, the most famous of which is *A Woman Killed with Kindness* (1603).

High Tor. Drama by MAXWELL ANDERSON, first performed New York, 1936.

Hindle Wakes. Drama by STANLEY HOUGHTON, first performed Manchester, 1912.

Hippolytus. Tragedy by EURIPIDES, first performed Athens, 428 B.C.

His House in Order. Drama by ARTHUR WING PINERO, first performed London, 1906.

Hit the Deck. Musical by VINCENT YOUMANS, book by Herbert Fields (based on the play *Shore Leave*, by R. P. Weston and Bert Lee), lyrics by Leo Robin and Clifford Gray; first performed New York, 1927.

H.M.S. Pinafore. 'Savoy opera' by W. S. GILBERT (book and lyrics) and Arthur Sullivan (music), first performed Savoy, London, 1878.

Hobson, Harold (b. 1904). English dramatic critic, on the *Sunday Times* since 1947; author of a number of books on the theatre.

Hobson's Choice. Comedy by HAROLD BRIGHOUSE, first performed New York, 1915.

Hochhuth, Rolf (b. 1932). German dramatist. His chief success has been his documentary drama on the subject of the Papacy and the Jews during the Second World War, *Der Stellvertreter* (1963), translated as *The Representative* in Britain and *The Deputy* in the U.S.A. His most notable later work is *Die Soldaten* (*Soldiers*) (1967), a similarly controversial piece based on the supposed involvement of Winston Churchill in the wartime death of the Polish general Sikorksi.

Hochwälder, Fritz (b. 1911). Austrian dramatist, best known internationally for his historical drama *Das heilige Experiment* (1943; known in English as *The Strong Are Lonely*). Other works include *Donnerstag* (1959), a modern miracle play written for the Salzburg Festival, *Der öffentliche Ankläger* (*The Public Prosecutor*, 1949), an historical drama set in the French Revolution, and *Donadieu* (1953), set in the Huguenot wars. Both the latter concern awakenings of conscience.

Hofmannsthal, Hugo von (1874–1929). Austrian poet and dramatist. Early in his career he wrote several poetic dramas conceived in Romantic terms as dream studies of a life of sensations (notably *Der Tor und der Tod*, *The Fool and Death*, 1893). Later he turned to classical themes and a more energetic form of drama in *Elektra* (1903), *Oedipus and the Sphinx* (1905), and *Ariadne auf Naxos* (1912), and also produced a succession of adaptations and elaborations: *Das gerettete Venedig* (*Venice Preserved*, after Otway, 1905); *Jedermann* (*Everyman*, after the medieval morality, 1912); *Das grosse Salzburger Welttheater* (after Calderón's *auto*, *The Great Theatre of the World*, 1922). Apart from *Jedermann*, which remains a regular feature of the Salzburg Festival, Hofmannsthal is best remembered now in the theatre at Richard Strauss's regular librettist in such operas as *Der Rosenkavalier*, *Ariadne auf Naxos*, *Die Frau ohne Schatten*, *Die ägyptische Helena*, *Elecktra*, and *Arabella*.

Hole, The. One-act comedy by N. F. SIMPSON, first performed by the English Stage Company, Royal Court, London, 1958.

Holly and the Ivy, The. Drama by WYNYARD BROWNE, first performed London, 1950.

Home, William Douglas (b. 1912). English dramatist who began his career as an actor. His first play was *Great Possessions* (1937); his most successful works are the prison drama *Now Barabbas* (1947) and a series of light comedies, *The Chiltern Hundreds* (1947), *The Manor of Northstead* (1954), *The Reluctant Debutante* (1955), *The Reluctant Peer* (1964), *The Secretary Bird* (1968), *The Kingfisher* (1977).

Home and Beauty. Farce by W. SOMERSET MAUGHAM, first performed London, 1919 (and at the same time in U.S.A. as *Too Many Husbands*).

Home at Seven. Drama by R. C. SHERRIFF, first performed London, 1950.

Homecoming, The. Drama by HAROLD PINTER, first performed by the Royal Shakespeare Company, London, 1965.

Horace. Tragedy by PIERRE CORNEILLE, first performed Paris, 1640.

Horniman, Miss A. E. F. (1860–1937). English theatre manager. A woman of considerable means, she sponsored the production of Shaw's *Arms and the Man* in London in 1894, and as a result of assisting W. B. YEATS as his secretary for a while she became interested in the possibilities of the Irish dramatic movement. In 1903 she built for Yeats and LADY GREGORY the ABBEY THEATRE, Dublin, and remained associated with the theatre until a disagreement in 1910 made her withdraw. In 1907, however, she had bought and redecorated the Gaiety Theatre, Manchester, for a repertory company specializing in new plays by local authors, who came to be known as the MANCHESTER SCHOOL. In 1921 she sold the theatre, after staging more than two hundred plays, over a hundred of which were new.

Hostage, The. Comedy-drama by BRENDAN BEHAN, first performed by Theatre Workshop, Stratford East, London, 1958. (Elaborated from *An Giall*, the author's own Gaelic original, Dublin, 1958.)

Hostage, The (L'Ôtage). Drama by PAUL CLAUDEL, first produced Paris, 1914.

Hotel Paradiso (L'Hôtel du libre échange) Farce by GEORGES FEYDEAU and Maurice Desvallières, first performed Paris, 1894. English adaptation by Peter Glenville first performed London, 1956.

Houghton, Stanley (1881–1913). English dramatist of the MANCHESTER

SCHOOL, author of realistic dramas and comedies, among them *The Dear Departed* (1906), *The Younger Generation* (1910), and his most famous play, *Hindle Wakes* (1912), an ironic story about a working girl who will not marry the rich man's son who has seduced her.

House of Bernarda Alba, The (La Casa de Bernarda Alba). Folk tragedy by FEDERICO GARCÍA LORCA, written 1936, first publicly performed Madrid, 1945.

Howard, Sidney (1891–1939). American dramatist. Author of many solid dramas, the only one which has retained its appeal being *They Knew What They Wanted* (1924), a comedy-drama about a mail-order bride which has been filmed several times and turned into a musical as *The Most Happy Fella.*

Hroswitha (*c.*932–83). Benedictine nun and author of six religious dramas in Latin, modelled on TERENCE in style and form but drawing their material from Christian history: *Paphnutius*, *Dulcitius*, *Gallicanus*, *Callimachus*, *Abraham*, and *Sapientia.* They are something of a 'sport' in dramatic history, being essentially CLOSET DRAMAS, but they form an interesting bridge between classical and medieval drama and are perfectly actable; they have, indeed, been acted on a number of occasions in modern times.

Hugo, Victor (1802–85). French poet, dramatist, and novelist. His plays were mostly verse dramas of an extreme and exaggerated Romanticism; the preface to his first, *Cromwell* (1827), was a trumpet-call to arms on behalf of a new Romantic drama and his first performed play, the tragedy *Hernani* (1830), caused riots and instituted a whole new era in the French theatre. Among his later plays were such elaborate historical dramas as *Le Roi s'amuse* (1832), *Lucrèce Borgia* (1833), *Marie Tudor* (1833), and *Ruy Blas* (1838), as well as numerous minor pieces. Several of his novels, particularly *Notre-Dame de Paris* and *Les Misérables*, were adapted for the stage later, and these two have often been filmed. His plays, with all their grandiloquence and extravagant sentiment, are not now taken very seriously (except, perhaps, for *Ruy Blas*), but continue occasionally to be played, affording as they do spectacular roles for actors in the grand manner – as with MARIA CASARÈS in the T.N.P.'s revival of *Marie Tudor.*

Huis-clos (variously translated as *In Camera*, *No Exit*, and *Vicious Circle*). One-act drama by JEAN-PAUL SARTRE, first performed Paris, 1944.

110 in the Shade, see THE RAINMAKER.

Hunter, N. C. (Norman Charles; 1908–71). English dramatist. His first play appeared in 1934, but he was not really discovered until *Waters of the Moon*, a delicate sub-Chekhovian piece, was chosen as a vehicle for Edith Evans and Sybil Thorndike during the Festival of

Britain (1951). Other pieces in the same style followed: *A Day by the Sea* (1953), *A Touch of the Sun* (1958), *The Tulip Tree* (1963). The last two were more individual in their subject and treatment, and contain perhaps his best work.

Hurry, Leslie (b. 1909). English painter and stage designer. First made a name for himself in ballet, and has continued to specialize in rich, exotic plays, which he has supplied with dark, vibrant designs often tinged, especially in his early work, with Surrealism. Principal production designs: *Hamlet* (1944), *Tamburlaine* (1951), *Venice Preserved* (1953), *Timon of Athens* (1956), *Mary Stuart* (1958), *The Cenci* (1959), *The Duchess of Malfi* (1960).

I

I am a Camera. Comedy-drama by JOHN VAN DRUTEN, based on
'Sally Bowles' and other stories by CHRISTOPHER ISHERWOOD;
first performed New York, 1951.

Ibsen, Henrik (1828–1906). Norwegian dramatist, generally regarded as
the father of modern theatre. His career shows a gradual move towards the realistic study of contemporary life and then, once this had
been achieved, a move away from it in the direction of overtly symbolic drama. All through it, though – at least since the earliest works
of his maturity – there is an unflinching consistency in the development of his art. The symbols of the earlier plays may for a while go
'underground' in dramas which seem on the surface, despite their
meticulous construction, quite naturalistic, but they are always present in the fabric of the plays to deepen their effect on audiences. It is,
no doubt, to this richness and complexity beyond the trappings of
naturalism that Ibsen's plays in the main owe their lasting place in
the theatre.

His first play, *Catalina* (1850), was a romantic drama heavily influenced by SCRIBE in the construction and SCHILLER in the material. It was followed by a group of historical plays with a Scandinavian
background, the best of which were *The Vikings of Helgeland* (*Hoer-
moendene paa Helgeland*, 1858) and *The Pretenders* (*Kongsemnerne*,
1864). During this time he worked as a *dramaturg*, first at Bergen,
then in an Oslo theatre, where his satirical piece *Love's Comedy*
(*Kjaerlighedens Komedie*, 1862) was first produced. In 1863 he received a travelling fellowship, and in 1865 a state pension which
gave him freedom from major financial worries. The pension was
largely the result of the publication of his first major work, *Brand*,
in 1865: this vast symbolic drama in verse (not staged complete for
some years) about a sternly idealistic pastor's relations with God and
man, is the earliest of his plays to be revived at all frequently, and
states powerfully a number of themes which were to recur constantly
in his later work. Its main disadvantage is a certain humourlessness
and lack of a sense of proportion: faults corrected in his next play,
Peer Gynt (1867), though in a fashion which makes it clear that humour could never be Ibsen's strong point. *Peer Gynt* is a fantasy about
an ebullient hero who lives life to the full, good and bad, mixes
warm humanity with recklessness and ruthlessness and finds in the
end that he has never really existed except in the love of a simple
maiden he abandoned for the highest motives early in his life.

After two more plays belonging, one way or another, to the same emotional world, the satirical *League of Youth* (*De Unges Forbund,* 1869) and the vast two-part historical drama *Emperor and Galilean* (*Kejser og Galilaeer,* 1869–73), Ibsen turned to the sort of small-town social drama normally associated with his name. The first result was a series of four plays which perhaps had more immediate influence on the international drama than anything else he wrote: *Pillars of Society* (*Samfundets Støtter,* 1875–7), *A Doll's House* (*Et Dukkehjem,* 1878–9) *Ghosts* (*Gengangere,* 1881), and *An Enemy of the People* (*En Folkefiende,* 1882). In these Ibsen combined cast-iron theatrical construction (forgetting none of the lessons he had learnt from Scribe) with unusual boldness in his choice of subject – municipal corruption and hypocrisy in the first and fourth, the place of truth and falsehood in marriage in the second, and in *Ghosts,* the play which really made 'Ibsenism' an issue, venereal disease as an image of corruption in family life. After this group of plays, which mark the farthest point of 'realism' he reached in his drama, Ibsen began again to reintroduce symbolism, at first as an unobtrusive enrichment of his realistic observation in *The Wild Duck* (*Vildanden,* 1884), where the crippled duck in the attic is both a real duck and a symbol of the heroine's situation, and *Rosmersholm* (1886) in which the spirit of place becomes a character in the story of a 'new woman's' attempts to galvanize the man she loves into action. These plays and *Hedda Gabler* (1890), a dark comedy about affectation and pretension, mark the height of Ibsen's art. In later works like *The Lady from the Sea* (*Fruen fra Havet,* 1888), *The Master Builder* (*Bygmester Solness,* 1892), and *Little Eyolf* (*Lille Eyolf,* 1894) the symbolism (the heroine's dreams of the sea in the first; Solness's buildings; the Rat Wife's role in the third) tends to get out of hand and seem extraneous, tacked on to a basically realistic structure and constantly in danger of breaking it up. In his last two plays, *John Gabriel Borkman* (1896) and *When We Dead Awaken* (*Naar vi Døde Vaagner,* 1899), the symbolism becomes pervasive, and in both cases it is a return to the symbolism of *Brand*: the ascent of a mountain which brings man nearer and nearer to a confrontation with eternal truths.

Ibsen has continued to exert such power over the theatre that his bad plays as well as his good are constantly revived; his influence on contemporaries and following generations, whether directly or indirectly – by way of reaction against what he stood for – can hardly be overestimated. Though at the time his principal influence was in the direction of greater realism, this was rather in the sphere of subject-matter than of treatment; even at its most realistic his drama was never comparable with that of the French naturalists, who sought to represent man on the stage exactly as he was, with an absolute minimum of artifice. Ibsen, even at his most deliberately prosaic, was always a poet, and it is the extra imaginative charge that this fact gives his work which keeps it alive today, when that of most of the naturalists has been forgotten.

Iceman Cometh, The. Drama by EUGENE O'NEILL, written 1939, first performed New York, 1946.

Ideal Husband, An. Comedy by OSCAR WILDE, first performed London, 1895.

I Have Been Here Before. 'Time play' by J. B. PRIESTLEY, first performed London, 1937.

Importance of Being Earnest, The. Comedy by OSCAR WILDE, first performed London, 1895.

Improvisation. An element of improvisation by actors on a set theme or plot-structure has long been a part of drama, notably in the COMMEDIA DELL'ARTE. In modern times it has become an integral part of an actor's training as practised by Stanislavsky and his followers, particularly the American proponents of the 'METHOD', and there have been a number of attempts to build whole plays and shows on improvisation. Group improvisation has played an important role in the elaboration of the final acting versions of THEATRE WORKSHOP plays (see BRENDAN BEHAN, SHELAGH DELANEY) and WILLIAM SAROYAN wrote a play with the company entirely by improvisation: *Sam, The Highest Jumper of Them All* (1960). The American revue *The Premise* (1961) was improvised with assistance from the audience.

I'm Talking About Jerusalem. Drama by ARNOLD WESKER, third section of the 'Wesker Trilogy', first performed Coventry, 1960; in sequence with the other two sections, Royal Court, London, 1960.

Inadmissible Evidence. Drama by JOHN OSBORNE, first performed by the English Stage Company, Royal Court, London, 1964.

In Camera, see HUIS-CLOS.

Inge, William (1913–73). Kansas-born American dramatist, all of whose plays were emotional dramas situated in small towns in the mid-West. His first big success was *Come Back, Little Sheba* (1950), a quiet, gentle drama about a middle-aged woman living in the past; later plays along the same lines have been *Picnic* (1953), *Bus Stop* (1955), *The Dark at the Top of the Stairs* (perhaps his best, 1957), and *A Loss of Roses* (1959).

Ingénue. Type of role in the theatre: an innocent young girl.

In Good King Charles's Golden Days. Comedy by GEORGE BERNARD SHAW, first performed Malvern Festival, 1939.

Insect Play, The (Ze zivota hmyzu). Symbolic drama by KAREL and JOSEF ČAPEK, first performed Prague, 1921. (Also known as *The World We Live In* and *And So Ad Infinitum*.)

Inspector Calls, An. Drama by J. B. PRIESTLEY, first performed Old Vic, London, 1946.

Interlude. Species of early Renaissance drama, the link between medieval religious drama and fully developed Elizabethan comedy. It was called an interlude because originally it was a sort of passage of buffoonery in the complete evening's entertainment at a banquet; the first dramatist to develop this into a separate form as a short secular comedy was JOHN HEYWOOD. A special company of four or five men, the Players of the King's Interludes, was permanently employed by the Tudor court until the reign of Mary I, but afterwards the form and its players became antiquated and disappeared.

Intimate Relations, see LES PARENTS TERRIBLES.

L'Invitation au château, see RING ROUND THE MOON.

Iolanthe. 'Savoy opera' by W. S. GILBERT (book and lyrics) and Arthur Sullivan (music); first performed Savoy, London, 1882.

Ionesco, Eugène (b. 1912). Rumanian-born dramatist, writing in French; leading figure in the Theatre of the ABSURD. Most of Ionesco's childhood was spent in Paris, his mother being French, his early manhood in Rumania, where he began writing and teaching French. He returned to France in 1936, supposedly to work on a thesis, which never materialized. He began writing plays more or less by accident, while learning English: the nonsensical flat statements of undeniable facts in his teach-yourself course set him off sketching a 'tragedy of language' which would illustrate the extreme difficulty of communication in words. The result was the one-act play *La Cantatrice chauve* (*The Bald Prima Donna*), written in 1948 and first performed, with no great success, in 1950. Up to then Ionesco had disliked the theatre, but now he realized that what he had disliked was the attempt to simulate belief against the audience's better judgement: what he wanted instead was a more extreme, violent theatre, a theatre of shock, which would 'alienate' the audience in more senses than one, and certainly far more completely than BRECHT had envisaged. This sort of theatre he proceeded to practise himself in a series of one-act plays dealing with such subjects as the breakdown of language, the proliferation of objects and the absurd (or Absurd) vulnerability of man, threatened from both outside and inside (by the pit of nothingness at the centre of his own being). His next play, *La Leçon* (*The Lesson*, 1951) is primarily concerned with language (it is a language lesson at the end of which the teacher erotically stabs his pupil); *Jacques, ou la soumission* (*Jacques, or Obedience*, 1950) and its sequel *L'Avenir est dans les œufs* (*The Future is in Eggs*, 1951) are about the individual forced into conformism and the horrors of proliferation respectively; *Les Chaises* (*The Chairs*, 1951), in which an old couple fill a room with chairs occupied by imaginary guests in order to hear an oration which when it comes makes no sense, is about the oppressive force of vacancy, nothingness, in life; *Les Victimes du devoir* (*The Victims of Duty*, 1952) seems to be at once a satire on Sartrean existentialism and its opposite, Freudian psychoanalysis, in the form of a play which shows dramatically that the thriller and the psychological drama are identical.

After these one-act plays Ionesco decided in 1953 to write a full-length three-act play, and the result was *Amédée, ou comment s'en débarrasser* (*Amédée, or How to Get Rid of It*), in which the unsatisfactory aspects of a couple's marriage are symbolized by a corpse in the back room which grows constantly larger and larger. Other full-length plays have followed, in a cycle dealing with a Chaplinesque little man called Bérenger, who in the first, *Tueur sans gages* (*The Killer*, 1957) resolves to track down a maniac killer who is ruining life in an ideal city and in the end apparently becomes almost willingly the killer's next victim; in *Rhinocéros* (1958) he finds that everyone else is turning into a rhinoceros and only he cannot do so, but must make the best of a bad job by sticking up for humanity; in *Le Roi se meurt* (*Exit the King*, 1961) he reappears as the king of an imaginary country, torn between two women. None of these works has been as satisfactory as the best of Ionesco's one-act plays, which have included more recently *Le Nouveau Locataire* (*The New Tenant*, 1953), *Le Tableau* (*The Picture*, 1955), and *L'Impromptu de l'Alma, ou le caméléon du berger* (*The Shepherd's Chameleon*, 1955), and it seems that his most effective form may be the clear, uncluttered elaboration of one image throughout a short, unbroken action. In these terms, though, several of his early one-acters, particularly *La Cantatrice chauve*, *La Leçon*, and *Les Chaises*, remain among the most brilliant works in the whole Theatre of the Absurd.

Iphigenia in Aulis. Tragedy by EURIPIDES, first performed Athens, *c*.406 B.C.

Iphigenia in Tauris. Tragedy by EURIPIDES, first performed Athens, *c*.414 B.C. Also a tragedy by JOHANN WOLFGANG VON GOETHE, inspired by Euripides (*Iphigenie auf Tauris*), written 1779–87.

I Remember Mama. Family comedy by JOHN VAN DRUTEN, based on Kathryn Forbes's book *Mama's Bank Account*; first performed New York, 1945.

Irish Dramatic Movement, see ABBEY THEATRE.

Irma La Douce. Musical; book and lyrics by Alexandre Breffort, music by Marguerite Monnot, first performed Paris, 1956; English version, book and lyrics by Julian More, David Heneker, and Monty Norman first performed London, 1958. International success because of its tinkling, sub-*bal musette* music and mildly *risqué* story of a prostitute and her protector.

Irving, Henry (1838–1905). English actor-manager, the leading classical actor of the later nineteenth century. Made his first appearance on the stage in 1856, arrived in London ten years later, and in 1871 made his name with an enormous success in a melodrama adapted from the French, *The Bells*, at a theatre subsequently to be more than any other linked with his name: the Lyceum. In 1874 he played Hamlet for the first time, in a controversial reading with the accent laid on the Prince's gentleness of spirit. In 1878 he took over the Lyceum as manager, and there staged, with himself and ELLEN TERRY in the leading roles, a succession of triumphs, artistic and commercial. The great Shakespeare productions under his rule were *The Merchant of Venice* (1879), *Romeo and Juliet* and *Much Ado About Nothing* (1882), *Twelfth Night* (1884), *Henry VIII* and *King Lear* (1892), and *Cymbeline* (1896). The most interesting of the other productions were two plays by Tennyson, *The Cup* (1881) and *Becket* (1893), which gave Irving one of his greatest roles. Irving was above all an *interesting* actor, striking to look at, powerful and dynamic in movement, more curious than melodious in diction; as a manager he was responsible for some important innovations in stage LIGHTING and DESIGN, but did little for the new drama of his day and continued throughout his career to mingle the most elementary melodrama with his greatest comic and tragic creations. He was the first actor to be knighted for services to the theatre (1895).

Isherwood, Christopher (b. 1904). English novelist and occasionally dramatist, principally in collaboration with W. H. AUDEN. 'Sally Bowles' and other stories in *Goodbye to Berlin* have been successfully adapted for the stage by JOHN VAN DRUTEN.

J

Jackson, Barry (1879–1961). English director, manager, and dramatist. Began his career as an architect, but soon became involved in drama as part of an amateur group called the Pilgrim Players, who turned professional in 1913 and occupied the Repertory Theatre he built them in Birmingham, backed with his own money. The company's programmes were extraordinarily enterprising, including modern-dress productions of Shakespeare, many foreign plays presented in England for the first time (often adapted by Sir Barry himself), and the first British performances of Shaw's *Back to Methuselah* (1923). In 1929 he founded the MALVERN FESTIVAL; and from 1945 to 1948 he was director of the Memorial Theatre at Stratford on Avon. Knighted 1925.

Jacques (Jacques, ou la soumission). One-act play by EUGÈNE IONESCO, written 1950, first performed Paris, 1955.

James, Henry (1843–1916). American-born novelist who lived and worked mostly in England. Throughout most of his life he had aspirations to become a dramatist, wrote extensively about the theatre, was the author of a number of plays (published 1948). However he never had any theatrical success and gave up playwriting after the failure of *Guy Domville* (1895). Several of his novels have subsequently been adapted for the stage with some success: among such adaptations are *Berkeley Square* (1928), based by John L. Balderston and J. C. Squire on *The Sense of the Past*; *The Heiress* (1947) adapted. by Ruth and Augustus Goetz from *Washington Square*; *The Innocents* (1950) adapted by William Archibald from *The Turn of the Screw*; Benjamin Britten's opera *The Turn of the Screw* (1954); Michael Redgrave's version of *The Aspern Papers* (1959); and Christopher Taylor's of *The Wings of the Dove* (1963).

Jarry, Alfred (1873–1907). French dramatist and poet. His earliest works were poems in the fashionable SYMBOLIST manner, but his main claim to fame is the play *Ubu Roi*, performed at the Théâtre de l'Œuvre in 1896. This wild symbolic farce, a sort of Rabelaisian parody of *Oedipus Rex*, had a *succès de scandale*, savagely attacking bourgeois complacency and placing before its audience a crude, violent image of the world as reflected in the activities of the monstrous tyrant Ubu, the bourgeois who makes himself king. Jarry wrote a sequel, *Ubu enchaîné*, published in 1900 but not performed till 1937, and various other works concerning Ubu and other figures from his own private mythology. In his novel *Gestes et opinions du Docteur*

Faustroll (published 1911) he elaborated 'pataphysics', the 'science of imaginary solutions, which symbolically attributes the properties of objects, described by their virtuality, to their lineaments'. This idea has been very influential among a number of modern French intellectuals and is at the root of the Theatre of the ABSURD.

J.B. Verse play by ARCHIBALD MACLEISH, based on the story of Job; first performed Yale, 1958.

Jellicoe, Ann (b. 1927). English dramatist and director. Studied at the Central School of Speech and Drama, London, where she subsequently became an instructor; in 1952 founded an open stage theatre club, the Cockpit Theatre, which she ran for two years. Her first play, *The Sport of My Mad Mother*, won a third prize in the *Observer* drama competition of 1956, and was subsequently produced by the English Stage Company at the Royal Court. It is a violent and ritualistic blend of words, sounds, and action suggested by aspects of teddy-boy life. Her next play, *The Knack* (1961), applies a similar technique to comedy of manners: it is a witty study of the relations of three contrasted housemates with an innocent girl who wanders in. *Shelley* (1965) is a relatively straightforward, almost documentary account of the poet's life, and *The Giveaway* (1969), a farce slightly suggestive of *The Knack* in its technique. She has also translated Ibsen (*Rosmersholm, The Lady from the Sea*) and Chekhov (*The Seagull*).

Jerome K. Jerome (1859–1927). English humorist, novelist and dramatist, best known as the author of *Three Men in a Boat* and *Three Men on the Bummel*. He wrote amusingly about the theatre of his day, and was also responsible for a number of plays, the only one of which now remembered is *The Passing of the Third Floor Back* (1908), a story of the return of Christ as a mysterious tenant in a London boarding-house.

Jessner, Leopold (1878-1945). German director, much influenced by Reinhardt and, as director of the Berlin State Theatre 1919–25, a very influential figure in the early days of EXPRESSIONISM. His most notable contribution to the theatre (and cinema) was his abolition of representational scenery in favour of a number of different acting levels connected by flights of steps (*spieltreppe*, or *jessnertreppe* as they were known).

Jew of Malta, The. Tragi-comedy by CHRISTOPHER MARLOWE, first performed London, *c.*1590.

Jew Süss. Tragi-comedy by ASHLEY DUKES, based on Lion Feuchtwanger's novel. First performed London, 1929.

Jig. Afterpiece in Elizabethan public theatres, sung and danced by three or four performers, generally including a clown. The material was often topical, the verses being set as a rule to traditional tunes.

John, Errol (b. 1924). West Indian dramatist and actor. His principal work, a picturesque drama of Caribbean life called *Moon on a Rainbow Shawl*, won first prize in the *Observer* drama competition (1956) and was subsequently produced at the Royal Court, London, 1958.

John Bull's Other Island. Drama by GEORGE BERNARD SHAW, first performed Royal Court, London, 1904.

John Gabriel Borkman. Drama by HENRIK IBSEN, first performed Helsingfors (Helsinki), 1897.

Johnson Over Jordan. Drama by J. B. PRIESTLEY, first performed London, 1939.

Johnston, Denis (b. 1901). Irish dramatist who did most of his most notable work between the wars. His first produced play, *The Old Lady Says No!* (1929), is a satirical panorama of Irish life at that period. His second, *The Moon in the Yellow River* (1931) is much more realistic in its study of a visionary Irish revolutionary and his romantic opposition to the building of a power plant near Dublin. Later plays mix reality and symbolism uncomfortably, and the only one which has been revived from time to time is *The Dreaming Dust* (1940), a complex evocation of the life of Swift.

Jones, Henry Arthur (1851–1929). English dramatist. Began his adult life as a commercial traveller, wrote a number of plays and works of fiction before his first play to be produced, *It's Only Round the Corner* (Exeter, 1878). In 1882 he scored his first major success as a dramatist with *The Silver King*, which he wrote in collaboration with Henry Herman. Thereafter he wrote an extraordinary number of plays, many of which featured the leading players of the day and were very successful with the public; the best-remembered is probably *Mrs Dane's Defence* (1900), the most ambitious *Michael and His Lost Angel*, a drama of conscience about a puritanical clergyman which caused something of a scandal in 1896. Jones was regarded in his day as a major dramatist and as a leading 'Ibsenite' (though he strenuously disclaimed the connexion). In fact, though he had the urge to deal with big social and moral issues, his plays seldom if ever rose above the level of well-made topical melodrama. They are marked by great facility in the creation of natural-sounding dialogue and the management of plot but have proved unable to survive long after the immediate circumstances which gave them life.

Jones, Inigo (1573–1652). English architect and stage designer. In 1605 he joined the household of Prince Henry as resident designer, and one of his most important functions was designing and staging MASQUES

– which he continued to do until 1613. His designs for settings, costumes, and machinery were often of the utmost elaboration, and he had a considerable influence on the spectacular theatre which succeeded the Commonwealth after his death. He seems to have been the first person in the English theatre to use revolving screens to indicate changes of scene and to introduce painted scenery designed to produce a 'stage picture' in perspective, framed by the proscenium arch, which he also introduced into England.

Jonson, Ben (1572–1637). English dramatist. His career lasted nearly forty years, during which his considerable output included comedy of nearly every sort, tragi-comedy, satire, tragedy, and masques, as well as a variety of unclassifiable pieces. He was better educated than most of his contemporaries among dramatists, or considered himself so, though he never went to university, and his work was notable for its intellectual force and honesty – on occasion to such an extent that it landed him in prison for the outspokenness of his views. This happened, in fact, with one of his earliest plays, *The Isle of Dogs* (1597), and again with *Eastward Ho!* (1605), on which he collaborated with MARSTON. His first major success was *Every Man in His Humour* (1598), a comedy in which each character was made the embodiment of a particular 'humour' – jealousy, irascibility, etc – and given an *idée fixe* to go with it: the amusement of the action deriving from the various ways the characters thus obsessed come into collision and interact. This is the basic principle of the 'comedy of humours' always associated with Jonson's name, though in fact nearly all his major comic creations escape from such summary classification, and his comedy is at its least effective the more closely it follows his theoretical pronouncements – as in *Every Man out of His Humour* (1599) for example. Some of his work at this time was also taken up with the working off of private grievances, particularly against fellow-writers, and has consequently retained only an historic interest (*Cynthia's Revels*, 1600; *Poetaster*, 1601). But from 1606 on he wrote a series of plays which have constantly been revived ever since and remain among the classics of English comedy: *Volpone* (1605–6), *Epicoene, or The Silent Woman* (1609), *The Alchemist* (1610), and *Bartholomew Fair* (1614). *Volpone* and *The Alchemist* are both essays on human gullibility, with some of the theatre's great rogues to do the gulling – Volpone in particular becomes a character of epic proportions and at the last, in his downfall, of almost tragic dignity. *Epicoene* is a complex and brilliantly constructed comedy of intrigue, while *Bartholomew Fair* is a loosely organized, bustlingly realistic panorama of contemporary London at fair-time.

During the same period Jonson acted as court poet and was responsible between 1605 and 1612 for devising the elaborate court MASQUES of the day, often with Inigo Jones, with whom he seems for the most part to have been on bad terms. None of his later plays lived up to the great works of his maturity, and they have rarely been revived since; similarly his tragedies *Sejanus* (1603) and *Cataline* (1611) have generally been found by later critics cold and dull, and though they make fascinating reading it is possible they would not act well on the stage. His major works, however, survive more certainly as part of the normal dramatic repertoire than any of his age except SHAKE-SPEARE'S.

Joruri. A type of Japanese puppet-theatre for which many major works of Japanese drama have been written, including several of the masterpieces of CHIKAMATSU. Joruri was originally a sort of epic recitation, which around 1630 became associated with puppet performance to form *ningyo-joruri*. From this it was a short step to the Joruri's becoming a fully-fledged drama on legendary or historical themes, as it was at its greatest period. The productions given to these puppet plays are very elaborate, with full scenery; the puppets, about two thirds life size, are put through their motions by manipulators in full view of the audience, the principal puppeteer wearing a ceremonial costume but no mask, and his assistants (usually three) wearing simpler costumes and plain hoods. The words are delivered to music by a group at the side of the stage.

Journey's End. War drama by R. C. SHERRIFF, first performed London, 1928.

Jouvet, Louis (1887–1951). French actor and director, best known for his long and close collaboration with the dramatist GIRAUDOUX. In 1913 he became a member of COPEAU's company at the Vieux-Colombier and in 1922 set up his own company at the Théâtre des Champs-Élysées, where in 1923 he had two great successes, both by Jules Romains, *Monsieur le Troubades* and *Knock*; the second of these was throughout his career one of his most famous roles. In 1927 he directed Giraudoux's first play, *Siegfried*, and thereafter directed the first productions of all Giraudoux's plays except one, as well as working with infinite care and patience on the drafting and revision of the texts with the author. As a director Jouvet developed slowly, tending in his early days to carry Copeau's principles of faithfulness to the text to quite fanatical lengths, but with his famous production of Molière's *L'École des femmes* (1936) he reached a perfect balance between fidelity and apt invention which he subsequently preserved with great consistency. In the process he revolutionized the accepted

French approach to the classics (especially when in the same year he was appointed a resident director at the Comédie-Française). Himself an intensely serious man, on stage he shone chiefly in comic roles, among them Knock and such important Molière characters as Tartuffe, Don Juan, and Arnolphe (*L'École des femmes*).

Judith. Drama by JEAN GIRAUDOUX, first performed Paris 1931; English adaptation by CHRISTOPHER FRY, first performed London, 1962.

Julius Caesar. Historical drama by WILLIAM SHAKESPEARE, written 1599–1600.

Juno and the Paycock. Tragedy by SEAN O'CASEY, first performed Dublin, 1924.

Justice. Drama by JOHN GALSWORTHY, first performed London, 1910.

Juvenile. Type of role, or actor generally cast in that role; clean-cut, uncomplicated young man.

K

Kabuki. Type of Japanese theatre, a popular off-shoot of NO, from which it takes many of its subjects and conventions, in a modified form. The Kabuki dramas are based on popular legends and myths, or sometimes on historical events; they are performed on a wide shallow stage with a sort of causeway running from the left-hand side of the stage to the back of the hall along which the actors make their entrances and exits – all this being at about the level of the audience's heads. Most Kabuki plays are long and episodic, being adapted in the main from the texts of the older forms, No and JORURI, but they are rarely if ever played in their entirety: the normal practice is for an evening's programme to mingle scenes from a variety of different plays – sections, perhaps, from *jidaimono* (historical dramas), *sewamono* (melodramas about private individuals), and *shosagoto* (dances). The form of staging adopted makes use of elaborate scenery and costumes, and always of a revolving stage. The actors are not masked as in No, but have heavily conventionalized make-up for the classical roles and for female roles, which are always played by men specializing in female impersonation. The precise form of musical accompaniment varies somewhat depending on the origin of the play performed: in general the conventions of the original genre are preserved: if the play comes from Joruri a reciter is used, if from No the usual group of samisen players is augmented by drums and transverse flute. Scenery is changed by two stage hands, one hooded and one not, who are conventionally regarded as invisible.

Kaiser, Georg (1878–1945). German dramatist and leader of the EXPRESSIONIST movement. He began by writing a satirical comedy, *Die jüdische Witwe* (*The Jewish Widow*, 1911) and an historical drama, *Die Bürger von Calais* (*The Burghers of Calais*, 1914), but created a great impression with *Von Morgens bis Mitternachts* (*From Morn to Midnight*, 1916) which rejected realism entirely and instead made all its characters types, boldly conventionalized to give a nightmarish picture of modern life as experienced by a bank clerk who steals a lot of money but finds that it does not lead him to the paradise he had expected. The impetus which gave life, at least briefly, to this play and made Kaiser an influential figure in the theatre carried him successfully through a sort of trilogy, *Die Koralle* (*The Corral*, 1917), *Gas I* (1918), and *Gas II* (1920), in which he traced the rise of industrial civilization, its enslavement and degradation of man, and its inevitable end in universal destruction. But in his later plays he proved to have nothing more to say, and they became increasingly repetitive: perhaps the best is *Der Floss der Medusa* (*The Raft of the Medusa*, 1943), in which the form of a children's adventure-play is used for social criticism.

Kálidása. Sanskrit dramatist, variously dated between the first and fifth centuries A.D. Three plays by him survive, *Malavikagnimitra*, a romantic comedy full of adventures and disguises, *Vikramorvasiya*, a fantasy about a nymph who falls in love with a human, and his best-known work, *Sakuntala*. This is a five-act drama of romantic adventure about a king who falls in love with and marries a hermit's foster-child, forgets her as the result of a curse but finally overcomes the curse and is reunited with his wife and son. *Sakuntala* is a charming work: to Western readers rather reminiscent of Shakespeare's later later plays as is all Kálidása's work. It also had some influence on European drama by offering, on its first Western appearance in 1789, a rallying-point for romantic taste and reaction against classical canons.

Kanin, Garson (b. 1912). American dramatist and director. Author of the satirical comedy *Born Yesterday* (1946) and the romantic drama *The Rat Race* (1949), as well as, alone or in collaboration with his wife, Ruth Gordon, of many successful film-scripts (*Adam's Rib*, *Pat and Mike*, *The Marrying Kind*, *It Should Happen to You*).

Kaufman, George S. (1889–1961). American dramatist, nearly always in collaboration, and director. During the 1920s his most constant collaborator was MARC CONNELLY, with whom he wrote several plays, among them *Merton of the Movies* (1922) and *Beggar on Horseback* (1924). During the 1930s he collaborated with, among others, Edna Ferber, Morris Ryskind and MOSS HART: his most successful works in this period were, with Edna Ferber, *The Royal Family* (1927), *Dinner at Eight* (1932), *Stage Door* (1936); with Ryskind *Animal Crackers* (1927), *Of Thee I Sing* (1931), *Let 'Em Eat Cake* (1933); and with Hart *You Can't Take It With You* (1936), *I'd Rather Be Right* (1937), *The Man Who Came to Dinner* (1939). His biggest post-war success has been *The Solid Gold Cadillac*, written with Howard Teichmann (1953).

Kazan, Elia (b. 1909). American director, born in Turkey. During the 1930s he worked as an actor and occasionally as a director with GROUP THEATRE. He came to prominence as a director in the 1940s with productions as varied as *The Skin of Our Teeth* (1942), *One Touch of Venus* (1943), *Jacobowsky and the Colonel* (1944), and *Deep are the Roots* (1945). His post-war reputation, though, is based largely on his association with the best new American drama of the period, particularly the works of Tennessee Williams and Arthur Miller, and with Actors' Studio, the school at which the METHOD has most influentially been propagated to young actors, directors, and writers. Among the plays Kazan has directed, generally in a lovingly naturalistic style, are *All My Sons*, *A Streetcar Named Desire* (1947), *Death of a Salesman* (1949), *Camino Real, Tea and Sympathy* (1953), *Cat on a Hot Tin Roof* (1955), *The Dark at the Top of the Stairs* (1957), *Sweet Bird of Youth* (1959). From 1962 to 1964 he was co-director of the theatre company of the new LINCOLN CENTER for the Performing Arts, New York, drawing talent freely from trainees of Actors' Studio and elsewhere. Kazan has been an influential director, with such films as *Viva Zapata!, On the Waterfront, East of Eden*, and *Baby Doll* and latterly a best-selling novelist with *America, America* (1962) and *The Arrangement* (1968).

Kean, Edmund (1787–1833). English actor, first of the great romantic players on the British stage. His family background and early history were themselves highly romantic, even making all allowances for exaggeration and mythologizing in his own life-time. As an actor he had his first major success in London in 1814, when he played Shylock at Drury Lane, and ever after that, despite his occasional flirtations with nobility and comedy, he was associated in the public mind with villainy and untameable passion. He depended in his acting almost entirely on forcefulness and personal magnetism: his voice seems to have been harsh and his physical appearance unimpressive. Among his best roles were Richard II, Iago (he also played Othello successfully), Macbeth, Sir Giles Overreach in *A New Way to Pay Old Debts*, and Barabas in *The Jew of Malta*. His career and personality were the subject of a play by ALEXANDRE DUMAS *père*, subsequently rewritten by JEAN-PAUL SARTRE.

Keep, The. Welsh dialect comedy by Gwyn Thomas, first performed by the English Stage Company, Royal Court, London, 1962.

Kenny, Sean (1932–73). British stage designer and architect, trained under Frank Lloyd Wright. Though he designed a number of fairly conventional productions he created most stir as a manipulator of stage mechanics, both in the arrangement of actual stages – the Chichester Festival Theatre (subsequently modified), the Dunes Hotel Theatre Restaurant, Las Vegas, projects for the National Theatre – and in the virtuoso use of the resources of the traditional stage, notably with Lionel Bart's musicals *Oliver!* and *Blitz*, in which the scenery was automated to be managed by a minimum stage-crew (in *Oliver!*, indeed, by only one).

Kern, Jerome (1885–1945). American composer of musicals. Started in the traditional fashion as a song-plugger and hack contributor to musical shows. His first solo Broadway score was for *The Red Petti-coat* (1912). His early hits included *Oh Boy* (1917), *Sally* (1920), and *Sunny* (1925), but his most important show was *Show Boat* (1927), which broke new ground by taking its subject from a fairly serious novel and integrating the songs and dances closely into the action of the story. In the early 1930s he had a number of lesser successes, one of them, *Music in the Air* (1932), written, like *Show Boat*, by OSCAR HAMMERSTEIN II, but in later years he worked more and more in the cinema and less in the theatre.

King and I, The. Musical play by RICHARD RODGERS, book and lyrics by OSCAR HAMMERSTEIN II, based on Margaret Landon's book *Anna and the King of Siam*; first performed New York, 1951.

King John. Historical drama by WILLIAM SHAKESPEARE, written *c*.1596–7.

King Lear. Tragedy by WILLIAM SHAKESPEARE, first performed London, 1606.

Kingsley, Sidney (b. 1906). American dramatist. Won a Pulitzer Prize with his first play, *Men in White* (written 1930, produced 1933), a well-made piece about doctors' professional and private lives and the conflicts which arise between the two. Kingsley's greatest hit was *Dead End* (1935), an elaborately realistic study of New York slum life which captured vividly the mood of the Depression years. None of his later works has achieved anything like the same success.

King's Men, see CHAMBERLAIN'S MEN.

King's Rhapsody. Musical play by IVOR NOVELLO, lyrics by Christopher Hassall, first performed London, 1949.

Kismet. Oriental fantasy by EDWARD KNOBLOCK, first performed New York, 1911. Also musical based on this play, book by Charles Lederer and Luther Davis, music (adapted from Borodin) and lyrics by Robert Wright and George Forrest, first performed New York, 1953.

Kiss Me Kate. Musical by COLE PORTER, book by Sam and Bella Spewack, suggested by *The Taming of the Shrew*. First performed New York, 1948.

Kitchen, The. Drama by ARNOLD WESKER, first performed for the English Stage Society in a production-without-décor, Royal Court, London, 1959; first public production in an expanded version by the English Stage Company, Royal Court, 1961.

Kitchen-sink drama. Term which became popular in the mid 1950s as a usually slightly insulting label for the newly current realistic working-class drama of the time – the plays of ARNOLD WESKER, the television plays of ALUN OWEN. The implication, more or less justified, was that the drama revolved, physically or psychologically, around the kitchen sink.

Kleist, Heinrich von (1777–1811). German dramatist. Whereas the practical theatrical reputation of most exponents of Romanticism in German drama has declined in subsequent years, Kleist's reputation has continued to increase, his subtlety and complexity, especially in the handling of morbid psychological states, endearing him especially to the modern sensibility. For many years *Der zerbrochene Krug* (*The Broken Jug*, 1808), a brilliantly worked out comedy about a corrupt judge made to preside over a trial for a crime he himself has committed, was regarded as his masterpiece. More recently considerably more attention has gone to his classical tragedy *Penthesilea* (1808), about an Amazon's fatal love for Achilles, and his strange 'psychological drama' (there is really no other term for it) *Der Prinz von Homburg* (*The Prince of Homburg*, 1811), an analysis of the nature of courage and the role of duty in life, which mixes moods in a poetically unpredictable fashion. His other plays include an extravagant family tragedy *Die Familie Schroffenstein* (1793), a masochistic picture of morbid womanly devotion, *Käthchen von Heilbronn* (1810), and another historical drama, *Die Hermannschlacht* (*The Battle of Arminius*, 1808). Kleist committed suicide at the age of thirty-four.

Knack, The. Comedy by ANN JELLICOE, first performed by the English Stage Company, Cambridge, 1961.

Knight of the Burning Pestle, The. Comedy by FRANCIS BEAUMONT, first performed London, *c*.1607–10.

Knights, The. Comedy by ARISTOPHANES, first performed Athens, 424 B.C.

Knoblock, Edward (1874–1945). American dramatist (real name Knoblauch). Noted mainly as an adaptor, sometimes in collaboration with the original author (with J. B. Priestley on a stage version of *The Good Companions*, for instance), sometimes by himself (Vicki Baum's *Grand Hotel*, 1931). The most famous of his original plays are the Oriental fantasy *Kismet* (1911) and *Milestones* (1912), written in collaboration with Arnold Bennett.

Knock, ou le triomphe de la médecine, see DOCTOR KNOCK.

Komisarjevsky, Theodore (1882–1954). Russian director. Began his career as a director working with his sister Vera Fedorovna Komisarjevskaya, one of the great Russian actresses, from 1896 to her death in 1910. After this he ran his own theatre in Moscow, and became director of the Imperial and State Theatres in Moscow until 1919, when he left for England. He was much influenced in his approach to the creation of character by STANISLAVSKY, placing great emphasis on building up performances from the inside: of his many dramatic productions in England probably the most important and influential were his versions of CHEKHOV staged with a regular company (one of them John Gielgud) at Barnes, which helped to take the pervasive gloom out of Chekhov productions in England.

Kopit, Arthur (b. 1938). American dramatist, prolific author of dramas while at university, where he wrote the play which gave him his international reputation, *Oh Dad, Poor Dad, Mamma's Hung You in the Closet and I'm Feeling So Sad*, described by the author, not inaccurately, as 'a pseudo-classical farce in a bastard French tradition'. It is a fantasy about an impossibly possessive mother and her down-trodden son's ineffectual attempts at rebellion, and has been successfully produced in New York and in Paris (with Edwige Feuillère) after an unsuccessful try-out in London (1961). Subsequently he has written a number of one-act plays, and *Indians* (1968), an ambitious attempt to tell the story of white America's relationship with the Indians in terms of a Wild West show.

Kops, Bernard (b. 1926). English dramatist and poet, most of whose plays are based on Jewish life and folklore. His first, *The Hamlet of Stepney Green* (1956), is a comic variation on the *Hamlet* story, set in Kops's native East End. *Change for the Angel* (1960) and *The Dream of Peter Mann* (1961) both extended this line with further studies of rebellious Jewish youth trying to come to terms with the world around. *Enter Solly Gold*, performed by Centre 42 at their first local festival at Wellingborough (1962) marked a new development in his work with a tough, fairly ruthless comedy about hypocrisy, and more recently a series of radio plays (*Home Sweet Honeycomb*, *The Lemmings*), have also suggested a new toughmindedness set against the frequent sentimentality of Kops's earlier work.

Korneichuk, Alexander Yevdokimovich (b. 1905). Ukrainian dramatist and one of the most successful stage writers in Soviet Russia. His first big success was the prize-winning *Wreck of the Squadron* (1934), about the scuttling of a fleet by communist sailors to keep it out of the hands of the White Russians. His emotional study of the career of a youthful surgeon, *Platon Krechet* (1935), and his Lenin play, *Truth* (1937), were both among the great successes of the 1930s, and immediately before the war he wrote one of his most lastingly successful plays, the historical drama *Bogdan Hmelnitsky* (1939). Korneichuk's range also includes satirical comedy, one of his better plays of the 1940s being *Mr Perkins in the Land of the Bolsheviks*

(1944), about an American millionaire's mission to Russia to find out the truth of things for himself. One of his later successes, *Wings* (1954), was about the new Soviet intelligentsia.

Kotzebuë, August Friedrich Ferdinand von (1761–1819). German dramatist who lived and worked for many years in Russia. He was immensely prolific, writing in every conceivable genre, and his works were vastly popular at the time. He could write sensational historical dramas, full of blood and thunder, like *Die Spanier in Peru* (1796, translated by Sheridan as *Pizarro*), *Johanna von Montfaucon* (1800), and *Graf Benyofsky* (1795); or soulful dramas on humanitarian subjects, like *Die Negersklaven* (*The Negro Slaves*, 1795); or strong bourgeois dramas like *Menschenhass und Rene* (*Misanthropy and Repentance*, known in English as *The Stranger*, 1789), *Armuth und Edelsinn* (*Poverty and Nobleness of Mind*, 1795), *Der Opfertod* (*Self-Immolation*, 1798), and *Das Kind der Liebe* (*The Child of Love*, 1791); or broad comedies like *Die deutschen Kleinstädter* (*The German Provincial*, 1803). Despite his great contemporary reputation and his great technical skill, though, little of his work has survived in the theatre up to the present.

Krapp's Last Tape. One-act monodrama by SAMUEL BECKETT, first performed by the English Stage Company, Royal Court, London, 1958.

Kyd, Thomas (1558–94). English dramatist. His most famous work, and indeed the only surviving play which can certainly be assigned to him, is *The Spanish Tragedy*, a melodramatic story of revenge which started a whole fashion in revenge-tragedies. Though coarse-grained it has great vitality and appears to have influenced SHAKESPEARE much in *Titus Andronicus*, if, indeed, Kyd did not have a hand in that play. He is also widely credited with two plays, now lost, on which Shakespeare is presumed to have based his works: an earlier *Hamlet* and *The Taming of a Shrew*, traces of which some scholars have professed to see in the 'bad' quartos of the relevant Shakespeare plays.

L

Labiche, Eugène (1815–88). French dramatist, prolific specialist in farces, of which he wrote, alone or in collaboration (most frequently with Marc Michel) more than 150. His very first play, *Monsieur de Coislin, ou l'Homme infiniment poli* (1838) was a great success, and from then until the 1870s he poured out a constant stream of plays, mostly for the Palais Royal theatre, in which the whole social world of his era was humorously but none the less acutely depicted. His most famous plays are *Le Chapeau de paille d'Italie*, written in collaboration with Marc Michel (1851), *Le Voyage de Monsieur Perrichon*, in collaboration with Édouard Martin (1860), and *La Cagnotte* (1864), all of which are regularly revived and figure in the permanent repertoire of the Comédie-Française. But many other of his plays reappear from time to time, among them *La Poudre aux yeux* (with Martin, 1861), *Si jamais je te pince* (with Michel, 1856), and *Les Trente-sept sous de Monsieur Montaudoin* (with Martin, 1863). Labiche never made the mistake of stepping outside his chosen genre (except for a single sentimental comedy, *Maman Sabouleux*, written with Michel in 1852); in farce he combined mechanical dexterity with a clear, unsentimental appreciation of human realities. He was invited to write a piece for the Comédie-Française in 1864 (*Moi*), and in 1880 was made a member of the Académic.

Laburnum Grove. Comedy by J. B. PRIESTLEY, first performed London, 1933.

Lady, Be Good. Musical comedy by GEORGE GERSHWIN, book by GUY BOLTON and Fred Thompson, lyrics by Ira Gershwin. First performed New York, 1924.

Lady from the Sea, The (Fruen fra Havet). Drama by HENRIK IBSEN, first performed Christiania (Oslo) and elsewhere, 1889.

Lady Precious Stream. Play by S. I. Hsiung, based on a traditional Chinese play. First performed London, 1934. Familiarized British audiences with some of the conventions of the Chinese theatre, presented in a quaint and easily palatable form.

Lady's Not for Burning, The. Verse comedy by CHRISTOPHER FRY, first performed Arts Theatre, London, 1948.

Lady Windermere's Fan. Comedy by OSCAR WILDE, first performed London, 1892.

Lagerkvist, Pär (b. 1891). Swedish novelist and dramatist. Though little known as a dramatist abroad, in Scandinavia he is regarded as second in importance only to IBSEN and STRINDBERG. He began as a poet, and his first play, *The Last Man* (*Sista mänskan*, 1917), is a choric drama (never staged), owing much to Strindberg and MAETERLINCK about the extinction of mankind. The following year his important essay *Modern Theatre* appeared, calling for a new fusion of realism and symbolism which could use the resources of the twentieth century theatre to the full and requiring the dramatist to see 'the fantastic in things themselves, and in very reality'. He put this programme into practice with a group of experimental one-act plays heavily influenced by Strindberg, *The Difficult Hour* (*Den svara stunden*, 1918) and other plays, before gradually throwing off Strindberg's influence in the mid 1920s to produce a series of plays tending more to realism, generally slightly more optimistic in subject-matter and often with a religious theme implied. Among the most important of his later plays are *The King* (*Koningen*, 1932), *Victory in the Dark* (*Seger i mörker*, 1939), *Midsummer Dream in the Poor House* (*Midsommar-dröm i fattighuset*, 1941), and *Barabbas* (1953), a subject he has also treated in a novel and a film script.

Land of Heart's Desire, The. Verse drama by W. B. YEATS, first performed London, 1894.

Lang, Matheson (1879–1948). English actor-manager. Early in his career he acted with Benson and with Ellen Terry, then in Ibsen and Shaw under the Barker–Vedrenne management at the Royal Court. In 1907 he had a major success in Hall Caine's *The Christian* at the Lyceum, and from then on headed his own company playing in modern romantic drama leavened with Shakespeare. In 1914 he directed and acted in the first Shakespeare season at the Old Vic; his most famous modern roles were in *Mr Wu*, by Harry M. Vernon and Harold Owen (1907), *The Wandering Jew*, by E. Temple Thurston (1920), and Ashley Dukes's adaptations of *Such Men are Dangerous* (1928) and *Jew Süss* (1929). His autobiography, *Mr Wu Looks Back*, was published in 1940.

Langtry, Lillie (1852–1929). English actress, born in Jersey (daughter of the Dean) and known as the 'Jersey lily'. A capable enough actress, especially in lightweight roles, and an excellent businesswoman. She owed more of her notability to her social position and her striking good looks than to her acting abilities.

Lardner, Ring (1885–1933). American humorist who wrote a number of brief 'nonsense plays' in the 1920s in a manner suggesting at once the English nonsense tradition and contemporary continental manifestations of DADA. Among them are *The Tridget of Griva*, *I Gaspiri* (*The Upholsterers*), and *Clemo-Uti/The Water Lilies*.

Lark, The (L'Alouette). Historical drama by JEAN ANOUILH, based on the life of Joan of Arc, first performed Paris, 1953, English adaptation by CHRISTOPHER FRY, first performed London, 1955; American adaptation by LILLIAN HELLMAN, first performed New York, 1955.

Last of Mrs Cheyney, The. Comedy-thriller by FREDERICK LONSDALE, first performed London, 1925.

Late Christopher Bean, The. Comedy by EMLYN WILLIAMS, adapted from *Prenez garde à la peinture*, by René Fauchois (1932), first performed London, 1933.

Lauder, Harry (1870–1950). Scottish singer and comic. First appeared in London in 1900, and was knighted in 1919 for his work entertaining the troops during the war. Among his most famous songs were *Roamin' in the Gloamin'*, *I Love a Lassie*, and *Stop Yer Tickling, Jock*.

Laughton, Charles (1899–1963). English actor. Achieved his first major success in *The Happy Husband* in 1927, and subsequently as Hercule Poirot in *Alibi*, a role he later played in New York (1932). In 1933–4 he was a member of the Old Vic Company, playing among other roles Lopakin in *The Cherry Orchard*, Henry in *Henry VIII*, Angelo in *Measure for Measure*, Macbeth, and Prospero in *The Tempest*. Meanwhile he had made a new reputation as a film actor, and scored an international success in *The Private Life of Henry VIII*. For eleven years from 1936 he worked entirely in the cinema, his most famous films being *The Barretts of Wimpole Street*, *Ruggles of Red Gap*, *Rembrandt*, and *Mutiny on the Bounty*. In 1947 he returned to the stage in Brecht's *Galileo*, which he adapted into English with the author, and thereafter appeared occasionally in the theatre, notably in the dramatic reading *Don Juan in Hell* (1951), and as Bottom in *A Midsummer Night's Dream* and *King Lear* at Stratford-on-Avon (1959).

Laurents, Arthur (b. 1920). American dramatist, author of a number of capable plays such as *Home of the Brave* (1945) about the colour problem and *The Time of the Cuckoo* (1952) about a middle-aged woman finding love in Italy. He has also written the books of the musicals *West Side Story* (1957) and *Gypsy* (1959).

Lawler, Ray (b. 1922). Australian dramatist and actor. His great success, *Summer of the Seventeenth Doll* (1955) is a straightforward drama about how an unthinking man of action comes to terms with the fact that he is growing old, written with unforced vigour and insight. Such later plays as *The Piccadilly Bushman* (1959) and *The Unshaven Cheek* (1963) have handled more ambitious subjects with considerably less ease and flair.

Legitimate theatre. Straight drama without songs, dances or musical interludes of any kind. The term derives from the old regulations governing the licensing of theatres, which were framed to cover only non-musical presentations, and could therefore be evaded by the addition of musical interludes to produce a bastard form beyond the licensor's control.

Leigh, Vivien (1913–67). English actress. Made her debut in films; first stage success in *The Masque of Virtue* (1935). The most important role in her career was probably Scarlett O'Hara in the film of *Gone With the Wind* (1939), which made her a major international star. Subsequent stage roles include Jennifer Dubedat in *The Doctor's Dilemma* (1942), Sabina in *The Skin of Our Teeth* (1945), Blanche du Bois in *A Streetcar Named Desire* (1949), which she repeated in the film, Cleopatra in *Antony and Cleopatra* and *Caesar and Cleopatra* (1951) opposite her then husband SIR LAURENCE OLIVIER, Viola, Lady Macbeth, and Lavinia in *Titus Andronicus* at Stratford (1955), Paola in *Duel of Angels* (1958), and Lulu d'Arville in *Look After Lulu* (1959).

Leighton, Margaret (1922–76). English actress. First London season with the Old Vic, 1944–5, where she remained for the next two seasons. Among her subsequent successes were the roles of Celia in *The Cocktail Party* (1950), Masha in *The Three Sisters* (1951), Orinthia in *The Apple Cart* (1953), Lucasta in *The Confidential Clerk* (1953), Mrs Shanklin and Miss Railton-Bell in *Separate Tables* (1954), Beatrice in *Much Ado About Nothing* with Sir John Gielgud in the United States (1959), and Elaine Lee in *The Wrong Side of the Park* (1960). After some years in the U.S.A. she returned to Britain and played Cleopatra in *Antony and Cleopatra* (1969) and Mrs Malaprop in *The Rivals* (1971), both at the Chichester Festival.

Lemaître, Frédérick (1800–76). French actor, one of the great Romantic actors, combining to a remarkable degree force and finesse, romantic ardour and professional discipline. His first great successes were in melodramas like *L'Auberge des Adrets* which gave him his famous role of Robert Macaire (1823), and *Trente ans, ou la vie d'un joueur* (1829), but he rapidly proved himself equally at home in great tragic roles like Hamlet and Othello. He reached the height of his career as first interpreter of the extravagant dramas of Dumas *père* (*Kean, ou désordre et génie*, 1836) and Hugo (*Ruy Blas*, 1838). Despite his almost unbroken string of successes he ended his life in poverty when the vogue for the sort of drama in which he had made his name passed. He appears as a leading character (played by Pierre Brasseur) in the Carné–Prévert film *Les Enfants du paradis*.

Leno, Dan (1860–1904). Leading figure of the Victorian music hall, where he specialized in cockney comedy, and of pantomime at Drury Lane, where he appeared regularly from 1889 in 'dame' parts such as Widow Twankey and Cinderella's step-mother.

Lenya, Lotte (b. *c*.1901). German singer and actress, wife of the composer KURT WEILL and a leading interpreter of his collaborations with BRECHT, among them *The Rise and Fall of the City of Mahagonny* (1927, and Brecht's production, 1931), *The Threepenny Opera* (1928), and *The Seven Deadly Sins* (1933). More recently she has been influential in their revival and has done much to popularize them, as well as appearing in the compilation *Brecht on Brecht* in New York and London (1961–2).

Léocadia, see TIME REMEMBERED.

Lermontov, Mikhail Yurevich (1814–41). Russian poet and dramatist. His plays were profoundly influenced by German Romanticism of the STURM UND DRANG era, particularly the first two, *The Spaniards*, which attacked the Tsar's rule under the guise of an historical drama about the Spanish Inquisition, and *Men and Passions*, an emotional drama based on his own family background. His greatest play is *Masquerade*, written in 1835 but not produced until 1852 (in a censored form) and not really properly appreciated until Meyerhold's production in 1917. It is an intense psychological drama about obsessive jealousy, which finally drives the hero to murder his wife, whom he wrongly believes to have been unfaithful. This theme is used as a pretext for a brilliantly ironical dissection of the sort of society which could give rise to such a situation, and the play remains one of the masterpieces of Russian drama.

Lerner, Alan Jay, see LOEWE, FREDERICK.

Lessing, Doris (b. 1921). South African novelist and dramatist. In 1953 she wrote a group of plays, of which the most successful, *Each His Own Wilderness*, was given a production-without-décor at the Royal Court in 1958. None of them showed much flair for the stage, but the later *Play with a Tiger* (1958, produced 1962) suggested in its impassioned central duologue that she might after all have a gift for emotional melodrama.

Lessing, Gotthold Ephraim (1729–81). German dramatist and drama theorist. From his earliest years Lessing was interested in the theatre, and unlike most intellectuals of his period carried this interest as far as spending much time among actors and backstage, learning theatrical craft at first hand. He began writing with several light comedies along French lines, as well as copious journalism on theatrical and artistic subjects (a line of activity which eventually produced his great treatise on aesthetics *Laokoon* in 1766). In 1755 his first important play, *Miss Sara Sampson*, appeared; it is a bourgeois tragedy written in an easy, naturalistic style, conforming to the unities but strongly influenced by the contemporary realistic English novels of Richardson and Fielding. In 1767 the first of Lessing's plays to become a regular part of the dramatic repertory, *Minna von Barnhelm*, was staged; it is a lively comedy of intrigue which set the tone for the thriving middle-class theatre springing up in Germany at the time. The same year Lessing was given a more extensive opportunity to put his ideas into practice when he was appointed *dramaturg* of Hamburg Theatre, in which position he wrote his most ambitious theoretical work, the *Hamburgische Dramaturgie* (1768). This reaffirms most of ARISTOTLE's ideas about tragedy, but modifies them in favour of middle-class subjects closer to a middle-class audience than the elevated personages recommended by Aristotle.

In 1769 the Hamburg Theatre ran into financial difficulties, and Lessing's later years were spent mainly in academic philosophical work. He did, however, write two tragedies: one, *Emilia Galotti* (1772), being a *pièce à thèse* designed to illustrate his ideas of the tragic in bourgeois life but not entirely avoiding melodrama, and the other, *Nathan der Weise* (first produced posthumously in 1783), a noble and eloquent if rather stiff play designed to demonstrate the truth in all religions.

Lesson, The (La Leçon). One-act drama of the ABSURD by EUGÈNE IONESCO; first performed Paris, 1951.

Lewes, George Henry (1817–78). English critic, dramatist, and philosopher, for long associate of the novelist George Eliot. His plays are now forgotten, but his dramatic criticism, especially the essays collected in *On Actors and the Art of Acting* (1875), is among the most vivid and penetrating of the nineteenth century, and his studies of Kean, Rachel, and others are invaluable.

Lewis, Matthew Gregory ('Monk') (1775–1818). English novelist, dramatist, and poet; leading exponent of the 'Gothick' craze in early Romantic literature. His most famous work is his novel *Ambrosio, or the Monk* (1795) – hence his nickname – but he also wrote a group of sensational dramas with titles such as *The Castle Spectre* (1797), *Adelmorn the Outlaw* (1801), *The Wood Daemon* (1807), and *Timour the Tartar* (1811), most of which enjoyed vast if short-lived success.

Lighting (stage). The whole question of stage lighting does not arise until the advent of the private, indoor theatre in the early seventeenth century. Up to then theatrical performances, classical and Renaissance, normally took place by daylight, in the open air, and the only special lighting introduced was in the form of props – torches and lanterns – used to indicate night scenes. Even with the first indoor theatre the performances were generally in the afternoon, and when they extended also to the evening the idea of special stage lighting was slow to develop: it was still a matter almost entirely of achieving satisfactory illumination over the whole area of the auditorium, by lamps and chandeliers. In the Baroque theatre theorists already began to advocate the darkening of the audience area and the more elaborately artificial illumination of the stage, but this was not put into practice until well into the nineteenth century. With the introduction of the proscenium stage in the Restoration theatre a more specialized form of stage lighting developed, however, with the gradual introduction of footlights (lights at floor level along the front of the stage, often concealed from the audience) and side-lights behind the proscenium arch, as well as the overhead illumination from one or more chandeliers. Reflectors were used to increase the intensity of lighting, and a variety of optical devices were used for special effects – an overall lightening or darkening of the stage, a sudden shaft of light, etc. GARRICK experimented with all sorts of stage effects, including lighting effects, and during the late eighteenth and early nineteenth centuries varied lighting for spectacular highlights, transformation scenes, etc., was widely used, though as a rule these effects remained isolated and the general lighting of the stage shows was constant and unatmospheric. Gas lighting was introduced in the 1800s, first for house-lighting then for the stage (Drury Lane, 1817), and was used mainly for its possibilities of brilliant illumination, until in the 1880s Irving began to darken the auditorium consistently during performances and to break up the main concentration of lights in batteries or 'floats' above the stage to produce far more delicate gradations of colour and intensity than had previously been achieved. In fact, he used gas lighting with such virtuosity that he long resisted the introduction of electricity (first London theatre completely lit by electricity: Savoy, 1881). This rapidly replaced gas in most places, and even, more slowly, the limelight, a sort of calcium lamp which gave an unusually brilliant white light, and was used for special effects, particularly moonlight, on the Victorian stage. Electricity permitted a far more flexible approach to stage lighting even than gas: batteries of lights could be directed on to the stage from the roof of the auditorium or from the front of the dress circle, and further batteries of lights above and behind the stage, used either directly or indirectly (reflected, generally, from a cyclorama), enable the modern lighting director (since 1945 often a separate, highly skilled post in the theatre) to produce any variation at the flick of a switch. Since the 1920s there has been an increasing reaction against footlights, and now they are often dispensed with even on a conventional proscenium stage, while open stages, apron stages, and in-the-round presentation tend to make them quite impractical.

Lilac Domino, The. Romantic operetta by Charles Cuvillier and Howard Carr, book by Harry B. Smith, lyrics by A. J. Adair Fitzgerald; first performed London, 1918.

Lilac Time. Operetta by G. H. Clutsam and Heinrich Berté, based on music by Schubert; book by Adrian Ross. First performed London, 1922.

Liliom. Drama by FERENC MOLNAR, first performed Budapest, 1909. See also CAROUSEL.

Lillie, Beatrice (b. 1898). Canadian actress and comic. Made her London debut in 1914, and achieved her first major successes in revue (*The Nine O'Clock Revue*, 1922; *André Charlot's Revue of 1924*; *This Year of Grace*, 1928), singing grotesque songs and playing in strange, often slightly Surrealistic sketches, many devised by herself. Though she has played a number of straight roles in comedies (notably *Auntie Mame*, 1958), she is best known in cabaret and revue on both sides of the Atlantic. In 1954 she scored a great personal success with her one-woman show *An Evening with Beatrice Lillie*, and has followed it with other, similar shows; in 1964 she played Madame Arcati in *High Spirits*, a musical version of *Blithe Spirit*, in New York.

Lillo, George (1693–1739). English dramatist, author of the famous bourgeois tragedy *The London Merchant: or the History of George Barnwell* (1731) in which a young man is led into murder for profit by a bad woman and pays the penalty for his crime. It created a vogue for this sort of play in England and on the Continent, was praised by Pope, and remained in the repertory until the mid nineteenth century. Another play, *The Fatal Curiosity* (1736) was also successful and influential, particularly in Germany.

Lincoln Center for the Performing Arts. A large-scale city project occupying a large site on the West Side of New York, intended to bring together an opera house, concert halls, a repertory theatre, art galleries, music, ballet, and drama schools. The first section completed, the large concert hall, was opened in 1962; the Vivian Beaumont Theater in autumn 1965. The theatre company was originally conceived as long ago as 1958 by Robert Whitehead, to constitute a sort of national company on rather the same lines as Britain's NATIONAL THEATRE, mixing classics of all nations with the best of modern drama in an eclectic repertory. Whitehead took as his co-director ELIA KAZAN and appointed HAROLD CLURMAN as 'executive consultant'; the first productions of the company were staged in a temporary home in 1962. Whitehead concentrated mainly on organization, Kazan principally on the actual staging, and ARTHUR MILLER was enrolled as a sort of resident playwright, two of his recent plays, *After the Fall* and *Incident at Vichy*, being written for and first played by the company. Late in 1964 disagreements led to the withdrawal of Whitehead from the company, followed by Kazan and Miller; their place was taken by Herbert Blau and Jules Irving, from San Francisco.

Linden Tree, The. Drama by J. B. PRIESTLEY, first performed London, 1947.

Lindsay (or Lyndsay), Sir David (1490–1555). Scottish poet and dramatist. His *Ane Pleasant Satyre of the Thrie Estaitis*, first performed at Cupar in 1540, is a long and lively political morality play with much rough humour and grotesque characterization; it was successfully revived by Tyrone Guthrie on an apron stage at the Edinburgh Festival in 1948. Lindsay, in his alternative role of statesman and diplomatist, is a leading character in JOHN ARDEN'S *Armstrong's Last Goodnight*.

Linklater, Eric (b. 1899). Scottish novelist and dramatist, author of a number of comedies not dissimilar from the works of JAMES BRIDIE. The best known are *Love in Albania* (1949), *The Atom Doctor* (1950), a modern variation on the theme of *The Alchemist*, and *Breakspeare in Gascony*, an historical play written for the 1959 Edinburgh Festival.

Lion in Love, The. Drama by SHELAGH DELANEY, first performed Coventry, 1960.

Little Eyolf (Lille Eyolf). Drama by HENRIK IBSEN, first performed Berlin, 1895.

Little Foxes, The. Drama by LILLIAN HELLMAN, first performed New York, 1939.

Little Minister, The. Comedy by J. M. BARRIE, based on his own novel, first performed London, 1897.

Little Tich (real name Harry Relph; 1868–1928). English music-hall comic, whose trade mark was a pair of immensely long boots. He began as a black-face comedian, but made his name on the English halls in a selection of comic sketches in which he played a wide variety of characters, male and female. He also appeared in pantomime.

Littlewood, Joan (b. 1914). English director, founder and motive force of THEATRE WORKSHOP. After brief studies at R.A.D.A. and some desultory painting in Paris Joan Littlewood settled in Manchester in the 1930s and founded there, with the folk singer and dramatist Ewan MacColl, the Theatre of Action, a political theatre rehearsing and performing whenever opportunity offered. Towards the end of the 1939–45 war she worked as a radio documentary producer in the North of England, and in 1945 she founded Theatre Workshop, again in Manchester, as a popular theatre for working-class audiences. From then until 1953 the company toured, mainly in the North but with occasional trips to Wales and the West. The repertoire consisted of classics (Shakespeare, Jonson, etc.) and a number of specially written plays on vaguely topical subjects by Ewan MacColl. In 1953 the company found a permanent home at the Theatre Royal in the working-class East London suburb of Stratford, continuing with the same sort of repertory as before, and had its first transfer to a West End theatre in 1955 with MacColl's version of *The Good Soldier Schweik*.

By this time the characteristics of Joan Littlewood's production style and approach to actors and texts were becoming evident. Much influenced by BRECHT (in 1955 she directed and played the title role in *Mother Courage*), she makes all her productions specifically theatrical in their effect, discouraging passive identification on the audience's part and making use of whatever tools come to hand – music and song, elaborate action like the bricklaying in *You Won't Always Be on Top*, jokes and asides to the audience in the best music-hall style – to bring home a point. As far as actors are concerned, the productions are very much a cooperative effort, with a lot of improvisation and frequently a rather cavalier treatment of the text. All the group's most famous productions – Brendan Behan's *The Quare Fellow* (1956) and *The Hostage* (1958), Shelagh Delaney's *A Taste of Honey* (1958), and Frank Norman's *Fings Ain't Wot They Used T'Be* (1959) – were along these lines, and the texts finally seen were considerably altered from the originals in the process. The classics directed by Joan Littlewood in the same period included *Volpone*, *The Dutch Courtesan*, and *Every Man in His Humour*. In 1961 Joan Littlewood left Theatre Workshop for eighteen months to work elsewhere and make a film, but returned in 1963 with *Oh What a Lovely War!*, a musical evocation and critique of the First World War, evolved collectively by her and the whole company. Subsequently she has directed a conflated version of the two parts of Shakespeare's *Henry IV* at the Edinburgh Festival (1964) and been involved in the foundation of a theatre school in Tunisia and the planning of a series of 'fun palaces', entertainment centres in various parts of Britain.

Living Newspaper. A sort of topical documentary revue in a series of short scenes based on current social and political problems, devised in the 1930s in the U.S.A. by the Federal Theater, and used elsewhere for propaganda during the war.

Living Room, The. Drama by GRAHAM GREENE, first performed London, 1953.

Livings, Henry (b. 1929). English dramatist. For a time actor with THEATRE WORKSHOP, when he began to write plays he specialized in North Country farces with a minimum of plot, starting with *Stop It Whoever You Are* (1961). All Livings's plays are based on his own principle of 'ten-minute takes' exploring one line of character-development at a time: other comedies by him include *Big Soft Nellie* (1961), and *Nil Carborundum* (1962), and *Eh?* (1964), both produced by the Royal Shakespeare Company, while *Kelly's Eye* is an unconventional love story with a strong undercurrent of violence, produced by the English Stage Company (1963).

Living Theatre. An Off-Broadway company founded by the director Judith Malina and the writer-designer Julian Beck in 1947. Between then and 1964 it became the most influential centre of advanced theatre in the U.S., particularly in its emphasis on group improvisation and its presentation of such pieces of free, physical theatre as JACK GELBER'S *The Connection* and *The Apple* and Kenneth H. Brown's *The Brig*, a shattering picture of life in a military prison. In 1964, finding themselves in financial difficulties, they moved to Europe, first touring *The Brig*, then settling down as a sort of acting school and centre of activity which every now and then mounts entertainments very much in the Theatre of CRUELTY manner, such as their *Frankenstein* show seen in London in 1969.

Lloyd, Marie (1870–1922). One of the best-known figures of the English music-hall in its Edwardian heyday. She made her debut in 1885, and had her first big success shortly afterwards with the song *The Boy I Love is up in the Gallery*. Among her most famous songs were *The Old Cock Linnet*, *Oh! Mr Porter*, *One of the Ruins that Cromwell Knocked Abaht a Bit*, and *A Little of What You Fancy Does You Good*. She continued to play the halls right up to her death and probably still symbolizes more than any other performer the best of music-hall in popular estimation today.

Lock Up Your Daughters. Musical based on Henry Fielding's play *Rape upon Rape* (1730); book by BERNARD MILES, lyrics by LIONEL BART, music by Laurie Johnson. First produced Mermaid Theatre, London, 1959.

Lodge, Thomas (c. 1558–1625). English dramatist and writer of romances. His most notable play was *Wounds of the Civil War* (1587–8), the earliest Roman history play in English and somewhat influenced by Marlowe's *Tamburlaine*. But his best-known work is the romance *Rosalynd* (1590), from which Shakespeare derived the plot of *As You Like It*.

Loewe, Frederick (b. 1904). Austrian-American composer; with lyricist Alan Jay Lerner responsible for the successful musicals *Brigadoon* (1947), *Paint Your Wagon* (1951), *My Fair Lady* (1956), and *Camelot* (1961); also the musical film *Gigi* (1959), staged with additions in 1973.

Logan, Joshua (b. 1908). American director and dramatist. Studied under STANISLAVSKY in Moscow, began directing in Britain in 1933, subsequently working mainly in New York. Has specialized in the direction of musicals and comedies, himself writing, alone or in collaboration, the books of the musicals *South Pacific* (1949), *Wish You Were Here* (1951), and *Fanny* (1954), and the comedy *Mister Roberts* (1948), all of which he also directed. Other productions include *Knickerbocker Holiday* (1938), *By Jupiter* (1942), *Annie Get Your Gun* (1946), *Picnic* (1953), *Middle of the Night* (1956), and *The World of Suzy Wong* (1958).

Long and the Short and the Tall, The. Service drama by WILLIS HALL. First performed by the Oxford Theatre Group at the Edinburgh Festival, 1958, as *The Disciplines of War*; London, English Stage Company, 1959.

Long Day's Journey into Night. Drama by EUGENE O'NEILL, written 1940–41, first performed (in Swedish) Stockholm, 1956, first American production New York, 1956.

Long Voyage Home, The. One-act play of the sea by EUGENE O'NEILL, first performed Provincetown Players, Massachusetts, 1917. It is one of a cycle of seven one-act plays, which are often known collectively under the same title: the others are *The Moon of the Caribbees*, *In the Zone*, *Bound East for Cardiff*, *Where the Cross is Made*, *The Rope*, and *'Ile*, all written 1916–17 and performed by the Provincetown Players 1916–18. Broadway production of first four, under title *S.S. Glencairn*, 1924.

Lonsdale, Frederick (1881–1954). Prolific English dramatist, specialist in lightweight comedy of manners, somewhat in the manner of MAUGHAM. His best-known plays date from the 1920s, among them *Aren't We All?* (1923), *The Last of Mrs Cheyney* (1925), and *On Approval* (1927); though often dismissed as the short-lived products of a capable commercial journeyman, they have shown an unexpected gift for survival, if only because of Lonsdale's impeccable craftsmanship and easy way with the sub-Wildean epigram. He also wrote the books of a number of musicals, the most successful being *The Maid of the Mountains* (1917) and *Madame Pompadour* (1923).

Look After Lulu. Free version by NOËL COWARD of FEYDEAU'S farce *Occupe-toi d'Amélie*, first performed New York, 1959.

Look Back in Anger. Drama by JOHN OSBORNE, first performed by the English Stage Company, Royal Court, London, 1956.

Lorca, Federico García (1898–1936). Spanish poet and dramatist. His first play, a one-act symbolic fantasy *El Malificio del mariposa* (*The Butterfly's Evil Spell*), was written while he was still in his teens, and was a failure. His first major play, however, a full-length 'popular ballad' called *Mariana Pineda* (1927), about a heroine of a revolution in the 1830s, went far towards establishing his mature style, though its mixture of violent action and expansively lyrical elements did not completely fuse together. The following years brought a number of short experiments: a group of poetic folk-plays with strong farcical elements (*El Amor de Don Perlimplin con Belisa en su jardin, La Zapatera prodigiosa, Retabillo de Don Cristobal*) and two Surrealist plays, *Asi que pasan cinco años* and *El Publico*. But in 1933 Lorca finally evolved his true personal form, the peasant tragedy written in a condensed poetic style, sometimes with pronounced supernatural elements, sometimes severely realistic. His first major play was *Bodas de sangre* (*Blood Wedding*), a savage story of family feuds, illicit love and sudden death cast into an increasingly symbolic mould, with the Moon and Death personified taking part in the action. *Yerma* (1934) is a strong drama about a woman torn between a passionate desire for the children her husband cannot give her and her inflexible code of honour which will not allow her to find another father for them. *Doña Rosita la soleva* (*Dona Rosita the Spinster*, 1935) is a subdued account of a spinster's life of pretence after her fiancé has jilted her, and Lorca's final play, *La Casa de Bernarda Alba* (*The House of Bernarda Alba*, 1936) is also a study of female frustration, this time of a whole household of sisters ruled over by a bigoted and tyrannical mother. *La Casa de Bernarda Alba* is considered by many Lorca's finest play, and certainly shows his mastery of dramatic technique at its most complete and assured. What he would have gone on to write had he not been killed in the Spanish Civil War at the age of thirty-eight it is impossible to guess, but there seems little doubt that it would have been remarkable.

Love for Love. Comedy by WILLIAM CONGREVE, first performed London, 1695.

Love in a Village. Ballad opera by ISAAC BICKERSTAFFE, first performed Covent Garden, London, 1762.

Love of Four Colonels, The. Comedy by PETER USTINOV, first performed London, 1951.

Love on the Dole. Drama by Ronald Gow and Walter Greenwood, from the novel by Walter Greenwood (1933); first performed London, 1935. Most famous British drama of the Depression.

Love's Labour's Lost. Comedy by WILLIAM SHAKESPEARE, written c.1594–5.

Lower Depths, The (Na dne). Drama by MAXIM GORKY, first performed Moscow Art Theatre, 1902.

Loyalties. Drama by JOHN GALSWORTHY, first performed London, 1922.

Lugné-Poë, Aurélien-Marie (1869–1940). French actor-manager. Early in his career he appeared at Antoine's Théâtre Libre, and later at Paul Fort's Théâtre d'Art, which in 1892 he took over and developed into the Théâtre de l'Œuvre. He was director and leading actor with this group until 1929, during which time he introduced to the French stage many plays by Ibsen, Strindberg, Hauptmann, Bjørnson, and d'Annunzio as well as first bringing MAETERLINCK to prominence in the theatre with productions of *Pelléas et Mélisande, L'Intruse,* and *Intérieur,* and introducing CLAUDEL with *L'Annonce faite à Marie* (1912).

Lunacharsky, Anatoli (1875–1933). Russian dramatist and theatre organizer. He played a vital part in the preservation of pre-Revolutionary Russian theatre and the development of new forms of dramatic writing and production: as first Commissar for Education in Soviet Russia he was responsible for the reorganization of the theatre after the Revolution, and evolved the theory of SOCIALIST REALISM, which entailed equally the deliberate development of a specifically Soviet form of theatre and the careful nurturing of all that was best in the drama of the past as a cultural heritage. His own plays, several of them – like *Oliver Cromwell* and *Thomas Campanella* – on historical subjects, have proved ephemeral.

Lunts, The: Alfred Lunt (1893–1977) and **Lynn Fontanne** (b. 1887). American husband-and-wife acting team (she of English origin) who almost invariably acted together from their marriage in 1922. Before that both had achieved some distinction, he scoring a big success in *Clarence,* by Booth Tarkington (1919), and she playing, among other things, the central role in *Chris* (1920), Eugene O'Neill's first version of *Anna Christie.* Together they have been identified mainly with elegantly sophisticated comedy, notably a series by S. N. Behrman, among them *The Second Man* (1927), *Meteor* (1929), *Amphitryon '38* (adapted from Giraudoux, 1937, and in London, 1938), *The Pirate* (after Ludwig Fulda, 1942), and *I Know My Love* (after Marcel Aymé, 1949). Other successes include Molnar's *The Guardsman*

(1924), *Arms and the Man* (1925), *Pygmalion* (1927), Noël Coward's *Design for Living* (1933), *The Taming of the Shrew* (1935), Robert Sherwood's *Idiot's Delight* (1936), Terence Rattigan's *Love in Idleness* (London, 1944, and in the U.S.A., 1946, where it was known as *O Mistress Mine*), and Noël Coward's *Quadrille* (London, 1952; New York, 1954). On the more serious side there were few memorable appearances, but Copeau's adaptation of *The Brothers Karamazov* (1927), *Strange Interlude* (Lynn Fontanne only, 1928), *The Seagull* (1938), and Dürrenmatt's *The Visit* (New York, 1958, London, 1960) should perhaps he mentioned.

Luther. Historical drama by JOHN OSBORNE, first performed London, 1961.

Lyly, John (*c.* 1554–1606). English dramatist and fiction-writer. His most famous and in its day influential work was his story *Euphues* (1597) and its sequel *Euphues and his England* (1580), which are written in an involved and elaborately artificial style which gave the term 'euphuistic' to the language. His plays were all courtly entertainments intended for small sophisticated audiences: some of them were on classical themes, like *Alexander and Campaspe*, *Sappho and Phaon*, and *Endimion, the Man in the Moon*; others, like *Midas* and *Mother Bombie*, were based on the conventions of TERENCE's plays.

Lyndsay, Sir David, see LINDSAY.

Lysistrata. Comedy by ARISTOPHANES, first performed Athens, 411 B.C.

M

Macbeth. Tragedy by WILLIAM SHAKESPEARE, written c.1605–6.

MacCarthy, Desmond (1877–1952). English dramatic critic, renowned for his wit and urbanity. Began writing on the theatre in 1904, and in 1913 joined the *New Statesman* as dramatic critic. He emerged at just the time that SHAW was creating a revolution in the English theatre, and proved one of Shaw's justest and most perceptive supporters. The fourth volume of his collected essays, *Drama* (1940), contains a selection of his writings on the theatre of the previous thirty years; other writings are contained in *Theatre* (1954) and *Shaw* (1957). Knighted 1951.

McCracken, Esther (b. 1902). English dramatist; her greatest successes were the cosy domestic comedies *Quiet Wedding* (1938) and *Quiet Weekend* (1941).

McCullers, Carson (1917–67). American novelist and dramatist, author mainly of atmospheric fiction about the deep South in decay. Her most successful play has been *The Member of the Wedding*, adapted from her own novel; it was followed by an original stage play, *The Square Root of Wonderful* (1958). Another story by her, *The Ballad of the Sad Café*, has been adapted to the stage by EDWARD ALBEE, and was first performed in 1963.

MacDougall, Roger (b. 1910). Scottish dramatist, author of a series of light comedies relying on verbal wit and eccentric invention a little reminiscent of BRIDIE. Principal plays: *The Gentle Gunman* (1950), *To Dorothy, a Son* (1950), *Escapade* (1952).

McGrath, John (b. 1935). English dramatist and television director; began play-writing at Oxford, where his first play, *A Man Has Two Fathers*, was staged by the O.U.D.S. Later plays include *The Tent* (one-act) and *Why the Chicken*. His most successful work, *Events While Guarding the Bofors Gun* (1966), a tense psychological drama with a military background, was later filmed.

Machiavelli, Niccolò di Bernardo dei (1469–1527). Italian dramatist and political theorist, best remembered as the author of *The Prince*, which outlined his unscrupulous view of political organization. He was also the author of a number of comedies, one of which, *La Mandragola* (1513–20), a witty piece of social criticism in the form of a classic Italian comedy of intrigue, remains in the repertory.

McKenna, Siobhan (b. 1923). Irish actress. One of her earliest roles was Lady Macbeth, in Gaelic (1940); from 1943 to 1946 she was at the

Abbey Theatre, and made her London debut in 1947. In 1954 she played Shaw's St Joan for the first time, a role with which she has subsequently been regularly associated; later roles include Miss Madrigal in *The Chalk Garden* (New York, 1955), Viola in *Twelfth Night* (Stratford, Ontario, 1957), Lady Macbeth (Cambridge, Mass., 1959), and Pegeen in *The Playboy of the Western World* (Dublin Festival, then London, 1960), another of her best roles.

MacLeish, Archibald (b. 1892). American poet and dramatist; author of a number of verse plays for stage and radio, mostly for small and specialized audiences; he achieved a major Broadway success in 1958 with *J.B.*, a verse parable play on the theme of Job which was directed by ELIA KAZAN.

MacLiammóir, Micheál (b. 1899). Irish actor and dramatist. After varied acting experience in London he returned to Ireland in 1925 and opened first the Galway Gaelic Theatre, where he directed twenty plays, then, in collaboration with Hilton Edwards, the Dublin Gate Theatre, the most dynamic Irish theatre group of the inter-war years, for which he has since acted in, and designed, nearly three hundred productions. In 1931 he was appointed director also of the government-subsidized Dublin Gaelic Theatre. Among his most famous roles as an actor are Robert Emmett in *The Old Lady Says No!* and Hamlet (both on many occasions), Larry Doyle in *John Bull's Other Island* (1947), Brack in *Hedda Gabler* (1954), and Oscar Wilde in his own compilation *The Importance of Being Oscar* (1960); his plays include *Ill Met by Moonlight* (1946), *The Mountains Look Different* (1948), and *Home for Christmas* (1950).

MacNeice, Louis (1907–65). Irish poet and dramatist. Though he has written for the theatre (*Out of the Picture*, 1937), most of his best dramatic work was for radio, in verse plays such as *Christopher Columbus*, *The Dark Tower*, and *The Queen of Air and Darkness*. He also translated successfully the *Agamemnon* of Aeschylus and Goethe's *Faust*.

Macready, William (1793–1873). Leading English actor of the early nineteenth century, noted particularly for his distinction in the great tragic roles. He made his debut in 1810 (as Romeo), and by 1819 had become famous enough to be regarded as KEAN's chief rival. His best roles were Hamlet, Lear, and Macbeth, and in these he won the plaudits of HAZLITT as, with Kean, the best tragic actor of his age. He was one of the most intelligent and discriminating actors and managers of the period, too, and the friend of poets and writers: he first staged Browning's *Strafford* (1837) and Byron's *The Two Foscari* (1838), and had major successes in two plays by Bulwer-Lytton, *The*

Lady of Lyons and *Richelieu*, in the same years. He was also influential in returning for practical theatrical purposes to the original texts of Shakespeare instead of using the various 'adaptations' then normal on the stage. He kept a diary, published after his death, which gives a vivid picture of the London theatre in his day.

Madame Sans-Gêne. Historical comedy-drama by VICTORIEN SARDOU, first performed Paris, 1893.

Maddermarket Theatre. Amateur theatre in Norwich, built in a dilapidated building as a home for the Norwich Players by Nugent Monck, their producer, in 1919. The theatre itself is on Elizabethan lines, Monck being a disciple of WILLIAM POEL, but it is adaptable to a variety of production styles. The company, organized on 'little theatre' lines, play one week in every four.

Madras House, The. Comedy by HARLEY GRANVILLE BARKER, first performed London, 1910.

Mad Woman of Chaillot, The (La Folle de Chaillot). Tragi-comedy by JEAN GIRAUDOUX, written 1943, first performed Paris, 1945.

Maeterlinck, Maurice (1862–1949). Belgian poet and dramatist, writing in French. He achieved an early success with a series of poetic plays on symbolic and legendary subjects, which all reflected in various ways the theory of drama put forward in his essay 'The Tragic in Everyday Life': that the business of drama was less with character in action than with the implied interaction of soul-states. Two of his earliest one-act plays in the style, *Les Aveugles* and *L'Intruse* (1890) seem to foreshadow the subject-matter, if not the style, of the Theatre of the ABSURD. His first big success was the wan legendary love-story *Pelléas et Mélisande* (1892), best known now in Debussy's operatic version. Later plays include *Intérieur* (1894), *Aglavaine et Selysette* (1896), and *Monna Vanna* (1902). His biggest international success was *L'Oiseau Bleu* (1908), a fairy play first produced by Stanislavsky at the Moscow Art Theatre. Though Maeterlinck went on writing plays for the rest of his long life, none of the later ones had comparable success, not even the sequel to *L'Oiseau Bleu*, *Les Fiançailles* (*The Betrothal*, 1922).

Magistrate, The. Farce by ARTHUR WING PINERO, first performed London, 1885.

Maids, The (Les Bonnes). One-act drama by JEAN GENET, first produced by Jouvet, Paris, 1947.

Mains Sales, Les, see CRIME PASSIONNEL.

Major Barbara. Dramatic comedy by GEORGE BERNARD SHAW, first performed Royal Court, London, 1905.

Make-up. In primitive and ritual proto-drama make-up was mainly the assumption of disguise, generally in the form of MASKS. In Renaissance drama make-up was used almost entirely for special effects – angels, devils and the like – but rarely if ever in normal roles, even, seemingly, when boys played the roles of women, though the usual resources of character make-up – wigs, beards, false noses, and a certain amount of paint to indicate scars, wrinkles, etc – were of course employed. All this was in a theatre habituated to daylight performances, but the advent of evening performances by artificial light did not bring in the general use of make-up immediately – except that women players obviously used all the make-up artifices they would have used off-stage. Indeed the rule holds good in general that, apart from special character disguises, make-up on stage was used by men and women to about the extent on the stage that they would have worn it off until early in the nineteenth century, when the introduction of gas lighting made some form of make-up almost essential. Grease-paints as we know them today were introduced as a commercial practicality around the mid 1870s; before that various combinations of greasy rouge and tinted powders were widely used. In the modern theatre make-up is normal for all roles, whether straight or character, and a vast and carefully graded range of grease-paints is available to cover every possible requirement.

Making of Moo, The. Satirical comedy by NIGEL DENNIS, first performed by the English Stage Company, Royal Court, London, 1957.

Malade imaginaire, Le. Comedy by MOLIÈRE, first performed Paris, 1672.

Malatesta. Historical drama by HENRY DE MONTHERLANT, first performed Paris, 1950.

Male Animal, The. Comedy by James Thurber and Elliot Nugent, first performed New York, 1940. The principal attempt by the American humorist Thurber to transfer his personal type of humour to the stage.

Malleson, Miles (1888–1969). English actor, director, and dramatist. As an actor is chiefly known for his series of elderly grotesques, principally in comedy; has played the leading roles in a number of his own adaptations of Molière, among them *The Miser* (1950), *The Prodigious Snob* (1951), and *Sganarelle* (1959).

Malraux, André (b. 1901). French novelist, critic and Minister for Culture in the de Gaulle government. In this latter role he has played an important part in the reorganization of the French national theatres: in 1959 the Comédie-Française was reformed, given a new director, and deprived of one of its theatres, the Salle Luxembourg, which became the Théâtre de France under the direction of Jean-

Louis Barrault. The reform also created two subsidized experimental theatres, one of them under the direction of Jean Vilar. Malraux himself has written no plays, but his book *Le Temps du mépris* was adapted by CAMUS (1936), and *La Condition Humaine* by Thierry Maulnier and Marcelle Tassencourt (1954).

Malvern Festival. Annual drama festival founded in the Midland spa of Malvern by SIR BARRY JACKSON in 1929, and devoted most notably to the works of SHAW, twenty of whose plays were produced there between 1929 and 1939, seven for the first time in England. Other plays performed there included revivals of many rare and interesting pieces of the Tudor, Jacobean and Restoration periods, as well as Bridie's *The Sleeping Clergyman* and plays by J. B. PRIESTLEY, John Drinkwater, and Lord Dunsany. The festival was revived under new management in 1947.

Maly Theatre. The oldest theatre company in Moscow (founded in 1806) occupying the oldest theatre building (opened 1824). The name means small – as opposed to Bolshoi, large – and the theatre from the first, though a department of the official Imperial Theatre, was able to choose its material with more freedom than the other, larger departments; it was here, for example, that GOGOL's anti-bureaucratic satire *The Government Inspector* was first staged. The style of production at the theatre was always essentially realistic, whether in contemporary drama or the classics: its repertoire included many works of Shakespeare – translated straight from English into Russian instead of via French, as was normal at the time – and also a series of plays by OSTROVSKY, who became virtually the theatre's own dramatist. The theatre and its company survived the Revolution and proved well able to adapt themselves to the new conditions, feeling their way cautiously at first by keeping to the standard classics and then in 1926, with Trenov's *Lyubov Yarovaga*, launching boldly into the new drama based on problems of the Soviet state.

Manager. The person responsible for the whole financial side of a theatrical production: he chooses the play, arranges for the hire of a theatre if he does not own one, and engages director, actors, etc, as well as controlling the takings. In America he is known as the 'producer', and with the gradual acceptance in Britain of the term 'DIRECTOR', for the man who actually stages the play, 'producer' is beginning to be used in Britain as an alternative for 'manager'.

Man and Superman. Drama by GEORGE BERNARD SHAW, written 1901–3, first performed by the Stage Society, Royal Court, London, 1905 (excluding the act 'Don Juan in Hell', usually omitted and sometimes performed separately).

Manchester School. A group of dramatists, writing realistic comedy or drama in a North Country setting, which gathered round the Gaiety, Manchester, during the period it was run by Miss A. E. F. HORNIMAN, 1907–21. Among the writers in this group were STANLEY HOUGHTON, HAROLD BRIGHOUSE, Alan Monkhouse and Elizabeth Baker.

Mandragola, La. Satirical comedy by NICCOLÒ MACHIAVELLI, first performed Florence, c. 1520.

Man for All Seasons, A. Historical drama based on the life of Sir Thomas More, by ROBERT BOLT (based on his own radio play of 1954), first performed London, 1960.

Mankowitz, Wolf (b. 1924). English novelist and dramatist. Author of some straight plays, notably *The Bespoke Overcoat*, after GOGOL (1953), and of several musicals, among them *Expresso Bongo* (1958), *Make Me an Offer* (1959), *Belle* (1961), *Pickwick* (1963) and *Passion Flower Hotel* (1965).

Man Who Came to Dinner, The. Comedy by GEORGE S. KAUFMAN and MOSS HART, first performed New York, 1939.

Man with a Load of Mischief, The. Period comedy by ASHLEY DUKES, first performed London, 1924.

Marat/Sade, The, see PERSECUTION AND ASSASSINATION OF MARAT AS PERFORMED BY THE INMATES OF THE ASYLUM OF CHARENTON UNDER THE DIRECTION OF THE MARQUIS DE SADE.

Marceau, Félicien (b. 1913). Belgian dramatist, writing in French. His first play was a strong drama, *Caterina* (1954), but his later works, like *L'Œuf* and *La Bonne Soupe*, tend more in the direction of lightweight social comedy.

Marceau, Marcel (b. 1923). French mime. Began to explore the possibilities of mime-expression while teaching children, and then started to appear as a solo performer with a group of little wordless sketches. In these he evolved a constant persona, the amiable, foolish, white-faced Bip, who was seen chasing a butterfly, taking part in a tug of war, smelling a flower, and so on. Later Marceau gathered a company round him to perform complete mime-dramas, the richest and most elaborate being based on Gogol's *The Overcoat* (1951). More recently he has alternated seasons with his company and solo seasons, and has appeared a number of times in London.

Marcel, Gabriel (1889–1974). French dramatist and critic. Has written numerous plays of a somewhat philosophical temper, all published but several never performed. His most successful plays, *Un Homme de Dieu* (written 1925, produced 1949), *La Chapelle ardente* (written 1931, produced 1950), *Le Chemin de Crète* (translated as *Ariadne,* written 1936, produced 1953), and *Rome n'est plus dans Rome* (1951), all deal with problems of conscience, but without any great dramatic urgency.

Marching Song. Drama by JOHN WHITING, first performed London, 1954.

Marco Millions. Drama by EUGENE O'NEILL, written 1923–5, first performed by Theatre Guild, New York, 1928.

Maria Marten. Victorian melodrama on the subject of a real-life murder which took place in 1827. There are various versions, mostly anonymous; one of the earliest was that performed in Marylebone in 1840, and another dates from 1833.

Maria Stuart. Tragedy by SCHILLER, first performed Weimar, 1800.

Marionettes, see PUPPET THEATRE.

Marius. Family drama by MARCEL PAGNOL, set in Marseilles; first performed Paris, 1930.

Marivaux, Pierre Carlet de Chamblain de (1688–1763). French dramatist and novelist. His novels are immensely long and solid; his plays short, slight, and infinitely delicate. They are comedies of extreme grace and subtlety, bitter-sweet fantasies on the traditional themes of love and deception, a sort of theatrical equivalent of the paintings of Watteau. His first great success was *Arlequin poli par l'amour* in 1720, played at the Comédie-Italienne, where most of his best plays were subsequently given. Among them are *La Surprise de l'amour* (1722), *La Double Inconstance* (1723), *Le Jeu de l'amour et du hasard* (1730), and *Les Fausses Confidences* (1737). None of them has much in the way of external plot: all the action is a matter of psychological nuances and fluctuations of mood, quite unlike the popular sentimental comedies of the day, and though they achieved a reasonable measure of success at the time Marivaux's main fame came in the nineteenth century and after. In all Marivaux wrote thirty-five plays, nearly all between 1720 and 1740; after 1746 he retired from the professional theatre.

Marlowe, Christopher (1564–93). English dramatist, predecessor of SHAKESPEARE and powerful influence on the whole course of Elizabethan drama. Educated at Cambridge, he came to the London stage and had a great success when only twenty-three with *Tamburlaine the Great* (1587), a spectacular, flamboyant historical drama more notable for its blazing poetry than for its coherent construction. A second part followed the next year. Possibly his next play (the exact chronology of his work is very confused) was *The Tragical History of Doctor Faustus*, the first dramatic treatment of the FAUST story, derived from a German prose treatment of a few years before; the text of the play survives only in versions generally considered to be garbled and corrupt. His two other major plays, possibly the last he wrote before his murder (apparently for political reasons), *The Jew of Malta* and *Edward II*, seem to have been first acted in 1590–3. *The Jew of Malta* is a violent melodrama shot through with ruthless comedy, while *Edward II* is a sober and quite subtle historical drama. Marlowe also had a hand in *Dido, Queen of Carthage*, which is probably the earliest work of his we have, and may also have collaborated on one or two other plays. His talent was essentially youthful, extravagant and undisciplined, but within these limitations among the most exciting of an exciting period in the theatre. *Edward II* suggests that he might have achieved an interesting maturity had he lived longer.

Marlowe Society. Cambridge University dramatic society, founded in 1908, which puts on an annual production, usually an Elizabethan or Jacobean play.

Marriage à la Mode. Comedy by JOHN DRYDEN, first performed London, 1672.

Marriage of Blood, see BLOOD WEDDING.

Marshall, Norman (b. 1901). English director. Began his directing career at the Festival Theatre, Cambridge, in 1926, and in 1932 took over management of the theatre. In 1934 he became director of the Gate Theatre, London, one of the most enterprising and influential of the inter-war club theatres, and there he directed such plays (mostly banned by the Lord Chamberlain for one reason or another) as *Victoria Regina* (1935), *Lysistrata, Oscar Wilde, The Children's Hour* (1936), and *Tobacco Road* (1937). Later he became a West End manager, worked for C.E.M.A. during the war, and was subsequently one of the first notable theatre men to go into television, being Head of Drama for Associated-Rediffusion 1955–9. His books include *The Other Theatre* (1947), on non-commercial theatre in Britain, and *The Producer and the Play* (1957).

Marston, John (*c*.1575–1634). English dramatist and satirist. Educated at Oxford and intended for the law, he turned instead to writing satirical verses, and by 1599 to drama. His first works were a revenge tragedy, *Antonio and Mellida*, and its sequel, *Antonio's Revenge*. In the following year he wrote a comedy, *What You Will* (1601), and most of his other works were comedies with a characteristic harsh, bitter, satirical tone: the best of them are *The Malcontent* (1604) and *The Dutch Courtesan* (1603–5). In 1605 he collaborated with JONSON and CHAPMAN on *Eastward Ho!*, and had to flee to escape prison; possibly as a result of this episode, he and Jonson became sworn enemies and constantly pilloried each other thereafter. In 1616 Marston suddenly gave up the stage, went into the Church, and spent most of the rest of his life as a country vicar.

Martin, Mary (b. 1913). American musical star. First appeared on the stage 1938, then in films until 1943. Later stage successes include *One Touch of Venus* (1943), *Pacific 1860* (1946), *South Pacific* (1949), *The Sound of Music* (1959), and *Hello, Dolly!* (London, 1965).

Martinez, Sierra Gregorio (1881–1947). Spanish dramatist, specialist in subdued, amiable comedy and lightweight drama. His best-known play is *Cancion de cuna* (*Cradlesong*, 1911); others include a new treatment of the Don Juan story, *Don Juan de Mañara* (1921). He was also the regular Spanish translator of the plays of Shaw.

Mary Rose. Supernatural drama by J. M. BARRIE, first performed London, 1920.

Mask and the Face, The (La Maschera e il Volto). Comedy by Luigi Chiarelli, first performed Rome, 1916; best known in a free English adaptation by C. B. Fernald, first performed London, 1924; also translation by W. SOMERSET MAUGHAM, first performed New York, 1933. A successful early exploitation of notions of character akin to Pirandello's.

Masks. Carried over from proto-dramatic religious ritual, masks indicating comedy or tragedy were an invariable part of Greek and Roman drama. Thereafter they fell into disuse in the West except for the occasional extraordinary and fantastic disguise, where they can be regarded as an extension of MAKE-UP until modern times. In the early twentieth century new study of Eastern drama, particularly NO, inspired a number of attempts to reinstate the mask, notably in some plays of YEATS and in EXPRESSIONIST drama. At present they are little used, though there have been eccentric exceptions (e.g. in WILLIAM GASKILL's production of JOHN ARDEN'S *The Happy Haven*, 1960).

Masque. Form of spectacular entertainment developed as a court diversion for special occasions in Elizabethan times and brought to the peak of elaboration in the reigns of James I and Charles I. It seems to have evolved from the simple mummers' play, and arrived in England via Italy and France as a suite of songs, dances, and rich poetical recitation, all cast in the form of an intricate compliment to the patron of the festivities, usually the ruler. The principal geniuses of the masque were BEN JONSON as writer and INIGO JONES as designer and stager; unfortunately they did not get on well, as they were working to different ends, and Jonson retired in 1634, leaving Jones to make the visual side increasingly elaborate and ingenious without corresponding splendour in the words. The form died a natural death with the Commonwealth, but contributed something to the spectacular 'English opera' which came in with the Restoration. The anti-masque was a comic-grotesque prelude to the main business; the device, also found in very primitive forms of mummers' song and dance, seems to have been invented or re-invented by Jonson.

Massinger, Philip (1583–1640). English dramatist, of a more prosaic type than most of the leading Jacobeans, hence probably his relative neglect. His best play is *A New Way to Pay Old Debts* (1631 or 1632), a satirical comedy-drama with a splendid actor's role, Sir Giles Overreach, which has helped to keep it in the repertory; other works include the tragi-comedy *A Maid of Honour* (*c*.1621), the comedies *The City Madam* (1632) and *The Guardian* (1633), and the tragedy *The Roman Actor* (1626), as well as many collaborations, of which the most notable are *The Virgin Martyr* (with DEKKER, 1620) and *Beggars' Bush*, a rustic comedy (with FLETCHER, 1615–22). Massinger's plays are all straightforward, solidly built and unsensational; qualities which do not help him in competition with his gaudier and more picturesque contemporaries.

Master Builder, The (Bygmester Solness). Drama by HENRIK IBSEN, first performed Berlin, 1893.

Master of Santiago, The (Le Maître de Santiago). Historical drama by HENRY DE MONTHERLANT, first performed Paris, 1948.

Matchmaker, The. Comedy by THORNTON WILDER, based on his earlier adaptation from Nestroy, *The Merchant of Yonkers* (1938), first performed Edinburgh Festival, 1954. Musical version, *Hello, Dolly!*, book by Michael Stewart, music and lyrics by Jerry Herman, first performed New York, 1964.

Matinée. Early performance, not, as the name suggests, in the morning as a rule, but in the afternoon or early evening. Most British theatres have an early evening matinée on Saturdays and one afternoon matinée earlier in the week.

Maugham, W. Somerset (1874–1965). English novelist and dramatist. Wrote innumerable plays, novels, short stories, essays, travel books, and books of all sorts. His great period as a dramatist was in the 1920s, when he wrote in quick succession several of the wittiest and most elegant comedies of manners in the English language. Before that he had been for some fifteen years one of London's most successful dramatists, beginning spectacularly in 1907 with *Lady Frederick*, followed at once by *Mrs Dot*, *Jack Straw*, and *The Explorer*, which were all running simultaneously in the West End by the middle of

1908. The first three were light comedies, and so were most of his other successes. When he turned to more serious themes the public seemed less ready to accept his work, though there were exceptions, notably *Caesar's Wife* (1919), *East of Suez* (1922), *The Letter* (1927), and *The Sacred Flame* (1928), only the first and last of which, however, could really qualify as 'serious'. But the plays of his which survive now are the social comedies of the 1920s: *Our Betters, Caroline, Home and Beauty, The Circle, The Constant Wife, The Breadwinner.* They remain very much of their period, but their wit and acuteness of observation, which helped at the time to give Maugham a great reputation for cynicism, keep them permanently fresh and attractive. The relative failure of his bitter comedy *Sheppey* in 1933 confirmed Maugham in his resolve to abandon the theatre, and he did not write another play. Apart from his own plays, a number of his stories have been adapted by other dramatists, the most famous example being *Rain*, adapted by John Colton and Clemence Randolph.

Mauriac, François (b. 1884). French novelist and dramatist, very much in that order: he had already been a leading novelist for some years when he first wrote a play, *Asmodée*, staged by the Comédie-Française in 1939. It is a rather gloomy drama of temptation, set in the upper middle class, like most of his works. His later plays are along much the same lines, though they have in general had less success: they are *Les Mal Aimés* (1939), *Le Passage du malin* (1947), and *Le Feu sur la terre* (1950).

Mayakovsky, Vladimir (1893–1930). Russian poet and dramatist, deeply involved in the theatrical experiments of the just post-Revolutionary period. He wrote the first Soviet play, *Mystery-Bouffe*, produced in Moscow in 1918: an ecstatic vision of communist revolution spreading to all corners of the world. Then, after ten years devoted largely to poetry, came one of his two enduring masterpieces, *The Bed Bug* (1929), which recounts in extravagantly satirical terms the efforts of an old-fashioned bourgeois and a bed bug, catapulted into a communist future, to come to terms with it all. In 1930 he turned on contemporary Soviet society, and in *The Bath House* produced a wildly comic but biting picture of the way elements of the old bourgeois mentality lived on in Soviet Russia. In both plays Mayakovsky was closely associated with the experimental director MEYERHOLD, who gave them highly formalized productions full of extravagant invention. Mayakovsky committed suicide in 1930, and at the same time the trend of Soviet drama was directed away from what he stood for; his plays, however, despite periods of official disapproval, have continued to be revived ever since. In Moscow a theatre has been named after him.

Me and My Girl. Musical comedy by Noel Gay, book by L. Arthur Rose and Douglas Furber. First performed London, 1937. The great success of the war years, and originator of the 'Lambeth Walk'.

Measure for Measure. Dark comedy by WILLIAM SHAKESPEARE, written *c*.1604.

Medea. Tragedy by EURIPIDES, first performed Athens, 431 B.C.

Medieval theatre. After the disappearance of drama in Europe at the end of the classical era, it began to revive in the Middle Ages as a by-product and in certain respects an elaboration of Church ritual. Much of this already fell naturally into elementary dialogue form, with responses and antiphonal singing, and one of the regular parts of the Easter services, the '*Quem quaeritis*', which reproduces the conversation between the angel and the two Marys at the tomb, came to be regularly enacted as a little dramatic tableau. This gradually evolved, by the addition of other scenes and lyrical elements, into a liturgical play, and soon other festivals of the Church were also marked in the same way, particularly Christmas. In the twelfth century too scholars started writing plays on biblical themes for performance in churches (the plays of HROSWITHA were not intended for performance and are quite outside this tradition, being isolated essays in a classical style). By the end of the thirteenth century there was a flourishing tradition of vernacular religious drama closely allied with the Church all over Europe. Little by little, though, the drama began to be moved from church to churchyard and from churchyard to market place, and there more and more secular influences were able to creep in, even though the themes remained essentially religious. The most common form at first was the mystery or miracle play, a series of dramatized scenes on subjects from the Bible, though often enlivened with broad humour and grotesque detail. In England and elsewhere these became the concern of the trade guilds, each of which would take over a particular episode for the performances (which usually took place on the feast of Corpus Christi, near mid-summer): the whole cycle would run from the Creation to the Last Judgement in the course of one day. Four cycles survive in England, those of York (forty-eight episodes), 'Coventry' (possibly not really from Coventry: forty-two), Wakefield (or 'Towneley': thirty-two) and Chester (twenty-five). There were also plays on the lives of saints, no English examples of which survive.

The greatest vogue of the mystery play was during the fourteenth and early fifteenth centuries. About half way through the period, though, they began to be supplanted in popularity by a new form, the morality play. This was an allegorical piece in which personified virtues and vices grappled for the soul of man; the main liveliness in the form tended to come in the depiction of the vices, where a lot of grotesquerie and broad humour was carried over from the mystery. The best known of the surviving moralities is *Everyman*, perhaps adapted from a Dutch original; others include John Skelton's *Magnyfycence* and the anonymous *Castell of Perseverance*. From the morality play evolved in Tudor times the moral interlude, where abstractions were partially replaced by individual human characters, and from that developed the fully fledged comedy and drama of Elizabethan times.

Meilhac, Henri (1831–97). French dramatist, author of many ephemeral comedies and vaudevilles, and, with Ludovic Halévy (1834–1908), librettist for many of Offenbach's operettas.

Meiningen Players. Troupe of actors formed by the Duke of Saxe-Meiningen in 1874, and one of the first in which ensemble playing shaped by a director in the modern sense of the term was a prominent feature. Many innovations were made in the company's productions between 1874 and 1890, especially in stage lighting and in the field of costume and scenery, where a meticulous attention to detail and period accuracy was enforced. The Duke excelled particularly as a director of crowd scenes, and his company had considerable influence on theatrical practice in this and other departments all over Europe as a result of its numerous and extensive tours.

Melodrama. Originally either (in Germany) a passage in an opera spoken with musical accompaniment or (in France) a passage in which the character says nothing while music expresses his emotions. From these contradictory senses, current from about 1780, emerged the modern meaning of an extravagant drama making full use of all the possibilities inherent in music, lighting, and stage machinery for the artificial heightening of emotion: the word first seems to have been applied in this way during the Empire in Paris, where Guilbert de Pixerécourt was the most popular writer of the day. His first play to be seen in England was *A Tale of Mystery*, adapted (without acknowledgement) by Thomas Holcroft in 1802. Many others followed, still using music as an important part of the play, but gradually the practice died out, and the popular theatres continued to exploit the genre simply as a straight drama of an unusually sensational type. During the Victorian period melodrama continued happily on two levels: as naïve popular entertainment and as a more elevated diversion (sometimes with pretensions to social significance) for the middle classes. Despite the advocacy of Irving, who had one of his biggest successes with *The Bells*, melodrama gradually became a derogatory term in the late nineteenth century; in the twentieth, though a natural taste for strong drama persists, it generally has to be disguised as something else.

Member of the Wedding, The. Drama by CARSON MCCULLERS, adapted from her own novel, first performed New York, 1950.

Menander (*c*.343–292 B.C.). Greek dramatist, leading figure of the New Comedy. For the rough topicalities of ARISTOPHANES Menander substituted an urbane social comedy with romantic overtones, and was immensely influential on the Roman comedy-writers TERENCE and PLAUTUS. He banished the chorus to the incidental role of providing irrelevant song and dance interludes between scenes and may be regarded as the father of modern comedy. Though his reputation was so high in antiquity none of his works survived, except in reference and quotation, until 1905, when a substantial group of fragments from four plays was found in Egypt. These were *Hero, Samia*, the *Epitrepontes*, and *Periciromene*, of which last enough survived to allow several conjectural restorations, the best known of which is Gilbert Murray's *The Rape of the Locks*. In 1957 a complete manuscript of another play by Menander, the *Dyskolos*, was discovered, and it has since had a number of performances. About half of another, *The Man from Sicyon*, was found in 1963.

Men without Shadows (Morts sans sépulture). Drama by JEAN-PAUL SARTRE, first performed Paris, 1946.

Mercer, David (b. 1928). British dramatist who made his name first in television with his ambitious play-trilogy *The Generations* (1961–3). Later television works, among them *A Suitable Case for Treatment* (1962), *In Two Minds* (1967) and *Let's Murder Vivaldi* (1968), have continued to treat Mercer's twin preoccupations, politics and mental illness, in various guises, as have his stage plays *Ride a Cock Horse* (1965), *Belcher's Luck* (1966), *After Haggarty* and *Flint* (both 1970).

Merchant of Venice, The. Comedy by WILLIAM SHAKESPEARE, written *c*.1596–7.

Mercury Theatre. Small theatre in Notting Hall Gate, London, opened by ASHLEY DUKES in 1933. It has always been the home of the Ballet Rambert; its principal claim to a place in dramatic history is as the post-war centre of the revival of poetic drama. Before the war it housed a production of *Murder in the Cathedral* (1935) and a season of verse plays under the management of Rupert Doone in 1937; after the war the tradition was renewed with showings of verse plays by CHRISTOPHER FRY, RONALD DUNCAN, Norman Nicholson, Anne

Ridler and other dramatists during seasons there by the Pilgrim Players.

Merman, Ethel (b. 1909). American star of musicals, noted for her direct, extravert style of playing (much admired by BRECHT) and for her ability to blast audiences out of their seats with a song. Began her career in vaudeville; her first straight stage part was in *Girl Crazy* (1930), and the success which really established her as an institution was in Cole Porter's *Anything Goes* (1934). Later shows include: *Red Hot and Blue* (1936), *Du Barry was a Lady* (1939), *Panama Hattie* (1940), *Something for the Boys* (1943), *Annie Get Your Gun* (1946), *Call Me Madam* (1950), *Gypsy* (1959).

Merrie England. Comic opera by Edward German, book by Basil Hood, first performed London, 1902. Remembered best for its 'English Dances', a favourite light orchestral selection, and for its bluff Edwardian patriotism.

Merry Widow, The (Die lustige Witwe). Operetta by Franz Lehar, book by Victor Leon and Leo Stein, first performed Vienna, 1905. Most famous and enduring of Viennese operettas from the period after the Strausses.

Merry Wives of Windsor, The. Comedy by WILLIAM SHAKESPEARE, written c.1598-9.

Messel, Oliver (b. 1905). English stage designer. Began career designing for COCHRAN revues from 1926 to 1931; here his light and sophisticated touch made him a reputation for wit and elegance; later work has added a romantic flavour to his image, establishing him as an expert in cobwebs and draped tulle, decaying summerhouses and Ruritanian rococo. Among the plays he has designed in London are *Glamorous Night* (1936), *A Midsummer Night's Dream* (1938), *The Lady's Not for Burning* (1949), *Ring Round the Moon* (1950), *The Dark is Light Enough* (1954); in New York he has designed, among others, *House of Flowers* (1954) and *Rashomon* (1959). He also worked on films such as *Caesar and Cleopatra*, *The Queen of Spades*, and *Suddenly Last Summer*.

Method. American adaptation of STANISLAVSKY's teachings on acting and direction, stressing mainly the building of the role (as detailed in *An Actor Prepares*) rather than the technical side of its presentation. The leading idea here is the complete losing of the actor in the role; the chief exponents of the Method (particularly LEE STRASBERG, ELIA KAZAN and others connected with the New York Actors' Studio) place great emphasis on improvisation and exercises to improve the actor's gifts of empathy, and the usual criticism of Method-trained actors, often if not always justified, is that they neglect diction and are effectively limited to naturalistic acting. If this is so, it is the result of the lop-sided view of Stanislavsky's ideas on the theatre presented by Method teachers, based as it is in effect on only one of his books which dealt rather specifically with the actors' preparation for performance rather than the performance itself.

Meyerhold, Vsevolod (1874–1940). Russian actor and director of primarily experimental interests. He began as an actor, and joined the Moscow Art Theatre at its inception in 1898. From 1902 to 1905 he toured in the provinces with his own Society of New Drama, acting and directing, and then went back to the Moscow Art Theatre at Stanislavsky's invitation to run the theatre's short-lived experimental studio. Subsequently he worked with Vera Komisarjevskaya's company, elaborating and putting into practice his own version of GORDON CRAIG's ideas, which reduced the role of the actor to a mere cog in the wheel of the director's vehicle. This led to disagreements, and from 1907 he worked at the Imperial Theatre and elsewhere until 1913, when he set up his own theatre studio. With the Revolution he threw himself enthusiastically into the Bolshevik cause, advocating a complete reorganization of the theatre (which was not carried out) and directing the first Soviet play, Mayakovsky's *Mystery-Bouffe*, in 1918. During the 1920s he had his own theatre, where he developed BIO-MECHANICS, a species of dramatic training which involved a considerable amount of almost acrobatic physical exercise and a detailed study of all the body's mimetic possibilities. His most brilliant productions at this time were two later plays by Mayakovsky, *The Bed Bug* and *The Bath House*. In the thirties, with the institution of SOCIALIST REALISM as the official style of Soviet theatre, he fell increasingly out of favour and his theatre was closed in 1938. In 1939 he was called to account for his 'formalist' tendencies and shortly afterwards disappeared: he is presumed to have died in prison.

Middle Comedy, see GREEK THEATRE.

Middleton, Thomas (1570?–1627). English dramatist, worked extensively in collaboration; also wrote a few notable plays himself. His best solo efforts are *A Trick to Catch the Old One* (1604–5), an ironic comedy of humours, and *Women Beware Women* (c.1621), a savagely witty tragedy of court manners; his most notable collaboration is *The Changeling* (with ROWLEY, 1622), an intense psychological drama. Elsewhere Middleton excelled especially in the vivid depiction of London low-life: among the plays exploring this vein are *The Honest Whore* (1604) and *The Roaring Girl* (1610), both written in collaboration with DEKKER, and *A Mad World, My Masters* (1606) and *Your Five Gallants* (1607). Standing rather apart from his other work is the political satire *A Game at Chess* (1624), which pictured the plots and plans to unite the royal families of England and France in terms of a chess game. Both *The Changeling* and *Women Beware Women* have been revived in the 1960s with considerable success.

Midsummer Night's Dream, A. Fantastic comedy by WILLIAM SHAKE-SPEARE, written *c.* 1695–6.

Mielziner, Jo (b. 1901). American stage designer, originally actor. His first designs were for *The Guardsman* (1924); has since designed numerous productions, ranging from Shakespeare (notably Gielgud's *Hamlet*, 1935) to musicals and light comedy to heavy drama. Among his designs (all in New York) are *Winterset* (1935), *The Women* (1937), *The Boys from Syracuse* (1938), *Knickerbocker Holiday* (1939), *Pal Joey* (1940), *Carousel* (1945), *Annie Get Your Gun* (1946), *A Streetcar Named Desire* (1947), *Summer and Smoke* (1948), *Death of a Salesman*, *South Pacific* (1949), *Guys and Dolls* (1950), *The King and I* (1951), *Picnic, Can-Can, Tea and Sympathy* (1953), *Cat on a Hot Tin Roof*, *The Lark* (1955), *The Most Happy Fella* (1956), *Sweet Bird of Youth, Gypsy* (1959). Also designed, with Eero Saarinen, the repertory theatre for the Lincoln Center for the Performing Arts in New York.

Mikado, The. 'Savoy opera' by W. S. GILBERT (book and lyrics) and Arthur Sullivan (music), first performed London, 1885.

Miles, Bernard (b. 1907). British actor, manager, and director. Most notable achievement the foundation of the Mermaid Theatre, first as an Elizabethan-style theatre in St John's Wood (1951) when productions included Purcell's *Dido and Aeneas* with Kirsten Flagstad and *Macbeth* in Elizabethan pronunciation, then later in a permanent building at Puddle Dock in the City of London, the first new theatre in the City for some three hundred years. He was also responsible for the text of the theatre's first production, *Lock Up Your Daughters* (adapted from Fielding), and has acted in or directed many more. Knighted 1969.

Miller, Arthur (b. 1915). American dramatist. Concerned mainly with a tragic view of the predicament of mid-century man and with expressing that view in a fairly prosaic way, drawing its strength from an Ibsenish brand of stage realism: even if Miller's plays move formally beyond these limits. His first success (1947) was *All My Sons* (though he had been writing plays since university days in the mid 1930s). It is a highly-wrought denunciation of war-profiteering. In 1949 came *Death of a Salesman*, in which, approaching his death, an unsuccessful commercial traveller comes to terms for the first time with the unsatisfactory nature of his own life. Then in 1953 came *The Crucible*, in which witch-hunting in seventeenth-century Salem was, by implication, equated with witch-hunting under McCarthy in contemporary America. *A View from the Bridge* (1955) appeared in New York as a one-act play (with *A Memory of Two Mondays*) and then in an expanded version in London; again it concerns characters brought face to face with the truth about themselves. After an interval during which he wrote an original screenplay, *The Misfits*, came *After the Fall* (1964), another ambitious attempt to make the central character trace the root of his actions and understand them for what they are, which opened the new Lincoln Center theatre project in New York. A later play, *Incident at Vichy*, based on an inquiry which actually took place under the Nazis during the Second World War, was also produced by the Lincoln Center Company (1964). With *The Price* (1968) Miller returned to Broadway, and to the same sort of subject-matter as in *All My Sons*, a jockeying for position between two sons in a Jewish family dominated by its past. The result was generally regarded as his most satisfactory play for some years.

Millionairess, The. Comedy by GEORGE BERNARD SHAW, first performed Vienna, 1936.

Milne, A. A. (1882–1956). British novelist, dramatist, and essayist. He wrote a number of successful light comedies, among them *Mr Pim Passes By* (1919), *The Dover Road* (1923), and *The Truth about Blayds* (1923), but is best remembered now for his children's books *Winnie the Pooh* and *The House at Pooh Corner*, and for his children's play *Toad of Toad Hall* (1929), based on Kenneth Grahame's *The Wind in the Willows* and revived almost annually in London at Christmas-time.

Milton, John (1606–74). English poet and scholar. His only dramatic works meant for performance are two MASQUES (with rather more plot than usual in the form), *Arcades* (1633) and *Comus* (1634), on the subjects respectively of family affection and maiden purity. In 1671 he published another play, *Samson Agonistes*, this time a CLOSET DRAMA taking its subject from the Bible and its form from Greek tragedy; though not primarily meant for performance, it has been staged on a number of occasions.

Mime. Literally 'representation' (from the Greek). In the ancient world both popular and literary forms existed: the former being broad comic shows with a strong emphasis on action and gesture, the latter literary monologues and dialogues often, though not always, meant to be read rather than acted. In modern usage mime means specifically acting without speech; it evolved from certain aspects of the COMMEDIA DELL'ARTE and, as well as being used as a part of the ballet's and straight drama's repertory of expression, has found a place as a theatrical entertainment in its own right. In the early nineteenth century the great mime artist was the Frenchman DEBURAU and the form has subsequently been practised more in France than elsewhere; a revival begun in the 1920s by Étienne Decroux has subsequently found such powerful advocates as JEAN-LOUIS BARRAULT and MARCEL MARCEAU.

Miracle, The. Wordless mystery spectacle by Karl Volmöller, music by Engelbert Humperdinck, directed by MAX REINHARDT; first performed at Olympia, London, 1911.

Miracle Plays, see MEDIEVAL THEATRE.

Misalliance. Comedy by GEORGE BERNARD SHAW, first performed London, 1910.

Misanthrope, Le. Tragi-comedy by MOLIÈRE, first performed Paris, 1666.

Miser, The (L'Avare). Comedy by MOLIÈRE, first performed Paris, 1668.

Miss Julie (Fröken Julie). Drama by AUGUST STRINDBERG, first performed Copenhagen, 1889.

Mrs Dot. Comedy by W. SOMERSET MAUGHAM, first performed London, 1908.

Mrs Warren's Profession. Play by GEORGE BERNARD SHAW, written 1893–4, first performed London, 1902.

Mister Roberts. Service comedy by Thomas Heggen and JOSHUA LOGAN, first performed New York, 1948.

Mistinguett (real name Jeanne Bourgeois; 1875–1956). French star of music hall, legitimate comedy (briefly), and revue. Starting as a singer and character-comedienne, she became the leading star of the Moulin Rouge and then of the Folies-Bergère between the wars, her extravagant costumes and the settings for her songs and sketches being as renowned as the material itself and the way she performed it. She wrote an autobiography called simply *Mistinguett*.

Modjeska, Helena (1844–1909). Polish actress. Her career began in a touring company in 1861; she settled in Warsaw in 1866, proving herself capable in a variety of roles, but only achieved fame after her emigration to America in 1876. There, after a period away from the stage, she made a comeback acting in English in San Francisco (1877), had a triumphant success, and thereafter toured continuously until her retirement in 1905. She specialized in tragedy and strong drama, and was considered comparable to, if not the equal of, BERNHARDT and DUSE.

Moiseiwitsch, Tania (b. 1914). British stage designer. Worked at the Abbey Theatre, Dublin, 1935–9; joined the Old Vic in 1944–6; has designed many Shakespeare productions at Stratford on Avon and Stratford, Ontario, as well as at the Old Vic. Others of the innumerable productions she has designed include *Bless the Bride* (1947), *The Deep Blue Sea* (1952), *The Cherry Orchard* (Milan, 1955), and *The Wrong Side of the Park* (1960).

Molière (real name Jean-Baptiste Poquelin; 1622–73). French dramatist and actor; greatest French writer of comedy. He studied at the Jesuit College of Clermont and was intended for the law, but in 1643 threw up his prospective career and joined forces with a family of actors called Béjart to form a theatrical company, the Illustre-Théâtre. This company failed, but after a period in prison for debt Molière set out again with a company to tour the provinces, 1645–58. For this group he seems to have written short, partly improvised farces in the COMMEDIA DELL'ARTE tradition, but his first real success as a writer was a farce, *Le Docteur amoureux*, which the company played before the king on their arrival in Paris and which helped to secure them royal patronage and a permanent home, shared by an Italian company, at the Petit-Bourbon. The company had its first big successes, again with farces by Molière, and at the end of 1658 he wrote his first famous play, *Les Précieuses ridicules*, which satirized the affectations of the new élite. From then on Molière had an almost unbroken series of successes, as well as being called upon to devise court entertainments (the best known *L'Impromptu de Versailles*, 1663). After *Sganarelle, ou le cocu imaginaire* (1660), Molière's company moved to a larger home, the Palais-Royal, and there he produced in rapid succession *L'École des maris* (1661), *L'École des femmes* (1662) and *La Critique de l'école des femmes* (1662). In 1664 he wrote another famous play, *Le Tartuffe*, an attack on hypocrisy wearing the cloak of religion, but religious factions had the play suppressed and for some years it was given only in private or in a watered-down version. Among his later plays were *Don Juan, ou le festin de pierre* (1665), *Le Misanthrope* and *Le Médecin malgré lui* (1666), *Amphitryon*, *L'Avare*, and *Georges Dandin, ou le mari confondu* (1668), and the most lavish of the court entertainments, *Les Amants magnifiques* (1670). In 1671 Molière wrote for the court *Le Bourgeois Gentilhomme*, and for the Palais-Royal *Les Fourberies de Scapin*, and in 1672 and 1673 two of his most famous plays, *Les Femmes savantes* and *Le Malade imaginaire*. It was after acting in a performance of this latter that Molière died on stage in 1673. He was an excellent comic actor (though he failed in tragedy) and a good director, as well as being the first writer in the French theatre to raise comedy to the point where it could rank with tragedy as an entertainment for intelligent and cultured people.

Molina, Tirso de (1584–1648). Spanish dramatist and ecclesiastic, real name Gabriel Tellez. He claimed to have written four hundred plays, of which about eighty survive. Many of his plays are sophisticated and witty comedies, excelling particularly in the depiction of female characters; the most famous of them is *Don Gil de las Calzas Verdes*. He also wrote historical dramas, and the first notable dramatic treatment of the Don Juan story, *El Burlador de Sevilla y Convidado de Piedra* (published 1630).

Molnár, Ferenc (1878–1952). Hungarian dramatist whose farces and fantasies had some vogue between the wars. His most famous plays are *The Guardsman*, played in America by Alfred Lunt and Lynn Fontanne, and *Liliom* (1909), a fantasy about a return to earth by a dead man which is now most familiar as the basis of the Rodgers and Hammerstein musical *Carousel* (1945).

Monsieur Beaucaire. Romantic comedy by Booth Tarkington and Mrs E. G. Sutherland, based on the former's novel (1900); first performed New York, 1901. Also operetta based on the play and the novel, book by FREDERICK LONSDALE, music by André Messager, first performed London, 1919.

Montherlant, Henry de (1896–1972). French novelist and dramatist. Most of his playwriting was done in the relatively brief span of twelve years, 1942–54, during which he wrote eight plays. The first, *La Reine morte*, is an account of a conflict between love and politics, based on an incident in Spanish history. Other plays which turned back to history in order to study modern problems (the relation of Church and State, the spiritual and the practical) are *Malatesta* (written 1943–4, produced 1950), *Le Maître de Santiago* (written 1945, produced 1948), and *Port-Royal* (1954). His plays in modern settings are on the whole less successful: they are *Fils de personne* (1943) and its sequel *Demain il fera jour* (1948), and *Celles qu'on prend dans ses bras* (1950). *La Ville dont le prince est un enfant* (1951) stands rather apart, being a study of emotional attachments in a Paris boys' school which the author refused to let be performed on the stage for some years; it was finally staged in 1968. After *Port-Royal* Montherlant announced he would write no more plays and published a definitive collection, but since then three more have appeared: *Brocéliande* (1956), *Don Juan* (1958), and *Le Cardinal d'Espagne* (1960).

Month in the Country, A (Mesiats v derevne). Drama by IVAN TURGENEV, written 1850, first performed Moscow, 1872.

Moon for the Misbegotten, A. Drama by EUGENE O'NEILL, written 1943, first performed on tour in U.S. 1947; first New York production, 1957.

Moon in the Yellow River, The. Comedy by DENIS JOHNSTON, first performed Abbey Theatre, Dublin, 1931.

Moon on a Rainbow Shawl. Drama by ERROL JOHN, first performed Royal Court, London, 1958.

Morality play, see MEDIEVAL THEATRE.

Morgan, Charles (1894–1958). English novelist, dramatist, and dramatic critic. Was dramatic critic of *The Times* 1926–39. His plays – *The Flashing Stream* (1938), *The River Line* (1952), and *The Burning Glass* (1954) – are written in self-consciously beautiful mandarin prose which has not worn well.

Morley, Robert (b. 1908). English actor and dramatist. Has made a career in playing bumbling, blustering eccentrics; his first big success was in the title role of *Oscar Wilde* (1936); later roles include George IV in *The First Gentleman* and the lead in his own play (written in collaboration with Noel Langley) *Edward, My Son* (1947).

Mortimer, John (b. 1923). English novelist and dramatist. His first notable dramatic success was a one-acter, *The Dock Brief* (1957), which began life on radio, then went on to television and the stage. Subsequently he has written full-length stage plays, *The Wrong Side of the Park* (1960), *Two Stars for Comfort* (1962) and *The Judge* (1966), *A Voyage Round My Father* (1972), and several one-act plays, the best of which is *What Shall We Tell Caroline?* (1958), as well as numerous radio and television plays. All his works show great facility in the invention of lively dialogue and a gift for characterization of Dickensian grotesquery, though his full-length plays are not so satisfactory as the one-acters.

Moscow Art Theatre. The most famous and influential of Russian theatres, founded as a cooperative in 1898 by STANISLAVSKY and NEMIROVICH-DANCHENKO with a group made up partly of amateurs and partly of new graduates from the dramatic class of the Philharmonic Society. The company played (and still plays) in the easy, naturalistic style advocated by Stanislavsky, in contrast to the elaborately histrionic style then in vogue in Russia; it began to achieve success with the public when it put on as its fifth production a revival of Chekhov's *The Seagull*, which had previously been unsuccessfully staged elsewhere. The company then gave the first productions of Chekhov's *Uncle Vanya*, *Three Sisters*, and *The Cherry Orchard*; the most interesting other new play it produced in the period before the Revolution was Gorky's *The Lower Depths*. At the time of the Revolution the company was permitted by LUNACHARSKY to go on a long tour of Europe and America, which it did with great success, and on its return he allowed it to ease itself gradually into the Soviet scene. Few of the new plays produced by the company in its Soviet days (except Gorky's *Yegor Bulychev*) have been particularly notable, but it has remained the main inheritor of Stanislavsky's teaching (some of his productions are still in the repertoire) and the incomparable interpreter of Chekhov. Many of its first actors – among them Chekhov's widow Olga Knipper-Chekhova – remained with the company for the rest of their working lives, and the continuity of membership has produced a standard of ensemble playing almost without parallel elsewhere. As by-products of the main company the Moscow Art Theatre has supported from time to time studios to do experimental work. MEYERHOLD began one, somewhat abortively, in 1905, and another was set up by L. A. Sulerzhirsky in 1913, to be reconstituted in 1924 under the direction of Michael Chekhov.

Most Happy Fella, The. Musical by Frank Loesser (book and music), based on SIDNEY HOWARD's *They Knew What They Wanted*. First performed New York, 1956.

Mother, The (Die Mutter). Play by BERTOLT BRECHT, based on the novel by MAXIM GORKY and (partly) on an earlier dramatization by G. Stark and G. Weisenborn. First performed Berlin, 1932.

Mother Courage and Her Children (Mutter Courage und ihre Kinder). Chronicle play by BERTOLT BRECHT, written 1938–9, first performed Zürich, 1941.

Motley. Pseudonym of a group of three English stage designers, Sophia Harris (1901–66), Margaret F. Harris (b. 1904), and Elizabeth Montgomery (b. 1902). Their first production design was for the O.U.D.S. production of *Romeo and Juliet* (1932), since when they have designed three or four productions a year, including a lot of Shakespeare and a fair scattering of drawing-room comedy and drama, for which their rather negative, tasteful style is admirably suited; one of the partnership now lives permanently in New York.

Mourning Becomes Electra. Three-part drama by EUGENE O'NEILL, modelled on the ORESTEIA of Aeschylus; first performed by Theatre Guild, New York, 1931.

Mousetrap, The. Thriller by AGATHA CHRISTIE, first performed London, 1952, and still running, holding by several thousand performances the record for the longest run in British theatre.

Much Ado About Nothing. Comedy by WILLIAM SHAKESPEARE, written c.1598–9.

Muni, Paul (1895–1967). Real name Muni Weisenfreund. American actor. Began his career in the Yiddish theatre in 1918, and was then a member of the New York Jewish Art Theatre until 1926; his first

English-speaking part was in *We Americans* (1926). He had a great success in *Counsellor-at-Law* (1931) and then appeared exclusively in films until 1939, when he returned to Broadway in *Key Largo*. Major later roles were Willie Loman in *Death of a Salesman* (London, 1949) and Henry Drummond in *Inherit the Wind* (1955).

Munk, Kaj (1898–1944). Danish playwright. He was also a parish priest, and his most famous play, *Ordet* (*The Word*, 1932), had a religious theme, concerning a modern raising from the dead. His historical play *Cant*, based on the story of Henry VIII and Anne Boleyn, had some success also, and his last play, *Niels Ebbesen* (1943) achieved at least a temporary fame by being banned and published just before his death at the hands of the Nazis.

Murder in the Cathedral. Historical verse play by T. S. ELIOT, first performed in Canterbury Cathedral chapter-house during the Canterbury Festival, 1935.

Musical Chairs. Drama by Ronald Mackenzie, first performed London, 1931. One of the most highly-regarded British plays of the 1930s; famous partly for its (discreet) treatment of the subject of homosexuality.

Musical comedy. Form of play with interpolated songs and dances (not necessarily comical, though usually tending to the light-hearted) which evolved from the light opera and operetta in the 1890s and 1900s. The line between operetta and musical comedy has never been very clearly drawn, though most would agree that Lehar's *The Merry Widow* is operetta while the perceptibly lighter *Floradora* (by Leslie Stuart) is musical comedy. In the early days, with shows like *The Arcadians* (1909) in England or *The Belle of New York* in America, the form was primarily one for actor-singers; the principals might well require singing voices of almost operatic calibre. After the 1914–18 war, though, the genre became in general lighter, slighter, and faster-moving, with more dancing and less accent on romance but more comedy. For a while the old-fashioned romantic operettas of SIGMUND ROMBERG (*The Student Prince*, 1924; *The Desert Song*, 1926; *The New Moon*, 1928) and RUDOLPH FRIML (*Rose Marie*, 1924; *The Vagabond King*, 1925) flourished alongside the slicker, quicker entertainments of GEORGE GERSHWIN (*Lady, Be Good*, 1924; *Oh Kay*, 1926; *Funny Face*, 1927) and RODGERS and HART (*The Girl Friend*, 1926), but gradually the latter supplanted the former and during the 1930s reigned supreme in the work of Gershwin, Rodgers and Hart, COLE PORTER, IRVING BERLIN, and others. A solitary straw in the wind was the JEROME KERN–OSCAR HAMMERSTEIN *Show Boat* (1928), which told a quite serious dramatic story and integrated the songs with the narrative. When the vogue of the fast-talking, sophisticated musical comedy began to pass early in the war Hammerstein was able to return to this form (in collaboration with Richard Rodgers) in *Oklahoma!* (1943), which pushed the musical (as it now came to be called, dropping the 'comedy') in the direction of a sort of light folk-opera. This quasi-operatic tendency in the musical continued in the later works of Rodgers and Hammerstein, while the desire to integrate singing, dancing, and the spoken word into one continuous texture reached its culmination in *West Side Story* (1957). Meanwhile, some of the other spectacularly successful musicals of the period, notably *My Fair Lady* (1956), seemed to be looking back nostalgically towards the old operetta form. More recently devisers of musicals have turned increasingly to the making-over of recent dramatic successes, sometimes selected with desperate disregard for the reasonable possibilities of the musical form.

Music hall. Variety entertainment of songs and comic turns at which the audience could buy drink. The form flourished in Britain from about the middle of the nineteenth century to the First World War. It developed from the earlier tavern entertainments, which had grown to the proportions of minor theatres though still attached to public houses, thereby circumventing the laws which protected the theatrical monopoly of stage entertainments. Gradually with changes in the theatrical licensing laws, the pub connexion vanished, though it was normal for there to be bars around the main music hall so that the entertainment could be combined with alcoholic refreshment. The programmes of the music hall in its heyday really were 'variety': along with songs and comedy were acrobats, animal acts, and even interludes by legitimate actors, ballet dancers, etc. Most of the great stars of the halls devoted themselves entirely to them, each with his own material and his own stage character, immediately recognizable – ALBERT CHEVALIER as the cockney costermonger, GEORGE ROBEY with his eyebrows, LITTLE TICH with his elongated boots, VESTA TILLEY with her dandyish masculine rig. Others who decorated the music hall boards at the turn of the century were MARIE LLOYD, HARRY CHAMPION, HARRY LAUDER, Gus Elen, and George Formby, Sr.

With the introduction of licensing laws (1902 onwards), banishing drink from the auditorium, and the new competition of films and later radio, music hall proper faded out until it was kept up only as a faint reminder in spectacular West End variety shows at the Palladium or, with self-conscious antiquarian enthusiasm, at the Players' Theatre Club. The 1960s have seen something of a revival, however, starting just where music hall did originally: as free entertainment in bars of working-class public houses.

Musset, Alfred de (1810–57). French poet and dramatist who wrote some of the most enduring French plays of the nineteenth century. His first play, *La Nuit venétienne* (1830) was a failure, but many of his later plays, though written in the first instance as CLOSET DRAMAS, proved perfectly stageable and, when finally staged (the first, *Un Caprice*, by the Comédie-Française in 1847), were very successful. Though Musset as a poet is much given to Romantic attitudinizing, his plays are for the most part coolly ironical, mingling humour and melancholy in a manner slightly reminiscent of MARIVAUX and as much classical as Romantic. His major plays, *Fantasio* (1833, acted 1866), *Lorenzaccio* (1834, acted 1883), and *Les Caprices de Marianne* (1851) are romantic, fantastic, funny and bitter all together, though tending towards a romantic extravagance. This is absent from his one-act 'proverbs' – *Un Caprice*, *Il faut qu'une porte soit ouverte ou fermée* (1848), *Il ne faut jurer de rien* (1848), and *On ne saurait pas penser à tout* (1849) – and moderated in his *On ne badine pas avec l'amour*, an ironic picture of heartless love intrigues. All these remain in the regular French repertory.

My Fair Lady. Musical by Alan Jay Lerner (book and lyrics) and FREDERICK LOEWE (music) based on GEORGE BERNARD SHAW'S *Pygmalion*; first performed New York, 1956.

Mystery plays, see MEDIEVAL DRAMA.

N

Nash, N. Richard (b. 1916). American dramatist; real name Nusbaum. His best-known plays are the whimsical-philosophical fantasy *The Rainmaker*, based on an earlier television script and later filmed and turned into a musical, and *Second Best Bed*, a farce about Shakespeare.

Nathan, George Jean (1882–1958). American dramatic critic, one of the most famous and influential of his day. Became dramatic critic of the *New York Herald* in 1905, and from there carried on a campaign for the modern drama of ideas rather similar to that waged a decade or two earlier by GEORGE BERNARD SHAW in Britain. He championed IBSEN, STRINDBERG, and SHAW when they were unpopular minority tastes, and was one of the first to discover O'NEILL and to support O'CASEY and SAROYAN. Author of many books on the theatre, including *The Critic and the Drama* and *Testament of a Critic*; for many years he brought out an annual review of New York theatre.

Nathan the Wise (Nathan der Weise). Tragedy by GOTTHOLD LESSING, first performed posthumously, Berlin, 1783.

National Theatre. An issue and a dream since the time of GARRICK, a British national theatre only finally came to realization in 1963–4. The stages by which this came about have been many and complicated. Garrick advocated that a national theatre under direct patronage of the Crown (somewhat on the model of the COMÉDIE-FRANÇAISE) should be set up in the eighteenth century, while in the nineteenth Bulwer Lytton and IRVING, among others, were vocal champions of the cause. A more positive step was taken in 1910, when HARLEY GRANVILLE BARKER and WILLIAM ARCHER published *The National Theatre: A Scheme and Estimates* (revised and rewritten by Granville Barker in 1930), and at the same time a national agitation started for the marking of the tercentenary of Shakespeare's death (1916) by the building of a Shakespeare Memorial Theatre in London. The two schemes combined, and a joint committee was set up, but the First World War intervened to put an end to the plans. After the war the idea was again taken up, and in 1930 an appeal for subsidy was made to the Government, which rejected the possibility at that time but raised no objection in principle. By 1938 the money at the committee's disposal (through subscription and investment) had reached £150,000, and a site was bought in South Kensington and designs for the theatre drawn up, but again war intervened. After the war the committee arranged to exchange the South Kensington site for one on the South Bank, and in 1951 a foundation stone was actually laid, though no theatre showed any sign of following. Finally in 1963 the idea of, in effect, turning the OLD VIC into a national theatre was put into practice (other groups involved in the scheme, including the Royal Shakespeare Company, having withdrawn), the Old Vic formally ceased to exist, and in its place a new National Theatre Company under the directorship of SIR LAURENCE OLIVIER moved into its premises in the Waterloo Road, pending the building of a special theatre designed for it by Denys Lasdun on a new site on the South Bank, for opening in 1974.

National Youth Theatre, The. Organization founded in 1955 by the director Michael Croft to channel the energies of young people interested in the drama. In 1959 they had a notable critical success with a production of *Hamlet*, seen in the West End, and have since had frequent seasons presenting classics and latterly new, specially written plays such as PETER TERSON's *Zigger-Zagger* and *The Apprentices*. Many of the brighter young British actors in the commercial theatre and cinema today have been members of the company in their teens.

Naturalism. Late-nineteenth-century movement in the theatre, aimed at banishing artifice and making the theatre mirror life with the utmost directness and even crudity. In this it meant to move a step beyond the realism of IBSEN: the forerunner of Naturalism was ZOLA with his dramatization of his novel *Thérèse Raquin* (1873), and its major dramatist in France was HENRI BECQUE, with *Les Corbeaux* (1882) and *La Parisienne* (1885). Towards the end of the 1880s ANTOINE provided Naturalism with a home in his Théâtre Libre, and there Becque and others, among them the early STRINDBERG, found sympathetic audiences. The movement spread to Germany, Britain, Russia, and America, producing some notable works – perhaps the most notable GORKY's *The Lower Depths* (1902) – before its chief proponents – STRINDBERG, HAUPTMANN, and others – began to drift away into SYMBOLISM and new vogues in the theatre dismissed Naturalism as old-fashioned.

Nazimova, Alla (1879–1945). Russian actress who made her name on the St Petersburg stage and then in 1906 emigrated to America, where she achieved a major success in her first English-speaking role, Hedda Gabler. She specialized in Ibsen roles until she went into films, where she did much to raise the level of intelligence in the American cinema by adapting important stage works (her most famous film being a *Salome* inspired equally by Wilde and Beardsley). Later she returned to the stage, playing with such companies as THEATRE GUILD and the Civic Repertory Theatre in a variety of modern classics, among them *A Month in the Country* and *Mourning Becomes Electra*.

Nekrassov. Satirical comedy by JEAN-PAUL SARTRE, first performed Paris, 1955.

Nemirovich-Danchenko, Vladimir (1859–1943). Russian man of the theatre. With STANISLAVSKY founder and director of MOSCOW ART THEATRE. In his early days a successful novelist and author of light comedies, he was made director of the Moscow Philharmonic Society's Drama Course in 1891, and there began to put into practice ideas which his experience and observation had given him about the need for a more naturalistic style of acting in the Russian theatre. In 1897 he met Stanislavsky and decided to set up a new theatre company with him, bringing into the organization some of his own pupils from the Philharmonic Society. In the new theatre his responsibilities were principally literary, as he exercised the function of a *dramaturg*, selecting plays for production and so on as well as directing a number of productions himself, especially after Stanislavsky's death. Apart from the Moscow Art Theatre, Nemirovich-Danchenko also founded the Moscow Musical Studio, in which the same principles which underlay the Art Theatre's practice were applied to musical comedy and operetta; this was his principal activity in Russia during the period just after the Revolution, when Stanislavsky and the main company were on extended tour in Europe and America.

New Comedy, see GREEK THEATRE.

New Moon, The. Musical comedy by SIGMUND ROMBERG, book and lyrics by OSCAR HAMMERSTEIN II, Frank Mandel, and Lawrence Schwab; first performed New York, 1928.

New Tenant, The (Le Nouveau Locataire). One-act play by EUGÈNE IONESCO, written 1953, first performed Finland, 1955 (in Swedish), first French performance Paris, 1957.

New Way to Pay Old Debts, A. Comedy by PHILIP MASSINGER, first performed London, c. 1632.

Nichols, Peter (b. 1927). British dramatist, prolific author of television plays who made a name in the theatre with *A Day in the Death of Joe Egg* (1967), a tragi-comic study of the predicament of parents with a spastic child. His next stage play, *The National Health* (1969), concerns the dying in a hospital ward, and was first performed by the National Theatre. It was followed by *Forget-Me-Not Lane* (1971), *Chez Nous* (1974), *The Freeway* (1974), and *Privates on Parade* (1977).

Nicoll, Allardyce (b. 1894). British theatre historian, author of many books on the history of British and world drama and on various aspects of theatrical theory and practice. His magnum opus is perhaps his six-volume *History of English Drama 1660–1900* with check-lists of plays arranged by dramatists; other important books are his popular comprehensive volumes *British Drama* and *World Drama*, and such more specialized works as *Stuart Masques and the Renaissance Stage* and *The World of Harlequin* (on *commedia dell' arte*), as well as the annual *Shakespeare Survey*, which he edits. Allardyce Nicoll has also been a professor of English at London University, Professor of History of Drama at Yale, and Director of the Shakespeare Institute, Stratford-on-Avon.

Night Must Fall. Thriller by EMLYN WILLIAMS, first performed London, 1935.

Noah (Noé). Biblical drama by ANDRÉ OBEY, first performed by the Compagnie des Quinze, Paris, 1931.

Noddy in Toyland. Fairy play for children by Enid Blyton, music by Philip Green; first performed London, 1954, and subsequently revived regularly as a Christmas attraction.

No Exit, see HUIS-CLOS.

No, No, Nanette. Musical comedy by VINCENT YOUMANS, book by Otto Harbach and Frank Mandel (based on a play, *His Lady Friends*, by Frank Mandel and Emile Nyitray, adapted from a novel by May Edginton), lyrics by Otto Harbach and Irving Caesar. First performed Chicago, 1925.

No (or Noh) play. Form of Japanese theatre, a species of lyrical drama which evolved around the beginning of the fifteenth century, traditionally in the work of Kwanami and his son Seami, though the language in which the plays attributed to them are written suggests a century or so earlier and the maturity of the form seems to indicate a century or two of tradition behind them. The form as it now exists has remained fixed since the early seventeenth century, and consequently it remains, as it has always been, a more specialized, highbrow taste than the decadent popular version KABUKI. No plays are performed on a square stage raised slightly from the ground (on which the audience sit on two sides); to one side is a balcony housing a chorus of ten singers, and at the back there is another, smaller stage occupied by four musicians and two stage hands. The actors make their entrances and exits along a long slanting walk which recedes from the left-hand side of the stage. The stage has no scenery, and locations are represented only by a small conventionalized framework with a roof to indicate the presence of a building. The plays are performed by two actors essentially, though they have companions in various scenes; the second actor (*waki*) introduces the action with a chant explaining the type of play to be performed, then the first actor (*shite*) appears disguised (he wears a mask as well as a very elaborate costume), delivers a chant of his own, then converses with the second actor so that the theme of the play and the real character of the first actor, a god or hero, emerge. The rest of the play then consists of highly formalized dances, generally in five movements, by the first actor; preceded by an interlude in which an actor in ordinary costume tells the story of the play in plain prose. An evening's No entertainment would consist of five plays separated by three *kyogen*, short farcical interludes performed generally in ordinary costume and frequently parodying the themes and characters of the No plays themselves. The whole entertainment lasts for about seven hours, beginning at ten in the morning or one in the afternoon.

Norman, Frank (b. 1931). English novelist and dramatist, deviser of two musicals presented by Theatre Workshop and elaborated under the guidance of JOAN LITTLEWOOD: *Fings Ain't Wot They Used T'Be* (1959) with music by LIONEL BART, and *A Kayf Up West* (1964) with music by Stanley Myers. Both are lively and picturesque excursions into Soho low life.

No Room at the Inn. Drama by Joan Temple, first performed London, 1945. Sensational story of evacuee children and their sufferings at the hands of an unscrupulous landlady.

Novello, Ivor (1893–1951). Real name David Ivor Davies. British composer, dramatist, and actor. Coming of a family of musicians, he began his career as a composer, and achieved a spectacular success in the First World War with his song *Keep the Home Fires Burning*, as well as contributing numbers to various musicals and revues, starting with *Theodore and Co* (1916). During the 1920s he became an actor on stage and screen, and began writing straight plays, his first and one of his most successful being *The Rat* (1924), which he wrote in collaboration with Constance Collier, and starred in himself. His best remembered works, though, are the series of romantic musicals he wrote, composed, and (generally) starred in between 1935 and his death: the first four of them, *Glamorous Night* (1935), *Careless Rapture* (1936), *Crest of the Wave* (1937), and *The Dancing Years* (1939), were presented successively at Drury Lane, and the last, revived in 1942, became a permanent feature of the war-time theatre scene. Later musicals by Novello include *Arc de Triomphe* (1943), *Perchance to Dream* (1945), *King's Rhapsody* (1949), in which he was appearing at the time of his death, and *Gay's the Word* (1951).

Nymph Errant. Musical comedy by COLE PORTER, book by Romney Brent, based on a novel by James Laver; first performed London, 1933.

O

Oberammergau. See PASSIONPLAY.

Obey, André (1892–1975). French dramatist, best known for the works
produced during his three years with Copeau's COMPAGNIE DES
QUINZE which he joined in 1929. For them he wrote three plays, all
produced in 1931: *Le Viol de Lucrèce*, *La Bataille de la Marne*, and
Noé. They are written in a free, non-realistic form, using in some
cases lyrical narration and always giving much opportunity for
formalized, mimetic staging. After leaving the Compagnie des Quinze
he wrote French adaptations of Shakespeare and Sophocles, and a
Don Juan (1934), rewritten in 1950 as *L'Homme de cendres*. His most
interesting later works are *Lazare* (1951), a severe dramatic handling
of the story of Lazarus, and *Plus de miracles pour Noël* (*Frost at
Midnight*, 1957), a medieval drama built around the performance of
a nativity play.

Obratsov, Sergei (b. 1901). Russian puppeteer and director of the
Russian State Puppet Theatre. As an individual artist Obratsov is
best-known for his burlesque songs and musical sketches with glove
puppets, which caricature a number of perennial types – the vain
soprano, the bumptious artiste, the drunk – with Gogolian gusto.

O'Casey, Sean (1880–1964). Irish dramatist who made his reputation
in the 1920s with a group of bitter comedy-dramas set in the Dublin
slums. His first play, *The Shadow of a Gunman* (1923) is set in a
Dublin tenement and shows the effect of the battles in Ireland in
1920 on the people living there. It was followed by *Juno and the
Paycock* (1924), a tragedy of slum life, and *The Plough and the Stars*
(1926), which concerns the 1916 Easter Rising; these remain
O'Casey's most famous and arguably his most successful plays. With
The Silver Tassie (1928) O'Casey began to modify his realistic style
somewhat by introducing symbolic elements, at first with mixed success, although *Purple Dust* (1940) and *Red Roses for Me* (1946),
respectively a rustic comedy contrasting the English and Irish
temperaments and a high-charged symbolic drama about the state of
Ireland, can compare with his best work. Later plays, such as *Cock-
a-Doodle Dandy* (1949) and *The Drums of Father Ned* (1956) have been
more capricious but burst with life and energy not altogether successfully harnessed. From 1928, when the ABBEY THEATRE, which had
produced O'Casey's earlier plays, rejected *The Silver Tassie*, O'Casey
lived in England, and for some years refused to allow his plays to be

performed in Ireland, or at least at the Abbey – a restriction he finally relaxed.

Occupe-toi d'Amélie. Farce by GEORGES FEYDEAU, first performed Paris, 1908. See also LOOK AFTER LULU.

Odets, Clifford (1906–1963). American dramatist, associated during the most fruitful years of his career with GROUP THEATRE. His first great success was the one-act play *Waiting for Lefty* (1935), a somewhat doctrinaire left-wing study of a taximen's strike which worked on stage because of its great flair in handling a free, almost cinematic form. He followed this with a revision of an earlier-written play, *Awake and Sing* (1935), an effective drama of a working-class Jewish family's struggles, and with *Golden Boy* (1937), which concerned a young musician forced to make a living prize-fighting. None of his later plays lived up to these, though after failures with *Night Music* (1940) and *Clash by Night* (1941) he retrieved his position commercially with *The Big Knife* (1949) and *The Country Girl* (1950, called *Winter Journey* in Britain), both set in show-business milieux. His best later writing is probably to be found in another show-business story, the script of the film *The Sweet Smell of Success* (1957).

Ocdipus at Colonus. Tragedy by SOPHOCLES, first performed Athens after the author's death in 406 B.C. Sequel to *Oedipus Rex*.

Oedipus Rex. Tragedy by SOPHOCLES, first performed Athens, c.425 B.C.

Off-Broadway. A group of theatres in New York, clustered round Greenwich Village and mid- and uptown on the east side, which are organized on shoe-string budgets and present new plays of a more or less experimental (or at least non-commercial) type, foreign plays, revivals, etc. The theatres are smaller than on Broadway, often improvised in halls or cellars, and the actors and technicians are paid at lower rates than the American unions require for full-scale Broadway shows, while various other union restrictions are also waived. Much of the most lively American theatre today comes from, and often stays, off-Broadway.

Oh Dad, Poor Dad, Mamma's Hung You in the Closet and I'm Feelin' So Sad. Comedy by ARTHUR KOPIT, first professionally performed London, 1961.

Oh What a Lovely War! Musical evocation and critique of the First World War evolved by JOAN LITTLEWOOD, Charles Chilton and the THEATRE WORKSHOP company, first performed Theatre Royal, Stratford, London, 1963.

Oklahoma! Musical by RICHARD RODGERS, book and lyrics by

OSCAR HAMMERSTEIN II, based on the play *Green Grow the Lilacs* (1931) by Lynn Riggs, first performed New York, 1943.

Old Bachelor, The. Comedy by WILLIAM CONGREVE, first performed Drury Lane, London, 1693.

Old Comedy, see GREEK THEATRE.

Old Vic. Theatre and theatre company taking their name from the Victoria Theatre (built in 1818 as the Coburg Theatre) in the Waterloo Road. It was taken over in 1880 by Emma Cons as a temperance music hall, under the name of the Royal Victoria Hall and Coffee Tavern; later Emma Cons's niece LILIAN BAYLIS introduced into its programme of music and lectures, films, opera, and in 1914 drama, in the shape of a Shakespeare season. By 1923 all Shakespeare's plays had been performed there. From then on until 1940 the theatre had a company contracted for a season at a time – through which passed virtually every British actor to make a mark between the wars – and concentrated mainly on Shakespeare, with occasional revivals of other dramatists. From 1931, shortly after Lilian Baylis opened Sadler's Wells as a new home for opera, it concentrated entirely on drama. In 1940 the theatre was bombed, but the company continued its activities on tour or at the New Theatre, London, which became its temporary home until the Waterloo Road theatre was reopened in 1950. After the war it was devoted less exclusively to Shakespeare, aiming rather to provide an all-round classical repertoire in keeping with its position as an unofficial national theatre. In 1963 negotiations for it to be merged into a new permanent national theatre were completed, and the company was officially dissolved, to be replaced at Waterloo Road (pending completion of new premises on the South Bank) by the NATIONAL THEATRE Company.

Oliver! Musical by LIONEL BART, based on Charles Dickens's *Oliver Twist* (1839), first performed London, 1960.

Olivier, Laurence (b. 1907). English actor and director. His first stage appearance was as Katharine in *The Taming of the Shrew* in 1922 at the Festival Theatre, Stratford-on-Avon, in a special boys' performance. From 1926 to 1928 he was with the Birmingham Repertory Company, and made his first notable London appearance with them in 1928 in various parts, among them the Young Man in *The Adding Machine* and Marcellus in *Back to Methuselah*. From then on he was established as a leading actor, generally in romantic drama (*Beau Geste*, 1929) or comedy (Victor in *Private Lives*, 1930), until in 1935 he returned to Shakespeare with JOHN GIELGUD's memorable production of *Romeo and Juliet* in which he alternated the roles of Romeo and Mercutio with John Gielgud. During his first season (1937) with the Old Vic he confirmed his position as one of our leading Shakespearian actors by playing Hamlet (complete), Henry V, Macbeth, and Sir Toby in *Twelfth Night*, his reading of the more extravert roles being in general preferred to his forthright version of the gloomy Dane. The following year with the Old Vic he played Iago in *Othello*, Caius Marcius in *Coriolanus*, and Vivaldi in Bridie's *The King of Nowhere*. After a period in America and in films he returned to the Old Vic in 1944 as co-director, and played a variety of roles with the company, including the Button Moulder in *Peer Gynt*, Sergius in *Arms and the Man*, Richard III, Astrov in *Uncle Vanya*, Hotspur in *Henry IV* Part I and Shallow in *Henry IV* Part II, Oedipus Rex, and Puff in *The Critic*. He remained with the Old Vic until 1949, taking part in its visits to Paris, New York, Australia and New Zealand and adding to his repertoire King Lear, Mr Antrobus in *The Skin of Our Teeth*, Sir Peter Teazle in *The School for Scandal*, and the Chorus in Anouilh's *Antigone*. Later roles have included the Duke in Christopher Fry's *Venus Observed* (1951), with which he began a period of management at the St James's Theatre, Caesar in *Caesar and Cleopatra* and Antony in *Antony and Cleopatra* (1951), the Grand Duke in Rattigan's *The Sleeping Prince* (1953), Macbeth, Titus Andronicus and Malvolio in *Twelfth Night* at Stratford (1955), Archie Rice in John Osborne's *The Entertainer* (1957), Coriolanus at Stratford (1959), Bérenger in Ionesco's *Rhinoceros* (1960), and first Becket, then Henry II in Anouilh's *Becket* in New York (1961). In 1962 he became director of the CHICHESTER FESTIVAL at the new Festival Theatre there, and himself played in *Uncle Vanya*, Ford's *The Broken Heart*, and Fletcher's *The Chances*; in 1963 he was appointed director of the NATIONAL THEATRE, and in 1964 played Othello there for the first time. During the following years he remained very active as an acting member of the National Theatre Company, sometimes in relatively small roles; his major performances have included the Captain in *The Dance of Death* (1967) and Shylock (1970). He has also acted in many films, and directed and starred in three notable films of Shakespeare plays, *Henry V*, *Hamlet* and *Richard III*. He has been married to three actresses, Jill Esmond, VIVIEN LEIGH, and JOAN PLOWRIGHT. He was knighted for services to the theatre in 1947 and made a life-peer in 1970.

On Approval. Farce by FREDERICK LONSDALE, first performed London, 1927.

Ondine. Fantasy by JEAN GIRAUDOUX, first performed Paris, 1939.

O'Neill, Eugene (1888–1953). American dramatist. Son of a successful actor, James O'Neill, he began his career as a journalist, but then turned to the stage and wrote a number of plays which first reached performance in Provincetown, Massachusetts, by an enterprising summer stock company, the Provincetown Players – most notably the group of one-act plays of the sea (1916–18) later grouped under the titles *S.S. Glencairn* (for New York production, 1924) or *The Long Voyage Home* (for filming and later in book form). His first full-length play produced in New York, *Beyond the Horizon* (1920), a realistic rural drama, was a success and won him his first Pulitzer Prize. From then until 1934 he poured out plays in an almost continuous flow. Among the successes were *The Emperor Jones* (1920), a romantic drama about a self-appointed Negro ruler; *Anna Christie* (1921) a melodrama about the redemption by love of a fallen woman; *The Hairy Ape* (1922), a symbolic drama along rather EXPRESSIONIST lines; *All God's Chillun Got Wings* (1924), a drama about a mixed marriage; *Desire Under the Elms* (1924), a tense emotional drama set on a New England farm; *The Great God Brown* (1926), another Expressionist-influenced symbolic drama; *Marco Millions* (1928), a comedy-satire on big business; *Strange Interlude* (1928) a vast, nine-act emotional drama which studies the mental processes of its characters by extensive use of asides and soliloquies; *Mourning Becomes Electra* (1931), an equally lengthy re-enactment of the *Oresteia* set in New England after the Civil War; and *Ah, Wilderness!* (1933), a graceful, nostalgic comedy. In 1936 he was awarded the Nobel Prize for literature.

After this O'Neill disappeared from the theatre until 1946, when he allowed *The Iceman Cometh* (written 1939) to be produced. A philosophical drama about emotional derelicts, it had some success, particularly with the critics, unlike its companion-piece, *A Moon for the Misbegotten* (written 1943), which closed on tour in 1947. This was the last new play by O'Neill to be produced until after his death, when in 1956 his autobiographical *Long Day's Journey into Night* (written 1940–41) was performed in Stockholm and New York. With an off-Broadway revival of *The Iceman Cometh*, this started up a major revival in his reputation; it has been followed by another play from the same autobiographical series, *A Touch of the Poet* (written 1940, produced 1957), and yet another, *More Stately Mansions* (written 1938, produced Stockholm, 1963). O'Neill's reputation as a dramatist still remains, however, more a matter of controversy than that of any other major figure in twentieth-century drama, mainly because of his seeming insensitivity to words, which works against his ambitious conceptions and his evident dramatic flair.

One-night stand. Production given in a particular theatre or hall for one night only. A tour of one-night stands is one of the most gruelling forms of theatrical activity, and is usual only in popular entertainments – musical and variety. Plays are staged thus only in isolated areas with no other theatrical activity or accommodation for it.

One Way Pendulum. 'Farce in a new dimension' by N. F. SIMPSON, first produced by the English Stage Company, Royal Court, London, 1960.

Only Way, The. Romantic drama by Freeman Wills and Frederick Langbridge, based on Charles Dickens's novel *A Tale of Two Cities* (1859), first performed London, 1899. Sidney Carton was the most famous role of the actor-manager Sir John Martin Harvey.

O.P., see PROMPT.

Open-air theatre. Until the institution of permanent roofed theatres in Elizabethan times nearly all dramatic performances were given in the open air, but thereafter the practice was abandoned, except for occasional MASQUES and PAGEANTS, until the late nineteenth century, when again it became fashionable, especially among amateurs. The most famous open-air theatre in Britain is that in Regent's Park, founded in 1933, where seasons of Shakespeare and occasionally other suitable plays are given each summer – under cover when wet.

Open stage, see STAGE.

Opéra comique, see COMIC OPERA.

Operetta, see MUSICAL COMEDY.

Operette. Musical play by NOËL COWARD, first performed London, 1938.

Oresteia. Trilogy of plays by AESCHYLUS, consisting of the *Agamemnon*, the *Choephori* (or *Libation-Bearers*), and the *Eumenides*, first performed Athens, 485 B.C.

Orpheus Descending. Drama by TENNESSEE WILLIAMS, first performed New York, 1956; based on the author's earlier play *Battle of Angels*, first performed Boston, 1940.

Orton, Joe (1933–67). British dramatist, specialist in black comedy full of innuendo conveyed in tones of precarious gentility. Most successful play, *Entertaining Mr Sloane* (1964) followed by *Loot* (1966) and the posthumously produced *What the Butler Saw* (1968), in similar style.

Osborne, John (b. 1929). English dramatist. Began his career as an actor, and wrote three plays in collaboration before *Look Back in Anger* (1956), which was the first play by a new dramatist produced by the ENGLISH STAGE COMPANY at the Royal Court and in effect set off a whole revival of British drama. Its success was mainly due to the angry rhetoric voiced by the central character, Jimmy Porter. Osborne's next play to appear, *Epitaph for George Dillon* (produced 1957 but written earlier, in collaboration with ANTHONY CREIGHTON), had greater complexity in depiction of character-conflicts, but *The Entertainer* (1957), despite the advocacy of SIR LAURENCE OLIVIER, failed to integrate the realistic style of the body of the work with the BRECHT-inspired, non-realistic, music-hall framework. The following work, the musical *The World of Paul Slickey* (1959), was generally agreed to be a failure, but with *Luther* (1961) Osborne scored another major success with critics and public. This he followed with two one-act plays under the general title *Plays for England: The Blood of the Bambergs* and *Under Plain Cover,* the first a feeble semi-satirical farce but the second a quite accomplished character-study on the theme of sexual fetishism in marriage. Then came *Inadmissible Evidence* (1964), a savage piece of character-analysis widely regarded as his best play since *Look Back in Anger*, and *A Patriot for Me* (1965), a loosely organized historical drama telling the story of the spy Redl and his career in the pre-1914 Austrian army. In 1968 two further plays, *Time Present* and *The Hotel in Amsterdam*, both modern dramas, were produced consecutively at the Royal Court. Later plays here included *West of Suez* (1971) and *A Sense of Detachment* (1973). Osborne has also written for television (*A Subject of Scandal and Concern*, 1960).

Ostrovsky, Alexander (1823–86). Russian dramatist. He trained as a lawyer, though he never qualified, and spent some years around the courts in Moscow before writing the first play to bring him fame, *The Bankrupt* (later known as *It's All in the Family*, 1848). This realistic picture of life among the unscrupulous merchant class was banned by the censors but circulated in manuscript and gave Ostrovsky a considerable reputation even before it was performed. Meanwhile his comedy *Poverty is No Disgrace* had had a considerable success and between 1855 and his death Ostrovsky wrote more than eighty plays, as well as numerous translations of Molière, Dumas, and Shakespeare. Among them were historical dramas such as *Kozma Minin* and *Vassilissa Melentyeva* and the fantasy *The Snow Maiden*, later made into an opera by Rimsky-Korsakov, but his most successful works were his social dramas and comedies, usually set among the middle class and minor aristocracy; they include *A Profitable Job* (1857), *Wild Money* (1859), *The Ward* (1859), *Without Dowry* (1863), *The Forest* (1870), *Wolves and Sheep* (1872), *Talents and Suitors*

(1882), and his most famous play, *The Storm* (1860), a gloomy study of life in the Russian provinces. Most of Ostrovsky's plays were produced at the MALY THEATRE, which became generally known as the House of Ostrovsky. In 1885 Ostrovsky was made manager of the Moscow Imperial Theatre, the first professional to hold this post; he also founded the Society of Russian Playwrights and a dramaitc school at which he trained actors in the style most suitable for his own plays.

Othello. Tragedy by WILLIAM SHAKESPEARE, written *c.*1602–3.

Otway, Thomas (1652–85). English dramatist, best remembered now as the author of *Venice Preserved* (1682), much praised at the time and since as the finest post-Jacobean tragedy. Otway's first play, *Alcibiades* (1675) was an instant success, and was followed by another tragedy, in rhymed verse, *Don Carlos*, and a comedy, *Friendship in Fashion*, before the author joined the army, supposedly because of a disappointment in love. His two best plays, *The Orphan, or The Unhappy Marriage* (1680) and *Venice Preserved, or A Plot Discovered* (1681), were both written and performed on his return. He also adapted various works from the French, among them Racine's *Bérénice* (as *Titus and Berenice*, 1676) and Molière's *Les Fourberies de Scapin*.

O.U.D.S. Oxford University Dramatic Society, founded 1885 by a group of undergraduates including Arthur Bourchier and Cosmo Gordon Lang, later Archbishop of Canterbury and cousin of the actor Matheson Lang. Since then, except for periods of suspension during the wars, 1914–19 and 1939–49, it has presented annual productions, usually of Shakespeare and the classics, as well as open-air productions in college gardens in the summer. The female roles were generally played by professionals up to 1939, female undergraduates being debarred from performing until then, and the producers are usually professionals.

Our Betters. Comedy by W. SOMERSET MAUGHAM, first performed London, 1923.

Our Town. Drama by THORNTON WILDER, first performed New York, 1938.

Outward Bound. Supernatural drama by Sutton Vane, first performed London, 1923; popularized the notion of an ocean liner as a microcosm of society.

Owen, Alun (b. 1926). British dramatist of Welsh origin. He was born in Liverpool, which has provided the background for several of his very successful television plays (notably *No Trams to Lime Street*, 1959) as well as his stage drama on religious and cultural conflicts, *Progress to* *the Park* (1959), and his musical with LIONEL BART, *Maggie May* (1964). His other stage plays include *The Rough and Ready Lot* (1959), set in a Latin American republic during a revolution, *A Little Winter Love* (1963), an emotional drama set in a red-brick university and *The Goose* (1967), a battle for power in a building contractor's firm.

P

Pageant. Originally the word referred to the movable stage on which scenes of medieval religious plays were performed; later it came to be applied to the entertainment enacted upon them, and so to its modern usage to describe a procession made up of spectacular tableaux and usually including songs, dances, and dramatic scenes with some bearing on local history. The great era of this sort of entertainment was in the 1900s and 1920s, but it still lingers on and elements of it are to be found in the annual Lord Mayor's Shows in London.

Pagnol, Marcel (1896–1974). French dramatist and film-maker born near Marseilles and using Marseilles and the south of France as the background for many of his works. After writing a number of plays he had his first success with the bitter satire *Les Marchands de gloire* (1925), written in collaboration with Paul Nivoix. Next came *Jazz* (1926), rewritten in 1931 as *Phaéton*, and then in 1930 one of his most famous plays, *Topaze*, about a humble teacher who becomes a ruthless tycoon. Though most widely known in their film versions, two of his Marseilles trilogy on the fortunes of one group of characters began as stage plays – *Marius* (1930) and *Fanny* (1931) – but the third reversed the process by being filmed in 1933 and adapted for the stage in 1946. From the early 1930s on he devoted himself almost entirely to the cinema, apart from translation-adaptations of *Hamlet* and *A Midsummer Night's Dream*, but returned to the theatre in 1955 with the curious and not very successful *Judas*.

Pajama Game, The. Musical by Richard Adler and Jerry Ross, book by GEORGE ABBOTT and Richard Bissell, based on Bissell's novel *Seven and a Half Cents*; first performed New York, 1954.

Pal Joey. Musical by RICHARD RODGERS, book by John O'Hara based on his own novel, lyrics by LORENZ HART; first performed New York, 1940.

Pantaloon. The old man in the HARLEQUINADE, usually COLUMBINE's father, husband, or guardian and anyway the principal sufferer from the pranks of the others. In COMMEDIA DELL'ARTE Pantalone was an old merchant, usually enamoured of a young wife or girl, but mean, grasping, jealous, and ripe for deception.

Pantomime. The principal modern meaning of the term, when it is not used as interchangeable with 'MIME', is an exotic and irrational Christmas entertainment. Based remotely on fairy tales but padded out with popular songs of the moment, topical comedy, and audience participation routines, it requires the hero (principal boy), to be played by a girl in tights and the comic older woman (dame) to be played by a man. This species of entertainment began life as an appendage to or variation on the HARLEQUINADE, and by the early nineteenth century had grown and developed to the point where it became the main item on the bill, with perhaps a one-act comedy to start and a vestigial harlequinade to round things off. The most popular subjects for pantomimes are *Cinderella* (which has two principal boys, the Prince and his valet Dandini, taken over from Rossini's opera on the subject), *Aladdin* (from a burlesque of the 1860s), *Dick Whittington*, *The Babes in the Wood*, and *Jack and the Bean Stalk*, though most other familiar fairy-stories have been called on as an excuse at least once.

Other meanings of the term pantomime include entertainments in ancient Rome given by one actor who, with the aid of a compartmented mask, played several roles in enactments of fabulous tales; eighteenth-century mythical ballets; mime-plays as performed by DEBURAU's company at the Funambules; and dumb-show melodrama.

Paolo Paoli. Drama by ARTHUR ADAMOV, first performed at Lyons by the Roger Planchon Company, 1957.

Paper. Papering a house means filling the theatre with invited guests on complimentary tickets, who may be assumed to be friendly towards plays and performers.

Parents terribles, Les. Drama by JEAN COCTEAU, first performed Paris, 1938.

Partage de midi. Drama by PAUL CLAUDEL, written 1906, first performed Paris (privately, by Groupe Art et Action), 1916; first public performance Paris, 1948.

Pass door. Fire-proof door between the auditorium and the backstage area of a theatre, not generally used except by theatre staff.

Passing of the Third Floor Back, The. Religious drama by JEROME K. JEROME, first performed London, 1908.

Passion play. Religious drama concerning the crucifixion of Christ, widely performed on Good Friday in the Middle Ages, but surviving after the Reformation mainly in Switzerland, Austria and southern Germany. The most famous is that given every ten years by the villagers of Oberammergau, Bavaria, which has been performed regularly since 1633.

Pastoral. Dramatic eclogue or play in rustic setting. The vogue began in Italy in the mid sixteenth century, and the two most famous examples are Tasso's *Aminta* (1573) and Guarini's *Il Pastor fido* (*c.*1590). There were attempts to adapt the pastoral to British taste in the seventeenth century, but the only one to have any success was Fletcher's *The Faithful Shepherdess* (1609); pastoral elements may be found in some of Shakespeare's plays, particularly *As You Like It*.

Pataphysics. Supposed philosophical system invented by ALFRED JARRY, described as 'the science of imaginary solutions'. After the Second World War a group of admirers of Jarry founded the Collège de Pataphysique, with an elaborate hierarchy and a set of nonsense rules and regulations as a sort of serious joke: among the members have been EUGÈNE IONESCO, the poet and novelist Raymond Queneau, BORIS VIAN, the poet Jacques Prévert, and the painter Jean Dubuffet. Pataphysics in literature and drama represents mainly the liberating incursion of nonsense and anarchy into the realms of solemnity and reason – a function performed after the First World War in similar circumstances by DADA – and the most telling dramatic expressions of it in drama, apart from the works of Jarry himself, are to be found in the plays of Ionesco and Vian.

Patate, see ROLLO.

Patience. 'Savoy opera' by W. S. GILBERT (book and lyrics) and Arthur Sullivan (music), first performed London, 1881.

Patriot for Me, A. Historical drama by JOHN OSBORNE, first performed by the English Stage Society at the Royal Court, 1965.

Pauvre Bitos, ou le dîner de têtes. *Pièce grinçante* by JEAN ANOUILH, first performed Paris, 1956.

Paxinou, Katina (1900–1974). Major Greek actress of her generation and, with her husband Alexis Minotis, leader of her own company. She has acted frequently in English, both in films and on the stage (her most famous roles being Mrs Alving in *Ghosts* and Bernarda Alba in Lorca's *La Casa de Bernarda Alba*); in modern Greek she has played most of the great tragic roles – Medea, Jocasta in *Oedipus Rex* – as well as contemporary roles like Abbie in O'Neill's *Desire Under the Elms*.

Pedrolo, Manuel de (b. 1918). Spanish dramatist and novelist, writing in Catalan. He has written a number of plays, but it is to two recent works somewhere in the convention of the Theatre of the ABSURD that he owes what international reputation he has. They are *Cruma* (1957) and *Homes i No* (1958), both symbolic investigations of human individuality and the nature of liberty.

Peele, George (1558?–97?). English dramatist, one of the Elizabethan 'university wits'. He wrote in a variety of styles: biblical drama (*David and Bethsabe*, *c*.1587), history play (*Edward I*, 1591), pastoral-mythological comedy (*The Arraignment of Paris*, *c*.1581), and broad burlesque (*The Old Wives' Tale*, c.1590). The last two are his best known and most successful works.

Peepshow. A miniature theatre in a box designed for viewing through a single eye-hole. Depending on the degree of elaboration, peepshows can include moving scenery and movable wooden or cardboard figures, or be reduced to a mere succession of coloured slides; the device was invented in the fifteenth century, and reached its apogee in the eighteenth and early nineteenth centuries.

Peer Gynt. Poetic drama by HENRIK IBSEN, written in 1867, first performed Christiania (Oslo), 1876.

Pelléas et Mélisande. Legendary drama by MAURICE MAETERLINCK, first performed Paris, 1893.

Penny for a Song. Comedy by JOHN WHITING, first performed London, 1951; revised version first performed Royal Shakespeare Company, London, 1962.

Perchance to Dream. Musical romance by IVOR NOVELLO, first performed London, 1945.

Pericles, Prince of Tyre. Romantic comedy-drama by WILLIAM SHAKESPEARE, written c.1608–9.

Period of Adjustment. Comedy by TENNESSEE WILLIAMS, first performed New York, 1960.

Persecution and Assassination of Marat as Performed by the Inmates of the Asylum of Charenton under the Direction of the Marquis de Sade, The (Die Ermordung des Jean-Paul Marat, dargestellt von der Truppe des Marquis de Sade im Irrenhaus von Charenton). Drama by PETER WEISS, first performed Berlin, 1964.

Peter Pan. Fairy play by J. M. BARRIE, first performed London, 1904.

Petrified Forest, The. Drama by ROBERT EMMET SHERWOOD, first performed New York, 1935.

Phèdre. Tragedy by JEAN RACINE, first performed Paris, 1677.

Philadelphia Story, The. Comedy by PHILIP BARRY, first performed New York, 1939.

Philipe, Gérard (1922–59). French actor on stage and screen. He began in the theatre, after studying at the Paris Conservatoire, and made his first major impact in 1944 as the Angel in Giraudoux's *Sodome et Gomorrhe*, followed in 1945 by the title role in Camus's *Caligula*. During the next few years he devoted himself almost entirely to the cinema, with occasional returns to the stage, notably in Henri Pichette's *Les Épiphanies* (1948); then in 1951 he played *Le Cid* with JEAN VILAR at Avignon and re-established himself at once as the most brilliant young heroic actor for many years. Later stage roles included *The Prince of Homburg* (also at Avignon), Musset's *Lorenzac-*

cio (1953), Hugo's *Ruy Blas* (1954), Shakespeare's *Richard II* (1954), and more Musset: *Les Caprices de Marianne* (1958) and *On ne badine pas avec l'amour*, directed by René Clair (1959).

Phillips, Stephen (1864–1915). English poetic dramatist whose plays had a considerable though short-lived vogue in the 1900s, particularly *Herod* (1901), produced by BEERBOHM TREE, and *Paolo and Francesca* (1902) produced by George Alexander.

Phillpotts, Eden (1862–1960). English novelist and dramatist, author of many rustic comedies, mostly set in his native Devon. His greatest success was *The Farmer's Wife* (1916), which was first produced at Birmingham Repertory Theatre, like several of his later plays, among them *Devonshire Cream* (1924), *Jane's Legacy* (1925), and *Yellow Sands* (1926).

Philoctetes. Tragedy by SOPHOCLES, first performed Athens, 409 B.C.

Picture stage, see STAGE.

Pierrot. In modern English usage member of a seaside concert-party, especially if wearing the traditional floppy white silk suit and dunce's cap. The costume derives remotely from that of the COMMEDIA DELL'ARTE character Pedrolino, one of the servant roles, or of his French successor Pierrot, whose childlike pleasures and fears were memorably mimed in the nineteenth century by DEBURAU and have contributed much to the character of Bip, created by MARCEL MARCEAU. The character's vogue in Britain dates from the success of *L'Enfant prodigue*, a wordless mime play in which he featured (1891), and soon 'pierrot troupes' of men and women singers, dancers, and comics, whose only connexion with Pierrot was their costume, spread throughout Britain's holiday resorts; in the West End they were represented by the CO-OPTIMISTS; since the Second World War they have virtually died out.

Pillars of Society (Samfundets Støtter). Drama by HENRIK IBSEN, first performed Copenhagen, 1877.

Pinero, Arthur Wing (1855–1934). English dramatist who made his name chiefly with two sorts of play: the broad farce and the well-made emotional drama. In general the farces came first: after a few years as an actor and not particularly successful dramatist (his first play £200 *a Year*, was produced in 1877) he had a major triumph with his farce *The Magistrate* (1885) and followed it in rapid succession with *The Schoolmistress* (1886), *Dandy Dick* (1887), *The Cabinet Minister* (1890), and *The Amazons* (1893). Meanwhile he essayed sentimental drama successfully in 1888 with *Sweet Lavender*, and in 1889 began his succession of intelligent social dramas and occasional comedies with *The Profligate*, followed by *The Second Mrs Tanqueray*

(1893), *Trelawny of the 'Wells'* (1898), *The Gay Lord Quex* (1899), *Iris* (1901), *His House in Order* (1906), and *Mid-Channel* (1909). Thereafter he hit less consistently the taste of the time, though his 'fable' *The Enchanted Cottage* (1922) had a certain success. He was one of the English theatre's most brilliant craftsmen, and despite many subsequent attacks on his reputation as a dramatist his plays continue to be successfully revived.

Pinget, Robert (b. 1919). French novelist and dramatist whose plays incline to the Theatre of the ABSURD. The best known of these are two one-acters, *Lettre morte* (1960), about a man who keeps hopelessly writing to his absent son and awaiting the reply that never comes, and *La Manivelle* (1960, translated by SAMUEL BECKETT as *The Old Tune*), a radio play about two old men uncertainly reminiscing about their past.

Ping-pong, Le. Drama by ARTHUR ADAMOV, first performed Paris, 1955.

Pinter, Harold (b. 1930). English dramatist whose works are allied to the Theatre of the ABSURD. After some years as an actor he wrote his first play, *The Room* (1957), and then the full-length *The Birthday Party*, which was staged in London in 1958 and failed spectacularly despite the enthusiasm of several critics. Subsequently it was successfully produced on television and in 1960 his next full-length play, *The Caretaker*, became a long-running success in the West End. Other works include another one-act stage play, *The Dumb Waiter* (1958) and several short plays originally written for radio or television but most of them later staged, among them *A Slight Ache* (1959), *A Night Out* (1960), *The Dwarfs* (1961), *The Collection* (1961), *The Lover* (1963), and *Tea Party* (1965). In his earlier plays Pinter evolved his own sort of 'comedy of menace', having his characters humorously but horrifically menaced by mysterious outsiders; his later works have become more psychological, and his most recent television plays as well as his film script (based on a story by Robin Maugham), *The Servant*, and his latest full-length stage play, *The Homecoming* (1965), show a further shift into social comedy which still has about it a distinctive flavour of the Absurd. His double bill of short, gnomic one-acters, *Landscape* (1968) and *Silence* (1969), lead the way to *Old Times* (1971) and *No Man's Land* (1975).

Pirandello, Luigi (1867–1936). Italian dramatist with a view of life similar to that of proponents of the Theatre of the ABSURD: the pointlessness of human endeavour, the impossibility of defining reality or of pinning down individual characters are themes which recur again and again in his plays. The best-known of them, and the one which made his international reputation, was *Sei personaggi in cerca d'autore* (*Six Characters in Search of an Author*, 1921), in which a group of characters invade a theatre during rehearsal and reality and illusion are inextricably mixed. Before this he had written a number of plays in which the themes of his later work appeared in embryonic form, starting with a group of one-act plays, adapted from his Sicilian stories. His first notable plays were *Pensaci Giacomino* (*Think of It, Giacomino*, 1916) and *Così è* (*se vi pare*) (*Right You Are If You Think You Are*, 1916), both of which have a general message of live and let live. Among the other plays before *Six Characters* the best known is the bitter farce *L'Uomo, la bestia et la vertu* (*Man, Beast and Virtue*). The play of reality and illusion is taken up subsequently in two more plays directly about acting and the theatre, *Ciascuno al suo modo* (*Each in His Own Way*, 1924) and *Questa sera si recita a soggetto* (*Tonight We Improvise*, 1930), and in another, about a modern man who has taken on the identity of the German Emperor Henry IV, *Enrico Quarto* (1922), which poses the same problems more obliquely. Further studies of the nature of personality are found in *Vestire gli ignudi* (*Naked*, 1922) and *Come tu mi vuoi* (*As You Desire Me*, 1930). During this period, Pirandello was developing another style, more overtly symbolic, as in *La Sagra del Signore della nave* (*Our Lord of the Ship*, 1925) or his last play of all, *I giganti della montagna* (*The Giants of the Mountain*, 1937). His works, particularly *Six Characters* and *Enrico Quarto*, are frequently revived and continue to exert a powerful influence on later dramatists. He was awarded the Nobel Prize for Literature in 1934.

Pirates of Penzance, The. 'Savoy opera' by w. s. GILBERT (book and lyrics) and Arthur Sullivan (music), first produced London, 1880.

Piscator, Erwin (1893–1966). German director. He began as a follower of REINHARDT, but from the start used what he had learnt from Reinhardt for the purposes of propaganda in the theatre, holding with BRECHT, whom he greatly influenced, that conveying social and political messages was the prime aim of theatre in a dynamic modern society. In his EXPRESSIONIST productions of the 1920s (the most famous of which was his dramatization, with Brecht, of *The Good Soldier Schweik* in 1927) he used all the mechanical resources of the theatre to put over the points he wished to make, and from here he gradually felt his way towards the concept of EPIC THEATRE which he shares with Brecht. In 1931 Piscator was for a while director of the International Theatre in Moscow, and again in 1933 he left Germany to become director of the Dramatic Workshop of the New School for Social Research in New York. He remained there until 1951, both running the acting school and controlling for some years two theatres, one off-Broadway and one commercial. *Inter alia* he staged Sartre's *Les Mouches* and his own epic adaptations of Dreiser's *An American Tragedy* and Robert Penn Warren's *All the King's Men* (the latter in collaboration with the author). During the 1950s he worked in various German theatres, producing most notably his own dramatic version of *War and Peace* (1955; written 1936, in collaboration with Walter Neumann), and in 1963 opened his own theatre, the Free People's Theatre in West Berlin.

Pit. Ground floor of theatre; originally the cheapest part.

Pitoëff, Georges (1887–1939) and **Ludmilla** (1896–1951). Russian–French actors and directors of the company which bore their name. Georges Pitoëff had acted and directed in Russia before he settled in France in 1918; there he acted with COPEAU's company (among others) before founding his own in 1924; it specialized in introducing the work of foreign writers to the French stage, notably Pirandello, Shaw, and – a particular favourite of the Pitoëffs – Shakespeare, as well as works of such relatively new and difficult French dramatists as Anouilh, Cocteau, and Claudel. After Georges Pitoëff's death the direction of the company was taken over by his wife Ludmilla, who was also for long the company's leading actress; after her death it passed to their son **Sacha Pitoëff**.

Plain Dealer, The. Comedy by WILLIAM WYCHERLEY, first performed Drury Lane, London, 1674.

Planché, J. R. (James Robinson; 1796–1880). English dramatist, best remembered for his pantomimes in pun-laden rhymed verse and for his opera librettos, which included that for Weber's opera-pantomime *Oberon*. He was also an expert on costume, and designed the costumes for Kemble's *King John* (1824), the first production seriously to aim at historical accuracy.

Planchon, Roger (b. 1931). French director, self-declared follower of BRECHT in his conception of didactic theatre. Began his professional life as a bank clerk, but opened the small Théâtre de la Comédie de Lyon (ninety-eight seats) in 1950, before he was twenty. In 1957 he moved to the Théâtre de la Cité Villeurbanne, and two years later he was appointed director of the Théâtre Populaire de Provence, one of the government's sponsored CENTRES DRAMATIQUES. His productions combine elements from many sources – an enthusiastic study of the theories of ARTAUD as well as the practice of JEAN VILAR and Brecht – but combine them into a direct, forthright, wholly personal style, perfectly mirroring his determination to produce a genuinely popular theatre to appeal to mass audiences in areas which have lost or never had the habit of theatre-going. His famous production of Shakespeare's *Henry IV*, the two parts conflated into one, used action devices from Western films, a map of medieval England as a back-cloth, and projected captions to help the audience with the plot; his free version of Dumas's *Les Trois Mousquetaires* was a joyous collective improvisation which made sense of the complex plot and at the same time cheerfully burlesqued the whole thing. Other classic plays he has had signal successes with are Marlowe's *Edward II*, which he has returned to repeatedly, and Molière's *Georges Dandin*; on the other hand his treatment of Marivaux's *La Seconde Surprise de l'amour* showed little gift for delicacy or for the high style necessary. Among contemporary dramatists Planchon has concentrated mainly on ADAMOV, producing *Professor Taranne*, *Le Sens de la marche*, and *Paolo Paoli*. Despite Planchon's didactic intentions his productions remain lively, often very funny, and brilliantly inventive.

Plato (427–348 B.C.). Greek philosopher, less notable in dramatic history for his views on drama than for provoking ARISTOTLE to reply to his strictures in the *Poetics*. Plato mistrusted poetry and drama as tending to have a debilitating effect on society, since they derived from inspiration rather than reason, appealed primarily to their audience's emotions, showed characters unable to control their emotions, and spread doubts and fears about the gods by showing them to be as irresponsible and quarrelsome as humans. Despite this, Plato's own philosophical works were cast in dialogue form and, though not intended for performance, often show an unexpected grasp of dramatic effect.

Platonov. Drama by ANTON CHEKHOV, discovered posthumously in 1923. The manuscript is untitled; the play was called *Platonov* in Dmitri Makaroff's translation, first performed Royal Court, London, 1960; it had previously been translated by Basil Ashmore as *Don Juan in the Russian Manner*. The play was not performed in Russia until 1960.

Plautus (third–second centuries B.C.). Roman playwright of whom virtually nothing is known apart from his twenty-one surviving comedies, two of which, the *Mercator* and the *Asinaria*, may not in fact be his. His comic style derives from the 'New Comedy' of MENANDER, and it is quite possible that some if not all the plays of his that we have are largely or entirely translations from Greek originals. Most of them have very involved plots full of disguises, substitutions, and mistaken identities (notably the *Menaechmi*, on which Shakespeare based his *Comedy of Errors*, and the *Amphitruo*), not to mention the restoration of long-lost relatives (the *Captivi* and the *Rudens*); the settings are often in low-life brothels, which feature prominently in the *Truculentus*, the *Bacchides* and the *Pseudolus*. Plautus was immensely popular on the Roman stage, his effects being considerably broader than those of his near-contemporary TERENCE, and has continued to find favour even with modern audiences – the hit musical *A Funny Thing Happened on the Way to the Forum* is based on material from his plays.

Playbill. Originally a small ticket advertising a play-production, distributed to houses in the seventeenth century. The earliest surviving posters for plays come from the mid eighteenth century, and from very few details they rapidly came to include all the information of a modern theatre programme. As they got bigger they became increasingly difficult to use as programmes, and in the mid nineteenth century smaller versions of the bill for easy reading in the theatre were introduced – from which come our modern theatre programmes. Theatre posters, or playbills, continued of course to be used, but less from the end of the 1930s on, since after that most theatres relied more on advertisements in newspapers and magazines, plus a few playbills displayed outside the theatre and in ticket agencies, rather than posters widely disseminated, to draw the public's attention to their shows.

Playbill. Double bill by TERENCE RATTIGAN, consisting of *The Browning Version* and *Harlequinade*; first performed London, 1948.

Playboy of the Western World, The. Comedy by J. M. SYNGE, first performed Abbey Theatre, Dublin, 1907.

Playfair, Nigel (1874–1934). English theatre manager and director. Originally an actor, he achieved his greatest fame and success as manager of the Lyric, Hammersmith, which he took over in 1918 and ran until 1934. The production which really established his management was the revival of *The Beggar's Opera* (1920), designed by Lovat Fraser, which ran for 1,462 performances in all; it was followed by Gay's sequel, *Polly*, by revues, and by revivals of classic comedies, such as *The Way of the World* (with Edith Evans as Millamant, 1924), *The Beaux' Stratagem* (with Edith Evans as Mrs Sullen, 1927), and *The Importance of Being Earnest* (with John Gielgud as Jack Worthing, 1930). Playfair acted in many of these productions himself, and wrote two books about his management, *The Story of the Lyric Theatre, Hammersmith* (1925) and *Hammersmith Hoy* (1930); he was knighted in 1928.

Playhouse (see also STAGE, SCENERY, LIGHTING). The form of the average playhouse now in use (not including, that is, deliberately and radically experimental forms) is a combination of elements from a variety of quite distinct sources. The English playhouse, which always has been primarily a house of drama rather than opera, has probably contributed most in the long run, since it was by tradition both more specifically adapted to spoken drama and more suited by its form to the requirements of a popular audience, unlike the characteristic Continental theatre. The English playhouse originated in the inn courtyard with one or two tiers of galleries all round, and has never entirely escaped this pattern, even when roofed in and equipped with a proscenium to separate stage from audience: separate boxes for small groups have always played a relatively minor part in the arrangement of the whole, the galleries developing into unpartitioned upper levels of seats known as the Dress Circle (so called because evening dress used to be required in it), the Upper Circle, and the Balcony or 'Gods', which were the cheapest, unreserved seats just beneath the roof. This form of theatre developed on the whole quite independently of contemporary Continental practice, though a theatre built in Amsterdam by Jacob van Campen in 1637 seems to have had some influence on Wren in his DRURY LANE (1674), combining as it did certain elements of the English 'medieval' tradition and the Continental neo-classical, and arranging the seats on the various levels into a horseshoe with the proscenium across what would be the open end.

The origin of the Continental theatre was quite different: in Italy, from which most Continental theatre architecture ultimately derived, the theatre originated really in the aristocratic whim of Duke Ercole d'Este in the fifteenth century to revive classical comedy in a 'classical' playhouse built along the lines laid down in the writings of Vitruvius. All the theatres built under this influence were arranged on vaguely classical lines, varying only according to the architect's lights, and were usually built within a large existing hall (in France they were generally converted tennis-courts). Nearly all Continental theatres in the early days were built primarily as private houses for aristocratic patrons, and so did not need to provide a lot of accommodation for the public. Later, when opera was the general vogue, the place of the single patron tended to be taken by the moneyed upper-classes, and the same thing applied: the emphasis, consequently, was upon individual boxes which normally occupied the whole of the upper tiers, except, perhaps, for some small accommodation for the lower orders right at the very top. This type of theatre left much to be desired acoustically, and if elaborated to be suitable for the wilder flights of baroque opera-spectacle was likely not to suit straight drama very well. Consequently, where drama was the staple diet of a Continental theatre, as happened increasingly often from the beginning of the nineteenth century, it was likely that a new theatre built to accommodate it would arise much nearer to the English model.

In modern times there have been all sorts of attempts to modify the form of the theatre, generally inhibited to some extent by the existence of so many theatres along the lines described and the prohibitive expense of replacing them. See STAGE, however, for details of theatres-in-the-round, theatres with arena and apron stages, etc.

Play of Daniel, The. Medieval religious drama with music, dating from the twelfth century. It has been revived on a number of occasions in the 1960s, in a new version with an explanatory narration by W. H. AUDEN.

Plays for England. Double bill by JOHN OSBORNE, consisting of *Under Plain Cover* and *The Blood of the Bambergs*, first performed by the English Stage Company, Royal Court, London, 1962.

Plowright, Joan (b. 1929). English actress, particularly identified with the work of the new British dramatists. She was first noticed as the cabin-boy in Orson Welles's *Moby Dick* (1955), and in 1956 she joined the permanent company of the English Stage Company, making her first mark in a leading role as Marjery Pinchwife in *The Country Wife* (1956). Other notable roles include the Old Woman in *The Chairs* and the Pupil in *The Lesson* (1957–8), Jean Rice in *The Entertainer* (1958), Major Barbara (1958), Beatie Bryant in *Roots* at Coventry and in London (1959), Daisy in *Rhinoceros* (1960), Josephine in *A Taste of Honey* (New York, 1961), St Joan at Chichester (1963), and Hilde in *The Master Builder* at the National Theatre (1964). She is married to SIR LAURENCE OLIVIER.

Poel, William (1852–1934). English actor and director, noted chiefly for his Shakespearian productions and his attempts in them to perform Shakespeare in as nearly as possible the conditions of Shakespeare's day. In 1894 he founded the Elizabethan Stage Society, and in 1895 gave his first production on a reconstructed Elizabethan stage, *Twelfth Night*. Between then and the society's dissolution in 1905 he produced plays by most of the major Elizabethans and Jacobeans, as well as the first revival of *Everyman* for four hundred years; later he continued to be associated primarily with plays of this period.

Pogodin, Nikolai (b. 1900). Russian dramatist. He began his writing career as a journalist and his early plays, such as *Tempo* (1929) and *Aristocrats* (1934), were topical dramas based on events of the moment – the building of Stalingrad Tractor Plant, the digging of a canal from the White Sea to the Baltic. His most famous later works are a trilogy on Lenin, *Man with a Gun* (1937), *Kremlin Chimes* (1942), and the third, *Pathetic* (1955), but he has written many others, notably *Creation of the World* (1946), a patriotic drama about postwar reconstruction, and *Missouri Waltz*, a satire on President Truman.

Point of Departure (Eurydice). *Pièce noire* by JEAN ANOUILH, first performed Paris, 1942.

Porgy and Bess. Negro folk-opera by GEORGE GERSHWIN, book by DuBose Heyward (based on his novel), lyrics by DuBose Heyward and Ira Gershwin; first performed New York, 1935.

Porter, Cole (1892–1964). American composer of innumerable popular songs and stage and screen musicals, for which he has almost invariably written his own lyrics. He came of a prosperous family and studied music at Harvard, after which he joined the Foreign Legion, returned, married a wife as rich as himself, and lived the life of a complete dilettante until 1928, when he was persuaded to write the music for a revue, *Paris*, which was an immediate success. He composed some twenty stage shows, all showing a characteristic wit and sophistication; among them are *Fifty Million Frenchmen*, *Wake Up and Dream* (1929), *Gay Divorce* (1932), *Nymph Errant* (1933), *Anything Goes* (1934), *Du Barry was a Lady* (1939), *Panama Hattie* (1940), *Kiss Me Kate* (1948), *Can-Can* (1953), and *Silk Stockings* (1955).

Posters, see PLAYBILL.

Potash and Perlmutter. Comedy by Montague Glass and Charles Klein, first performed New York, 1913. The two title characters and the play itself have become part of theatrical vocabulary as summing up a certain type of broad Jewish dialect humour.

Potting Shed, The. Drama by GRAHAM GREENE, first performed New York, 1957; re-written version London, 1958.

Pour Lucrèce, see DUEL OF ANGELS.

Present Laughter. Comedy by NOËL COWARD, first performed London, 1943.

Priestley, J. B. (b. 1894). English dramatist, novelist, and essayist. After achieving considerable success as a novelist he came to the drama by adapting (in collaboration with EDWARD KNOBLOCK) his own novel *The Good Companions* to the stage (1931). During the 1930s the nature of time interested him greatly, and one of his first original plays, *Dangerous Corner* (1932), presents two alternative versions of a series of events starting from the same innocent remark; the idea of parallel time was taken up again in two 'time plays', *Time and the Conways* and *I Have Been Here Before* (both 1937). Other plays of the period, such as the comedy dramas *Laburnum Grove* (1933) and

Eden End (1934) and the farce *When We Are Married* (1938) were more straightforward, but he also wrote experimental plays like *Music at Night* (1938) and *Johnson Over Jordan* (1939) and, with more popular success, the war-time allegory *They Came to a City* (1943). Since the war his most interesting plays have been the dramas *An Inspector Calls* (1945) and *The Linden Tree* (1947); during the later 1950s he virtually gave up the stage and the only new play by him to be seen in London for some years is an adaptation in collaboration with Iris Murdoch of her novel *A Severed Head* (1964).

Princess Ida. 'Savoy opera' by W. S. GILBERT (book and lyrics) and Arthur Sullivan (music), first produced London, 1884.

Principal boy, see PANTOMIME.

Private Lives. Comedy by NOËL COWARD, first performed London, 1930.

Producer. A confusing term, since it means, or has until recently meant, different things in Britain and the U.S.A. In traditional British usage it has usually meant the person who actually stages a play, called in America the 'DIRECTOR', but now the American usage is becoming general in Britain. In America 'producer' means the person financially and otherwise responsible for the management of the company (known in Britain as the 'MANAGER'), but again the American term is now coming into general use in the same sense in Britain.

Professor's Love Story, The. Comedy by J. M. BARRIE, first performed London, 1894.

Professor Taranne (Le Professeur Taranne). Dream play by ARTHUR ADAMOV, first performed Lyons, 1953.

Progress to the Park. Drama by ALUN OWEN, first performed Royal Court, London, in a production-without-décor, 1959; first public performance Theatre Royal, Stratford, London, 1961.

Prologue, see EPILOGUE.

Prompt. The prompter is the person detailed to give actors lines they forget and generally see that performances do not depart too far from the form laid down by author and director. To do this he follows the performance in a **prompt copy** of the play with all the stage directions, movements, etc., noted. In the English theatre he normally sits in the **prompt corner** to stage left, just behind the proscenium arch; from this fact stage left is often known as **Prompt side,** or **P.S.,** and stage right as **Opposite prompt,** or **O.P.** On the Continent the prompter usually occupies a **prompt box,** a cubby-hole in the centre of the footlights concealed from the audience by a covered hood; this arrangement is sometimes to be found in British opera houses.

Properties (usually shortened to **Props**). Everything required during the action of a play which does not count as furniture, costume, or scenery – such as letters, spectacles, cigarettes, knitting, weapons of various sorts (known as **hand props**, since they are carried by the actors), and food, drink, china and cutlery, telephones, and other oddments of the sort. They are looked after by the **property-man** and kept by him in a special room or cupboard when not actually in use.

Proscenium, see STAGE.

Provincetown Players. A company of American actors set up to 'give American playwrights a chance to work out their ideas in freedom'. In their first year, 1916, they put on the first of EUGENE O'NEILL'S plays to be staged, *Bound East for Cardiff*, at the tiny Wharf Theatre in Provincetown, Massachusetts, and followed it with a number of other one-acters by O'Neill. In 1916 too they gave their first New York season, and later moved entirely to New York, where they played in various theatres until disbanded in 1929. During this time they were directed by Kenneth Macgowan, Robert Edmond Jones, and O'Neill himself, and were involved in the production of most of the plays O'Neill wrote at that time.

Provok'd Wife, The. Comedy by SIR JOHN VANBRUGH, first performed London, 1697.

Pulcinella. Comic servant in COMMEDIA DELL'ARTE, hump-backed and stupid. In France he became Polichinelle, and in England Punchinello, or simply Punch, in which guise he achieved new life and fame as the central figure of the PUNCH AND JUDY show.

Punch and Judy. Puppet show, usually given in the open-air at the seaside or at fairs and fêtes. It is operated by one man concealed in a square striped tent the size of a telephone box with a stage opening in the upper half at which the hand-operated puppets are seen. Punch and Judy are husband and wife, Punch acting throughout with the utmost brutality: he throws the baby out of the window, beats and kills Judy, a Doctor, and various other characters, cheats the hangman into hanging himself, and even disposes of the Devil, all in a manner intended to amuse rather than horrify a predominantly juvenile audience. The Punch and Judy show as we know it developed about 1800. Punch still wears a striped Italian costume, has an exaggerated beaked nose and a conventionalized hump back, and talks in a high-pitched squeak.

Puppet theatre. Form of drama acted by puppets: rounded miniature figures controlled from below stage directly by the operator's hands or by rods, or marionettes: rounded miniature figures controlled from above the stage by strings or wires. Puppets and marionettes go back to the earliest times, and seem to have provided popular folk entertainment since the dawn of drama. In this form they were usually seen in travelling shows presented in temporary open-air theatres, as is the case with the principal surviving modern form, the PUNCH AND JUDY show. In the sixteenth and seventeenth centuries more refined versions of these folk entertainments were developed for aristocratic audiences and indoor theatres; Italian puppets had a great vogue in Britain at the time of the Restoration, and hardly a city in Europe did not have its puppet show in the eighteenth century. During the nineteenth century puppets and marionettes were widely used for their possibilities in caricature and satire, but there was a gradual fading of interest in them until the renewed interest of intellectuals (spurred at least partly by the newly fashionable influence of Japanese art, where puppets had long had an honoured place: see JORURI) brought about a renaissance of puppet and marionette entertainments in the twentieth century. Though they still often suffer from the popular tendency to regard them as primarily for children, they have many brilliant professional exponents today, notably Vittorio Podrecca's Teatro dei Piccoli in Milan and OBRATSOV's Central Puppet Theatre in Moscow. See also SHADOW PLAYS.

Purple Dust. Drama by SEAN O'CASEY, written 1940, first performed Liverpool, 1945.

Pushkin, Alexander (1799–1837). Russian poet and dramatist. Though his most memorable work was done in the lyrical forms, he was always deeply interested in drama, particularly that of Shakespeare. His major completed play, *Boris Godunov* (written 1819, first performed 1870) is a drama from Russian history, heavily influenced by Shakespeare; his only other plays are a group of short scenes written in 1836–7, among them a *Don Juan* and *Mozart and Salieri*. *Boris Godunov* was set to music by Mussorgsky, and *Mozart and Salieri* by Rimsky-Korsakov.

Pygmalion. Comedy by GEORGE BERNARD SHAW, first performed Vienna, 1913.

Q

Quaker Girl, The. Musical play by Lionel Monckton, book by James Tanner, lyrics by Adrian Ross and Percy Greenbank; first performed London, 1910.

Quality Street. Period comedy by J. M. BARRIE, first performed London, 1902. A musical version under the title *Dear Miss Phoebe*, book and lyrics by Christopher Hassell, music by Harry Parr Davies, first performed London, 1950.

Quare Fellow, The. Tragi-comedy by BRENDAN BEHAN, first performed Dublin, 1954; revised version produced by Theatre Workshop at Theatre Royal, Stratford, London, 1956.

Quayle, Anthony (b. 1913). English actor and director. First appeared on the professional stage in 1931; before the war he played a variety of minor roles, and was for three seasons a member of the Old Vic Company before going into the forces. After demobilization in 1945 he rapidly came to prominence, particularly after being appointed director of the Shakespeare Memorial Theatre Company in 1948. He stayed there until 1956, running the company, himself directing several productions, and playing among other roles Iago, Claudius, and Petruchio (1948), Falstaff in *Henry IV* (1950), Othello, Bottom, and Pandarus (1954), and Falstaff in *The Merry Wives of Windsor* (1955). Other notable performances include Tamburlaine (New York, 1956), Eddie in *A View from the Bridge* (1956), Moses in *The Firstborn* (New York, 1958), James Tyrone in *Long Day's Journey into Night* (1958), and Cesareo in *Chin-Chin* (1960).

Queen After Death (La Reine morte). Historical drama by HENRY DE MONTHERLANT, first produced Comédie-Française, Paris, 1942.

Queen and the Rebels, The (La Regina e gli insorti). Drama by UGO BETTI, first produced Rome, 1953.

Queen's Men. The most famous Elizabethan theatre company, formed in 1583 and of which the twelve original members were Grooms of the Chamber, was called Queen Elizabeth's Men, or more shortly the Queen's Men. It gradually faded out after 1594, and the next company to hold the title was Queen Anne's Men, founded on James I's accession, which was succeeded in its turn by Queen Henrietta's Men founded in 1625 and finally disbanded at the closure of the theatres in 1642.

Quiet Wedding. Family comedy by ESTHER MCCRACKEN, first performed London, 1938.

Quiet Weekend. Family comedy by ESTHER MCCRACKEN, first performed London, 1941.

Quintero, The Brothers: Serafin (1871–1938) and Joaquin (1873–1944). Writing team responsible for over 150 plays, mostly light comedies and sentimental dramas. Eight of their plays were successfully translated by HARLEY GRANVILLE BARKER and his wife: *The Women Have Their Way, A Hundred Years Old, Fortunato, The Lady from Alfaqueque, Love Passes By, Don Abel Wrote a Tragedy, Peace and Quiet*, and *Doña Clarines*.

Quintero, José (b. 1924). American director, founder of the off-Broadway Circle-in-the-Square theatre in New York. His most famous productions have been of two works by O'Neill, *The Iceman Cometh* (1956, off-Broadway) and *Long Day's Journey Into Night* (1956, on Broadway), both elaborately detailed, giving the text in full and staying very close to it, with a minimum of directorial invention beyond that explicitly required in the stage directions.

R

Rachel (real name Élisa Félix; 1820–58). French actress, greatest tragedienne of her day. Born of a poor Jewish family, she sang in the streets as a child, studied at the Théâtre Molière and briefly at the Conservatoire, and was first discovered by the critic Jules Janin. She first appeared at the Comédie-Française in 1838, playing Camille in *Horace*, and rapidly became the unrivalled interpreter of French classical tragedy in such roles as Phèdre, Hermione, and Roxane, as well as playing in a number of modern plays, among them Scribe and Legouvé's *Adrienne Lecouvreur* (1848). She was at her best in powerful, dynamic roles, and more or less burnt herself out, touring widely and fighting consumption until her early death at the age of thirty-eight.

Racine, Jean (1639–99). French dramatist, greatest and most meticulously disciplined exponent of the classical tragedy in alexandrines. He was orphaned at an early age, and brought up by his aunt, a fervent Jansenist and later Abbess of Port-Royal, where he was educated and which did much to shape his view of life. His first play, *La Thébaïde, ou les frères ennemis*, was staged by MOLIÈRE in 1664, and had some success, but after his second play, *Alexandre le Grand* (1665) there was a breach between the two dramatists, and Racine's later works were produced by rival companies. His first major success, which established him as the main rival of CORNEILLE, was *Andromaque* (1667), a superbly organized tragedy with, as usual in Racine's work, a woman as the central figure. This Racine followed with his one comedy, *Les Plaideurs* (1668) and then with another of his greatest plays, though not a particularly successful one at the time, *Britannicus* (1669). A competition, accidental or deliberate, with Corneille when both wrote plays on the subject of Berenice in 1670 found Racine generally regarded as the victor with his *Bérénice*; his three following plays, *Bajazet*, *Mithridate*, and *Iphigénie* were equally successful. In 1677 a further competition, this time with a dramatist of only passing interest, Pradon, who wrote a play on the subject of Phaedra for a rival company to compete with Racine's, brought Racine's career to an abrupt end, since Pradon's was slightly more successful than his *Phèdre*; an appointment as Louis XIV's historiographer, coming at the same time, decided Racine to give up the theatre. This he did for twelve years and then broke his silence only at the request of Mme de Maintenon to write two plays on biblical themes, *Esther* (1689) and *Athalie* (1691), for private performance at her girls' school at Saint-Cyr. Both were subsequently performed, after Racine's death, at the Comédie-Française, *Athalie* with great and continuing success. Racine carried French classical tragedy to its ultimate in intensity and refinement, and remains one of the world's greatest tragic poets.

R.A.D.A. Royal Academy of Dramatic Art. One of the leading acting schools in Britain, founded by BEERBOHM TREE in 1904 at His Majesty's Theatre and moved to its present home in Gower Street in 1905. The traditional strong point of R.A.D.A. training is fine diction; many of the leading actors and actresses in Britain today have studied there.

Raimu (real name Jules Muraire; 1883–1946). French actor. Began his career in music hall and graduated to straight theatre around 1915, achieving his first big success in Sacha Guitry's *Faisons un rêve* and confirming his reputation as one of the great character actors of the French stage in Pagnol's *Marius* (1929) and its sequels, in which he also appeared on the screen. During the 1930s and 1940s he devoted most of his time to the cinema, notably in Pagnol's *La Femme du boulanger* and *La Fille du puisatier*, but in 1943 he joined the Comédie-Française and had particular successes in *L'Avare* and *Le Malade imaginaire*.

Rain. Drama by John Colton and Clemence Randolph, based on a short story by W. SOMERSET MAUGHAM; first performed New York, 1922.

Rainmaker, The. Dramatic comedy by N. RICHARD NASH, first performed New York, 1954. A musical version, *110 in the Shade*, book by Nash, lyrics by Tom Jones, music by Harvey Schmidt, first performed New York, 1963.

Raisin in the Sun, A. Drama by LORRAINE HANSBERRY, first performed New York, 1958.

Rake. Angle of incline of a stage from back to front normal in eighteenth and nineteenth century theatres but now rarely found. Its principal function was to help the illusion of scenery painted in perspective.

Ralph Roister Doister. Comedy by NICHOLAS UDALL, first performed Eton, 1534–41.

Rattigan, Terence (b. 1911). English dramatist, one of the most phenomenally successful of his era. His second play, *French Without Tears* (1936), a light comedy, ran for over a thousand performances and so, later, did a war-time farce, *While the Sun Shines* (1943). Though his earlier successes were generally lightweight, and he has continued to write comedies such as *Love in Idleness* (*Oh Mistress Mine* in the U.S.A., 1944), *Who is Sylvia?* (1950), and *The Sleeping Prince* (1953), he has broadened and deepened his talents with *Flare Path* (1942),

The Winslow Boy, a careful, serious drama suggested by the Archer-Shee case (1946), *The Browning Version* (1948), and *The Deep Blue Sea* (1952). Other plays include a flirtation with costume drama, *Adventure Story* (1949), based on the life of Alexander the Great, a linked double-bill, *Separate Tables* (1954), a life of T. E. Lawrence, *Ross* (1960), *Man and Boy* (1963) and *A Bequest to the Nation* (1970). He has also written successful television plays (*Heart to Heart*, 1962) and original film scripts (*The Way to the Stars*, 1945; *The V.I.P.s*, 1963; *The Yellow Rolls-Royce*, 1965). An extremely efficient craftsman, he remains one of the most reliable entertainers in the English theatre. Knighted 1976.

Realism. A late-nineteenth-century movement in drama, in effect a less extreme form of NATURALISM. Its exponents aimed to rid the theatre of histrionics in acting and the too-evident artifice of the sub-SARDOU well-made play, replacing them with a more natural-seeming acting style and with plays which, while still carefully constructed, depended less on contrived *coups de théâtre* and a mechanical snapping of pieces into place. One of the main instigators of the movement was IBSEN, and his work continued to be an inspiration to those of like mind in other countries – SHAW in England, for example, and GEORGE JEAN NATHAN in the United States. Realism too was the basis of STANISLAVSKY's practice, and by extension has greatly influenced modern American practitioners of the METHOD.

Rebecca. Romantic drama by Daphne Du Maurier, based on her own novel, first performed London, 1940.

Recruiting Officer, The. Comedy by GEORGE FARQUHAR, first performed Drury Lane, London, 1706.

Redgrave, Michael (b. 1908). English actor, director, and dramatist. His parents were both actors, but he began his career as a schoolmaster before joining Liverpool Repertory Company in 1934, where he stayed for two years. His first appearances in London were with the Old Vic, where in 1936–7 he played a variety of roles, the most prominent being Orlando in *As You Like It*. A later season in John Gielgud's company at the Queen's (1937–8) helped to establish him as an actor of unusual intelligence with a subtle sense of style, especially in the classics, and in 1940 successful appearances as Macbeth in *The Beggar's Opera* and Charleston in *Thunder Rock*, allied with some notable appearances in films, helped to bring him a wide popular following. After a period of war service he soon re-established himself, particularly with his Rakitin in *A Month in the Country* (1943), and scored a popular success with the title-role in *Uncle Harry* (1944). His great period dates from 1947, with his appearance at the Aldwych as

Macbeth, followed by such roles as the Captain in *The Father* (1948), Berowne in *Love's Labour Lost*, Marlow in *She Stoops to Conquer*, and Hamlet with the Old Vic (1949–50), Richard II, Hotspur, and Prospero at Stratford on Avon (1951), Shylock, Lear, and Antony in *Antony and Cleopatra* at Stratford on Avon (1952–3), Hector in *Tiger at the Gates* in London and New York (1955), Benedick and Hamlet again at Stratford on Avon (1958), 'H.J.' in his own dramatization of *The Aspern Papers* (1959), Jack Dean in *The Tiger and the Horse* (1960), Vanya in *Uncle Vanya* at Chichester (1962) and Vanya, Solness in *The Master Builder*, and Hobson in *Hobson's Choice* at the National Theatre (1964). In 1965 he directed the first season at the new Yvonne Arnaud Theatre, Guildford, and himself appeared in two of the three productions, *A Month in the Country* and *Samson Agonistes*. He was knighted in 1959. Among his writings are two books of lectures on acting, *The Actor's Ways and Means* (1955) and *Mask or Face* (1958).

Almost all Redgrave's family are also on the stage: his wife **Rachel Kempson** (b. 1910), their daughters **Vanessa** (b. 1937) and **Lynn** (b. 1944) and son **Corin** (b. 1939). Vanessa Redgrave first appeared with her father in *A Touch of the Sun* (1958) and rapidly established herself as a leading lady in her own right, particularly with her playing of Stella Dean in *The Tiger and the Horse* (1960), her Rosalind in *As You Like It* at Stratford and the Aldwych (1962), and her appearances in *The Taming of the Shrew*, *The Lady from the Sea*, *The Seagull*, and other plays.

Red Roses for Me. Drama by SEAN O'CASEY, first performed London, 1946.

Régisseur. A synonym for DIRECTOR, widely used on the Continent, particularly in Germany and Russia; in France itself '*metteur-en-scène*' is more usual, '*régisseur*' normally meaning stage manager.

Rehearsal, The. Burlesque comedy by George Villiers, DUKE OF BUCKINGHAM, first performed Drury Lane, London, 1671.

Rehearsal, The (La Répétition, ou l'amour puni). *Pièce brillante* by JEAN ANOUILH, first performed Paris, 1950.

Reine morte, La, see QUEEN AFTER DEATH.

Reinhardt, Max (real name Goldmann; 1873–1943). Austrian actor, director, and manager. He began his career as an actor in 1893, and specialized particularly in playing old men before changing over entirely to direction in 1903. As a director he made his main popular reputation with his most spectacular productions, like the *Oedipus Rex* at the Zirkus Schumann, Berlin, in 1910 and *The Miracle*, a mimed religious drama, at Olympia, London, in 1911. Certainly his management of crowds on stage was masterly, putting into practice with great brilliance some of GORDON CRAIG's ideas on the nature of the stage picture, the relation of actors to settings, lighting, and so on. But Reinhardt's work was not confined to large-scale spectacle: during the early 1920s he directed regularly in three Berlin theatres, the vast Grosses Schauspielhaus, the medium-sized Deutsches Theater, and the tiny Kammerspiele, holding an audience of only three hundred, where he specialized in intimate chamber-dramas full of nuances and psychological subtleties. As well as playing in Germany and Austria his company toured extensively, having their major success in the U.S.A., 1927–8, when they gave a season including *A Midsummer Night's Dream*, *Danton's Death*, and Hofmannsthal's version of *Everyman*. Reinhardt himself directed a number of productions for English and American companies, among them Martin-Harvey's *Oedipus Rex* (1912), *A Midsummer Night's Dream* for the O.U.D.S. in 1933 and in Hollywood in 1934 (the latter subsequently filmed by Reinhardt himself), and Offenbach's *La Belle Hélène*, as *Helen*, for Cochran in 1932. Another major enterprise of Reinhardt's was the founding and running of the Salzburg Festival (1920), for which he regularly staged Hofmannsthal's *Jedermann* in front of the cathedral as well as a variety of straight plays in the theatre. After the advent of Hitler in 1933 he spent most of his time abroad, and left Europe permanently for the United States in 1938.

Réjane (real name Gabrielle Charlotte Réju; 1857–1920). French actress, specialist in comedy, and leading Parisian player in her line during the 1890s and 1900s. She seldom acted in plays of any great interest (her most famous role was in *Madame Sans-Gêne*) but her personality and technique were praised by Shaw and she had a prosperous career from her debut in 1875 to her retirement in 1915.

Relapse, The. Comedy by SIR JOHN VANBRUGH, first performed Drury Lane, London, 1697.

Reluctant Debutante, The. Light comedy by WILLIAM DOUGLAS HOME, first performed London, 1955.

Renaud, Madeleine, see BARRAULT, JEAN-LOUIS.

Rendez-vous de Senlis, Le, see DINNER WITH THE FAMILY.

Repertory. The essential of a repertory company, strictly speaking, is that it should have several productions – a repertory of productions, in fact – ready at the same time, so that the play presented can change from night to night. This ideal has rarely been realized in practice, except in a number of London companies: in the BARKER–VEDRENNE management at the Royal Court (1904–7), and the ENGLISH STAGE COMPANY at the same theatre in 1956 and again 1965–6, the

Royal Shakespeare Company at the Aldwych, the OLD VIC and the NATIONAL THEATRE COMPANY. The term is more usually used to denote companies which play each production for only a limited period – generally two or three weeks – and have a certain continuity of acting personnel from one production to the next. This is the case with most of the provincial companies which form part of the Repertory Theatre Movement, which began in effect with the work of Miss A. E. F. HORNIMAN in Dublin and Manchester. Other early provincial repertories along the same lines were Glasgow (1909–14), Liverpool (founded 1911), and Birmingham (founded 1913), which were followed by similar companies in every town of any size in England and to a lesser extent Wales and Scotland. At the height of the movement's success there were over one hundred such theatres, but after the Second World War audiences began to decline, partly because of the spread of television and partly because new, younger audiences failed to be attracted by the generally conservative choice of plays (usually the West End successes of a year or two before, though there are some enterprising exceptions, such as the Glasgow Citizens' Theatre, Birmingham Repertory, the theatres-in-the-round at Scarborough and Stoke, and the Belgrade Theatre, Coventry). By the beginning of the 1960s the number of repertory theatres outside London had been reduced to around forty.

Répétition, La, see THE REHEARSAL.

Representative, The (Der Stellvertreter). Political drama by ROLFHOCH-HUTH, first performed Berlin, 1963. (American title: *The Deputy*.)

Requiem for a Nun. Drama by William Faulkner, extracted from his novel in dramatic form by Ruth Ford: first performed by the English Stage Company, Royal Court, London, 1957. The only play by this leading American novelist.

Resounding Tinkle, A. Comedy by N. F. SIMPSON, first performed by the English Stage Company in a production-without-décor, Royal Court, London, 1957; publicly performed at the Royal Court in double bill with Simpson's *The Hole*, 1958.

Respectable Prostitute, The (La Putain respectueuse; more properly **The Respectful Prostitute).** Drama by JEAN-PAUL SARTRE, first performed Paris, 1946.

Revenger's Tragedy, The. Drama usually attributed to CYRIL TOUR-NEUR, first performed London, *c*.1606–7.

Revolve, see STAGE MACHINERY.

Revue. A hybrid form of theatrical entertainment, consisting of a rapid succession of short items – songs, dances, and sketches – often with a vaguely topical or satirical basis. The first real revue seems to have been *Under the Clock* (1893), written by Seymour Hicks and Charles Brookfield. Up to the early 1920s revues were chiefly spectacular entertainments, as represented by the work of Albert de Courville and ANDRÉ CHARLOT, and later Alfred Butt in Britain and FLORENZ ZIEGFELD and GEORGE WHITE in New York. During the 1920s this type of revue was less in favour, though latterly it has returned in the series of spectacular shows (something between revue and variety) staged by Robert Nesbitt at the Palladium, London, in the 1950s and 1960s. Between the wars and for some years after the most popular sort of revue was the 'intimate revue', for the invention of which C. B. COCHRAN can perhaps claim chief credit; the first real intimate revue was *Odds and Ends* in 1914. In Cochran's series of revues at the London Pavilion and later at the Ambassadors most of the major stars of the inter-war years appeared, among them Jack Buchanan, Jessie Matthews, Gertrude Lawrence, and BEATRICE LILLIE; he also employed writers like NOËL COWARD and Herbert Farjeon, choreographers like Massine and Fokine, and leading designers from all over the world. One of the biggest successes of the war and immediately post-war years was the really intimate *Sweet and Low* (1943), followed by *Sweeter and Lower* (1944), and *Sweetest and Lowest* (1946), which ran for a total of over a thousand performances at the Ambassadors: later successes along similar lines, all devised by Laurier Lister, were *Oranges and Lemons* (1948), *Penny Plain* (1951), and *Airs on a Shoestring* (1953). When this particular formula seemed to be wearing thin, *Cranks*, devised by the choreographer John Cranko (1955) brought in some strongly surrealistic elements, and *One to Another* and *Pieces of Eight* (both 1959) called in such new dramatists as HAROLD PINTER and N. F. SIMPSON to contribute sketches. In the 1960s the satire boom threw off a number of satirical revues, the most successful of which was the long-running *Beyond the Fringe* (1961). Another phenomenon deserving of mention is *Revudeville* at the Windmill Theatre, a form of continuous variety show with comedy and nudes which ran in various editions from the 1930s and owed its boast 'We never closed' to the fact that it was the only theatre to remain open all through the London blitz of 1940–42. It closed in 1964.

Rhinoceros. Play by EUGÈNE IONESCO, first performed Paris, 1960.

Rice, Elmer (real name Reizenstein; 1892–1967). American dramatist. His first play, *On Trial* (1914), a melodrama using a cinematic flashback technique, was a success, but his writing did not show much quality until *The Adding Machine* (1923), one of the first plays to adapt EXPRESSIONIST techniques to the English-speaking stage, picturing the regimentation of modern life through the career of the unfortunate representative figure of Mr Zero. Rice's other notable successes, *Street Scene* (1929) and *Counsellor-at-Law* (1931) were both realistic dramas; for the first he won a Pulitzer Prize. None of his later plays was so distinguished, or so successful, except for *Dream Girl* (1945), a pleasant fantasy. In 1937 he helped to set up and directed the Playwrights' Producing Company; in 1960 he wrote a controversial book on American drama, *The Living Theatre*, and in 1964 his autobiography, *Minority Report*.

Richard II. Historical drama by WILLIAM SHAKESPEARE, written c.1595–6.

Richard III. Historical drama by WILLIAM SHAKESPEARE, written c.1592–3.

Richardson, Ralph (b. 1902). English actor. Made his professional debut at Lowestoft in 1921, toured the provinces for four years, joined Birmingham Repertory Theatre in 1926, first London appearance in *Yellow Sands* (1926). He first attracted attention in Sir Barry Jackson's productions of *Back to Methuselah* and *The Taming of the Shrew* in modern dress at the Royal Court (1928) and his first leading roles were with the Old Vic Company at the Old Vic and Sadlers' Wells, 1930–31, where he played, most notably, Prince Hal in *Henry IV* Part I, Sir Toby Belch in *Twelfth Night*, and Bluntschli in *Arms and the Man*. For the next few seasons his best work was done for the Old Vic (Petruchio, Bottom, Henry V, Brutus, Iago, etc., 1931–2) and at the Malvern Festival (Face in *The Alchemist*, Sergeant Fielding in Shaw's *Too True to be Good*, 1932). In 1932 he appeared in Maugham's *For Services Rendered* and in 1933 in the same author's *Sheppey*; in 1934 he began a fruitful association with the work of J. B. Priestley in *Eden End*, continuing with *Bees on the Boatdeck* (which he co-directed with Laurence Olivier, 1936), Priestley's ambitious symbolic drama *Johnson over Jordan* (1939), and *An Inspector Calls* (1946). Also during the 1930s Richardson played Mercutio in Katharine Cornell's *Romeo and Juliet* (New York, 1935) and had a major commercial success in *The Amazing Dr Clitterhouse* (1936). After a period of war service he returned to the Old Vic as joint director (1944) and played among other roles Peer Gynt and Uncle Vanya; in 1945–7 with the same company he played Falstaff in *Henry IV* Parts I and II, Tiresias in *Oedipus Rex*, Inspector Goole in *An Inspector Calls* and Cyrano de Bergerac. Later roles include Dr Sloper in *The Heiress* (1949), David Preston in *Home at Seven* (1950), Vershinin in *The Three Sisters* (1951), Prospero, Macbeth, and Volpone (Stratford, 1952), Dr Farley in *A Day by the Sea* (1953), Timon of Athens (Old

Vic, 1956), General St Pé in *The Waltz of the Toreadors* (New York, 1957), Jim Cherry in *Flowering Cherry* (1957), Victor Rhodes in *The Complaisant Lover* (1959), Bottom in *A Midsummer Night's Dream* and Shylock in *The Merchant of Venice* (foreign tour, 1964), the Father in Graham Greene's *Carving a Statue* (1964) and Doctor Rance in Joe Orton's *What the Butler Saw* (1968). This last began a number of appearances in 'new drama', among them John Osborne's *West of Suez* (1971), David Storey's *Home* (1970), and Harold Pinter's *No Man's Land* (1975). He has always specialized in the transfiguration of the ordinary man on stage, and has had many of his biggest successes in this type of role (*Sheppey*, *Johnson over Jordan*, *Flowering Cherry*, *The Complaisant Lover*), but he can also encompass the big comic or tragi-comic role, like Falstaff, Peer Gynt, Volpone, or General St Pé and even play thoroughly unsympathetic roles like Dr Sloper with conviction. He was knighted in 1947.

Richardson, Tony (b. 1928). English director. Began directing with O.U.D.S. while an undergraduate, worked in television, and in 1955 became associate artistic director of the English Stage Company. There and elsewhere he has been associated with contemporary drama, notably that of JOHN OSBORNE, whose *Look Back in Anger*, *The Entertainer*, and *Luther* he has directed, as well as films of the first two, and Osborne's television play *A Subject of Scandal and Concern*. Among other plays he has directed are Ionesco's *The Chairs* and *The Lesson*, *Requiem for a Nun* (in London and New York), *Pericles* and *Othello* (both at Stratford), *Orpheus Descending* (London), *A Taste of Honey* (New York and as a film), *St Joan of the Stockyards* (London) and *Hamlet* with Nicol Williamson (London, the U.S. and as a film). Among his other films are *Tom Jones* (1963), *The Loved One* (1965) and *The Charge of the Light Brigade* (1968).

Riders to the Sea. One-act tragedy by J. M. SYNGE, first performed Dublin, 1904.

Ringer, The. Thriller by EDGAR WALLACE, first performed London, 1926.

Ring Round the Moon (L'Invitation au château). *Pièce brillante* by JEAN ANOUILH, first performed Paris, 1947. English adaptation by CHRISTOPHER FRY first performed London, 1950.

Rivals, The. Comedy by RICHARD BRINSLEY SHERIDAN, first performed Covent Garden, London, 1775.

River Line, The. Drama by CHARLES MORGAN, first performed Edinburgh Festival, 1952.

Robbins, Jerome (b. 1918). American choreographer and director. Dance-director for a number of musical shows, notably *The King and*

I, director of *The Pajama Game*, *Bells are Ringing*, and *Gypsy*, and deviser-director of *West Side Story* (1957). Has subsequently directed straight plays in New York: most successfully *Oh Dad, Poor Dad, Mamma's Hung You in the Closet and I'm Feelin' So Sad* (1962), and more controversially *Mother Courage* (1963), as well as continuing to run his own dance company, Ballet: U.S.A.

Robert and Elizabeth, see THE BARRETTS OF WIMPOLE STREET.

Robertson, T. W. (Thomas William; 1829–71). English dramatist, early advocate of stage realism. He was the son of an actor, and himself a child actor before taking up writing. His first success was conventional enough, being *Garrick* (1864), adapted from the French, but the next year he made his reputation with *Society*, a strong and, in its period, sober and realistic contemporary drama. This was followed by *Ours* (1866), *Caste*, his most famous play (1867), *Play* (1868), and *School* (1869), all of them similarly dramas of contemporary domestic life, what was called not unkindly 'cup-and-saucer drama', set in believable surroundings and avoiding the most melodramatic excesses normal in popular drama of the kind. Robertson was his own director, and paid particularly close attention to realism in sets and props; his success exerted a great influence on the development of English drama in the nineteenth century.

Robeson, Paul (b. 1898). American Negro actor and singer. Began his career as a lawyer, first acted professionally in 1921, and first achieved a major success in 1924, when he played Jim Harris in *All God's Chillun Got Wings* and Brutus Jones in *The Emperor Jones* with the Provincetown Players. In 1928 he played Joe in *Show. Boat* in London, in which he first sang *Ole Man River*. The most famous of his later stage roles is Othello, which he played in London in 1930, New York in 1943, and at Stratford on Avon in 1959.

Robey, George (1869–1954). English music-hall comedian and actor. In his music-hall act he affected a bowler hat, a cane, and two heavy black eyebrows, and was billed as 'the Prime Minister of Mirth', performing popular songs and humorous sketches. With the decline of the music hall around the 1914–18 war he transferred increasingly to revue, and also acted a number of straight roles: Falstaff in *Henry IV* Part I, Menelaus in *Helen* (Cochran's version of *La Belle Hélène*), and Sancho Panza opposite Chaliapin in a film of *Don Quixote*. He was knighted in 1954.

Robinson, Lennox (1886–1958). Irish dramatist, director, and critic. His first play, *The Clancy Name* (1908) was produced at the ABBEY THEATRE, Dublin, and from then on he was associated with it in one capacity or another until his death. In 1910 he became a producer there and gradually took over a major share of the theatre's management, as well as writing a regular succession of plays, including several political tragedies – *Patriots* (1912), *The Dreamers* (1913), *The Lost Leader* (1918) – and a number of skilful comedies – *The White-Headed Boy* (1916), *The Far-off Hills* (1928), *Church Street* (1934) – which have remained in the repertoire. His writings on drama include a history of the Abbey Theatre.

Robson, Flora (b. 1902). English actress. Studied at R.A.D.A., made her debut in Clemence Dane's *Will Shakespeare* (1921). One of her first major successes was the role of Mary Paterson in *The Anatomist* (1931); 1933–4 she was with the Old Vic, playing among other roles Varya in *The Cherry Orchard*, Queen Catherine in *Henry VIII*, Isabella in *Measure for Measure*, Lady Macbeth and Gwendoline Fairfax in *The Importance of Being Earnest*. After the war she appeared in two major popular successes, *Black Chiffon* (1949) and *The House by the Lake* (1956), as well as taking some more substantial roles, including Lady Cicely in *Captain Brassbound's Conversion* (1948), Paulina in *The Winter's Tale* (1951), Mrs Alving in *Ghosts* (Old Vic, 1958), Miss Tina in *The Aspern Papers* (1959), Mother Courage on television (1959), Mrs Borkman in *John Gabriel Borkman* (1963), and Miss Prism in a revival of *The Importance of Being Earnest* (1968). She was created D.B.E. in 1960; a new repertory theatre in Newcastle upon Tyne was named after her in 1962.

Rodgers, Richard (b. 1902). American composer of musicals. His career has been divided into two principal phases, his partnership with the lyric-writer LORENZ HART, which lasted from 1920 nearly to Hart's death in 1943, and his partnership with OSCAR HAMMERSTEIN II, which ran from 1943 until Hammerstein's death in 1961. The collaboration with Hart, beginning when Rodgers was at Columbia University and they worked together on a university show, first brought them success in 1925 with *Garrick Gaieties*, a revue marked by the wit and dexterity of Hart's lyrics, which brought out a corresponding wit and ingenuity in Rodgers's setting of them. Among the shows they worked on together were *The Girl Friend* (1926), *Evergreen* (London, 1930), *On Your Toes* (1936), *Babes in Arms* (1937), *The Boys from Syracuse* (1938), *Pal Joey* (1940), and *By Jupiter* (1942). Hammerstein's talents were more consciously poetic, perhaps excessively so, and with him Rodgers turned away from wit (though not humour) in a number of attempts to realize Hammerstein's dream of a musical which should be a sort of folk-opera. Together they wrote *Oklahoma!* (1943), *Carousel* (1945), *South Pacific* (1949), *The King and I* (1951), *Flower Drum Song* (1958), and *The Sound of*

Music (1959) – all phenomenally successful – as well as several less successful. After Hammerstein's death Rodgers took to writing his own lyrics rather in the style of Hart and with some success, notably in *No Strings* (1962), as well as collaborating with Stephen Sondheim in *Do I Hear a Waltz?* (1965).

Rollo (Patate). Comedy by MARCEL ACHARD, first performed Paris, 1958.

Romanoff and Juliet. Comedy by PETER USTINOV, first performed London, 1956.

Roman Theatre. Theatre, or at least drama, in ancient Rome was derived almost entirely from the GREEK; when drama proper first replaced rough folk entertainments at the public games of 240 B.C. it was with a Greek play in translations and virtually all the Roman plays written for public performance which have survived, whether of TERENCE, PLAUTUS, or some lesser writer, seem to be based more or less closely on Greek originals. The theatres in which the perform-ances took place were first of all temporary, then permanent open-air buildings, somewhat after the Greek pattern, except that the role of CHORUS was largely eliminated from Roman drama (or taken by a single speaker) and so the focus of attention was on the raised stage instead of the lower orchestra in front, which remained largely un-used. MASKS and costumes were employed, the latter in more and more elaborate forms to help satisfy the Roman taste for spectacle. Comedy seems to have predominated in the Roman theatre, and what we know of its tragedy shows the main emphasis falling on the grotesque, horrific, or spectacular elements present in embryonic forms in the Greek originals. Towards the end of the Republican era in Rome drama began to decline in popularity and the theatre in prestige; under the Empire straight drama was largely replaced by pantomimes and spectacular shows of various sorts, while the writing of drama became a literary pursuit indulged in by intellectuals such as SENECA, who never intended their works for performance. The final blow to Roman drama was the hostility of the Christian Church, and the institution of Christianity as the state religion brought about the closing of theatres in the sixth century A.D.

Romberg, Sigmund (1887–1951). Hungarian-American composer of musical comedies, mostly in a conservative romantic style. His first success was *The Whirl of the World* (1913), and his most famous shows were *The Student Prince* (1924), *The Desert Song* (1926), and *The New Moon* (1928).

Romeo and Juliet. Tragedy by WILLIAM SHAKESPEARE, written 1595–6.

Rookery Nook. ALDWYCH FARCE by BEN TRAVERS, first performed London, 1926.

Room, The. One-act drama by HAROLD PINTER, first performed Bristol, 1957.

Roots. Drama by ARNOLD WESKER, first performed Coventry, 1959; first performed with *Chicken Soup with Barley* and *I'm Talking About Jerusalem* as 'The Wesker Trilogy', Royal Court, London, 1960.

Rope. Thriller by PATRICK HAMILTON, first performed London, 1929.

Roscius, Quintus (*d*. 62 B.C.). Roman actor, the most famous comic of his day, praised by Cicero, who defended him in a law suit, and granted equestrian rank by the dictator Sulla.

Rose Marie. Musical play by RUDOLF FRIML and Herbert Stothart, book and lyrics by Otto Harbach and OSCAR HAMMERSTEIN II; first performed New York, 1924.

Rosencrantz and Guildenstern are Dead. Drama by TOM STOPPARD, first produced National Theatre, London, 1967.

Rose Tattoo, The. Drama by TENNESSEE WILLIAMS, first performed New York, 1950.

Rosmersholm. Drama by HENRIK IBSEN, first performed Bergen, 1887.

Ross. Dramatic biography of T. E. Lawrence by TERENCE RATTIGAN, first performed London, 1960.

Rostand, Edmond (1868–1918). French dramatist. A whole-hearted Romantic, he wrote a series of eloquent, often humorous verse plays which provided showy roles for the more important actors of his day. He began with a light comedy, *Les Romanesques* (1894) and a lyrical drama, *La Princesse lointaine* (1895), but his great lasting success came with *Cyrano de Bergerac* (1898), the part of the long-nosed poet (in fact an historical character, 1619–55, and playwright of some slight note) being first played by the elder Coquelin. *L'Aiglon* (1900) gave Bernhardt a telling role as Napoleon's pathetic son, the King of Rome. *Chantecler* (1910), Rostand's last completed play, was an ambitious and quite effective allegory.

Rough and Ready Lot, The. Drama by ALUN OWEN, first performed London, 1959.

Round, Theatre in the, see STAGE.

Roussin, André (b. 1911). French dramatist, specialist in light comedy and farce. His first successes were *Am Stam Gram* (1943) and *Une grande fille toute simple* (1944). The best known of his later plays are *La Petite Hutte* (1947, translated by Nancy Mitford as *The Little Hut*), *Nina* (1949), *Bobosse* (1950), and *Lorsque l'enfant paraît* (1952). Most of his comedies have a certain poetic element, but succeed best when this is least pronounced.

Rowe, Nicholas (1674–1718). English dramatist, leading tragic writer of the early eighteenth century. He became Poet Laureate in 1715 and was a capable if not particularly distinguished poet: his best plays are *The Fair Penitent* (1703), based on *The Fatal Dowry* by MASSINGER and Field, and *The Tragedy of Jane Shore* (1714), both with telling leading roles for women. Rowe was also an early editor of the works of Shakespeare.

Rowley, William (*c*.1585–*c*.1637). English dramatist and actor. Wrote a number of plays in collaboration, of which the most interesting are *The Witch of Edmonton* (1621), a topical drama written with FORD and DEKKER, and *The Changeling* (1622), a tragedy written with MIDDLETON. By himself he wrote *All's Lost by Lust* (1622), in which he himself played the clown, and as an actor he seems to have specialized in fat comic roles. Virtually nothing is known of his life outside his work.

Royal Court Theatre. Theatre outside London's West End proper, in Sloane Square on the edge of Chelsea. For two periods in its career (it was opened in 1870, rebuilt 1871 and 1887) it has housed important companies with a bias towards experiment, 1904–7, when it was the home of the BARKER–VEDRENNE Company, and from 1956, when it has been the home of the ENGLISH STAGE COMPANY.

Royal Shakespeare Company, see STRATFORD.

Rozov, Victor (b. 1913). Russian dramatist, author of several of the biggest commercial successes in post-war Moscow theatre. Many of his plays are about teenage problems and conflicts between the generations; one of the most popular, *Uneven Combat* (1961), was performed simultaneously at the Maly and at the Children's Theatre, for which he has specially written several plays. Other plays by him include *In Search of Happiness*, performed on British television, and *The Cranes are Flying*, best known from the film version.

Ruddigore. 'Savoy opera' by W. S. GILBERT (book and lyrics) and Arthur Sullivan (music), first performed London, 1887.

R.U.R. Drama by KAREL ČAPEK, first performed Prague, 1921.

Rutherford, Margaret (1892–1972). English actress. Made debut in 1925, after playing a variety of character roles in repertory and on the London stage (among them Miss Prism in *The Importance of Being Earnest*, 1939) had major successes with the roles of the sinister Mrs Danvers in *Rebecca* (1940), the eccentric medium Madame Arcati in *Blithe Spirit* (1941), and the equally eccentric headmistress, Miss Whitchurch, in *The Happiest Days of Your Life* (1948). Later roles include Lady Bracknell in *The Importance of Being Earnest* (New York, 1947; Dublin, 1947), Mme Desmortes in *Ring Round the Moon*

(1950), Lady Wishfort in *The Way of the World* (1952), the Duchess of Pont-au-Bronc in *Time Remembered* (1954). She was created D.B.E. in 1967.

Ruy Blas. Verse tragedy by VICTOR HUGO, first performed Paris, 1838.

S

Sabrina Fair. Light romantic comedy by Samuel Taylor, first performed New York, 1953, and subsequently all over the world.

Sachs, Hans (1494–1576). German dramatist and mastersinger, familiar chiefly as the hero of Wagner's opera *Die Meistersinger*. The historical Sachs was also a cobbler, and wrote an enormous number of tragedies, comedies and short carnival plays. Most of his more ambitious plays suffer from too evidently moralistic aims, but the carnival plays, of which he wrote some two hundred, are unpretentious folk-comedies in rough verse and generally colloquial language which remain pleasing even today.

Sacred Flame, The. Drama by W. SOMERSET MAUGHAM, first performed New York, 1928.

Sadler's Wells. Theatre away from the West End of London, in Islington. Began life as a music house in the pleasure gardens surrounding the medicinal wells. Rebuilt in stone as a theatre 1765, it reached the height of its glory in the 1840s and 1850s, when Phelps was manager and chief attraction. Later it declined and was derelict for some years until taken over by LILIAN BAYLIS as a North London companion-house to the Old Vic. She built a completely new theatre on the site in 1931, and the Old Vic Company alternated between the Old Vic and Sadler's Wells until 1934, when the Old Vic was made exclusively the home of drama and Sadler's Wells concentrated on opera and ballet.

Sail Away. Musical by NOËL COWARD, first performed New York, 1962.

Saint-Denis, Michel (1897–1971). French director and actor, nephew of COPEAU and founder and director of the COMPAGNIE DES QUINZE. After the company was disbanded Saint-Denis settled in London in 1936 and founded the London Theatre Studio, an acting school which closed in 1939; also staged a number of distinguished productions in London, among them *Macbeth* (1937), *The Three Sisters* (1938), and Lorca's *Marriage of Blood* (1939). During the war he worked as head of the French Section of the B.B.C., and then for a year with Radiodiffusion Française. From 1946 to 1952 he was general director of the Old Vic Theatre School; he also staged *Oedipus Rex* (1945), *A Month in the Country* (1949), and *Electra* (1951) for the Old Vic and in 1950 became a director of the theatre. From 1952 to 1957 he returned to France as director of the Centre Nationale Dramatique de l'Est, Strasbourg. He was a consultant for the foundation of the Lincoln Center Repertory Theater and Dramatic School,

New York, and in 1962 returned to Britain as a director of the Royal Shakespeare Company, for which he staged *The Cherry Orchard*.

Sainthill, Loudon (1919–69). Australian stage designer. Began designing sets and costumes for the theatre in Australia in 1940; established in Britain, he designed a number of ballets, Shakespeare productions (*The Tempest*, Stratford, 1951; *Romeo and Juliet*, Old Vic, 1953; *Pericles*, Stratford, 1958; *Othello*, Stratford, 1959), a few modern plays like *Moon on a Rainbow Shawl* (1958) and *Orpheus Descending* (1959), and a memorably elegant revival of *A Woman of No Importance* (1953). For the most part his designs were essentially romantic, with often a faint hint of Surrealism in the details, but he could also, as with the Wilde, recreate a period with brilliant exactness.

Saint Joan. Drama by GEORGE BERNARD SHAW, first performed New York, 1923.

Saint's Day. Drama by JOHN WHITING, first performed London, 1951.

Sakuntala. Drama by KÁLIDÁSA, date unknown.

Salacrou, Armand (b. 1899). French dramatist. Son of a chemist, he began by studying medicine, went on to journalism and wrote his first play, *Le Casseur d'assiettes*, in 1923. His early plays had little success, despite the enthusiasm of Jouvet and Giraudoux, but he finally had a major success with *Une Femme libre* (1931), a comedy-drama about love and freedom. In later works the subject of predestination and inevitability in life has recurred constantly, notably in *L'Inconnu d'Arras* (1935), in which a suicide relives the events which led to his death; *L'Archipel Lenoir* (1947), a savage burlesque; *Dieu le savait* (1950), which follows fatality through three generations; and *Les Invités du Bon Dieu* (1953), about God's attitude towards pain and unhappiness. Slightly apart from the main line of his work are three of his most interesting plays, *La Terre est ronde* (1939), a life of Savonarola given by the Comédie-Française, *Histoire de rire* (1939), an elegantly patterned sex comedy, and *Sens interdit* (1953), a poetic fantasy based on a consideration of what would happen if time started moving backwards. The principal criticism of Salacrou's drama has tended to be that he introduces serious themes into his plays but works them out too easily to carry complete conviction.

Salad Days. Musical by JULIAN SLADE, book and lyrics by Dorothy Reynolds and Julian Slade, first performed Bristol, 1954.

Salomé. One-act drama by OSCAR WILDE, written in French, put into rehearsal by Sarah Bernhardt for London production in 1892, but banned by the Lord Chamberlain and first performed Paris, 1896. First performance of Lord Alfred Douglas's English version, London, 1905.

Samson Agonistes. Tragedy by JOHN MILTON, published 1671, first performed London, 1900.

Sánchez, Florencio (1875–1910). Uruguayan dramatist, author of a number of realistic dramas about the adaptation of primitive elements in Spanish-American society to the problems of the modern world. His most famous play is *M' Hijo el doctor* (1903) about a conflict between generations and town and country ways in an old gaucho family.

Sardou, Victorien (1831–1908). French dramatist, one of the most brilliant and successful exponents of the WELL-MADE PLAY. For some time he was SARAH BERNHARDT's favourite contemporary dramatist, and devised for her a series of strong dramas, mostly titled with women's names: *Dora* (1877), later revised as *L'Espionne* (1905); *Fédora* (1882); *La Tosca* (1887), better known to succeeding generations by way of Puccini's opera; *Théodora impératrice de Bizance* (1884), one of the big spectacles of the day; *Cléopâtre* (1890); and *La Sorcière* (1903), a drama of the Inquisition. Sardou also wrote comedy, notably in the brilliantly constructed *Les Pattes de mouche* (1860) and *La Famille Benoiton* (1865), and, in his famous historical romance *Madame Sans-Gêne* (1893), one of Réjane's greatest successes. His last play, *L'Affaire des poisons* (1907) was a sensational historical drama set in the court of Louis XIV. Apart from *Madame Sans-Gêne* his plays do not survive in the normal repertoire, but in their day they were highly influential, and drove Shaw to coin the term 'Sardoodledom', a pejorative expression intended to sum up all that was most trashy and contrived in the mechanically 'well-made' play.

Saroyan, William (b. 1908). American dramatist of Armenian extraction. After achieving some success as a fiction writer he turned to drama in 1939 with *My Heart's in the Highlands*, a long one-act play about the poetic spirit in a materialist world, and *The Time of Your Life*, a sort of optimistic equivalent of *The Iceman Cometh*, celebrating sentimentally man's ability to overcome adversity with sweetness and light. A similar message is embodied in such other plays as *Love's Old Sweet Song* (1940), *The Beautiful People* (1941), *The Cave Dwellers* (1957), and even *Sam, the Highest Jumper of Them All* (1960), which he improvised during rehearsals with the Theatre Workshop Company at Stratford, London. Possibly his best play, certainly less affected by sentimentality than most, is *Hello Out There*, a one-act drama about a lynching (1942).

Sartre, Jean-Paul (b. 1905). French novelist, dramatist, and philosopher, leading figure in the Existentialist movement. His first play,

Les Mouches (1942) is almost an Existentialist thesis in dramatic form: a retelling of the myth of Orestes, it reverses its point, so that Orestes kills Clytemnestra as a free act to defy the anger of gods in whom he does not believe. *Huis-clos* (1944), a long one-acter about three characters in a stuffy second-empire room which represents for them hell, since within it they are destined to torture each other endlessly without issue, is perhaps Sartre's best play; within its limits at least it is a brilliant piece of theatre. As much cannot be said for *La Putain respectueuse* (1946), a crude tract on racism, but *Les Mains sales* in 1947 retrieved matters somewhat, being at least a very able political thriller. This was followed by one of Sartre's most ambitious plays, the vast *Le Diable et le Bon Dieu* (1951), which set out, rather too schematically for theatrical success, to demonstrate the uselessness of the concept of God. After two divertissements, *Kean, ou désordre et génie* (1953), rewritten from Dumas *père* for PIERRE BRASSEUR, and *Nekrassov* (1955), an entertaining enough political comedy, Sartre returned to more substantial themes with *Les Séquestrés d'Altona* (1959), a large-scale drama about a family which embodies in its various members the anguish of Germany in the post-Nazi era. Drama has remained a sideline, though an important sideline, in Sartre's career, but in *Huis-clos* and *Les Séquestrés d'Altona* he has provided contemporary French theatre with two of its most telling works.

Satyr play. Grotesque farcical drama presented in the Greek theatre in the same programme as each tragic trilogy. It usually provided a sort of burlesque footnote to the main work in the programme, involving a legendary hero – often from the accompanying tragedies – in some ridiculous situation and surrounding him with a chorus of satyrs, half-human beasts with a frankly indecent view of life. The satyr play was written by the same author as the tragic trilogy, and its writing was indeed part of the competition. A satyr play by Euripides, *The Cyclops*, survives complete, and there are fragments of one by Sophocles, the *Ichneutae*; none of Aeschylus' work in the form survives, though he was considered, with Pratinas, the great master of the genre. The origin of the satyr play and its place in the system of Greek drama, though the subject of much speculation, even in classical times, remain impenetrably obscure.

Saunders, James (b. 1925). English dramatist, somewhat influenced by the Theatre of the ABSURD. His first play to attract attention was *Alas, Poor Fred* (1959), an Ionesco-like fantasy in which a husband and wife talk about the vanished Fred, who seems to represent their dead past. Later works include *The Ark* (1959), a relatively straightforward dramatization of the story of Noah in which Noah turns out to be the villain of the piece; *Next Time I'll Sing to You* (1962), an eloquent series of fantastic excursions based vaguely on the facts of the life and death of the Great Canfield hermit Alexander James Mason; and *A Scent of Flowers* (1964), a sensitive tragi-comedy about the first few hours after the death of a young suicide. Saunders has also written a number of brief one-act plays.

Savory, Gerald (b. 1909). English dramatist, author mainly of light comedies. His first great London success was the domestic comedy *George and Margaret* (1937), long a repertory favourite; later works, particularly *A Likely Tale* (1956) and *Come Rain, Come Shine* (1958) show a delicate, poetic temperament at work within the framework of conventional West End comedy.

Savoy. London theatre built by D'OYLY CARTE in 1881 as a home for the comic operas of GILBERT and Sullivan, which are consequently known as the 'Savoy operas' (even those produced at other theatres before 1881). The first to be produced there was *Patience*, transferred from the Opéra Comique. The Savoy is also notable as the first theatre to have been completely lit by electricity.

Saxe-Meiningen, George, Duke of, see MEININGEN PLAYERS.

Scapa, see SEAGULLS OVER SORRENTO.

Scarron, Paul (1610–60). French dramatist and novelist, author of numerous comedies, many of them based on Spanish originals. The first two plays he wrote, *Jodelet, ou le maître-valet* (1643) and *Jodelet souffleté* (1645) were big successes, and so were most of his later works, particularly *Don Japhet d'Arménie* (1647) and *L'Écolier de Salamanque* (1654). His plays have slipped from the modern repertoire, but *Don Japhet d'Arménie* was successfully revived in 1955.

Scene bay, scene dock. Rooms in a theatre immediately adjacent to the stage, where scenery can be stored.

Scenery, theatrical. Scenery as such (unless we except the mysterious 'periaktoi' – see SOPHOCLES) was unknown in classical drama, which was normally performed against a permanent background, sometimes an elaborate architectural one. Equally, scenery, beyond a minimum of what could be regarded as props, was unknown in medieval drama, but began to be developed in Renaissance times, when painted backcloths making use of perspective effects appeared to make the halls in which plays were given look larger. The principles upon which set design might be based were first elaborated by Baldassare Peruzzi (1481–1531) and by his pupil SEBASTIANO SERLIO (1475–1554), who in his *Architettura* suggested three different types of setting for different genres of drama. In 1584 Vincenzo Scamozzi provided for changeable perspective scenes to be glimpsed through the doors of the permanent architectural setting in the Teatro Olimpico at Vincenza, and in 1589 Bernardo Buontalenti, or delle Girandole, introduced what look like 'wings' – changeable painted canvas side-pieces – and very elaborate settings for the Florentine intermezzi (see INTERLUDE). From these settings developed the work of many later Italians, and also, indirectly, of such foreigners as the Frenchman Jacques Callot (1592–1635) and the Englishman INIGO JONES.

The development of opera in the seventeenth century led to a further immense elaboration in theatrical scenery, and the appearance of the first full-time stage designers (as opposed to architects or painters for whom the stage was a sideline). The most notable of these was GIACOMO TORELLI (1608–78), the great master of Baroque stage design. He may have invented the system of wings installed at the Teatro Farnese in Parma and widely copied elsewhere. His methods of scene-setting and changing rapidly spread all over Europe, particularly to France, despite attempts to cling to the old permanent settings, and to England, where the theatre was beginning to revive after the Civil War. Meanwhile in Italy techniques continued to develop, particularly in the work of the BIBIENA family of designers. The eighteenth century saw the reappearance of neo-classic styles of stage decoration, especially on the Continent, and alongside it the introduction of elaborate naturalistic landscape backdrops. This latter impulse was particularly telling in England, where GARRICK encouraged the work of Philippe Jacques de Loutherbourg (1735–1810), a romantic landscape artist, and himself devised some technical innovations. Shortly afterwards William Capon (1757–1827), Kemble's designer, began to study documents of the period when designing for Shakespeare productions, thereby anticipating the nineteenth-century vogue for historical authenticity in settings and costume.

The nineteenth century in general saw a reaction against sets of painted canvas, and a new vogue for realism in sets and props began, which reached its climax in the naturalism of ANTOINE, who matched in his settings the determined, detailed naturalism of the sort of plays he favoured. From this there was bound to be a reaction, which came almost at once from the SYMBOLISTS, led by PAUL FORT and LUGNÉ-POË at the Théâtre d'Art, later Théâtre de l'Œuvre. For a while the two approaches existed side by side, STANISLAVSKY in Russia, under the influence of Antoine, remaining on the whole faithful to naturalism in stage design while APPIA and GORDON CRAIG preached and the latter practised a complete divorce between theatrical settings and real life. Gradually, however, an eclectic approach developed – best summed up in the work of REINHARDT – according to which no general principle should be applied indiscriminately to all drama, but the style of setting used which accorded best with the requirements of the particular play in question. And this has remained in general the case; apart from a definite swing away from spectacle and a taste for the economical effect in theatrical production (especially in Shakespeare, which no one now wants to produce with the elaboration of BEERBOHM TREE), almost any style from the most abstract to the most naturalistic is permissible in the modern theatre.

Schéhadé, Georges (b. 1910). French dramatist of Lebanese origin, author of a number of erratic, graceful, poetic tragi-comedies, among them *Monsieur Bob'le* (1951), *La Soirée des proverbes* (1954), and *Histoire de Vasco* (1956), all of them tales of journeys and quests in which the expected seldom happens and nothing is ever quite what it seems.

Schiller, Johann Christoph Friedrich von (1759–1805). German dramatist and poet, master of Romantic costume-drama imbued with the spirit of STURM UND DRANG. His first play, *Die Räuber* (1781) described a violent, intense hostility between brothers and became something of a rallying-point for young opinion. At the time of its production Schiller was in the army, but the next year he deserted and settled in Mannheim, where his *Kabale und Liebe* (1784), a lightweight satire on despotism, was successfully produced and where he began *Don Carlos* (1787), a large-scale romantic tragedy set in the court of Philip II of Spain. During the next twelve years he worked as a history professor at Jena and editor of a literary and philosophical magazine, *Thalia*, but in 1799 he completed his major historical trilogy *Wallenstein*. The next five years brought forward four more historical dramas in rapid succession, *Maria Stuart* (1800), *Die Jungfrau von Orleans* (1801), *Die Braut von Messina* (1803), and *Wilhelm Tell* (1804). In these later plays Schiller's stagecraft has been refined and perfected, so that they strike a balance between Romantic subject-matter (particularly the recurrent notion of redemption through the acceptance of suffering) and classical orderliness and precision in the form, which in *Die Braut von Messina* goes as far as imitation of the structure of Greek tragedy.

Schisgal, Murray (b. 1926). American dramatist, most of whose plays were first produced in Great Britain. The earliest to make a mark were a quartet of one-act plays, *Schrecks* (1960), which favoured the Theatre of the ABSURD; two of them, *The Typists* and *The Tiger*, were later produced on Broadway and in the West End. *Ducks and Lovers* (1961), a comedy-drama of gipsy life, and *Luv* (1963), a triangle comedy, are more conventional in style, and made little impression when produced at the Arts Theatre, London; *Luv*, however, went on to be a surprise success on Broadway.

Schlegel, August (1767–1845). German critic and translator of Shakespeare. His major work of criticism was his series of lectures *Über dramatische Kunst und Literatur* (1809–11), in which he outlined the history of world drama; his translations of Shakespeare still remain the most generally used in Germany.

Schnitzler, Arthur (1862–1931). Austrian dramatist who combined a cool cynicism about his characters and their motives with a romantically graceful and elegant surface. His best known plays are *Anatol* (1893), a collection of sketches about the life and loves of a somewhat unscrupulous man-about-town; *Liebelei* (1895), a gloomy story of the devotion of a working-class girl to an aristocrat who does not care for her; and *Reigen* (1902), which shows love as a bitterly comic merry-go-round. The last two are best remembered now as the basis of Max Ophül films, *Reigen* becoming *La Ronde*.

School for Scandal, The. Comedy by RICHARD BRINSLEY SHERIDAN, first performed Drury Lane, London, 1777.

School for Wives (L'École des femmes). Comedy by MOLIÈRE, first performed Paris, 1662.

Schwartz, Yevgeny (1897–1958). Russian dramatist, author of satirical fables in dramatic form, some so sharp that they have been temporarily or permanently banned by the Soviet government. His most successful plays are *The Naked King* and *The Snow Queen*, based on Hans Andersen, and *The Dragon*, a sub-Arthurian fantasy.

Scofield, Paul (b. 1922). English actor. Made his professional debut in 1940, played two seasons with Birmingham Repertory Company, then in 1946–7 joined the resident company at Stratford-on-Avon, where he was noticed as Henry V, Don Armado in *Love's Labour's Lost*, Mercutio, and Sir Andrew Aguecheek. At the Arts in 1946 he played Tegeus-Chromis in *A Phoenix Too Frequent*, and back at Stratford in 1948 Hamlet, the Clown in *The Winter's Tale*, and Troilus in *Troilus and Cressida*. His major popular success at this period was in the dual role of Hugo and Frederic in *Ring Round the Moon* (1950), a success later repeated in another Anouilh play, *Time Remembered* (1955). Meanwhile, in Sir John Gielgud's 1952–3 season at the Lyric, Hammersmith, he played Richard II, Witwoud in *The*

Way of the World, and Pierre in *Venice Preserved*. In 1956 he played a season, directed by Peter Brook, at the Phoenix, appearing in *Hamlet*, *The Power and the Glory*, and *The Family Reunion*. Later roles include Johnnie in *Expresso Bongo* (1958), Clive Root in *The Complaisant Lover* (1959), Sir Thomas More in *A Man for All Seasons* (1960), and King Lear with the Royal Shakespeare Company (Stratford 1962, London and Paris 1963, world tour 1964), *Timon of Athens* and *The Government Inspector*, also with the Royal Shakespeare Company (Stratford and London, 1965–6), and leading roles in Charles Dyer's *Staircase* (1966) and JOHN OSBORNE's *Hotel in Amsterdam* (1968).

Scribe, Eugène (1791–1861). French dramatist, best remembered as the inventor of the mechanically WELL-MADE PLAY so abominated by Shaw. He was an excellent theatrical craftsman, though nearly all the 400-odd plays and VAUDEVILLES he wrote (alone or in collaboration) are now forgotten. His first success was in 1820, with *Une Nuit de la Garde Nationale*, and from then until his death he continued to pour out works of all sorts, of which the only one anyone remembers now is *Adrienne Lecouvreur* (1849), written in collaboration with Ernest Legouvé, which tells with considerable dramatist's licence the life-story of the early eighteenth-century actress and gave RACHEL one of her greatest successes. Scribe also wrote a number of libretti for operas such as *Fra Diavolo*, *Les Huguenots*, and *Robert le diable*, which survive now only in so far as the music keeps them alive.

Seagull, The (Chaika). Drama by ANTON CHEKHOV, first performed Moscow, 1896.

Seagulls Over Sorrento. Long-running service comedy by Hugh Hastings, first performed London, 1949. Musical version, *Scapa*, book, lyrics, and music by Hugh Hastings, first performed London, 1962.

Second Mrs Tanqueray, The. Drama by ARTHUR WING PINERO, first performed London, 1893.

Seneca, Lucius Annaeus (*c*.4 B.C.–A.D. 65). Roman dramatist, statesman, and philosopher. His nine tragedies, the main surviving drama of the Roman Empire, were written to be read rather than performed, and indeed contain many scenes which would be quite impractical on stage. Unlike most Roman drama the plays, though on the Greek model, are original works, and have an individual climate of horror and brutality which perhaps reflects the atmosphere of Nero's Court, in which they were written, Seneca being for some time Nero's tutor and adviser. The subjects are all derived from Greek legend, but on the whole the most savage are chosen, as in Seneca's *Medea*, *Phaedra*,

Agamemnon, and *Hercules Furens* and *Oetaeus*. The sensational qualities of Seneca's plays made him favourite reading during the Renaissance, and his influence can be seen on much of the drama of the period, notably in the works of Marlowe, the whole school of revenge tragedy, and Shakespeare's *Titus Andronicus*.

Separate Tables. Double bill of linked plays by TERENCE RATTIGAN, *Table by the Window* and *Table Number Seven*; first performed London, 1954.

Serjeant Musgrave's Dance. Drama by JOHN ARDEN, first performed by the English Stage Company, Royal Court, London, 1959.

Serlio, Sebastiano (1475–1554). Italian architect and author of an ambitious treatise on architecture, the second book of which, published 1545, concerned perspective in theatrical design and gave instruction for the painting of three different types of perspective backdrops.

Seven Against Thebes. Tragedy by AESCHYLUS, first performed Athens, 469 B.C.

Shadow of a Gunman, The. Drama by SEAN O'CASEY, first performed Abbey Theatre, Dublin, 1923.

Shadow play. A type of puppet theatre originating in the far east, especially China and Indonesia, in which flat articulated figures are manipulated between a strong light and a translucent screen, so that the audience sees merely their shadows. Primitive forms of the shadow play are found as a folk entertainment in Greece and towards the end of the eighteenth century there was a short-lived vogue for '*ombres chinoises*', particularly in France, where Dominique Séraphin and his family ran a permanent shadow theatre from 1774 to 1859. An English version, known as a Galanty Show, was also popular for a while. A more self-consciously artistic type of shadow show had a revival in the 1880s, somewhat paralleling the general revival of interest in puppets.

Shadwell, Thomas (*c.*1642–92). English dramatist and Dryden's successor as Poet Laureate. He regarded himself as a disciple of BEN JONSON, and his comedies, among them *Epsom Wells* (1672), *The Squire of Alsatia* (1688), and *Bury Fair* (1689), have a crude vigour more suggestive of Jonson than of their Restoration contemporaries. He also made some very free adaptations of Shakespeare, such as *The Enchanted Island* (1674), garbled from *The Tempest* to suit the taste of the time.

Shaffer, Peter (b. 1926). English dramatist who achieved a major West End success with his first stage play, *Five Finger Exercise* (1958), an effective emotional drama of middle-class life. Later works include a double bill of comedy-dramas, *The Private Ear* and *The Public Eye* (1962), an ambitious play about the Spanish invasion of the Inca empire, *The Royal Hunt of the Sun*, produced at the Chichester Festival in 1964, and later at the National Theatre, and another one-act comedy, *Black Comedy*, first produced at the Chichester Festival in 1965. The most successful of his later plays has been *Equus*, a symbolic drama first staged at the National Theatre in 1973.

Shaftesbury Avenue. Street in the West End of London on or just off which are situated a number of theatres, among them the Lyric, the Apollo, the Globe, the Queen's, the Palace, the Saville, and the Shaftesbury, formerly the Prince's. By extension, the term has come to be used generically of commercial West End theatre, as opposed to anything experimental, non-commercial, and generally 'fringe'.

Shakespeare, William (1564–1616). English dramatist and actor, born in Stratford on Avon of a prosperous middle-class family. He is first mentioned in connexion with the London stage in Robert Greene's pamphlet *A Groatsworth of Wit bought with a Million of Repentance* (1592), by which time he was clearly well established. In 1595 he became a 'sharer' in the CHAMBERLAIN'S MEN; around 1610 he seems to have retired to Stratford, though he continued to visit London from time to time until his death. Apart from some poems – *Venus and Adonis* (1593), *The Rape of Lucrece* (1594), *Sonnets* (published 1609) – thirty-six plays by him, in whole or part, survive of which twelve were published in quartos (often dubiously authorized) during his life and nearly the whole body in the 'First Folio' edited by Heminge and Condell in 1623. The dates of very few of the plays can be established with certainty, but the general lines of a rough chronology between *Henry VI* Parts II and III, written around 1591, and *Henry VIII*, written around 1612, have been widely agreed by scholars. The pattern of Shakespeare's career as worked out on various evidences, internal and external, goes something like this: from about 1590 to 1600 a general concentration on history plays and comedies; 1600 to 1608 tragedies and 'dark comedies'; 1608 to 1612 dramatic romances.

The eight plays in which Shakespeare covered the whole course of English history from Richard II to Richard III were not written in order, though some sort of overall pattern has often been found in the resulting sequence; the second half of the period, that covered by the *Henry VI* plays and *Richard III*, came first, and then later on *Richard II*, *Henry IV* Parts I and II, and *Henry V*. Meanwhile Shakespeare was trying his hand at various sorts of comedy: the frankly farcical in *The Comedy of Errors*, the elaborately sophisticated in *Love's Labour's Lost*, the light fantastic in *A Midsummer Night's Dream*, and the romantic in *The Two Gentlemen of Verona, The Taming of the Shrew, The Merchant of Venice, Much Ado About Nothing, As You Like It,* and *Twelfth Night.* From this period, too, date the essay in SENECAN revenge drama *Titus Andronicus* (presumably very early) and the romantic tragedy *Romeo and Juliet.*

The second period opens with the Roman drama *Julius Caesar,* and there follow three bitter comedies, *Troilus and Cressida, All's Well that Ends Well,* and *Measure for Measure,* the classical dramas *Antony and Cleopatra* and *Coriolanus,* and the tragedies *Hamlet, Othello, King Lear, Macbeth,* and *Timon of Athens,* as well as one broad comedy, *The Merry Wives of Windsor,* traditionally the result of Queen Elizabeth's wish to see Falstaff from *Henry IV* in love. The last period, that of the dramatic romances, seems to reflect a mellower view of life (though one should probably beware of too ready an interpretation in terms of Shakespeare's own emotional states): the plays in this group are all loosely-knit comedy-dramas full of long-lost relatives, confused wanderings and belated reconciliations. They are *Pericles, Cymbeline, The Winter's Tale,* and *The Tempest* – after which come two plays written in collaboration (apparently with FLETCHER), *Henry VIII* and *The Two Noble Kinsmen,* the latter of which has never been accepted into the official canon of Shakespeare's works. Of the numerous other works attributed to him from time to time he may have had a hand in *Edward III* and almost certainly wrote a scene for the collaborative *Sir Thomas More,* which survives in what seems to be his own handwriting.

Shakespeare has been the most consistently popular of all English dramatists, both at home and abroad. During the seventeenth and eighteenth centuries his plays were almost invariably played in ruthlessly adapted versions altered to suit the tastes of the time – Nahum Tate's version of *King Lear* with a happy ending (1681) is the classic instance – and the original texts only began to be restored in the nineteenth century. Some or all of his works have been translated into nearly every language in the world and, especially since the dawn of Romanticism, have exerted a unique influence on subsequent drama as well as more generally on the life and thought of men.

Shanghai Gesture, The. Classic melodrama by John Colton, first produced New York, 1925.

Shaw, George Bernard (1856–1950). Anglo-Irish dramatist and theatre critic. He began his career, after an ineffective grapple with commerce, as an unpublished novelist and speaker on a variety of topical subjects, mainly for the Fabian Society. In the early 1880s he became a regular periodical critic, first of books for the *Pall Mall Gazette* and of art for the *World*, then of music (under the pseudonym of Corno di Bassetto) for the *Star*, then – and most influentially – of drama for the *Saturday Review* from 1895 to 1897. While a regular dramatic critic he developed very clear ideas of the stage and its proper uses for the putting-over of ideas – IBSEN, whose chief supporter in this country he was, provided the most important impetus here. In 1885 he started work on his first play, *Widowers' Houses*, which was finally staged in 1892. It was followed by a considerable success, *Arms and the Man* (1894), a comedy with a moral which has remained one of Shaw's most popular plays, and by *Mrs Warren's Profession*, written in 1893 but not staged until 1902, and not seen professionally in London until the Lord Chamberlain's ban was lifted in 1925. It was banned because it concerned prostitution, and it was one of a series of plays in which Shaw deliberately set out to deal realistically with subjects previously taboo in the theatre, or at best handled only in terms of sentimental melodrama. Other plays of this early period in his work are *Candida* (1895), *The Devil's Disciple* (1897), *Caesar and Cleopatra* (1898), *John Bull's Other Island* (1904), *Major Barbara* (1905), and *The Doctor's Dilemma* (1906), and in the middle of it came the gargantuan *Man and Superman* (1901–3), in which he first developed in detail his idea of the Life Force as the ruling factor in the life of man.

With the setting up of the BARKER–VEDRENNE management in 1904 Shaw was able for the first time to play a vital part in the production of his plays, and thereby to exert a stronger influence than ever on the theatre of the time. During the succeeding years before the First World War he wrote a group of comparatively lightweight but durable comedies, among them *Misalliance* (1910), *Androcles and the Lion* (1912), and *Pygmalion* (1913). Then, during the years 1913–19, he worked on what many regard as his finest play, the Chekhovian drama *Heartbreak House*, which he followed by the even more ambitious, if more patchily successful, play-sequence *Back to Methuselah* (1918–20), which traces in characteristically Shavian terms the history of man from Adam and Eve to the remotest future. The other major works of the 1920s were the popular historical play *Saint Joan* (1923) and the political comedy *The Apple Cart* (1929). During the 1930s Shaw remained as prolific as ever, but his plays were in general less interesting, with the possible exception of *The Millionairess* (1935) and *In Good King Charles's Golden Days* (1939). After nearly ten years away from the theatre Shaw returned with *Buoyant Billions* (1948) and *Far-Fetched Fables* (1950), both considerably below the level of his best work.

Shaw has been accused, with some justice, of a casualness about characterization and construction, and there is no doubt that he was sometimes too concerned with putting over his ideas to pay sufficient attention to their development in properly dramatic terms. But his wit still shines brilliantly, and many of his lighter plays stay firmly in the repertory even if his more overtly didactic pieces have faded with the passage of time.

Shelley, Percy Bysshe (1792–1822). English poet and dramatist. He wrote several poems in dramatic form, mostly, like *Prometheus Unbound* and *Hellas*, cosmic in range and grandly impractical for the stage, but including one, *The Cenci* (1818), a tragedy composed on the Elizabethan model, which has been staged several times (first by the Shelley Society in 1886) with fair success.

Sheppey. Drama by W. SOMERSET MAUGHAM, first performed London, 1933.

Sheridan, Richard Brinsley (1751–1816). Anglo-Irish dramatist and theatre manager. Son of the novelist Mrs Frances Sheridan, he studied law, but in 1775 made a spectacular debut as a dramatist with no fewer than three plays: a comedy, *The Rivals*, a farce, *St Patrick's Day; or the Scheming Lieutenant*, and a comic opera, *The Duenna*. In the following year he took over the management of DRURY LANE, which he rebuilt in 1794 and left only in 1809 when the new theatre was burnt down. In 1777 he wrote an adaptation of Vanbrugh's *The Relapse* called *A Trip to Scarborough*, and his own masterpiece *The School for Scandal*, and in 1779 *The Critic; or a Tragedy Rehearsed*, a burlesque on the dramatic fads of the time suggested by Buckingham's *The Rehearsal*. Thereafter he became increasingly involved in the management side of the theatre, and also in politics, writing virtually nothing except *Pizarro* (1799), a spectacular verse drama adapted from KOTZEBUË. Of his plays, *The School for Scandal* and *The Rivals* and, to a lesser extent, *The Critic* and *The Duenna* continue to be revived, in spite of a change of taste in recent years which finds their sentimental comedy a little anaemic compared with the genuine Restoration comedy of which it is evidently a watered-down version.

Sherriff, R. C. (Robert Cedric, 1896–1975). English dramatist and novelist who achieved sudden fame with his realistic drama of the First World War, *Journey's End* (1928). Of his numerous later plays the best are a rustic light comedy, *Badger's Green* (1930), and an effective psychological drama, *Home at Seven* (1950), which provided a showy leading role for Sir Ralph Richardson. Autobiography, *No Leading Lady* (1968).

257

Sherwood, Robert Emmet (1896–1955). American dramatist of varied talents; his first success was a satirical comedy about Hannibal's march, *The Road to Rome* (1927). *Reunion in Vienna* (1931) was also a comedy, but his next success was a gangster melodrama *The Petrified Forest* (1935). His principal works of the later 1930s were *Idiot's Delight* (1936), a grimly ironic piece of prophecy which won a Pulitzer Prize, and *Abe Lincoln in Illinois* (1938), a sober study of Lincoln's early years and unwilling start in politics. None of his postwar plays matched these in quality.

She Stoops to Conquer. Comedy by OLIVER GOLDSMITH, first produced Covent Garden, London, 1773.

Shirley, James (1596–1666). English dramatist, leading figure in Caroline theatre. He wrote about forty plays, tragedies and comedies, of which on the whole the better are the comedies such as *The Witty Fair One* (1628), *Hyde Park* (1632), *The Gamester* (1633), and *The Lady of Pleasure* (1635). The best of his tragedies are *The Traitor* (1631) and *The Cardinal* (1641); none of his plays survived in the repertoire after the eighteenth century.

Shoemaker's Holiday, The. Comedy by THOMAS DEKKER, first produced London, 1599.

Show Boat. Musical comedy by JEROME KERN, book and lyrics by OSCAR HAMMERSTEIN II, based on the novel by Edna Ferber (1926), first performed New York, 1927.

Showboat. Floating theatres which plied the major American rivers, especially the Mississippi, in the nineteenth century. Companies seem to have toured by boat from early days, but the first record of a company actually performing on a boat dates from 1817. During the century they became more and more elaborate, and despite a setback at the time of the Civil War continued to be popular and profitable until the mid 1920s, presenting a mixture of melodrama and vaudeville with later an occasional musical comedy thrown in. From 1930 on their numbers declined sharply, and now there are only one or two surviving as museum pieces.

Siddons, Sarah (1755–1831). English actress, the greatest tragedienne of her age. She played in the provinces almost exclusively until 1782, when she came to London and was immediately acclaimed. Among her most famous roles were Jane Shore in Rowe's tragedy, Belvidera in *Venice Preserved*, and Isabella in Thomas Southerne's *The Fatal Marriage*; later she had great successes as Zara in Congreve's *The Mourning Bride*, Constance in *King John*, and Lady Macbeth. She retired in 1815.

Sight line. The line of vision from any seat in the theatre to the stage.

This has to be taken into account when designing sets and staging action so that as far as possible everyone in the theatre can see everything vital to the play.

Silence, Theatre of. A theory of theatre – more properly called Theatre of the Unspoken (Théâtre de l'Inexprimé), evolved by JEAN-JACQUES BERNARD in the 1920s and based on the belief that dialogue alone could not express the whole of what was going on on stage; more important often was what the people on stage did not and could not express in words, and the dramatist's job was to arrange his dramas in such a way that this residue of the unexpressed could yet emerge and be understood by the audience.

Silver Box, The. Drama by JOHN GALSWORTHY, first performed by the BARKER–VEDRENNE COMPANY Royal Court, London, 1906.

Silver King, The. Melodrama by HENRY ARTHUR JONES and Henry Herman, first performed London, 1882.

Silver Tassie, The. Drama by SEAN O'CASEY, first produced London, 1929.

Simpson, N. F. (Norman Frederick; b. 1919). English dramatist, affiliated to the Theatre of the ABSURD. His first play, *A Resounding Tinkle*, won a prize in the *Observer* play competition in 1956 and was later performed at the Royal Court in a double bill with another play by Simpson, *The Hole* (1958). Both are rather arid logical explorations of one or several absurd initial premises. A later play, *One Way Pendulum* (1959), described as 'a farce in a new dimension', was successfully transferred from the Royal Court to the West End, and later its fantasies about singing weighing machines and a do-it-yourself Old Bailey found an appreciative repertory audience. After six years' silence he returned to the theatre in 1965 with *The Cresta Run*, a comedy about spying in much the same style as his earlier plays.

Six Characters in Search of an Author (Sei personaggi in cerca d'autore). Drama by LUIGI PIRANDELLO, first performed Rome, 1921.

Skin Game, The. Drama by JOHN GALSWORTHY, first performed London, 1920.

Skin of Our Teeth, The. A 'History of the world in comic strip' by THORNTON WILDER, first performed New York, 1942.

Slade, Julian (b. 1930). English composer and dramatist: wrote the songs for *The Duenna* (1953), a musical *Comedy of Errors* (1954), and *Vanity Fair* (1963), and wrote (in collaboration with Dorothy Reynolds) book, lyrics and music for *Salad Days* (1954), and such other anodyne whimsies as *Free as Air* (1957), *Hooray for Daisy* (1959),

Follow That Girl, and *Wildest Dreams* (1960). A return to the West End, after a long interval, with *Trelawny* (1972). *Salad Days*, with 2,283 performances, holds the record for the third longest run in the British theatre.

Sleeping Clergyman, A. Drama by JAMES BRIDIE, first performed Malvern Festival, 1933.

Smith, Dodie (b. 1895). English dramatist and novelist. First play professionally produced *Autumn Crocus* (1931), followed by *Service* (1932), *Bonnet over the Windmill* (1937), *Dear Octopus* (1938), and *I Capture the Castle* (1954), among others. Most of her plays are lightweight domestic comedies showing a particular talent for the depiction of children.

Smith, Oliver (b. 1918). American stage designer. His first professional stage design was for the ballet *Rodeo* (1942): subsequently he has designed many ballets and straight plays, but is best known for his work in the musical, which has used his special gift for bold stylization that manages not to lose touch with reality. Among musicals he has designed for Broadway are *On the Town* (1944), *Brigadoon* (1947), *Paint Your Wagon* (1951), *Pal Joey* (1952), *My Fair Lady*, *Candide* (1956), *West Side Story* (1957), *Flower Drum Song* (1958), *The Sound of Music* (1959). *My Fair Lady* and the last three he also designed in London.

Snow, C. P. (Charles Percy, Lord Snow; b. 1909). English novelist and dramatist. Though he has written plays himself – *View over the Park* (1950) – he is best known in the theatre for the adaptations of his novels made by Ronald Millar, including *The Affair* (1961), *The New Men* (1963), and *The Masters* (1963).

Socialist realism. A vague and loosely defined term in Russian criticism, originally invented by LUNACHARSKY to describe the sort of theatre he believed the Revolution should bring into being. This was to be a new realism approximating the theatrical experience more closely to life as known by the people, and involved also the representation and re-interpretation of existing theatrical classics in order to indicate their relevance to contemporary life. Later, socialist realism became a more directly political term, implying primarily a willingness on the part of writers and directors to submit themselves unquestioningly and entirely to the current propaganda requirements of the government.

Son et lumière. Form of open-air entertainment related to the PAGEANT, usually telling the history of a place in a series of episodes or tableaux. In this case, though, the text is pre-recorded and broadcast by loud-speaker, accompanied by a series of elaborate lighting effects on the site, which may be a palace, a castle, a cathedral, or a complex of buildings seen from some vantage point. The idea originated in France, where the form was used to 'dramatize' some of the châteaux of the Loire in the early 1950s, but it has rapidly spread all over the world, particularly successful examples being staged in Britain at Greenwich Palace and the Tower of London.

Sophocles (496–406 B.C.). Greek dramatist, author of more than a hundred plays, of which, apart from scattered fragments, only seven tragedies and parts of one satyr play survive. In the dramatic competitions he won the first prize eighteen times, and never, it is said, came worse than second. He was also something of a public figure, holding various administrative posts during his long life. The plays of his which survive – *Ajax* (*c.*450 B.C.), *Antigone* (*c.*442), *Trachiniae*, *Oedipus Rex* (*c.*425), *Electra*, *Philoctetes* (409), and *Oedipus at Colonus* (406) – show Greek tragedy at the height of its subtlety and expressiveness, between the monumental simplicity of AESCHYLUS and the more romantic, 'psychological' work of EURIPIDES; in fact, Sophoclean tragedy was used by ARISTOTLE as the basis of his dramatic theories in his *Poetics*. Sophocles was responsible for the introduction of a third character on the stage, and in his hands Greek tragedy developed in the direction of greater intimacy and more human interest: his plays concern the subtleties of human character in the relations between people, or between individuals and fate or the gods. Consequently he adopted much more complex plots than Aeschylus, and abandoned the trilogy in favour of groups of three separate plays. The chorus in his tragedies became primarily lyrical in function, intervening less frequently in the action but commenting on it between scenes, preparing changes of mood, and so on. Other innovations in Sophoclean drama were an increase in the number of the chorus from twelve to fifteen, the (apparent) introduction of a fourth actor in the very late *Oedipus at Colonus*, posthumously produced, and the use of the mysterious '*periaktoi*', which seems to have been some device, probably revolving screens painted with landscapes, for indicating changes of scene. Though the more sensational style of Euripides was more admired in the later classical times, for the modern reader and theatregoer Sophocles remains the great classic, the ancient dramatist who speaks most directly and immediately to our own day.

Soubrette. The young female member of a theatrical company specializing in vivacious, more or less comic roles.

Soulier de satin, Le. Drama by PAUL CLAUDEL, written 1924, first performed by the Renaud–Barrault Company, Paris, 1943.

Sound of Music, The. Musical play by RICHARD RODGERS, book by

Howard Lindsay and Russel Crouse, lyrics by OSCAR HAMMER-STEIN II; first performed New York, 1959.

Southerne, Thomas (1660–1746). English dramatist, best remembered for two tragedies adapted from novels by Aphra Behn and mingling heroic and sentimental elements, *The Fatal Marriage, or, The Innocent Adultery* (1694) and *Oroonoko* (1695).

South Pacific. Musical by RICHARD RODGERS, book by OSCAR HAMMERSTEIN II and JOSHUA LOGAN, based on James A. Michener's *Tales of the South Pacific* (1947), lyrics by Oscar Hammerstein II; first produced New York, 1949.

Spanish Tragedy, The. Drama by THOMAS KYD, first performed London, *c*.1584–9.

Sparrers Can't Sing. East End comedy by Stephen Lewis, first performed by Theatre Workshop, Stratford, London, 1960; subsequently filmed by Joan Littlewood, 1963.

Sport of My Mad Mother, The. Drama by ANN JELLICOE, first performed by the English Stage Company, Royal Court, London, 1958.

Spotlight, see LIGHTING.

Spring '71 (Printemps '71). Historical drama by ARTHUR ADAMOV, first performed (in English), Unity Theatre, London, 1962.

Stage. The area of a theatre (or for that matter outside a permanent theatre building altogether) where the acting takes place. In Greek and Roman theatres it was a platform across the diameter of the semicircular arena, the flat area in front being used by the chorus and the seats banked in tiers around. In medieval drama the stage was generally a temporary wooden affair, possibly with trap-doors to represent hell and some sort of raised structure to represent heaven. The stage in the ELIZABETHAN THEATRE was a development of this, jutting out into the audience (the 'apron' stage) and with a permanent architectural background. In the mid seventeenth century the proscenium stage was introduced, the stage itself consisting of two areas, the forestage on which most of the action took place, and the area framed by an arched opening, which revealed a scenic background and through which, from either side, the actor might enter, though normally he would come through the proscenium doors to either side of the opening. At first there were as many as three doors on each side, with windows and balconies above, but gradually during the eighteenth century the doors were reduced to one on each side and more and more of the action took place 'in the scene', i.e. in the area behind the proscenium arch. By the middle of the nineteenth century the picture-frame stage, in which the whole stage was framed by the proscenium with virtually no forestage at all, had become general. This allowed for the use of all sorts of elaborate STAGE MACHINERY, and also, paradoxically, led to increased naturalism in stage sets and conventions, which reached its climax in the concept of a stage setting as a room with the fourth wall removed.

Towards the end of the nineteenth century some impatience with this system and its limitations was already being felt. For producing Shakespeare WILLIAM POEL began to experiment with a reconstructed Elizabethan stage, while GORDON CRAIG advocated a stage with an infinitely variable proscenium shape, so that the stage picture could be any shape desired. From this the next step was to eliminate the proscenium altogether, or at least greatly reduce its importance. In the 1920s all sorts of experiments were tried: REINHARDT staged drama in converted circuses or exhibition halls; theorists of the German Bauhaus art movement advocated getting drama out of the theatres altogether and staging it in the street or on balconies and in windows of buildings; the Moscow Realist Theatre staged action all round or in the middle of audiences; the Vieux-Colombier Theatre had an open stage with no proscenium arch at all. Theatres-in-the-round, with the audience sitting all round the central acting area have been extensively adopted by amateur groups, but also by some professional theatres in Britain and elsewhere, while the arena stage has been tried at the Stratford (Ontario) Festival Theatre and Chichester Festival Theatre, the open stage with no proscenium arch at the Mermaid Theatre, and all sorts of variations on these formulas in other places. The stage has become in principle infinitely adaptable, though the problem remains that most existing theatres are built on picture-stage lines and cannot readily be converted to accommodate types of drama not suited to this form of presentation.

Stage door. The entrance to the back-stage area of the theatre, used by actors and technicians. It is here that people wanting to see actors and actresses chose to wait after the show, hence the Edwardian institution of the stage-door Johnnie, the rich young man who would wait for chorus-girls, in search of a good time.

Stage machinery. The use of machinery for stage effects began in classical times, when the appearance of the god, the DEUS EX MACHINA, was sometimes accomplished with a car of some sort that could be raised and lowered. At the time of the Renaissance there was a great elaboration in the sort of machinery used on stage, in the shape of cars and spectacular constructions of various sorts. The height of elaboration in the machinery of the stage itself was reached in the nineteenth century, after which the move was to greater and greater simplification of the stage's purely mechanical means. At the time of the stage's greatest physical intricacy the floor and under-floor area, the wings and the area above the stage were crowded with mechanical devices of all sorts, many of them now obsolete.

The floor of the stage had a series of traps in it: at the front the footlights trap, which enabled the footlights to be lowered below the stage for cleaning or for effects of darkness; then the carpet cut, an aperture in which the edge of a carpet on stage could be locked; then two corner traps, variously operated, but with the basic use of raising people rapidly through the stage floor; then several special traps, such as the grave trap (as in *Hamlet*), the cauldron trap (as in *Macbeth*), and a group of long narrow traps, through which flat scenes, especially rolled painted cloths, could be drawn up from below stage level. Finally, nearer the back of the stage, came a bridge, a whole section which could be raised and lowered with a group of actors or an elaborate tableau on it. Behind this the alternation of bridges and sloat-cuts (as the cuts with painted scenes, etc., were called) might be continued to the back of the stage, as far as it went. In the modern stage a revolve, electrically operated, often occupies the centre of the stage, enabling scenes to be changed merely by revolving from one set to another. The wings, or side areas of the stage behind the proscenium, housed a number of tall side-pieces for the settings which could be slid in and out in grooves. The wings also house on occasion the boat trucks or wagon stages, movable platforms which slide on to the stage on castors and on which whole scenes, or sections of scenes, can be set ready. Above the stage are the flies, where scenery can be 'flown' until required, when it can be lowered into position. This is done from the fly-floor, a gallery on which the fly-men work, and above that is the grid, an open floor from which the flown sets are suspended on pulleys and from which lights can be suspended.

In modern theatres most of the stage machinery is worked by electricity and is usually much simplified, since on the whole stage effects depend less on mechanical contrivance than on the play of lights, on suggestion rather than literal spectacle; when scenic elaboration is required, however, as in the musicals of LIONEL BART, the possibilities of automation in the modern theatre are quite capable of producing it.

Stage Society, The Incorporated. London group founded in 1899 to put on good but apparently uncommercial plays for one or two private, experimental performances in West End conditions, on Sundays when the theatres were not otherwise engaged. The first production was *You Never Can Tell*; later the society introduced other SHAW plays and works by GORKY, WEDEKIND, PIRANDELLO, COCTEAU and a variety of other foreign dramatists. With the appearance of several theatre clubs with similar aims in the 1930s there was a move to wind up the society, but this was defeated and it continued active until 1939.

Stalls, see PLAYHOUSE.

Stanislavsky, Konstantin Sergeyevich (real name Alexeyev; 1865–1938). Russian director, actor, and teacher, one of the most important theorists of the twentieth-century theatre. He began as an amateur actor, and then studied at a dramatic school under F. P. Komisarjevsky, father of Vera and Theodore, and took up acting professionally. In 1888 he founded the Society of Literature and Art, along with Fedotov and F. P. Komisarjevsky. The interests of the society were primarily dramatic, and Stanislavsky soon became its producer, achieving his first recognition in 1891 with productions of Tolstoy's *The Fruits of Enlightenment* and an adaptation of Dostoyevsky's *Selo Stepanchikov*. From the first Stanislavsky strove in his productions for an easy, realistic style of acting and a careful naturalism in sets and costumes, rejecting the histrionic style of acting in vogue in Russia at the time. In 1898 he founded the MOSCOW ART THEATRE in partnership with NEMIROVICH-DANCHENKO. His greatest triumphs as a director were his productions of CHEKHOV's plays, starting with *The Seagull* in 1898. Chekhov's writing matched Stanislavsky's chosen style of production perfectly, calling as it does for a detailed realistic production which yet has glints of poetry, depending more for its effect on atmosphere and psychological suggestion than on detailed literal re-creation. In fact, during the 1900s Stanislavsky came to place less emphasis on the naturalistic externals, and more on the actor's development of character, a line to which he returned after a brief flirtation with formalism and the symbolic dramas of MAETERLINCK and ANDREYEV in the years before the Revolution. Apart from his own practical work in the theatre (which may still be seen, since a number of productions by him are still in the Moscow Art Theatre's repertory), Stanislavsky had a great influence, both directly, through his books, and indirectly, through teachers trained by him, on the theatre outside Russia, especially in America. The emphasis of his teachings has been partly misunderstood, because only *An Actor Prepares* (1926), in which he concentrates mainly on the psychology of acting rather than on technique, was easily available, notably to those who evolved the American METHOD. His later books, *Building a Character* and *Stanislavsky Rehearses Othello*, correct this with a powerful insistence on the importance of style, and of matching the style to the role and fitting the role into the production as a whole. He also wrote a theatrical autobiography, *My Life in Art* (1926).

Stein, Gertrude (1874–1947). American novelist and dramatist, author of a variety of more or less experimental plays and playlets, the best known of which are *Four Saints in Three Acts* (1934), set to music by Virgil Thompson, and *In Savoy* (1945), a more straightforward drama of the French occupation.

Stock company. American term for a theatrical company operating along repertory lines in some out-of-town theatre during the summer months.

Stoppard, Tom (b. 1932). British dramatist whose major international success has been his ambitious Theatre of the Absurd play *Rosencrantz and Guildenstern are Dead* (1967), first produced by the National Theatre, which examines the Shakespearean characters in their lives when off the stage of *Hamlet*'s main action. Other plays include *Enter a Free Man* and *The Real Inspector Hound* (both 1968), *Jumpers* (1972), and *Travesties* (1974), staged at the National Theatre.

Strange Interlude. Drama by EUGENE O'NEILL, first produced New York, 1928.

Strasberg, Lee (b. 1901). American director and teacher; founder and artistic director of the New York Actors' Studio and principal exponent, there and elsewhere, of the METHOD. He was born in Austria, went to America at the age of eight, and studied drama with Richard Boleslavsky and Marie Ouspenskaya. He began directing in 1925, was a founder of GROUP THEATRE in 1930, acted in and directed a number of productions for them in the 1930s, began with the Actors' Studio in 1948, and has there taught most of the best of the younger American actors. During 1963–4 the Actors' Studio became also a producing organization on Broadway, with all-star revivals of *Strange Interlude*, *The Three Sisters*, and some less successful new plays.

Stratford. Stratford-on-Avon, as the birthplace of Shakespeare, began to attract attention in the eighteenth century, especially after Garrick's lavishly staged jubilee celebrations in 1769, and the idea gradually arose that the town should be the scene of regular festival performances of Shakespeare plays. In 1879 a site for a memorial theatre was donated, and the annual festival began, in a theatre specially built for the purpose. In 1925 the Memorial Theatre was granted a Royal Charter, but in 1926 it burned down. The new theatre, designed by Elizabeth Scott, was opened in 1932. Since then the Festival has continued regularly, under a succession of directors: after the war it was taken over by SIR BARRY JACKSON (1945–8), then ANTHONY

QUAYLE, then PETER HALL; in 1961 the Memorial Theatre Company became the Royal Shakespeare Company, dividing its activities between London and Stratford. Shakespeare Festivals have also been set up at other Stratfords, notably at Stratford, Connecticut, in 1955, and Stratford, Ontario, where a festival was instituted in 1953 by TYRONE GUTHRIE in a theatre built to his own specifications.

Streetcar Named Desire, A. Drama by TENNESSEE WILLIAMS, first performed New York, 1949.

Street Scene. Drama by ELMER RICE, first performed New York, 1929. Also musical version by KURT WEILL, book by Rice, lyrics by Langston Hughes, first performed New York, 1947.

Strife. Drama by JOHN GALSWORTHY, first performed London, 1909.

Strindberg, August (1849–1912). Swedish dramatist and novelist; a very prolific writer, with more than fifty plays as well as novels, short stories, poems, and an autobiography to his credit. He began in a fairly conventional way, writing historical dramas and farcical tales of rural life. Few of the plays from this earlier period, which began with *Hermione* (1869), are still remembered, except perhaps for *The Wanderings of Lucky Per* (*Lycko-Pers Resa*, 1882). In the 1880s a violent change was seen in his work, and in 1887, with *The Father* (*Fadren*) he began a new phase in his drama with a savage and intense study of human frailties and the implacable enmity of the sexes in a war which the woman seemed always bound to win. *The Father* was followed by the equally bitter *Miss Julie* (*Fröken Julie*, 1888), and *Creditors* (*Fordringsägare*, 1888), as well as a number of one-act plays such as *The Stronger* (*Den Starkare*, 1890) and *Playing with Fire* (written in German as *Das Spiel mit dem Feuer*, 1892). After these plays, which pushed theatrical realism to the very limit of its possibilities and sometimes beyond, there was a gap in Strindberg's theatrical work, after which emerged in 1898 the first two sections of his vast symbolic drama *To Damascus* (*Till Damaskus*). During the next ten years Strindberg worked with feverish energy, producing no fewer than twenty-eight plays in a variety of styles. Among them were fifteen historical dramas based on episodes in Swedish history and starting with *Gustaf Vasa* and *Erik XIV* (both 1899); a group of strange symbolic dramas, including *A Dream Play* (*Ett drömspel*, 1902), *To Damascus* Part 3 (1904), and *The Ghost Sonata* (*Spöksonaten*, 1907), which tried to capture in dramatic form the apparent discontinuity and unpredictability of the dream; one curious but charming fairy-play slightly suggestive of Maeterlinck, *Swanwhite* (*Svanehvit*, 1902); and a series of plays taking up in a more mature style the sort of subject he had formerly dealt with in the more hysterical plays of his middle period, though now heavy with symbolic and religious overtones. Among the most important of these last are *Advent* (1898), *Easter* (*Påsk*, 1900), and the two-part *Dance of Death* (*Dödsdansen*, 1901), along with which should be counted the late group of 'chamber plays' Strindberg wrote in 1907–9 for the Intima Teatern which he founded with August Falck in Stockholm in 1907. These, apart from *The Ghost Sonata*, showed a partial return to naturalistic style, suggested by the special conditions of the tiny theatre in which they were performed, which permitted no sort of histrionic exaggeration: among them the most notable are *The Storm* (*Oväder*, 1907) and *The Burnt Lot* (*Brända tomten*, 1907). Strindberg's significance in dramatic history lies partly in his technical experiments, especially his attempts to put the thought-processes of the unconscious on the stage, and, more influentially, in his exploration of new subject-matter for the stage, pushing the analysis of the sex war further than ever before. Of his large output many plays are forgotten, outside Sweden at least, but about a dozen remain in the international repertory.

Strong are Lonely, The (also called **Faith is not Enough; Das heilige Experiment**). Drama by FRITZ HOCHWÄLDER, first performed Biel, Switzerland, 1943.

Student Prince, The. Light opera by SIGMUND ROMBERG, book and lyrics by Dorothy Donnelly; first performed New York, 1924.

Sturm und Drang. Literally 'storm and stress'. A phase of the German Romantic movement in literature and drama during the late eighteenth and early nineteenth centuries. Adherents made Shakespeare their idol, and inclined to deal with violent and extreme emotions in freely formed, rambling poems and dramas. Favourite themes were the battle of the individual to live according to the dictates of his own ideas and emotions in a hostile environment and the power of passion to overthrow even the most highly principled natures. Most German writers of the period were affected to some extent by the movement: GOETHE's *Faust* and the earlier plays of SCHILLER are its most distinguished dramatic manifestations.

Suddenly Last Summer. One-act drama by TENNESSEE WILLIAMS, first performed New York, 1958, with *Something Unspoken* in a double bill entitled *Garden District*.

Sudermann, Hermann (1857–1928). German dramatist in the realistic style, who achieved a major success with his first play *Honour* (*Die Ehre*, 1889), a study of the divergence between workers and middle class in contemporary Germany. Most of his plays dealt with middle-class life, usually in a fairly melodramatic way, as in *Die Heimat*

(*Home: Magda* in English, 1893) and *The Battle of the Butterflies* (*Die Schmetterlingsschlacht*, 1895). Sudermann also wrote historical plays, and in *Morituri*, a sequence of three one-act plays (1896), combined past and present quite effectively.

Suë, Eugène (1804–57). French dramatist and novelist, author of a number of long and sensational novels which were vastly successful both in book form and when adapted for the stage. The most famous were *Les Mystères de Paris* and *Le Juif errant* (both 1844). *Le Juif errant* was dramatized by Suë himself in 1849 and an adaptation of *Les Mystères de Paris* made with Félix Pyat was staged in 1863. Other plays by Suë include *Mathilde* (1843) and *La Morne au diable* (1848).

Sullivan, Sir Arthur, see W. S. GILBERT.

Summer and Smoke. Drama by TENNESSEE WILLIAMS, first performed New York, 1948.

Summer of the Seventeenth Doll. Drama by RAY LAWLER, first performed Melbourne, 1955.

Super (i.e. Supernumerary). Players who are required for the action of a play but have no lines to speak.

Suppliant Women, The. Tragedy by AESCHYLUS, first performed Athens, c.490 B.C.

Surrealism. Movement in the arts during the 1920s, closely akin to and not clearly separable from DADA. It was defined by one of its founders, André Breton, as 'Pure psychic automatism, by which it is intended to express verbally, in writing or by other means, the real process of thought, in the absence of all control exercised by the reason and outside all aesthetic or moral preoccupation'. Unlike Dada, Surrealism expressed itself little in drama; its most important dramatic expressions were the two films of Salvador Dali and Luis Buñuel, *Un Chien andalou* (1928) and *L'Âge d'or* (1930). ANTONIN ARTAUD was for a while associated with the movement.

Swan, The (A Nattyú). Drama by FERENC MOLNAR, first performed Budapest, 1914.

Sweeney Todd. Various melodramas about the demon barber of Fleet Street have been written, among them those by George Dibdin Pitt (1842), Frank Hazleton (1862), and Matt Wilkinson (1870). Modern texts generally conflate them.

Sweet Bird of Youth. Drama by TENNESSEE WILLIAMS, first performed New York, 1959.

Symbolism. Theatrical movement expressing opposition to the principles of NATURALISM, originated by PAUL FORT at the Théâtre d'Art in the early 1890s and developed by LUGNÉ-POË at the same theatre, re-christened the Théâtre de l'Œuvre. The essential of Symbolism was the abandonment of the appearances of life in favour of its spirit, symbolically represented, and the search for a poetic rather than a prosaic drama. The principal dramatist of the movement was MAETERLINCK.

Synge, J. M. (John Millington; 1871–1909). Irish dramatist and one of the founders of the Irish Dramatic Movement. During his brief life he wrote, in addition to some poems and prose, six plays which remain among the classics of Irish drama, beginning with *In the Shadow of the Glen* (or *The Shadow of the Glen*, 1903), a tragi-comedy, and a one-act peasant tragedy, *Riders to the Sea* (1904). His next three plays were prose comedies drawing on the richness of Irish folk-speech for their distinctive flavour, *The Well of the Saints* (1905), *The Tinker's Wedding*, and *The Playboy of the Western World* (1907). This last is Synge's masterpiece; it caused a riot when first staged at the Abbey Theatre but has since been accepted as a regular part of the dramatic repertory. At the time of his death Synge had nearly finished a poetic drama, *Deirdre of the Sorrows*, which suggests that had he lived his talent might have taken a new turn, in favour of more formal, legendary drama which was yet enriched with the vital speech-patterns of the west of Ireland, selected and recreated with a poet's ear.

T

Tabs (i.e. tableau curtain). Usually, though not correctly, used for curtain-settings on stage; properly a front curtain.

Taïrov, Alexander Yakovlevich (1885–1950). Russian director. Founded the Kamerny Theatre in 1914 to put into practice principles of theatre diametrically opposed to STANISLAVSKY'S, replacing the lovingly realistic depiction of life by a 'THEATRICALIST' approach, using the lessons of the ballet and the circus to turn drama into a symphony of movement working on the audience largely through the instincts. Sets and lighting were of vital importance in Taïrov's theories, while actors tended to be reduced to puppets in the director's hands. To begin with Taïrov productions were somewhat misleadingly labelled 'neo-realistic', though his productions of Claudel's *Tidings Brought to Mary* (1920), *Romeo and Juliet* (1921), and *Phèdre* (1922), with their splintered, Cubist sets and balletic acting, would hardly qualify as 'realistic' in any normal sense of the term. Later he went through a Constructivist phase, akin to the contemporary work of MEYER-HOLD, and at this time directed O'Neill's *Desire Under the Elms* and *The Hairy Ape* (1926) and *All God's Chillun Got Wings* (1929), and Sophie Treadwell's *Machinal* (1933). In 1934 he directed *An Optimistic Tragedy*, but he was accused of FORMALISM, and forced to work under a management committee, adapting himself gradually to SOCIALIST REALISM – with some success, particularly in his 1939 production of *Madame Bovary*, though in general his last twenty years were less productive of exciting new work than before.

Talma, François Joseph (1763–1826). French actor. Made his debut at the Comédie-Française in 1787, and was soon responsible for a reform of diction (in favour of greater naturalness) and costume (in favour of historical accuracy). He supported the Revolution, and headed the Comédie-Française as reconstituted by Napoleon in 1803. He continued to act successfully until his death, specializing in tragedy though venturing occasionally into comedy.

Tamburlaine the Great. Two-part drama by CHRISTOPHER MARLOWE, first performed London, 1587–8.

Taming of the Shrew, The. Comedy by WILLIAM SHAKESPEARE, written c.1593–4.

Tardieu, Jean (b. 1903). French poet and dramatist. Early in his career he wrote some unpublished plays then, apart from writing an unproduced verse play, *Tonnerre sans orage*, in 1944, turned exclusively to poetry until he became head of Radiodiffusion Française's experi-

271

mental workshop in 1947. His plays, collected in two volumes, *Théâtre de Chambre* (1955) and *Poèmes à Jouer* (1960) are mostly very short, hardly more than sketches. The earliest, *Qui est là?* and *La Politesse inutile* (both 1947) anticipate IONESCO's style and type of subject-matter; others indulge in such typical devices of the Theatre of the ABSURD as the telescoping of time (*Faust et Yorick*) or construct dramatic dialogue in quasi-musical forms (*La Sonate des trois messieurs, Conversation-sinfonietta*), or even in one case make a drama out of an empty room and a disembodied voice (*Une Voix sans personne*). Tardieu's most ambitious play to date is *Les Temps du verbe, ou le pouvoir de la parole* (1956), a more conventional two-act piece based on the premise that our standpoint in time is governed by the tenses of the verbs we use. Tardieu is an interesting fringe-figure in the Theatre of the Absurd, his work perhaps more valuable for its explorations than for its achievement.

Tartuffe, Le. Comedy by MOLIÈRE, first performed Paris, 1664 (in private) and 1667 (in public), the latter an altered version entitled *L'Imposteur*.

Taste of Honey, A. Drama by SHELAGH DELANEY, first performed by Theatre Workshop, Stratford, London, 1958.

Tate, Harry (real name Ronald Macdonald Hutchinson; 1874–1940). English music-hall comedian, noted for his sketches on such topics as motoring, golfing, and fishing. He appeared also in revue and in pantomime.

Taylor, Laurette (1884–1946). American actress, wife of the dramatist John Hartley Manners, who wrote for her her most famous early success, the romantic *Peg o' My Heart* (1912). Later her career suffered an eclipse, but in 1945 she returned to the stage to give one of the greatest performances in the modern American theatre in Tennessee Williams's *The Glass Menagerie*.

Tea and Sympathy. Drama by ROBERT ANDERSON, first performed New York, 1953.

Teahouse of the August Moon. Long-running service comedy by John Patrick, based on the novel by Vern Sneider, first performed New York, 1953.

Tempest, Marie (real name Mary Susan Etherington; 1864–1942). English actress, specializing, after an apprenticeship in light opera, entirely in comedy. Among her early roles were Nell Gwynn, Peg Woffington, and Becky Sharp, and as Kitty in *The Marriage of Kitty* (1902), adapted by Cosmo Gordon-Lennox from the French, she played all over the world. The best of all her roles was that of the feckless actress Judith Bliss in *Hay Fever* (1925), which Noël Coward wrote for her; she continued acting until her death, and was created D.B.E. in 1937.

Tempest, The. Dramatic romance by WILLIAM SHAKESPEARE, written c.1611–12.

Ten Little Niggers. Thriller by AGATHA CHRISTIE, adapted from her novel, first performed London, 1943.

Tennyson, Alfred Lord (1809–92). English poet and dramatist. One of his earliest works was a verse comedy along Elizabethan lines, *The Devil and the Lady*, written when he was only fourteen, but after that he abandoned drama until 1876, when his historical drama *Queen Mary* was produced by Irving. Irving also staged his one-act drama *The Cup* (1881), with Ellen Terry, and *Becket*, in which he had one of his greatest successes. In spite of this, Tennyson had little real feeling for dramatic effect, and none of his plays has survived on stage, though *Becket* has had at least one revival.

1066 and All That. Comic history of England, in revue form, by Reginald Arkell, based on the book by W. C. Sellar and R. J. Yeatman; first performed London, 1935.

Terence (Publius Terentius Afer; c.190–159 B.C.). Roman dramatist, author of comedies more or less closely adapted from Greek originals of MENANDER and other writers of the New Comedy (see GREEK THEATRE); only six of his plays survive. They are subtler than those of PLAUTUS, with greater care taken over construction and more attention paid to the credibility of characters. We often know from his argumentative prologues what alterations he made in his adaptation of Greek plays (he was, apparently, much criticized for making any alterations at all): usually it was a matter of adding characters, seldom of bringing the plays up to date in any way, as Plautus did with topical allusions. However, Terence's earliest play, the *Andria* (166 B.C.) does introduce a specifically Roman situation, by showing his hero in love with a girl of his own class, something virtually inconceivable in terms of Greek society. His other surviving plays are *Hecyra* (165 B.C.), *Heautontimorumenos* (163), *Eunuchus* (161), *Phormio* (161), and *Adelphi* (160). In these he develops his own variant of Menander's sentimental comedy, verbally eloquent and tending gradually away from farce until in the last we reach something like a problem play, with a message about the importance of freedom in education and the harmfulness of excessively strict discipline. The work of Terence was less consistently popular than that of the more obvious Plautus, and by the time of his death the drama was already being threatened in public taste by the simpler charms of the circus and the gladiatorial contest, though his work remained popular with the reading public and a model of elegant Latin style even in the Middle Ages.

Terry, Ellen (1847–1928). English actress. Born into a theatrical family, she first appeared on stage at the age of nine, married the painter Frederick Watts at sixteen, returned to the stage for a while when the marriage broke up, left again for six years during her liaison with the architect Edward Godwin (by whom she had two children, EDWARD GORDON CRAIG and Edith Craig), before returning to the stage in 1874 in Charles Reade's *The Wandering Heir*. From then on she was rapidly established as the leading actress of her day, especially after 1878, when she joined Irving as his leading lady at the Lyceum. Here she played a vast variety of roles, particularly in Shakespeare, her best parts being Beatrice, Portia, Viola, Cordelia, Desdemona, and Olivia, as well as Lady Macbeth, on her interpretation of whom opinion was divided. She was also a notable Lady Teazle in *The School for Scandal*, and played in a number of modern plays, among them Tennyson's *Becket* and *The Cup*, and Edward Bulwer-Lytton's *The Lady of Lyons*. In 1903 she went into management herself, appearing in Ibsen's *The Vikings* and *Much Ado About Nothing*, under the direction of Edward Gordon Craig, and later she played in such new dramas as Barrie's *Alice-Sit-by-the-Fire* and Shaw's *Captain Brassbound's Conversion*. After marrying again in 1907 she virtually retired from the stage, devoting much of her time to lecturing on Shakespeare. Some of these lectures were published, and so were an autobiography and her correspondence with Shaw. She was created D.B.E. in 1925.

Terson, Peter (b. 1932). British dramatist, author of a number of plays set in and around the Vale of Evesham, among them *A Night to Make the Angels Weep* (1964), *The Mighty Reservoy* (1967) and *Mooney and his Caravans* (1968), but better known for his lively pieces specially written for the National Youth Theatre, *Zigger-Zagger* (1967) and *The Apprentices* (1968).

Thark. ALDWYCH FARCE by BEN TRAVERS, first performed London, 1927.

Theatre Guild. American theatrical company run along the lines of a corporate society, founded in 1919 to put on plays considered uncommercial or at least dubiously commercial. During the 1920s it followed this policy quite successfully, both commercially and artistically, building its own theatre in 1925. A number of distinguished actors appeared as guest stars with the company, among them HELEN HAYES in *Caesar and Cleopatra*, the LUNTS in *Arms and the Man* and *The Taming of the Shrew*, and NAZIMOVA in *A Month in the Country* and *Mourning Becomes Electra*, and during the 1920s the plays produced included Franz Werfel's *Goat Song* and *Juarez and Maximilian*, *The Brothers Karamazov* adapted and directed by Copeau, and *Marco Millions*. Later the Guild became more conservative in its choice of play, though in general keeping up its high standards of acting and production.

Theatre-in-the-round. A type of twentieth-century stage presentation in which the acting-area is entirely surrounded by the audience. It has been most popular in America; among the most successful examples have been André Villiers's Théâtre en Rond de Paris (1954), the Pembroke Theatre, Croydon (now defunct), and Stephen Joseph's Victoria Theatre, Stoke-on-Trent (1962).

Théâtre Libre, see ANTOINE, ANDRÉ.

Théâtre National Populaire (T.N.P.). Theatrical company founded by JEAN VILAR in 1951. It has divided its time between Paris and Avignon, where Vilar staged festivals from 1947, working with a permanent group of actors under contract and a number of distinguished guest stars, among them GÉRARD PHILIPE and MARIA CASARÈS. The company's most notable productions have nearly all been classics revivified, among them *The Prince of Homburg* (1951), *L'Avare* (1952), *Macbeth* (1954), *Marie Tudor* (1955), *Phèdre* (1958), and *A Midsummer Night's Dream* (1958), but there have also been modern plays, like *Mother Courage* (1951), Pirandello's *Henry IV* (1957), and *Ubu* (1958).

Théâtre Total. Concept of theatre as above all a director's medium, using the text only as one relatively minor part of an overall theatrical experience of lights, music, movement of all sorts, sets and costumes. Its chief exponent in the practical theatre has been JEAN-LOUIS BARRAULT.

Theatre Workshop. Cooperative theatre company founded by JOAN LITTLEWOOD and making its home at the Theatre Royal, Stratford, London, from 1953 to 1964.

Theatricalism. Theory of theatre evolved in Russia and Germany during the 1900s as a counter-blast to NATURALISM and based on the reasonable principle that 'theatre is theatre, not life'.

Thieves' Carnival (Le Bal des Voleurs). *Pièce rose* by JEAN ANOUILH, written 1932, first performed Paris, 1937.

This Happy Breed. Drama by NOËL COWARD, first performed London, 1943.

This Way to the Tomb. Verse drama by RONALD DUNCAN, music by Benjamin Britten, first performed London, 1945.

Thomas, Brandon (1857–1914). English dramatist, actor, and manager, remembered today entirely as the author of *Charley's Aunt* (1892). This classic farce is beloved of actors for the comic possibilities of its transvestite central role and has been constantly revived since its first production.

Thorndike, Sybil (1882–1976). English actress. Made her first professional appearance on stage in 1904; joined the company at the Gaiety Theatre, Manchester, in 1908, and made her first London appearance in 1909. Her first big success was in St John Irvine's *Jane Clegg* (1912) and in 1914 she joined the Old Vic Company for four years, playing among other parts Lady Mabceth, Beatrice, Rosalind, Portia, Ophelia and, rather surprisingly, Prince Hal in *Henry IV* Part I and the Fool in *King Lear*. In 1919 she had another success in Claudel's *The Hostage*, followed by Hecuba and Medea in Gilbert Murray's translations of Euripides. In 1920–22 she played in a season of *grand guignol*, and then in 1924 was given one of her greatest roles, Shaw's *St Joan*, followed in 1929 by *Major Barbara*. The 1930s brought her Volumnia in *Coriolanus* at the Old Vic (1938) and Miss Moffat in *The Corn is Green* (1938–40). In 1944 she again joined the Old Vic Company, at the New Theatre playing Aase in *Peer Gynt*, Catherine in *Arms and the Man*, and Queen Margaret in *Richard III*. The next year, with the same company, she played Mistress Quickly in *Henry IV* Parts I and II, Jocasta in *Oedipus Rex*, and the Justice's lady in *The Critic*. Later roles included Isabel Linden in *The Linden Tree* (1947), Lady Randolph in *Douglas* (Edinburgh Festival, 1950), Mrs Whyte in *Waters of the Moon* (1951), Laura Anson in *A Day by the Sea* (1953), Saint Teresa in Hugh Ross-Williamson's *Teresa of Avila* (1962), Claire in Marguerite Duras's *The Viaduct* (1967) and Mrs Basil in ENID BAGNOLD's *Call Me Jackie* (1968). She was created D.B.E. in 1931.

Three Estates, The (Ane Pleasaunt Satyre of the Thrie Estaitis). Morality play by SIR DAVID LINDAY (Lyndsay), first performed Cupar, 1540; modern version first performed Edinburgh Festival, 1948.

Threepenny Opera, The (Die Dreigroschenoper). Musical play by BERTOLT BRECHT, suggested by Gay's *The Beggar's Opera*; music by KURT WEILL. First performed Berlin, 1928.

Three Sisters, The (Try sestri). Drama by ANTON CHEKHOV, first performed Moscow Art Theatre, 1901.

Thunder Rock. Drama by Robert Ardrey, first performed New York, 1939; the most important attempt to dramatize the intellectual's crisis of conscience at the approach of world war.

Ticket-of-Leave Man, The. Drama by Tom Taylor, from the French, first performed London, 1863. Often-revived and very influential melodrama of contemporary life.

Tidings Brought to Mary (L'Annonce faite à Marie). Drama by PAUL CLAUDEL, first performed Paris, 1912.

Tiger and the Horse, The. Drama by ROBERT BOLT, first performed London, 1960.

Tiger at the Gates (La Guerre de Troie n'aura pas lieu). Drama by JEAN GIRAUDOUX, first performed Paris, 1935.

Tilley, Vesta (real name Matilda Ball or Bowles; 1864–1952). English music-hall performer, generally as a male impersonator. Her most famous songs were *Burlington Bertie, Jolly Good Luck to the Girl Who Loves a Soldier*, and *The Army of Today's All Right*. Retired in 1920.

Time and the Conways. Drama by J. B. PRIESTLEY, first performed London, 1937.

Time of Your Life, The. Comedy-drama by WILLIAM SAROYAN, first performed New York, 1939.

Time Remembered (Léocadia). *Pièce rose* by JEAN ANOUILH, first performed Paris, 1940.

Timon of Athens. Tragedy by WILLIAM SHAKESPEARE, written c.1604–5.

'Tis Pity She's a Whore. Tragedy by JOHN FORD, first performed London, between 1625 and 1634.

Titus Andronicus. Tragedy by WILLIAM SHAKESPEARE, written c.1592–3.

T.N.P., see THÉÂTRE NATIONAL POPULAIRE.

Toad of Toad Hall. Fantasy-play by A. A. MILNE, based on Kenneth Grahame's book *The Wind in the Willows*, first performed London, 1930.

Tobacco Road. Drama by Jack Kirkland, based on Erskine Caldwell's novel, first performed New York, 1933. The quintessential depiction of American rural squalor, frequently parodied, banned as sensational and immoral, and revived all over the world.

Tobias and the Angel. Comedy by JAMES BRIDIE, first performed Cambridge, 1930.

Toller, Ernst (1893–1939). German dramatist, best known for his earlier plays, among the most popular and widely produced works of the EXPRESSIONIST school. His first big success was *Masses and Men* (*Masse-Mensch*, 1921), an hysterical drama about the career of a woman revolutionary who is finally executed by the revolutionaries she once led. This was followed by *The Machine-Wreckers* (*Die Maschinenstürmer*, 1922), about the Luddite riots of 1812–15, and *Brokenbrow* (*Der deutsche Hinkemann*, 1923), about a soldier who returns impotent from the war and has troubles with an errant wife. Toller's later plays were less successful; he left Germany in 1933 and committed suicide shortly before the outbreak of war.

Tolstoy, Alexey Nikolayevich (1882–1945). Russian dramatist and novelist; though a count, he was a political *emigré* from Tsarist Russia, and returned only after the Revolution, which he celebrated in his first play. His major dramatic works were two historical trilogies on Peter the Great and on Ivan the Terrible; he also wrote plays on modern subjects, such as *The Road to Victory* (1939), another drama of the Revolution.

Tolstoy, Lev Nikolayevich (1828–1910). Russian novelist and dramatist. His plays were always a sideline, and show some impatience with the limitations of dramatic form; the last two were left unfinished. He began in 1887 with a short play on peasant drunkenness, *The First Distiller* (*Pervy vinokur*), which he followed in 1889 with *The Power of Darkness* (*Vlast tmi*), a strange and intense adaptation of naturalistic peasant drama to quasi-mystical ends. *The Fruits of Enlightenment* (*Plodi prosveshcheniya*, 1891) mixed social drama with a denunciation of contemporary spiritualism. *The Living Corpse*, also called *Redemption* (*Zhivoi trup*), was written in 1900 but never finally revised and produced only in 1911. This and *Light Shining in the Darkness* (*I svet vo tme tsvetit*), his last play, concern the impossibility of truly disinterested unworldliness in a world which is not adapted to it. Several of Tolstoy's novels have been successfully adapted to the stage, notably *Anna Karenina*, in various versions, and *War and Peace*, as adapted by PISCATOR.

Tonight at 8.30. Series of nine one-act plays by NOËL COWARD, eight of them first performed in various combinations London, 1935, the ninth, *We Were Dancing*, in New York the same year. The other plays concerned are *Family Album*, *The Astonished Heart*, *Red Peppers*, *Hands Across the Sea*, *Fumed Oak*, *Shadow Play*, *Ways and Means*, and *Still Life* (later called *Brief Encounter*, after its film adaptation).

Topaze. Ironic comedy by MARCEL PAGNOL, first performed Paris, 1930.

Torelli, Giacomo (1608–78). Italian stage designer, great master of the Baroque theatre. He was a pupil of Giambattista Aleotti, designer of the revolutionary Teatro Farnese at Parma, and may have been responsible for the complete set of wings installed there, the first on record. He seems to have been the first artist to work primarily and almost exclusively as a stage designer. From 1641 to 1645 he was designer for the Teatro Novissimo in Venice, after which he went to

Paris for seventeen years, and reconstructed the backstage area of Molière's theatre, the Petit-Bourbon, so that it could encompass the latest innovations in spectacular staging, as it did for Corneille's *Andromède* in 1650. Many of his set designs survive, and his innovations, particularly the sets of wings he devised which could be moved simultaneously on to the stage, were at once adopted into general theatrical practice.

Touch of the Poet, A. Drama by EUGENE O'NEILL, written *c.*1940, first performed Stockholm, 1957; in English, New York, 1958.

Tourneur, Cyril (1575–1626). English dramatist. Little is known of him, not even for certain that the best-known play associated with his name, *The Revenger's Tragedy* (published 1607), is actually by him. The arguments that it is are based mainly on *The Atheist's Tragedy* (published 1611), which has points of similarity but suggests an earlier work. Both have a dark intensity and passages of fine, morbid poetry; *The Revenger's Tragedy* is revived on occasion.

Tovaritch. Comedy by Jacques Deval, first performed Paris, 1933; English adaptation by ROBERT EMMET SHERWOOD, first performed New York, 1936.

Toys in the Attic. Drama by LILLIAN HELLMAN, first performed New York, 1960.

Toy theatre. Miniature theatres built out of cardboard, with cut-out wings and backdrops and cut-out standing figures of actors and actresses in costume. With them could be performed favourite dramas of the day, the vogue starting around 1810 and continuing until the 1860s. During this period toy theatres were a popular nursery amusement, and reached a high degree of elaboration; the materials for making them and for staging any given play could be bought penny plain and twopence coloured. The toy theatres of the period are an invaluable repository of information on the appearance of the real theatre and its settings at the time; one maker of toy theatres and their props still exists in London today, Benjamin Pollock's, who also have a fine collection of old theatres in their Toy Museum.

Trachiniae. Tragedy by SOPHOCLES, first performed Athens, between 420 and 414 B.C.

Tragedy. Form of drama so often and so variously defined that perhaps all which may safely be said of it is that it ends unhappily, usually if not invariably with the death of the principal character. The Greek view of tragedy was defined by ARISTOTLE; Elizabethan tragedy was influenced more by SENECA than directly by Greek precept, but kept at least the notion that tragedy should concern people of high estate, and should deal with man's relation to fate in a fairly lofty, poetic fashion. The French neo-classical theorists, and after them RACINE and CORNEILLE, favoured a return to the teachings of Aristotle, which they interpreted, especially as far as the unities are concerned, with a strictness foreign to Aristotle himself, who described rather than prescribed. The eighteenth century brought various attempts to acclimatize tragedy to middle-class surroundings; the Romantics sought formal freedom and a definition of true tragedy in relation to one vital flaw in the character of the protagonist, which derived more from Shakespeare than from Aristotle. In the twentieth century there have been few attempts at tragedy proper; more consonant with the mood of the time seem to be domestic and social drama with tragic overtones, or mixed media such as the tragi-comedy.

Trap, see STAGE MACHINERY.

Traveller without Luggage, The (Le Voyageur sans bagage). *Pièce noire* by JEAN ANOUILH, first performed Paris, 1937; English adaptation by JOHN WHITING, first performed London, 1959.

Travers, Ben (b. 1886). English dramatist, best known for the series of farces staged at the Aldwych Theatre in the 1920s and hence known as the ALDWYCH FARCES. The most successful of his later plays was *Banana Ridge* (1938). His autobiography, *Vale of Laughter* (1957), contains many illuminating comments on the art and craft of farce.

Tree, Herbert Beerbohm (1853–1917). English actor-manager, half-brother of Max Beerbohm and associated mainly with Shakespearian productions of extreme visual sumptuousness and elaboration. His first professional appearance on stage was in 1878; in 1887 he first went into management, and in the same year took over the Haymarket Theatre, where he produced among other plays a *Hamlet* starring himself (1892), *A Woman of No Importance* (1893), and George du Maurier's *Trilby* (1895), in which he scored one of his major successes as Svengali. In 1897 he opened the new Her Majesty's nearly opposite, and there staged a number of Shakespeare productions, the best of which was *Richard II* (1903), and some new plays, the most notable being *Pygmalion* (1914). Tree was a romantic actor, of no great range but of some brilliance on his own ground; he also wrote a number of books, the most interesting of which is *Thoughts and Afterthoughts* (1913). He was knighted in 1909.

Trelawny of the 'Wells'. Comedy by ARTHUR WING PINERO, first performed London, 1898. Also musical version, *Trelawny*, book by Aubrey Woods, George Powell and Julian Slade, music and lyrics by Julian Slade, first performed Bristol, 1972.

Trewin, J. C. (John Courtenay; b. 1908). English theatre critic, notably on the *Morning Post* (1934–7), *John O'London's Weekly* (1945–54), and the *Birmingham Post* (from 1955). Author of many books on the theatre, among them *The Theatre since 1900* (1951), *Dramatists of Today* (1953), and studies of *Edith Evans* (1954), *Sybil Thorndike* (1955), and *Paul Scofield* (1956); has also edited the annual *Plays of the Year* volumes since 1948.

Trial by Jury. 'Savoy opera' by W. S. GILBERT (book and lyrics) and Arthur Sullivan (music), first performed London, 1875.

Trip to Scarborough, A. Farce by RICHARD BRINSLEY SHERIDAN, based on Vanbrugh's THE RELAPSE; first performed Drury Lane, London, 1777.

Troilus and Cressida. Tragi-comedy by WILLIAM SHAKESPEARE, written *c.*1602.

Trojan Women, The. Tragedy by EURIPIDES, first performed Athens, 415 B.C.

Turgenev, Ivan Sergeyevich (1818–83). Russian novelist and dramatist. Though he wrote a number of plays, nearly all between 1847 and 1850, he is remembered as a dramatist today almost entirely for *A Month in the Country* (*Mesiats v derevne*, 1850), a subtle, atmospheric psychological drama which in many ways anticipates CHEKHOV and was not staged until 1872. His other plays are mostly bitter-sweet comedies similar in background and subject-matter to those of OSTROVSKY: among them are *Insolvency* (*Bezdenezhe*, 1846), *Where It's Thin It Breaks* (*Gde tonko, tam i rvyotsa*, 1848), *The Bachelor* (*Kholostiak*, 1849), and *A Provincial Lady* (*Privubtsialka*, 1851).

Turkey Time. ALDWYCH FARCE by BEN TRAVERS, first performed London, 1931.

Turner, David (b. 1927). English dramatist, author of a number of realistic television plays and several stage plays, the most successful of which is *Semi-Detached* (1962), a Jonsonian comedy of disreputable manners set in a Birmingham suburb. Other plays include *The Bedmakers* (1962), a sort of *King Lear* in a working-class setting, and *Bottomley* (1966), a panoramic biography of the famous swindler. All three were first produced at the Belgrade Theatre, Coventry.

Tutin, Dorothy (b. 1930). English actress. First professional appearance 1949, joined the Old Vic 1950–51, had her first major success in *The Living Room* (1953). Later notable roles: Sally Bowles in *I am a Camera* (1954), St Joan in *The Lark* (1955), Hedwig in *The Wild Duck* (1955), Jean Rice in *The Entertainer* (1957), Juliet, Viola, and Ophelia (Stratford on Avon, 1958), Portia, Viola, and Cressida (Stratford on Avon, 1960), Jeanne in *The Devils* (1961), Queen Victoria in William

Frances's *Portrait of a Queen* (1965), and Kate in Harold Pinter's *Old Times* (1971).

Twelfth Night. Comedy by WILLIAM SHAKESPEARE, first performed London, *c*.1601.

Two Gentlemen of Verona, The. Comedy by WILLIAM SHAKESPEARE written 1594–5.

Two Nobel Kinsmen, The. Romance by WILLIAM SHAKESPEARE and JOHN FLETCHER, based on Chaucer's *Knight's Tale*, written *c*.1613.

Tynan, Kenneth (b. 1927). English drama critic, noted in his early days for his enthusiastic support of THEATRICALISM and ANOUILH, latterly for his left-wing views and approval of drama with a pronounced social purpose. Drama critic of the *Observer* 1954–8, 1960–63, of the *New Yorker* 1958–60; 'Literary Manager' of the National Theatre from 1963 to 1969. Author of *Alec Guinness* (1953) and three volumes of collected criticism, *He That Plays the King* (1950), *Curtains* (1961) and *Tynan Right and Left* (1968). Deviser of the very successful New York revue *Oh! Calcutta!* (1969), noted mainly for pioneering the use of complete nudity in the commercial theatre.

U

Ubu Roi. Comedy by ALFRED JARRY, burlesquing *Oedipus Rex*, first performed Paris, 1896. *Ubu*, a conflation of this and other Ubu plays, performed by the T.N.P. in 1958.

Udall, Nicholas (1505–56). English dramatist and headmaster of Eton, where his comedy *Ralph Roister Doister* was probably first performed between 1534 and 1541. It is the first secular comedy in English, and is modelled on the works of PLAUTUS and TERENCE. Udall also wrote other plays, but none seems to have survived, except perhaps the doubtfully attributed *Thersites*.

Uncle Vanya (Diadia Vania). Drama by ANTON CHEKHOV, first performed Moscow Art Theatre, 1899; based on an earlier play by Chekhov, *The Wood Demon* (*Leshii*), privately performed in Moscow, 1889.

Under Milk Wood. Poetic drama by Dylan Thomas, written for radio and first broadcast, 1954, first staged London, 1956.

Under Plain Cover, see PLAYS FOR ENGLAND.

Unities, see ARISTOTLE.

Unity Theatre. London club theatre in St Pancras, run on little-theatre lines with largely amateur personnel. The company began as the Rebel Players, and in 1936 formed itself into the Unity Theatre Club with the avowed intention of rebelling against 'the escapism and false ideology of the conventional theatre' and setting up instead a left-wing 'agitational' theatre. In 1937 they made a permanent home in a converted mission hall, and have since presented a long series of social and revolutionary dramas, interspersed with satirical revues and pantomimes. Among the more important plays given first or first British productions there are Pogodin's *Aristocrats*, Clifford Odets's *Waiting for Lefty*, O'Casey's *The Star Turns Red*, and Adamov's *Spring '70*. The most notable British dramatist introduced by the Unity is TED WILLIS.

Upstage. Towards the back of the stage, once literally 'up' because of the RAKE. To 'upstage' an actor is to manoeuvre him into a less favourable position, literally or metaphorically, for catching and holding the audience's attention.

US. Show with songs collectively evolved by the Royal Shakespeare Company, with the dramatist DENIS CANNAN and the poet Adrian Mitchell, under the direction of PETER BROOK, London, 1966.

Ustinov, Peter (b. 1921). English dramatist and actor. Studied acting under MICHEL SAINT-DENIS, first made an impression as an actor performing his own sketches at the Players' Club (1939) and in the revues *Diversion* (1940) and *Diversion No. 2* (1941), in both of which he wrote his own material. Most of his later stage appearances have been in his own plays, which include *House of Regrets* (1942), *The Banbury Nose* (1944), *The Indifferent Shepherd* (1948), *The Love of Four Colonels* (1951), *Romanoff and Juliet* (1956), *The Empty Chair* (1956), and *Photo-Finish* (1963). His plays have been perpetually promising but flawed; the most successful were the fantastic comedies *The Love of Four Colonels* and *Romanoff and Juliet*.

Utopia Limited. 'Savoy opera' by W. S. GILBERT (book and lyrics) and Arthur Sullivan (music), first performed London, 1893.

V

Vagabond King, The. Musical comedy by RUDOLPH FRIML, book and lyrics by W. H. Post and Brian Hooker, first performed New York, 1925.

Vakhtangov, Yevgeny (1883–1922). Russian director and actor. A pupil of STANISLAVSKY at the Moscow Art Theatre, he became in 1914 head of the company's acting studio, where he handed on Stanislavsky's ideas on acting and production. Around the time of the Revolution he began to experiment on his own behalf, both in the studio and with a student's group called the Mansurov Studio, which in 1917 was reorganized as the Moscow Dramatic Studio under Vakhtangov and in 1920 was combined with the Art's acting studio to become the Third Workshop. With these actors he evolved a strongly non-realistic, EXPRESSIONIST style of production, the first fruit of which was his production of Maeterlinck's *The Miracle of Saint Anthony* (1918), in which he combined a strongly formalistic attitude to the structure and design of the production with a careful regard for the individuality of the actor and the creative contribution he could make (in contrast to MEYERHOLD's tendency to treat actors as puppets). Among his other famous productions of this period were Pushkin's *The Feast During the Plague*, Strindberg's *Eric XIV*, *The Dybbuk*, and Gozzi's *Princess Turandot*; these established him as one of the great figures in modern Russian theatre, combining the formal brilliance of Meyerhold with some of Stanislavsky's human warmth and understanding. He was taken ill during the final rehearsal of *Turandot* and died shortly afterwards, at the height of his powers.

Valle-Inclan, Ramón del (1869–1936). Spanish dramatist, author of a number of plays in a poetic-fantastic style, among them the best-known *The Farce of the True Spanish Queen* (*Farsa y licencia de la reina castiza*, 1920) and *Face of Silver* (*Cara de plata*, 1923).

Valmouth. Musical by SANDY WILSON, based on the novel by Ronald Firbank (1918), first performed London, 1958.

Vanbrugh, Sir John (1664–1726). English dramatist and architect. He was primarily an architect (his most famous work being Blenheim Palace) and eventually gave up the stage almost entirely for architecture. Before that he was responsible for a number of translations and adaptations, and for two classics of English comedy, *The Relapse: or Virtue in Danger* (1696) and *The Provok'd Wife* (1697), both rough, virile and a little coarse – to such an extent that for many years *The Relapse* was staged only in Sheridan's watered-down version, *A Trip to Scarborough*, though in the twentieth century it has been restored to favour along with other Restoration comedies. Vanbrugh's last play, *A Journey to London*, was left unfinished at his death, but completed by Colley Cibber as *The Provok'd Husband* (1728).

Van Druten, John (1901–57). Anglo-American dramatist. First came to fame with his drama *Young Woodley* (New York, 1925) a mild study of the sexual initiation of an adolescent which was brought to public notice by the Lord Chamberlain's ban. The best of his later plays were *Old Acquaintance* (1940), a drama about two very different women; *The Voice of the Turtle* (1943), a light romantic comedy; and *I am a Camera* (1951), adapted from stories in Christopher Isherwood's *Goodbye to Berlin*.

Vaudeville. More or less the American equivalent of British music hall: a series of turns, comic, musical, acrobatic, etc., deriving from the rough, vulgar beer-hall entertainments of the middle nineteenth century, and invading theatres as a family entertainment from the 1870s on. The heyday of vaudeville was almost exactly contemporary with that of music hall: from the early 1890s to the mid 1920s; and in America as here it was ousted mainly by the cinema, particularly the talkies. The word vaudeville is also used in French, and during the nineteenth century sometimes in English, to mean a very light-weight type of play with musical interludes.

Vedrenne, John E., see BARKER, HARLEY GRANVILLE.

Vega, Lope de (full name Lope Felix de Vega Carpio; 1562–1635). Spanish dramatist of the Renaissance, vastly prolific as a writer of plays (he is said to have written 2,000, and at least 470 survive) as well as of poetry and novels, and enormously varied in his style and output. The majority of his works, and probably the most influential, were tragi-comedies, and he more or less invented the cloak-and-dagger play, poised between comedy and drama, inclining now one way, now the other, and full of romantic incident. He also tried his hand at everything from dramatized lives of saints to the most basic farce. His views on dramaturgy are set forth in his *Arte nuevo de hacer comedias en este tiempo* (*The New Art of Writing Plays in this Age*, 1609), which set out the classic form for Spanish drama, of three acts in various metres, and laid it down that the prime aim of the drama-tist should be to catch and hold the interest of his audience rather than to conform to any cut-and-dried set of rules. It is difficult to pick the outstanding works from his vast output. The most famous for modern audiences is certainly *Fuente ovejuna* (*The Sheep Well*, *c.*1614), hailed in Russia and elsewhere during the twentieth century as the first true proleterian drama, in that the hero is really the whole rebellious population of a village. Among other plays of note by

Lope are *El castigo sin venganza* (*Punishment without Revenge*), the nearest he came to pure tragedy; *Castelvines y Monteses* (*c*.1608), a tragi-comic treatment of the Romeo and Juliet story; *La bella mal casada* (*Marriages of Convenience*), a drama of love and money on quite eighteenth-century lines; *El perro del hortelano* (*The Gardener's Dog*, *c*.1615), a light and elegantly artificial comedy which in some ways foreshadows MARIVAUX; and *La Dorotea*, a semi-autobiographical psychological drama which seems to anticipate MUSSET. Lope shows in many of his plays a startling modernity of outlook and, though he has never really had his due in the English-speaking world (his influence in France, particularly on MOLIÈRE, was considerable), there are now signs that the situation will be improved with the appearance of good new acting versions. Lope will no doubt soon take his place, in practice as well as in theory, among the world's great dramatists.

Venice Preserved. Tragedy by THOMAS OTWAY, first performed London, 1682.

Venus Observed. Verse drama by CHRISTOPHER FRY, first performed London, 1950.

Vestris, Madame (*née* Françoise Gourgaud; 1743–1804). French actress. Married into a notable Franco-Italian theatrical family and made her debut at the Comédie-Française in 1768. She was noted mainly as a tragic actress, her best roles being in Voltaire's *Irène* (1778), in which she was praised by the author, as Catherine de Medici in *Charles IX* (1789), and in *Gabrielle de Vergi* (1772), which offered her a spectacular death scene.

Vian, Boris (1920–59). French novelist and dramatist (as well as jazz trumpeter, engineer, film actor, and prolific translator from several languages); enthusiastic exponent of PATAPHYSICS. His best plays are *L'Équarrissage pour tous* (performed 1950), a bitter black comedy set in a knacker's yard in 1944, and *Les Bâtisseurs d'empire* (*The Empire-Builders*, performed 1959), a ruthlessly logical example of the Theatre of the ABSURD about a family constantly driven upward in their house by a terrible, unexplained noise and yet still finding time and energy to kick the Schmürz, a silent, bandaged figure who in the end, with his fellows, is left in sole possession of the house.

Vicente, Gil (*c*.1465–*c*.1539). Portuguese dramatist, author of a number of short comedies and also of a trilogy of religious plays along morality lines, *Barca do inferno* (*The Boat of Hell*, 1517), *Barca do purgatorio* (*The Boat of Purgatory*, 1518), and *Barca do gloria* (*The Boat of Glory*, 1519).

Vicious Circle, see HUIS-CLOS.

Victor. Comedy by ROGER VITRAC, first performed Paris, 1928.

Victoria Regina. Sequence of plays based on the life of Queen Victoria, by Laurence Housman, first performed London, 1937, after long delay owing to the Lord Chamberlain's doubts about allowing figures of such recent history to be seen on the stage.

Vidal, Gore (b. 1925). American novelist and dramatist, author of a number of satirical comedies, among them *Visit to a Small Planet* (1957), about the world as seen by a visitor from outer space, and *The Best Man* (1960), about the election of a presidential candidate.

View from the Bridge, A. Drama by ARTHUR MILLER. One-act version first performed New York, 1955; two-act version first performed London, 1956.

Vigny, Alfred de (1797–1863). French poet and dramatist. He was a passionate admirer of Shakespeare, and his first theatrical works were adaptations into French of *Romeo and Juliet* (in collaboration, 1827), *The Merchant of Venice* (1828) and *Othello* (1829), all conceived as weapons in the great Romantic rebellion against Racinian classicism in favour of freer Shakespearian ideas of tragedy. His first two original plays, *La Maréchale d'Ancre* (1831) and *Quitte pour la peur* (1833) were costume plays on the Shakespearian model, neither very successful. In 1835 he had a major success (largely *de scandale*) with his romantic tragedy *Chatterton*, which followed closely upon Hugo's *Hernani* as a rallying point for fervent Romantics in the theatre. Its success was brief, however, and it is seldom played today.

Vilar, Jean (b. 1912). French director, manager, and actor. Studied with CHARLES DULLIN; founded the Compagnie des Sept in 1943, the Festival d'Art Dramatique at Avignon in 1947, and the THÉÂTRE NATIONAL POPULAIRE in 1951. As a director he has adopted a straightforward, reasonably eclectic style, placing great emphasis on the 'classical' virtues of clear diction and economical movement even when presenting distinctly modern interpretations of classical texts.

Villiers, George, see BUCKINGHAM, DUKE OF.

Visconti, Luchino (1906–1976). Italian director and designer. Began his career in the theatre as a designer with two productions in 1937, went over to the cinema to make *Ossessione* (1942; often claimed as the first example of cinematic neo-realism), and returned to the theatre as a director in 1945, after which he alternated theatre and film productions. His first theatre productions were Cocteau's *Les Parents terribles* and *La Machine à écrire* and Hemingway's *The Fifth Column*; subsequently he directed an enormous variety of plays, old and new, and operas. Many of his best drama productions were for the Paolo Stoppa-Rina Morelli company: they included *Crime and*

Punishment and *The Glass Menagerie* (1946), *Eurydice* (1947), *Life with Father* (1948), *Death of a Salesman*, and Diego Fabbri's *Il Seduttore* (1951), Goldoni's *La Locandiera* and *Three Sisters* (1952), *Uncle Vanya* (1955), *A View from the Bridge* (1958), Fabbri's *Figli d'arte* (1959). Of his drama productions for other companies the most famous was his sumptuous Paris version of *'Tis Pity She's a Whore* (1961); of his opera productions the best known were his versions of *La Vestale* (1954), *La Sonnambula* and *La Traviata* (1955), all with Callas, and his Covent Garden *Don Carlos* (1958).

Visit, The (Der Besuch der alten Dame). Drama by FRIEDRICH DÜRRENMATT, first performed Zürich, 1955.

Vitrac, Roger (1899–1952). French dramatist, poet, and journalist. A founder, with Tristan Tzara, of the French DADA movement, a disciple of JARRY, and associate of ARTAUD, with whom he founded the Théâtre Alfred Jarry in 1927. This company presented his first two plays, *Les Mystères de l'amour* (1927) and *Victor, ou les enfants au pouvoir* (1928), the first an acting-out of the sado-masochistic fantasies of two lovers and a sort of manifesto of the Theatre of CRUELTY, the second a bitter farce about a nine-year-old child who snatches all the prerogatives of adulthood and dies of the knowledge he gains. *Le Peintre* (1930) rivals Jarry in its gross vigour; *Le Coup de Trafalgar* (1934) pillories human folly in a story of a group taking refuge from a bombardment during the First World War. Later plays include a political satire, *Le Camelot* (1936); a drama of jealousy, *Les Demoiselles du large* (1938); a farce set in a nursing home, *Le Loup-garou* (1939); and *Le Sabre de mon père* (1951), an extravagant Surrealistic farce. Vitrac's most notable play is *Victor*, misunderstood when it first appeared but successfully revived in 1946 and again, directed by ANOUILH (who has recognized Vitrac as an important influence on his own work), in 1962.

Volpone. Comedy by BEN JONSON, first performed London, 1605–6.

Voltaire (real name François-Marie Arouet; 1694–1778). French novelist, dramatist, poet, and philosopher. In his time he was a successful as well as a prolific dramatist, though none of his plays survives in the modern theatre. His tragedies, of which the best are *Zaïre* (1732) and *Mérope* (1743), are coldly correct, but lifeless; he also wrote satires and bourgeois dramas, one of the latter, *Nanine* (1749), based on Richardson's novel *Pamela*. Voltaire's novel *Candide* has been successfully dramatized by Lillian Hellman as a musical.

Vortex, The. Drama by NOËL COWARD, first performed London, 1924.

Voysey Inheritance, The. Drama by HARLEY GRANVILLE BARKER, first performed London, 1905.

W

Waiting for Godot (En attendant Godot). Drama by SAMUEL BECKETT, first performed Paris, 1953.

Waiting in the Wings. Drama by NOËL COWARD, first performed London, 1960.

Walkley, A. B. (Arthur Bingham; 1855–1926). English dramatic critic, particularly on *The Times* 1900–26. His interests were more literary than strictly theatrical: he always devoted much more space to the texts of the plays he reviewed than to their acting and production. Within this area he was generally moderate and acute: his best pieces are collected in such volumes as *Pastiche and Prejudice* (1921), *More Prejudice* (1923), and *Still More Prejudice* (1925).

Wallace, Edgar (1875–1932). English novelist, dramatist, and journalist. His most successful plays, like his novels (and indeed sometimes based on them), were thrillers of a fairly elementary but ingenious nature: the most famous were *The Ringer* (1926), *On the Spot* (1930), and *The Case of the Frightened Lady* (1931).

Wallace, Nellie (1870–1948). English music-hall comic and actress. Began her career as a clog-dancer in 1888, toured in a sister-act, played in a number of straight plays, and then extensively on the halls as an individual comic turn, the most famous of her songs being *I Lost Georgie in Trafalgar Square*. She was also one of the few successful woman dames in pantomime.

Waltz Dream, A (Ein Walzertraum). Operetta by Oscar Straus, book and lyrics by Felix Dormann and Leopold Jacobson; first performed Vienna, 1907.

Waltz of the Toreadors, The (La Valse des toréadors). *Pièce grinçante* by JEAN ANOUILH, first performed Paris, 1952.

Wanamaker, Sam (b. 1919). American actor and director. Made his British debut in 1952 in *Winter Journey*, which he also directed, and subsequently directed and starred in *The Shrike* (1953), *The Big Knife* (1954), *The Rainmaker* (1956), and *A Hatful of Rain* (1957). In 1957 he took over the management of the New Shakespeare Theatre, Liverpool, which he ran for two years on very enterprising lines, presenting among others the first production of *One More River* and the first British productions of *Bus Stop* and *The Rose Tattoo*.

Wandering Jew, The. Drama by E. Temple Thurston, first performed London, 1920. A successful piece of spectacular theatre based on the medieval legend.

War and Peace. Epic drama by ERWIN PISCATOR and Walter Neumann, based on Tolstoy's novel (1868–9); first performed Berlin, 1955.

Wasps, The. Comedy by ARISTOPHANES, first performed Athens, 422 B.C.

Waste. Tragedy by HARLEY GRANVILLE BARKER, first performed London, 1907; revised version London, 1936.

Watch on the Rhine, The. Drama by LILLIAN HELLMAN, first performed New York, 1941.

Waterhouse, Keith, see HALL, WILLIS.

Waters of the Moon. Drama by N. C. HUNTER, first performed London, 1951.

Way of the World, The. Comedy by WILLIAM CONGREVE, first performed London, 1700.

Webster, John (c.1580–1634). English dramatist. Almost nothing is known of his life except that he wrote a number of plays in collaboration and at least four unaided, as well as poems, pageants, etc. His earliest surviving play is *Appius and Virginia* (c.1608). a dignified Roman piece, but his reputation rests on *The White Devil* (1612), *The Duchess of Malfi* (1614), and to a lesser extent *The Devil's Law Case* (c.1620). These are dark, violent works, shot through with passages of extraordinary poetry, and obsessed, even the last and lightest, with death and decay. Next to Shakespeare Webster is the most frequently revived tragic dramatist of his time.

Wedekind, Frank (1864–1918). German dramatist and actor. His plays are a sort of half-way house between the NATURALISM of HAUPTMANN and the frenzies of EXPRESSIONISM. All his major plays are concerned with the effects of sex in life – sex frustrated, extravagantly indulged, brooded over, perverted. His two earliest plays, *Die Junge Welt* (*The World of Youth*, 1890) and *Frühlings Erwachen* (*Spring's Awakening*, 1891), both deal with adolescent problems, unusually frankly – so much so that in 1963 *Spring's Awakening* was banned in Britain by the Lord Chamberlain, and later passed only after cuts had been made. In *Der Erdgeist* (1895) and *Die Büchse der Pandora* (1903) he traced the career of one woman, Lulu, an embodiment of lust: the plays are best known today in Alban Berg's operatic version, *Lulu*. Gradually Wedekind's drama became more violent and extreme in its expression: in plays like *Totentanz* (1906); the trilogy *Der Kammersänger* (*The Tenor*, 1899), *Musik* (*Music*, 1907), and *Schloss Wetterstein* (*Castle Wetterstein*, 1910); *Samson, oder Scham und Eifersucht* (*Samson, or Shame and Jealousy*, 1914); and *Herakles* (*Hercules*, 1917) the dream progressively takes over from reality until we reach something like fully-fledged Expressionism.

Weigel, Helene (1900–1971). German actress, wife of BERTOLT BRECHT and a leading interpreter of his work, notably in *A Man's a Man* (1928), *Mother Courage* (1949), *The Mother* (1951), *The Caucasian Chalk Circle* (1954), and *Terror and Misery of the Third Reich* (1957). After Brecht's death in 1956 she directed the BERLINER ENSEMBLE.

Weill, Kurt (1900–50). German composer. In Germany during the 1920s and early 1930s he was a regular collaborator of BRECHT, most notably on *The Threepenny Opera* (1928), *The Rise and Fall of the City of Mahagonny* (1927–9), and *The Seven Deadly Sins* (*Anna-Anna*, 1933). In 1935 Weill went to America where he worked on a number of musicals, the most successful of them *Knickerbocker Holiday* (1938), *Lady in the Dark* (1941), *One Touch of Venus* (1943), *Street Scene* (1947), and *Lost in the Stars* (1949). He was married to LOTTE LENYA.

Weiss, Peter (b. 1916). German dramatist now a naturalized Swede. Author of some experimental fiction and director of several *avant-garde* films, he achieved international success in 1964 with the appearance of his first full-length play to be produced, *The Persecution and Assassination of Marat as Performed by the Inmates of the Asylum of Charenton under the Direction of the Marquis de Sade*, a piece of brilliant 'director's theatre' which engaged the attention of distinguished directors in many countries, notably PETER BROOK in Britain. His next work, *Die Ermittlung* (*The Investigation*), described as an oratorio on the subject of Auschwitz, was first produced by PISCATOR in 1965 and received several readings in English at the Aldwych in 1965–6. Later plays reflect on such popular current causes of international concern as Angola (*The Song of the Lusitanian Bogey*, 1967) and the Vietnam war (*The Vietnam Dialogue*, 1968), as well as a more straightforward historical piece, *Trotsky in Exile* (1969).

Welles, Orson (b. 1915). American director, actor and writer. Made his acting debut at the Gate Theatre, Dublin, in 1931; acted a variety of roles in his teens, and in 1936 became director of the Negro People's Theatre, New York, for which he directed a famous all-coloured version of *Macbeth*. In 1937 he was appointed a director of the Federal Theatre Project, for which he directed *Horse Eats Hat* (his own version of Labiche's *Italian Straw Hat*), *Doctor Faustus*, and *The Cradle Will Rock*. The same year he founded the Mercury Theatre, with John Houseman, directing there a modern-dress *Julius Caesar*, *The Shoemaker's Holiday*, *Heartbreak House*, and *Danton's Death*. Subsequently he moved also into radio (with his notorious dramatization of *The War of the Worlds*, which in 1938 panicked a continent) and films, starting with *Citizen Kane* in 1940. Since then he has alternated stage and film activity: among his most notable stage work has been a lavish musical version of *Around the World in Eighty Days*, written, directed by, and starring himself (New York, 1946); *Time Runs*, his own version of *Faust* which he starred in and directed (Germany, 1950); *Othello* which he directed and played the title role in (London, 1955); *King Lear*, which he directed and starred in (New York, 1956); and *Rhinoceros*, which he directed (London, 1960).

Well-made play. Concept of the superficial, mechanically efficient drama originated by SCRIBE and fanatically opposed by SHAW in the name of Ibsen and high seriousness.

Well of the Saints, The. Comedy by J. M. SYNGE, first performed Abbey Theatre, Dublin, 1905.

Werfel, Franz (1890–1945). Austrian dramatist and novelist. His best-known and most influential play was *Goat Song* (*Bocksgesang*, 1921), adapted from his own novel about a monster, half goat and half man, who leads a peasant revolt in the eighteenth century and symbolizes the bestial element in humanity. He also wrote an ambitious trilogy on the Faust theme, *Der Spiegelmensch* (1921) and a successful historical drama, *Juarez und Maximilian* (1924).

Wesker, Arnold (b. 1932). English dramatist. His first play, *Chicken Soup with Barley*, a drama following the life of an East End Jewish family from the 1930s to the 1950s, was successfully produced at the Belgrade Theatre, Coventry, in 1958, and was followed at the same theatre by two further plays, *Roots* (1959) and *I'm Talking About Jerusalem* (1960), concerning members of the same family and their further adventures in search of an ideal life. All these plays were transferred to the Royal Court, London, the last as part of a season in which the whole 'Wesker Trilogy' was presented consecutively. Another play, *The Kitchen*, was given a production-without-décor at the Royal Court in 1959 and, revised and enlarged, a full-dress production in 1961. This was followed by one of Wesker's major successes to date, *Chips with Everything* (1962), a play of army life in which the services are seen as a microcosm of the world at large, rather as the kitchen of a London restaurant was seen in *The Kitchen*. In 1962 Wesker was also instrumental in founding the CENTRE 42 organization, which has since occupied much of his time. His two-character love story *The Four Seasons* had a brief run in the West End in 1965; British managers fought shy of his elaborate new social drama *Their Very Own and Golden City*, and it received its first production in French, by the Belgian National Theatre (1965). It was produced at the Royal Court in 1966. His next play, *The Friends*, was also first produced abroad, in Stockholm (1970), then in London (1970); it was followed by *The Old Ones* at the Royal Court (1972).

West, Mae, see DIAMOND LIL.

West Side Story. Musical by LEONARD BERNSTEIN, book by ARTHUR LAURENTS, from an idea by JEROME ROBBINS, lyrics by Stephen Sondheim, first performed New York, 1957.

What Every Woman Knows. Comedy by J. M. BARRIE, first performed London, 1908.

What Shall We Tell Caroline? One-act comedy by JOHN MORTIMER, first performed London, 1958.

When We Dead Awaken (Naar vi Døde Vaagner). Drama by HENRIK IBSEN, first performed Christiania (Oslo), 1900.

Where the Rainbow Ends. Fairy play by Clifford Mills and John Ramsey (Reginald Owen), music by Roger Quilter, first performed London, 1911. For many years a regular part of London's Christmas entertainments for children.

While the Sun Shines. Farce by TERENCE RATTIGAN, first performed London, 1943.

Whip, The. Sporting drama by Cecil Raleigh and Henry Hamilton, first performed Drury Lane, London, 1909. The most famous of the Drury Lane melodramas, including as spectacular highlights a train-wreck and the Derby on stage.

White, George (b. 1890). American producer. Specialist in spectacular revues, the best known of which were the *George White's Scandals*, which began in 1919 and introduced many of the leading talents of the American musical stage, including GEORGE GERSHWIN, who wrote most of the scores for them from 1920 to 1924.

White Devil, The. Tragedy by JOHN WEBSTER, first performed London, 1612.

Whitehall farces. Series of farces played at the Whitehall Theatre under the management of the actor Brian Rix from 1950 on: the plays concerned are *Reluctant Heroes* (1950–54), *Dry Rot* (1954–8), *Simple Spymen* (1958–61), *One for the Pot* (1961–4), and *Chase Me Comrade!* (1964–6).

Whiting, John (1915–63). English dramatist and actor. After training at R.A.D.A. and some years acting he took to writing with *Saint's Day* (1947–9), an intense and obscure symbolic drama haunted by death which won first prize in the Arts Council's Festival of Britain play competition (1951), was produced at the Arts Theatre and caused a storm of controversy. Meanwhile a harmless fantastic comedy by Whiting, *A Penny for a Song*, had been produced with mild success; in 1954 another drama, *Marching Song*, appeared, and despite its clear and eloquent exposition of its subject – a matter of suicide for personal-cum-political reasons – failed in the West End. After some years' absence from the theatre (a bitter comedy, *The Gates of Summer*, closed on tour in 1956), Whiting returned with a psychological drama, *The Devils*, based on Aldous Huxley's *The Devils of Loudun*, concerning a case of supposed demonic possession in seventeenth-century France, and this proved a major success when produced by the Royal Shakespeare Company at the Aldwych in 1961. His only other stage plays were a gnomic one-act piece, *No Why*, posthumously produced at the Aldwych in 1964, and *Conditions of Agreement*, a very early play produced at Bristol in 1965.

Who is Sylvia? Comedy by TERENCE RATTIGAN, first performed London, 1950 .

Who's Afraid of Virginia Woolf? Drama by EDWARD ALBEE, first performed New York, 1962.

Widowers' Houses. Drama by GEORGE BERNARD SHAW, written 1885–7, first performed London, 1892.

Wild Duck, The (Vildanden). Drama by HENRIK IBSEN, first performed Christiania (Oslo), 1885.

Wilde, Oscar (1856–1900). Irish dramatist, novelist and wit. Educated at Oxford, he dabbled early in poetry and poetic drama, two of his early plays, *Vera* (1882) and *The Duchess of Padua* (1891), being produced in New York. In the main, though, he concentrated on fiction and essay writing until 1892, when he hit, in *Lady Windermere's Fan*, on the combination of (rather sentimental) social drama and corruscatingly witty dialogue which was to make his fame and fortune as a dramatist. *A Woman of No Importance* (1893) and *An Ideal Husband* (1895) followed, written in the same convention, and then *The Importance of Being Earnest* (also 1895), his best play, in which the elements of sentimental melodrama were dropped and the result was the most elegant and stylish high comedy written in English since CONGREVE. He also wrote at this time a one-act drama, *Salomé* (1892), in highly decorated French prose, which was banned in England but produced in France. In 1895, during the run of *The Importance of Being Earnest*, Wilde was tried and imprisoned for homosexual offences, and wrote nothing further for the theatre before his death. A one-act verse play, *A Florentine Tragedy* (written 1893–4) was completed by Sturge Moore and produced in 1906.

Wilder, Thornton (1897–1975). American dramatist and novelist. His most important plays are *Our Town* (1938), a loving recreation of small-town American life using a non-realistic form with a 'Stage Manager' on stage regulating the action, and *The Skin of Our Teeth* (1942), which the author described as 'a history of the world in comic strip', demonstrating that mankind has managed to survive through the ages only by the skin of its teeth. Both these plays won Pulitzer Prizes. Wilder's other plays include a Civil War drama, *The Trumpet Shall Sound* (1926); a free adaptation of a Nestroy farce, *The Merchant of Yonkers* (1938), rewritten even more freely in 1954 as *The Matchmaker* and made the basis of the hit musical *Hello, Dolly!* in 1964; *A Life in the Sun*, a new version of the ALCESTIS story produced at the Edinburgh Festival in 1955; and *Three Plays for Bleeker Street*, a group of one-act plays (1962). He also translated Obey's *Lucrèce* (1932).

Williams, Emlyn (b. 1905). Welsh dramatist and actor. Author of many plays, the most successful of which have been thrillers, among them *A Murder Has Been Arranged* (1930), *Night Must Fall* (1935), and *Someone Waiting* (1953), and the semi-autobiographical piece *The Corn is Green* (1938), about the education of a Welsh boy. Other plays have included the farcical (*The Late Christopher Bean*, adapted from the French, 1933), the historical (*Spring 1600*, 1934–5), and the supernatural (*The Wind of Heaven*, 1945; *Trespass*, 1947). As an actor he has appeared in many of his own plays, and in 1951 had a spectacular success as Charles Dickens in a series of readings from the novels, based on Dickens's own; in 1955 he devised another solo performance for himself, *Dylan Thomas Growing Up*, based on the writings of Dylan Thomas. He has written also two volumes of autobiography, *George* and *Emlyn*.

Williams, Tennessee (b. 1914). American dramatist. After earlier years variously spent as student, bohemian, and shoe-salesman he had his first full-length play professionally produced: *Battle of Angels*, which was put on by GROUP THEATRE in Boston (1940) and withdrawn before it reached New York. After a few more years of odd jobs and writing of various sorts, including *You Touched Me!* (1942), a dramatic adaptation of a D. H. Lawrence story in collaboration with Donald Windham, he wrote *The Glass Menagerie* (1945), which proved a big Broadway success and made his name. It has all the familiar props of his drama – a slightly grotesque faded-genteel older woman, a young innocent, a tough young hero, a run-down Southern background. These elements, some or all of them, recur in nearly all his plays, but most obviously in *A Streetcar Named Desire* (1947), *Summer and Smoke* (1948), *The Rose Tattoo* (1951), *Cat on a Hot Tin Roof* (1955), *Orpheus Descending* (a new version of *Battle of Angels*, 1957), *Sweet Bird of Youth* (1959), and *Night of the Iguana* (1962). He has occasionally ventured into slightly different territory, as with the overtly symbolic drama *Camino Real* (1953), the primarily comic film-script *Baby Doll* (1956), based on two one-act plays from his collection *Twenty-Seven Wagons Full of Cotton*, the unashamedly *grand guignol Suddenly Last Summer* (1958), and the domestic comedy *Period of Adjustment* (1960). None of his later plays, such as *The Milk Train Doesn't Stop Here Any More* (1962), *Slapstick Tragedy* (1966), *The Two-Character Play* (1967) and *In the Bar of a Tokyo Hotel* (1969), has anywhere near matched the commercial success of his early work. He is a brilliant creator of theatrical atmosphere, providing spectacular acting parts, especially for young men and older women, which have endeared him to Hollywood perhaps even more consistently than to Broadway. He published his *Memoirs* in 1976.

Williamson, Nicol (b. 1937). British actor. After a period in repertory first made an impression in 1962 in a season of small productions staged by the Royal Shakespeare Company at the Arts Theatre – most notably as Albert Meakin in HENRY LIVINGS's *Nil Carborundum* and as Leantio in *Women Beware Women*. He was established as one of the outstanding actors of his generation by his extraordinary creation of Bill Maitland, the tortured hero of *Inadmissible Evidence* (1964), a role he repeated in the film version. Outstanding later performances include *The Diary of a Madman* (1967) and a Hamlet (1969, also later filmed) in TONY RICHARDSON's production which was widely acclaimed as the definitive performance of its decade.

Willis, Ted (b. 1914). English dramatist, author of a number of stage plays set generally in working-class backgrounds, among them *No Trees in the Street* (1948), *The Blue Lamp* (1952), and *Hot Summer Night* (1958). He was the first British dramatist to concentrate on television as a writing medium, working on series (*Dixon of Dock Green*) and writing a number of original plays for television: among then *The Young and the Guilty*, *Look in any Window*, *Woman in a Dressing Gown* (adapted for the stage in 1964), and *The Four Seasons of Rosie Carr*. In 1964 he was created a Life Peer.

Wilson, Sandy (b. 1924). English composer and dramatist. Educated at Oxford, began his theatrical career writing songs for revues such as *Slings and Arrows* (1948) and *Oranges and Lemons* (1949), then had a major success with *The Boy Friend* (1953), a pastiche of 1920s musical comedy written and composed by him, originally for the Players' Club. This ran five years in the West End. His later musicals include *The Buccaneer* (1956), a fantasy set in the office of a boys' magazine, *Valmouth* (1958), based on the novel by Ronald Firbank, and *Divorce Me, Darling* (1965), which attempted to do for the 1930s what *The Boy Friend* did for the 1920s.

Wind of Heaven, The. Drama by EMLYN WILLIAMS, first performed London, 1945.

Wing. A painted, canvas-covered flat at the side of a stage, used as part of a setting backed by a backcloth and masking the side areas of the stage, which are by extension also known as the wings. There might have been seven or eight wings in recession on each side of the stage during their heyday, but since the introduction of the enclosed 'box set' they have become virtually obsolete, except in ballet. See also STAGE MACHINERY.

Winslow Boy, The. Drama by TERENCE RATTIGAN, first performed London, 1946.

Winter Journey. Drama by CLIFFORD ODETS, called in America *The Country Girl*; first performed New York, 1950.

Winterset. Poetic drama by MAXWELL ANDERSON, first performed New York, 1935.

Winter's Tale, The. Dramatic romance by WILLIAM SHAKESPEARE, first performed London, *c*.1611.

Witness for the Prosecution. Thriller by AGATHA CHRISTIE, first performed London, 1953.

Wodehouse, P. G. (Pelham Grenville; b. 1881). English humorous novelist and dramatist; his main contribution to the theatre has been as collaborator with GUY BOLTON on the books of more than twenty musical comedies.

Woffington, Peg (*c*.1714–60). English actress and mistress of GARRICK, celebrated by Charles Reade in his novel of the same name. She was an effective comedienne with a good figure which enhanced her appeal in breeches parts, among which was one of her most famous roles, Sir Harry Wildair. She retired in 1757.

Wolfit, Donald (1902–68). English actor-manager. Made his debut in 1920, first appeared in London in 1924, and joined the Old Vic in 1929–30, where he was noticed in such roles as Macduff, Tybalt, Cassius, and Claudius. In 1936–7 he went to Stratford on Avon for two seasons, playing Hamlet, Cassius, Kent, Ulysses, Iachimo, Touchstone, Autolycus, and other roles, and in 1937 he set up his own touring company, which existed for a number of years. Among his great roles during this period were Volpone, which he first played in 1938, Shylock, and King Lear (first played 1943); he was widely regarded as the greatest modern Lear. In 1951 he briefly joined the Old Vic, playing Tamburlaine and Lord Ogleby in *The Clandestine Marriage*; in 1953 he added *Oedipus Rex* and *Oedipus at Colonus* to his repertoire, as well as Sir Peter Teazle in *The School for Scandal*. In 1955 he played one of his most notable modern roles,

Father Fernandez in *The Strong are Lonely*, and in 1957 presented two plays by Montherlant, *The Master of Santiago* and *Malatesta*, at the Lyric, Hammersmith. Later roles included Pastor Manders in *Ghosts* (1959), and the title-role in *John Gabriel Borkman* (1963). He published his autobiography, *First Interval*, in 1955, and was knighted in 1957.

Woman Killed with Kindness, A. Tragedy by JOHN HEYWOOD, first performed London, *c*.1603.

Woman of No Importance, A. Comedy by OSCAR WILDE, first performed London, 1893.

Women, The. Comedy by Clare Boothe, first performed New York, 1936. A barbed comedy of manners with an entirely female cast.

Women Beware Women. Tragedy by THOMAS MIDDLETON, first performed London, *c*.1621.

Wonderful Town. Musical by LEONARD BERNSTEIN, book by Joseph Fields and Jerome Choderov (based on their play *My Sister Eileen*, 1940, based on the book of short stories by Ruth McKenney), lyrics by Betty Comden and Adolph Green; first performed New York, 1953.

Wood, Charles (b. 1932). British dramatist, born into a theatrical family; his childhood provided the background for his comedy *Fill the Stage with Happy Hours* (1966). Most of his other plays concern military life in some way: the three plays which make up his bill *Cockade* (1963), *Dingo* (1967) and *H, or Monologues at Front of Burning Cities* (1969), commissioned by the National Theatre. *Veterans* (1971), which provided Sir John Gielgud with a classic role, concerned the making of a film epic on location.

World of Paul Slickey, The. Musical play by JOHN OSBORNE, with music by Christopher Whelan, first performed London, 1959.

World of Susie Wong, The. Long-running comedy-drama by Paul Osborn, based on the novel by Richard Mason; first performed New York, 1958.

Worm's Eye View. Long-running service farce by R. F. Delderfield, first performed London, 1945.

Wrong Side of the Park, The. Drama by JOHN MORTIMER, first performed London, 1960.

Wycherley, William (1640–1716). English dramatist, author of a group of 'Restoration comedies' which are still fairly regularly revived. He spent some time in France and was influenced by MOLIÈRE, but his plays, in their robust, extravert humour and acute observation of contemporary types, remain very English, even when adapted from foreign models, as in the case of *The Gentleman Dancing Master*

(1672), based on Calderón. His first play was *Love in a Wood; or, St James's Park* (1671), but his best-known works are *The Country Wife* (1674–5), a lusty comedy of sexual manners, and *The Plain Dealer* (1674?), a satirical comedy suggestive in some details of *Le Misanthrope*. With the passing of the vogue for his sort of play and the purification of the stage, Wycherley gave up play-writing, fell into disgrace and debt, and concentrated latterly on poetry.

Y

Yeats, W. B. (William Butler; 1865–1939). Irish poet and dramatist. He was fascinated by drama from his youth, and, with LADY GREGORY, played an important part in the foundation of the Irish Dramatic Movement in 1899. He became a director of the ABBEY THEATRE on its foundation in 1904 and continued to take part in its running until his death, as well as outlining authoritatively the aims and intention of the Irish Dramatic Movement in his essays 'The Irish Literary Theatre' (1900) and 'The Irish Dramatic Movement' (1923). He wrote nearly thirty plays in a variety of styles, ranging from pale Celtic-Twilight romanticism in his earliest work to the stark severity of his last plays. His very earliest plays, *The Land of Heart's Desire* (1894), *The Countess Cathleen* (1889–99), and *The Shadowy Waters* (1885–1906) are tenuous, carefully poetic pieces not very far removed from the world of MAETERLINCK. In the 1900s he experimented with more realistic peasant drama in *Cathleen ni Houlihan* and *The Pot of Broth* (1901 and 1902, both written in collaboration with Lady Gregory), and with a type of poetic play which was intellectually tougher and dramatically more powerful in *The Hour Glass* (prose version 1902, verse 1903), *The King's Threshold*, and *The Unicorn from the Stars* (1903 and 1907, again both collaborations with Lady Gregory), and later on in the enigmatic *Player Queen* (1908). At the same time he began a series of plays on Irish legends with *On Baile's Strand* (1901–4) which continued through *Deirdre* (1905–6), *The Green Helmet* (1908–10), *At the Hawk's Well* (1915–16), *The Only Jealousy of Emer* (1916), and *The Death of Cuchulain* (1938), one of his last plays. Just before the First World War Yeats became interested in Eastern, particularly Japanese drama, and embodied some of what he learned in several of these plays, particularly those – *At the Hawk's Well*, *The Only Jealousy of Emer*, *The Dreaming of the Bones*, and *Calvary* – described by him as 'plays for dancers'. His later plays include a version of *Oedipus at Colonus* (1926) and two strange and intense one-act plays, *The Words upon the Window-pane* (1930), about the last days of Swift, and *Purgatory* (1938). In recent years Yeats's drama has been widely studied and revalued, and it is possible that some at least of it will find its way back into a theatre which was not ready for it at the time.

Yellow Sands. Comedy by EDEN and Adelaide PHILLPOTTS, first performed Birmingham, 1926.

Yeoman of the Guard, The. 'Savoy opera' by W. S. GILBERT (book and lyrics) and Arthur Sullivan (music), first performed London 1888.

Yerma. Tragedy by FEDERICO GARCÍA LORCA, first performed Madrid, 1934.

Yiddish theatre. A movement to create drama in Yiddish grew up towards the end of the eighteenth century among German Jews, and slightly later in Russia. The first permanent Yiddish theatre was not founded until 1876, when Abraham Goldfaden (1840–1908) set up a company, at first on a small scale, with programmes of songs and sketches, then with full-length plays of his own. He soon had rivals in other parts of Russia, and other playwrights sprang up, including Joseph Lateiner (1853–1935), who later founded the first Yiddish theatre in New York, and Joseph Yehuda Lerner (c. 1849–1907). But in 1883 all performances in Yiddish were banned in Russia, and the ban was not relaxed until 1908, by which time audiences were ready for a more literary, artistic form of theatre. In 1908 Peretz Hirshbein (1881–1949) set up the first Yiddish Art Theatre in Odessa – it failed after two years – and in 1916 David Hermann (1876–1930) founded an art theatre at Vilna, to concentrate entirely on Jewish folk-drama. Half of this company later went to America and combined with a group already functioning in New York under the direction of Maurice Schwartz (1889–1960) to form one of the most influential and productive Yiddish theatres of all, responsible for the production of a series of plays based on the stories of SHOLOM ALEICHEM and the plays of Halper Levick (b. 1888), the most famous of which is *The Golem.* Many other groups were formed, most notably the Moscow State Jewish Theatre, but towards the end of the 1930s Yiddish theatre began to die out in Britain and America for lack of support, and was replaced in Israel by theatre in Hebrew, though it still flourishes in Eastern Europe, particularly Poland and Russia.

Youmans, Vincent (1898–1946). American composer of musical comedies. His first Broadway show was *Two Little Girls in Blue* (1921), in which he collaborated with Paul Lannin; his biggest successes were *No, No, Nanette* (1925) and *Hit the Deck* (1927), from which such songs as *I Want to be Happy, Tea for Two, Sometimes I'm Happy,* and *Hallelujah* are still remembered. In 1933 he was forced to retire because of illness, and spent most of the rest of his life in sanatoriums.

You Never Can Tell. Comedy by GEORGE BERNARD SHAW, written 1895–6, first performed London, 1899.

Young, Stark (1881–1963). American dramatic critic of the *New Republic* 1921–47, apart from a season (1924–5) on the *New York Times,* and was generally held to be the most perceptive critic of acting in

America. His writings on the theatre have been collected in various volumes, outstanding among them *Immortal Shadows* (1948). He also translated the plays of CHEKHOV.

Young England. Patriotic drama by Walter Reynolds, first performed London, 1934. The classic case of a play succeeding in spite of its intentions: meant as a stirring patriotic call, it was taken as a riotous burlesque, and became something of an institution for audiences who went to laugh, heckle, and generally join in the unintentional fun.

Young Idea, The. Comedy by NOËL COWARD, first performed London, 1923.

Young Woodley. Drama by JOHN VAN DRUTEN, first performed New York, 1925.

Z

Zeffirelli, Franco (b. 1924). Italian director and stage designer. He began as a designer, working with VISCONTI on several productions, then made a name for himself with his stylish productions of opera, notably *Lucia di Lammermoor*, *Cavalleria Rusticana*, and *I Pagliacci* at Covent Garden. Since then he has specialized in revivifying the classics with often startlingly realistic productions, among them *Romeo and Juliet* at the Old Vic, *La Dame aux camélias* in New York, and *Hamlet* in Rome.

Ziegfeld, Florenz (1867–1932). American impresario, noted especially for the series of lavish revues he staged for twenty-four years from 1907 under the title of the *Ziegfeld Follies*. These were famed for their elaborate sets and glamorous showgirls, many of whom went on to distinguished careers in films or on the stage. Most of the best musical performers and comics appeared in the Follies, and virtually every important popular composer contributed material. Ziegfeld also produced other musical shows, the most famous of which were *Sally* (1920) and *Show Boat* (1927).

Zola, Émile (1840–1902). French novelist and dramatist. He was the great exponent of ruthless NATURALISM, to such an extent that several of his works were banned and all were placed on the Index. Many of his novels were adapted for the stage by others, and he himself wrote a number of plays for ANTOINE's Théâtre Libre, most notably *Thérèse Raquin*.

Zoo Story, The. One-act drama by EDWARD ALBEE, first performed Berlin, 1959.

Zuckmayer, Carl (1896–1977). German dramatist, who specialized mainly in comedy and satire. He began as an EXPRESSIONIST, but in 1923 led a reaction against the movement with his rustic comedy *The Happy Vineyard* (*Der fröhliche Weinberg*). His next big success was a satirical comedy, *The Captain from Kopenick* (*Der Hauptmann von Kopenick*, 1931), which ridiculed German militarism and was one of the reasons for Zuckmayer's seeking refuge first in Austria, then in Switzerland, after 1933. In 1939 he went to America, and there wrote his other big success, *The Devil's General* (*Des Teufels General*, 1946), a vivid picture of life in Nazi Germany. Of his later plays the most notable is *The Cold Light* (*Das kalte Licht*, 1956), a political drama about a nuclear scientist turned traitor.